THE ANATOMY OF ARSON

THE ANATOMY OF ARSON

Harvey M. French

ARCO PUBLISHING, INC.
NEW YORK

Published by Arco Publishing, Inc.
219 Park Avenue South, New York, N.Y. 10003

Copyright © 1979 by Arco Publishing, Inc.

Library of Congress Cataloging in Publication Data

French, Harvey M
  The anatomy of arson.

  Bibliography: p. 275
  Includes index.
  1. Arson investigation.   2. Arson.   I. Title

HV8079.A7F74   364.12   78-2472
ISBN 0-668-04423-3 (Library Edition)

Printed in the United States of America

CONTENTS

FOREWORD

This text does not presume to supply all the answers to the phenomenon of fire and its effects on exposures. The truth is, we do not know all the answers. It is generally agreed by those who are willing to face the facts, that much research is needed, particularly in the technical areas of ignition and flame spread in materials and exposures in common use before reasonably precise answers may be reached in a number of critical areas of fire scene examination.

A group of research people recently conducted a series of tests on explosive gases at the China Lake Naval Weapons Center on the California desert. These tests were accomplished in the interest of efficiency and public safety concerning the transportation and storage of flammable and explosive compounds. Relatively high volume tests were conducted under practical field conditions. Perhaps it should be stated that, over the years, numerous smaller scale and laboratory tests have been conducted with reportedly "predictable" results. Following the China Lake tests, it was reported that the results did not necessarily equate with the predicted ones. For example, Dr. C.D. Lind, chemist and Chief Investigator for the project, stated that liquid natural gas, released in large quantities, burned differently than predicted on the basis of laboratory tests and computer calculations. He further stated, "We could run a test ten times and it would not look the same. The current large scale field tests provide little help, to date, to predict how even larger spills will behave." The current tests were with controlled 1,500 gallon spills in an open environment. According to Dr. Roger A. Strehlow, Professor of Engineering, University of Illinois, and a recognized leading authority on gas cloud research, as quoted in the *Los Angeles Times,* August 29, 1977: "Unfortunately, the mechanism of such unconfined explosions is not well understood at this time." He further commented that the present "gap" in our knowledge of the behavior of gas clouds, other than in small scale, guided laboratory conditions, must be corrected by further study and research.

The above is simply illustrative of the fact that we still have a considerable amount to learn about the phenomenon of fire and explosion. Our scientific people recognize that our breadth of knowledge is far from complete and recommend further study and research to raise our level of understanding. What the scientists have said about "knowledge gap" concerning the behavior of gases under conditions of heat decomposition applies to many other areas of fire and explosion behavior in everyday arson and fire cause investigation. It applies to investigative analysis of fire patterns, rate of spread, depth of char in relation to time, and many other so-called physical pointers or "symptoms" of origin currently relied upon by most fire and arson investigators.

Much of the data relied upon is based upon limited laboratory or scientific verification and some of the guides or pointers have been factually discredited by actual structural fire field tests. Practical field tests under structural fire conditions have eloquently suggested the need for further scientific testing and analysis before some of the current investigative methods and so-called guides are fully credited.

Many experienced fire and arson investigators acknowledge that there are more voids in the expertise of fire cause investigation than some of the theorists would care to admit.

There has been considerable progress in the field of scientific investigation during the past thirty years. Having been closely associated with criminal investigation, including the investigation of incendiarism and arson, I would respectfully submit that the scientific side of arson investigation has *not* kept pace with other fields of criminal investigation. It is true there has been solid progress in raising the level of expertise in arson investigation. This has been evident in the increasing interest of Fire and Public Safety Services in cooperating with University- and College-sponsored fire and arson investigation seminars and related, specialized courses during the past twenty-five years. Many of the leading programs have been conducted under the sponsorship of such highly respected organizations as the International Association of Fire Chiefs, International Association of Arson Investigators, Western

Fire Chiefs, California Fire Chiefs, California Conference of Arson Investigators, and numerous law enforcement associations across the nation.

The National Fire Protection Association has long provided reliable data valuable to the fire and arson investigator on such subjects as fire growth, fire loading, and fire- and explosion- causing agencies and fuels. This data is available to investigators who know where to look and how to interpret the information presented.

Fire and arson investigation, regardless of what some would have us believe, is far from being an exact or precise science. For too long, we have "shadow boxed" with some of the basic problems in the field of research, knowledge, and training.

The crime of arson will continue to escalate so long as we continue to avoid appropriate research, training, and assignment of qualified personnel to deal with the prevention and investigation of incendiarism on a realistic basis.

It would be presumptuous to imply that all information set out in this text is original. Further, with the current areas of uncertainty and disagreement in the profession concerning certain physical aspects of fire origin and behavior, there may be some who might quite properly take exception to some areas of the text. So be it. In such case, the "exceptions" might produce verified documentation based upon much needed, qualified, scientific research.

Much has been written, over the years, about fire and arson investigation. There are many excellent texts and publications on general investigative procedures. The emphasis appears to have been on the general procedures rather than on the technical anatomy of the fire scene and specific cause. I have respectfully attempted to fill in some of the information gaps in a manner which may be of practical assistance to the investigator in establishing the origin and cause, whether the process is by physical analysis, by interview of witnesses and evaluation of their observations, or by a combination of both.

Much of the information in this book is based upon what has been learned from working on fire scenes and with fire investigators and experts with long-term, practical fire scene experience and laboratory expertise. While it might be said experience is an expensive teacher, it also happens to be, at least at the moment, the only way fire investigators can acquire knowledge of fire behavior. This may be supplemented in the form of the experience of others in assisting the younger investigators and thereby minimizing repetition of costly mistakes.

I would like to thank my former boss and old friend, Brendan P. (Pete) Battle, for encouraging this work and for his valuable suggestions.

Much of the information in this text has been passed along or suggested by long-time investigators who have been where it is and have seen it like it is. I respect each and every one of them and I am grateful for the assistance. I am thinking of officers like Chief Angelo Minchella, Chief Raymond Bachtelle, and Matt McCalla; Chief Bill (W.C.) Noller and Jim Upton; San Diego Sheriff's Inspector Robert Newsom; Chief Herb Johnson; Chief Wally Trotter, and Captain James O'Neill and his crew in the Los Angeles Arson Unit; the men in the Arson and Bomb Squad of the Los Angeles County Sheriff's Office; Santa Ana, Newport Beach, Orange, and Orange County Fire Departments; the Orange County District Attorney's Office; the many fine investigators across the country, including Dick Cole of the San Diego District Attorney's Office; and Edward J. Wallen, who has prosecuted many cases as a U.S. Attorney, and who has courageously represented defendants at the other end of the spectrum.

I would also like to thank some of my old friends and communicators: Walt Higgins; Bob May; John Stuerwald; Thor Fladwed; Don Morris; Lou Segal, long-time chemist for the California State Fire Marshal's Office, who many of us have called upon over the years when we needed reliable information on ignition and flammability characteristics of certain compounds or materials; and Ed Bent of the California Department of Education, Division of Fire Training, who has worked so long and hard to raise the standards of fire and investigative training.

I am indebted to many Fire Departments, law enforcement agencies, District Attorney's offices, and yes, public defenders and practicing attorneys for some very specific and practical comments on what should be expected from their individual points of view. Interestingly, investigative objectivity and complete factuality in reporting was a common thread throughout the fabric. Some of the departments have very kindly provided excellent fire scene photographs, with their specific comments on fire scenes of accidental and incendiary fires—photographs that tell each fire's particular story. It is their belief that actual investigative fire scene photography is a valuable educational and visual aid. I certainly agree.

Some of my earlier arson investigative assignments were under the exacting supervision of Samuel R. Waugh. I am certain he is generally remembered as one of the most highly respected arson investigators in the profession. Special Agent Waugh had previously been a staff investigator with the Royal Canadian Mounted Police. He was an infinitely patient and thorough investigator, and always humane, ethical, and objective in all of his investigations. He advocated the conservative and cautious approach. I hope I learned a few things from Sam. I recall one of his earliest, kindly, and timely admonitions—the advice of an old hand to a greenhorn who was probably "coming on too strong." He said, "Harvey, you will occasionally find that there are guys who would rather win than be right. That's a choice you gotta make sometimes in this business. You make the honest choice and you will sleep better each night. Also, you will be able to look yourself in the eye in the mirror next morning when you shave. It's important to win but more important to be right. This is particularly true in situations where a man's liberty and maybe even his life may be at stake."

I have always tried to remember and observe Special Agent Sam Waugh's admonition.

INTRODUCTION

Legal historians as well as authorities on law enforcement and human behavior have always regarded arson as a heinous offense in the sense that incendiary fires often result in fatalities, crippling injuries, suffering, and unrecoverable economic loss. It is well known that the arsonist often strikes with total disregard of the possible results of his act.

Arson is particularly sinister in that it is usually a crime of stealth, often committed in the dead of night and directed at places of human habitation or in areas of human congestion.

In 1976, nationally recognized authorities on public safety stated, for the record, that the incendiary fire loss situation in the United States is at the most serious level in our nation's history. The National Fire Protection Association stated, in 1976, "Arson has become one of the most common crimes in the last part of the twentieth century." In their latest publication, *Arson,* they have provided statistical data verifying what they describe as a "skyrocketing of arson during the past decade" and further commented, "There is no indication the rate of rise will slow down unless someone puts a stop to it." The findings of the National Fire Protection Association are supported by the International Association of Fire Chiefs who labelled arson in the 1960's and 1970's as the most costly act of violence perpetrated by man, with the exception of war, and resulting in the deaths and injury of untold thousands of American citizens and well over one billion dollars in property damage annually.

In June, 1977, Battalion Chief James J. O'Neill, Commander of the Los Angeles, California Fire Department Arson Unit, testified before the California Senate Select Committee on Fire Services that arson had increased 1000 percent in the city over the past ten years with an estimated cost of one million dollars per month to the taxpayers of that city. Senator William Campbell stated, "Arson's impact on the American economy, each year, may total as much as ten billion dollars through higher insurance premiums, lost jobs, and higher taxes."

Omaha, Nebraska reported a 28 percent increase in suspicious fires in mercantile establishments, taverns, and nightclubs. St. Louis, Missouri reported a 17 percent increase in economically related arsons in 1975. In 1973, a west coast city investigated an incendiary fire involving computer operations and resulting in major property loss. The motive was "fraud." The proprietors hired a "torch" to burn the premises to collect insurance. The torch and proprietors were apprehended and convicted. In the Pacific Northwest, arson-for-profit conspiracies were identified and arrests and convictions followed. In the summer of 1977, major arson ravaged New York City during a period of power failure in the area.

The arson problem is not unique to any particular part of the nation. Like some other types of violent crime, it appears to be spreading from the so-called "inner-city" areas into the suburbs. This is exemplified in all categories of arson from fires in distressed areas to commercial, fraud, school and church fires, and yes, even forest and wildland fires.

The nationwide arson problem amplifies the necessity of meaningful investigative attention. Once identified, the arsonist must be dealt with in accordance with the provisions of our justice system. During the past two decades, the courts have tightened investigative procedures including crime scene searches and seizures, interrogation of individuals, admissibility of extrajudicial statements, surveillance tactics, and invasion of privacy. These are basic constitutional guarantees which distinguish our democratic system from that of the police state. At the same time, the courts recognize the duty to protect the public from the acts of the criminal. This often requires a fine balance which may, at times, frustrate the fire and law enforcement authorities and even confuse the public. This balance cannot be maintained without the full cooperation of thoroughly trained, competent, and objective public safety officials and investigators.

This applies, full measure, to the fire or arson investigator who must be carefully selected and trained to do his job legally and in accordance with the facts.

Illustrative of the increase in arson over the past decade is the case of one major midwestern city reporting that 40 percent of their fires have been deliberately set. Various other communities, large and small, have placed the arson or incendiary incidence between 10 and 50 percent of their total reported fires.

It is recognized that the average act of arson causes more damage than the accidental fire. There are logical reasons; for example, the planned incendiary fire may be arranged for delayed discovery. Accelerants or boosters and even explosives may be utilized. Many incendiary fires are set during late night hours or on weekends in business districts when the chance of early discovery and report will be minimized.

Arson loss figures, admittedly sporadic and incomplete, are probably conservative. Further, extensive fire losses often discourage factual investigation, thereby negating discovery of the act of arson and resulting in the classification of the cause as "undetermined." The unsubstantiated or incomplete investigation always insures the criminal's chance of success—regardless of his motive. He is free to strike again at a time and place suited to his convenience.

During the past five years, there have been indictments and arrests exposing arson-fraud rings throughout the nation and with reasonably accurate evidence of involvement of well-organized criminal planning. Factual investigation, by competent, trained personnel, has resulted in prosecutions and convictions in arson cases where fraud, white collar profit, and even intimidation has appeared as motives.

Data from the records of the Federal Bureau of Investigation and the President's Commission on Fire Prevention and Control disclose that arson property loss accounts for at least 10 percent and possibly as much as 30 percent of the total fire loss figure. According to a U.S. Department of Commerce report, structural fire loss figures were projected at more than four billion dollars in 1976. The President's Commission reported, "This is greater than the loss caused by all other types of crime combined." Their studies disclose that "the arson rate has been rising faster than other classes of major crime." Knowledgeable authorities attribute at least some of this unprecedented rise to the neglect of meaningful investigation of incendiarism and arson by most law enforcement agencies. This neglect is a matter of record.

A report was prepared for the National Institute of Law Enforcement, U.S. Department of Justice,

by Aerospace Corporation, a scientific research group, dated October, 1976. This report was based upon a nationwide survey of the arson and incendiary problem and its impact on society. This report is probably the most comprehensive and objective analysis of the problem that has been conducted in this country during the past fifty years. The report defines the present magnitude of the arson problem, comparing it with the impact of other major crime in some detail. The report categorizes arson as the most costly act of violence except war and is, indeed, a major growing problem.

After detailed presentation of statistics and analysis, the report listed a summary of twenty recommendations including improvement of statistical data necessary in the confrontation of the problem and a crime index system. (There is no arson index system today; neither is there a uniform reporting system.) The upgrading of selection and training skills for personnel selected for fire and arson investigation, educational standards in the technical areas of fire and arson investigation, and instruction standards including requirements that instructors have a minimal amount of experience as field investigators specializing in arson investigation was stressed.

The recommendations further included "adequately trained" personnel assigned to arson investigation, increased practical fire research in fire behavior, as well as further meaningful laboratory research. The record shows that there are far too many unknowns in the area of physical evidence analysis and further serious scientific research is required before these unknowns can be defined. The report recommended development and upgrading of laboratory and field investigative equipment to insure more accuracy and integrity in fire scene examination and analysis of fire scene physical evidence.*

The National Fire Protection Association's records disclose that, in 1971, three times as many incendiary fires were recorded than in 1960. Federal Bureau of Investigation records disclose a general steady rise in arson over the past decade with a 75 percent increase between 1971 and 1974. In 1975 and continuing into 1976, increase in major crime, including arson, is projected in approximately the

*Aerospace Corporation, *Survey & Assessment of Arson & Arson Investigation,* (Washington, D.C., October, 1976). Prepared for the National Institute of Law Enforcement, U.S. Department of Justice.

same scale although current figures (1976) are not complete.

The record discloses that arson continues to be a multi-motive type of crime. A recent scientific study indicated approximately 17 percent of the arson fires were insurance motivated; other motives include urban unrest, social and inner city problems, old established motives including arson to cover other crimes, hate, jealousy, revenge, pyromania fires, and juvenile vandalism.

The size or circumstances of a fire often cause pre-judgment by supposedly experienced and knowledgeable officials and others. Further, insurance company loss executives are continually confronted with investigative pitfalls such as prejudgment of cause based upon the exigency of the moment.

Fire investigation is a highly sophisticated investigative activity which requires investigative and technical "know-how" and, very often, time and attention to detail. Much has been said about whether arson investigation should be handled by Police or by Fire Departments. There are excellent examples of responsible and productive investigations by Fire and Police Departments, Sheriff's Offices, District Attorney's investigative staffs, Federal and State agencies, and by certain qualified representatives of the insurance industry. Some of the outstanding cases have repeatedly illustrated the value of objective cooperation between all concerned and within the guidelines of our legal system.

It must be emphasized, however, that successful arson investigation usually demands the expertise, in the first instance, of a qualified investigator in establishing: (1) the origin of the fire; (2) the cause of the fire; and (3) approximate time of ignition, if reasonably possible. Certainly, the follow-up to identify and bring the arsonist to justice should also be assigned to qualified personnel.

Establishing the cause of the fire (in criminal fires, the *corpus delicti*) is a part of the investigation where the specialist may become an essential part of the investigative team—regardless of whether he comes from a police, Fire Department, or laboratory background. This investigator must be able to speak the fireman's language and evaluate the fire scene evidence. He must be able to qualify as an expert witness on cause and origin of fires if and when the matter proceeds to court. As I have suggested on a number of occasions throughout the text, establishing the cause of the fire is one of the most difficult bridges to cross in the investigative and prosecutive processes. This is a fact seldom appreciated by

those with a limited knowledge of investigative and legal procedures.

I know from experience that the arson investigator occasionally finds it very difficult to support his testimony as to origin and cause with credible evidence. Proving the cause is one of the major obstacles in the presentation of an arson case. One of the best tools that an investigator has at his disposal to maintain his credibility on the witness stand is the use of fire-scene photography. It is for this reason that I have included nearly 100 fire scene photographs in this book.

Arson investigation is an integral part of the fire prevention picture. It is well known that about 40 percent of the nation's fires are classified as undetermined. Common sense indicates that if we do not know the cause of these fires, we cannot effectively work to prevent their recurrence. The records also indicate that the larger the fire loss, the less is the likelihood of a supportable cause being established.

Until our society is fully informed and recognizes and meets the challenge presented by incendiarism, arson will continue to exact the toll on life and property it has in the past decade and with a reasonable probability of continuing to increase.

The bulk of educational and training data currently available in the field of arson investigation suggests a preoccupation with general procedures rather than with the anatomy of the fire scene and evaluation of physical evidence and relevant data which will identify the cause. While the *modus operandi* of arsonists, including "pyros," is interesting and important, and while motive and investigative procedure is also important, the record indicates that the investigative and prosecutive breakdown in most arson cases begins right back at the fire scene with the analysis and proof of cause. The second major road block to successful investigation and prosecution appears to be in the investigation and interrogation of witnesses and suspects.

I have attempted to include information which will help the field investigator when he takes the witness stand. It can be a very lonely place.

Experienced investigators and attorneys have long since recognized that courts and juries are frequently "turned off" by witnesses who resort to stereotyped and overly technical language when everyday English would have better explained the situation. Some investigators and attorneys call it communication.

The author hopes, in a modest way, to fill some of the informational gaps and thereby assist the field investigator in his difficult task at the fire scene. This text is not intended as a treatise on general investigation since there are many authoritative books dealing with general criminal procedural and legal investigative techniques; rather, it is hoped to assist the field investigator in the phenomenon of fire and the anatomy of the fire scene. The use of stilted and overly technical language is avoided wherever possible.

If this text assists any investigator in doing his job more ethically, legally, and efficiently, then this book has been worthwhile and I will be grateful.

THE ANATOMY OF ARSON

CHAPTER I

THE UNFOLDING OF AN ARSON CASE

Premeditated and carefully planned arson is seldom solved without investigative alertness, skill, and cooperation between fire and law enforcement authorities. In most circumstances, the evidence only appears in focus after long hours of careful work and complete objectivity.

Successful procedural techniques have much in common with assembling a picture puzzle in that the scene is not complete until all of the necessary pieces are in place. Thorough planning and systematization are essential.

Prejudging a fire scene is dangerous. The record is abundant with examples wherein presumptuous and inexperienced investigators, like the knights of old, have mounted their white chargers riding off in every direction at once. Following is a summary of facts developed during the investigation of a planned arson in a western city. The circumstances are not atypical of a number of other planned incendiary fires that have occurred, wherein the suspects were apprehended, prosecuted, and convicted. The case may be fairly illustrative of how some arson cases develop when the necessary investigative cooperation and expertise is provided. Arson and incendiarism *can* be detected and proved. Suspects can be identified, apprehended, and connected to the scene. Arsonists can be convicted under our system of law and justice. Statements to the contrary result from ignorance, indifference or 'myth.'

Mr. A was a respected and active member of his community who operated a furniture and appliance retail outlet in his city. This was a two-level, modern building on the main thoroughfare. Mr. A became involved in gambling debts. Neglect in his business, inflation, excess inventory and other circumstances were carrying him rapidly toward bankruptcy. Mr. A was bound to the premises by a long term lease which he had negotiated in more profitable times. He unsuccessfully attempted to negotiate an adjustment in his lease. He noted it contained a fire clause that would void the lease if the premises were destroyed by fire. He decided to terminate the lease by this process and, at the same time, liquidate his distressed inventory to the insurance companies.

Mr. A gradually increased the insurance coverage on his merchandise and equipment. He encountered no difficulty in this area since his brokers quickly recognized his increased values based upon inflation and in probable contemplation of the increased insurance premiums. Mr. A was already well covered by a liberal business interruption policy designed to compensate him if his business was interrupted by fire or other disasters.

Mr. A was indebted to a well-known gambler who was aware of his financial distress and who had "connections" in the East with groups familiar with the arrangement of insurance liquidations and fires. Following a conference, he put Mr. A in touch with an eastern "businessman" who arranged for a professional "torch" to meet with Mr. A at a predetermined spot to discuss arrangements for the fire. The meeting took place in a western city in a restaurant a few miles from Mr. A's home. The "torch" was a personable young man tastefully attired. We shall designate this young man as Mr. B.

Mr. B outlined suggestions and instructions which he cautioned Mr. A to follow explicitly. These instructions included discontinuance of his burglar alarm system with advice on what to tell the alarm company, establishment of a specific alibi for the evening of the fire, keys to the premises, and a date and time for the fire to occur.

The date for the fire was set for Halloween evening, the time for 8:10 p.m. The specific time was selected because the city planned a Halloween Parade down the main street which was to start from the plaza, two blocks from the furniture store, at 8:00 sharp. The conspirators estimated that the parade would be passing in front of the store at 8:10. The Fire Department was located such that it would be necessary to cross the main street and go through the parade en route to the fire. It was believed that the crowds and parade would delay arrival of the fire department sufficiently to allow the fire to gain headway and insure its success. It was also felt that the early hour of the fire would probably negate any suspicion.

Mr. A and his wife had arranged to be special guests in the VIP reviewing stand with one of the more prominent local citizens.

Following the final out-of-town planning conference, Mr. B was supplied with the necessary keys, including an entry key for a rear service door, and made his 'tactical' survey of the establishment and the neighborhood. In the meanwhile, Mr. A contacted the burglar alarm company instructing them to discontinue the alarm service because he considered the system troublesome and unsatisfactory. The service was terminated forthwith.

At a final meeting between Mr. A and Mr. B, the date and time of the fire was further confirmed. Mr. A arranged for suitable "storage" of sealed pacakages provided by Mr. B in locked spaces in the rear of the store on both levels. These sealed packages contained accelerants and other incendiary equipment needed by Mr. B. This preplanning made it possible for Mr. B to travel light on the evening of the fire. At this time, Mr. A provided Mr. B with a substantial downpayment on the job.

At shortly before 8:00 p.m. on the evening of the fire, Mr. B moved through the alley and entered the furniture store via the service door with a key he had previously tested. He unlocked the designated storage spaces on each floor, obtained his supplies, relocked the doors, and distributed his "plants" at desired locations on both levels. These "plants" were contrived combustibles saturated with gasoline. He then connected the "plants" with heavy synthetic wrapping cord soaked in flammable liquids, extending the "trailers" through the halls and onto a second level fire escape from which he planned to ignite the trailer. Exiting onto the fire escape, he checked the alley and noted that all was dark and observed no one. He checked his watch — it was 8:10 — and ignited the trailer, closed the exit, and began his descent into the alley. At this point, he observed a person in the alley with a flashlight approaching the area to the rear of the building. He utilized his alternate escape route: jumping from the fire escape to the roof of an adjacent building. At this point, he heard a dull explosion as the "plants" inside the furniture store ignited.

As Mr. B followed his escape route across the top of an adjacent building, he slipped on a skylight hatch and fell to the gravel and tar roof surface. He continued toward the building at the side street line and found a plumbing pipe extending down the rear to a concealed garden area. Making sure the alley was clear, he descended on the pipe and exited from the alley to the side street and walked to his rented automobile which he had parked several blocks from the scene. As he walked, he heard the sirens of the emergency vehicles responding to the fire. He failed to note, however, that the Halloween parade had not started. (Occasionally, the best laid plans cannot foresee contingencies such as the parade marshal arriving five minutes late. The parade could not start without the grand marshal.)

As Mr. and Mrs. A waited in the VIP reviewing stand for the parade to begin, they heard the dull explosion and observed flames emerge from the windows of the furniture store two blocks away from the reviewing stand. They watched as emergency apparatus proceeded unimpeded to the scene. Police authorities controlled the crowds while the fire department laid lines from hydrants into the front and rear of the involved premises. The fire was controlled after extensive damage to the interior.

An alert command officer observed the unusual fire patterns extending to both levels through the halls and along the carpeting toward the front of the store. He also discovered one of the trailers extending through the fire escape door on the second level and into the hall. He reported his findings to the Fire Chief who immediately sealed off the premises and posted guards. He then called for assistance of the police in further investigation of the cause of the fire. Further fire overhaul was suspended pending arrival of fire investigators and detectives.

Residue of plastic containers was found in the secured spaces and carpet samples were taken from suspected incendiary areas. The suspect materials were photographed in place, marked, sealed, and transported to FBI laboratories for analysis and report.

Meanwhile, authorities were canvassing the neighborhood for witnesses. Occupants of an apartment house across the alley from the store described a man who reportedly emerged from the fire escape door and, immediately following the sound of an explosion, leaped from the fire escape to the roof of the adjoining one story building and disappeared toward the side street across the rooftops. He was observed to fall at least once during this flight.

Investigators discovered fresh marks where someone had descended from the end building into an unpaved space at the rear. The descent marks and clear foot tracks were recorded and preserved by measurement, photography, and plaster casts.

Investigators found residue of torn fabric on a wire guide along the descent pipe. Examination of a roof skylight disclosed that someone had slipped along the steep roof pitch adjacent to the skylight. Tar and gravel samples were preserved from this location and also forwarded to the crime laboratory.

Police intelligence sources were able to connect Mr. A with Mr. B through fingerprints on a rented vehicle. This was accomplished with the aid of an informant who had seen Mr. A and Mr. B having dinner in a restaurant in a neighboring city. Through a court ordered utility communication record, the connection between Mr. A. and Mr. B was further established: The identification was corroborated by fingerprints on another rented vehicle.

Police investigators contacted police authorities in Mr. B's home city and briefed them on the evidence developed so far. The authorities in the eastern city, familiar with Mr. B's *modus operandi,* investigated further and learned that Mr. B had been visiting in the west coast area and had been expected to return shortly. A surveillance was arranged to monitor Mr. B's return to his home base.

Immediately following Mr. B's return, the authorities, armed with appropriate search warrants, examined Mr. B's person and premises and found one pair of shoes with bits of tar and gravel embedded in the soles and heels; the shoes were subsequently matched to the foot tracks in the alley space where the suspect had descended to the ground from the roof. Laboratory analysis matched the roof residue with residue found on the suspect's shirt and trousers. A torn section of his trousers matched with the torn fabric removed from the pipe area where the suspect had descended from the building.

Investigation disclosed that, several weeks prior to the fire, Mr. A rented a warehouse under a fictitious name. A search warrant disclosed that a considerable quantity of valuable merchandise had been moved from the furniture store — a little at a time — and replaced by distressed merchandise surreptitiously purchased from a bankruptcy outlet. Synthetic wrapping cord samples from merchandise in this warehouse was matched to the wrapping cord that had been saturated in flammable liquid and used for trailers inside the store.

Mr. A's records disclosed operating losses and stock manipulations over a period of several months prior to the fire; insurance coverage exceeded the value of the merchandise, including that in the store and in the hidden warehouse.

Mr. A and Mr. B were indicted by a county grand jury in the jurisdiction of the fire. Mr. B waived extradition and was returned for trial. Each defendant was convicted of arson and burning personal property (also a felony) for insurance fraud. Trial was by jury. Each defendant was sentenced to the State prison for the term prescribed by law.

Here was a case in which the fire authorities were alert and, sensing something was wrong with this fire, suspended further overhaul until experts could examine the scene. They promptly sealed the area off, thereby protecting the integrity of the physical evidence and the scene. The Fire Chief requested assistance from the Police who promptly assigned qualified criminal investigators. The physical evidence was identified, marked, packaged, and sent to the FBI Laboratory for analysis and report. (An FBI laboratory expert subsequently testified at the trial concerning his laboratory findings. This established the accelerants used, the *modus operandi* of the fire and the identity of the "torch.")

Detectives, initially assigned to the scene, were able to locate witnesses who directed them to the roof of the escape building from which evidence, later leading to the suspect, was obtained. Police intelligence sources were able to make appropriate contact with authorities in the East to insure appropriate investigation at that end when the suspect returned home. Police informants provided information which initially connected Mr. A and Mr. B and which identified the hidden warehouse.

Again, as will be shown throughout the text and as will be experienced in actual field investigation, the investigation of arson and incendiarism is seldom successful without the fullest cooperation between fire and law enforcement authorities.

Objective fire investigation, by qualified personnel, insures the protection of the innocent as well as the identification and processing of the guilty in accordance with the provisions of our constitutional and judicial system.

CHAPTER II

A GENERAL DEFINITION AND DISCUSSION OF THE LAW OF ARSON

This chapter is not intended as a fully embracing treatment of the subject of arson or incendiarism. What is said may serve to acquaint the fire investigator, in plain language, with some of the origins of the rules of human conduct concerning incendiarism and the specific act of arson which most jurisdictions have now codified for enforcement in modern society. Although there are basic similarities in fire setting laws in the various jurisdictions, the arson investigator must familiarize himself with the laws of the jurisdiction in which he functions. All law enforcement agencies, including the fire services, have access to expert legal advice from offices of the County Attorney, District Attorney, and Attorney General. The investigator should seek advice when he is in doubt as to the law or his investigative procedures. This applies to *all* aspects of his investigation.

Working knowledge of the basics of the common law origins of arson and codified application is essential if the investigator is to understand and apply the information he receives during his field investigation. Again, it is emphasized that when the investigator encounters a situation in which he is uncertain, he should contact appropriate legal authority. While this precaution may occasionally cause some delay, it may prevent days, weeks, or even months of investigative effort from being neutralized because of investigative legal error.

Although investigative mistakes may have been made in innocent ignorance, evidence may be excluded because of investigative fault and the case may collapse. The Courts have repeatedly stated that officers, or their agents, must not break the law to enforce the law.

Ignorance of the law does not excuse the criminal; neither does it excuse the investigator.

It may be said that the Law of Arson, as we know it, deals with definitive law governing the conduct of human beings in relation to the willful and malicious setting of fire to certain defined property, under cer-

tain defined conditions, and for which a certain defined punishment in the state's prison, upon conviction, is prescribed.

While it is the duty of certain public officials to investigate crimes, including arson, it is equally their duty, at all times and under all circumstances, to scrupulously observe and protect the basic constitutional guarantees of everyone in our society. Our system of government is one which equally represents the dignity of the State and the dignity of the individual. Our highest Courts have said, "The ideal that every man is entitled to due process of law and a fair and impartial trial is the very cornerstone of civilized government." This includes a fair and impartial investigation.

What is Arson? Britannica's World Language Dictionary defines Arson as "the malicious burning of a dwelling or other structure." The word is derived from the Latin *ardeo* meaning "to burn."

Basically, our modern codified system has grown out of the old English Common Law. With the early settlement of the American colonies came much of the English custom and system of jurisprudence. There were some exceptions but these are of no relevance to the subject at hand. Arson was one of the English Common Law crimes brought to this country with settlement of the colonies along with other major felony crimes such as murder, robbery, and burglary.

Following our independence, and by a process of sociolegal evolution, the codified versions of Arson and the fire related crimes have appeared, usually in accordance with the demands of society, legislative manifestation, and judicial interpretation. This is how our governmental system works. To cover this system of sociolegal evolution in detail is not the province of this text. Basically, however, the old English Common Law crime of arson was based upon apparent needs of the time. One of the legal authorities of the time, Lord Coke, defined arson as "the malicious and voluntary burning of the house of another by night or by day." *(Coke's Inst.* Chapter XLIX.) In brief, the concept of that time specified "the malicious and voluntary burning of the house of *another."* It should also be noted the scope of the crime was confined to the *house.* This seemed to have been the feeling of the time, since a dwelling house was where one lived and the willful or malicious burning of the house of another thereby threatened personal safety.

Under the Common Law of the American colonies and our formative years towards becoming a nation, arson was considered a crime against the habitation of another, as was common law burglary in those days. Both were serious crimes with arson being considered the more severe because of the killing potential of fire. But, remember, it was not arson if one set fire to his own house. Neither was it arson if he set fire to a school house, grocery store, bank, or other non-dwelling. In one early treatment of the matter, it was said, "If I burn down my tenant's house to get the insurance or for any other cause, it is arson; but, if he should burn it, with maliciousness and willfulness, it is not arson."

Some time later, Sir William Blackstone, in commenting upon the subject and its scope, stated, "Arson, *ab ardendo,* is the malicious and willful burning of the house or *outhouse* of another man." *(Blackstone's Commentaries,* Book IV, Chapter XVI.) It would appear that our courts generally adopted Sir William Blackstone's definition. It should be noted that outhouse was included in the above definition and it has been interpreted that it was included since, if one set fire to another man's outhouse, such fire might reasonably communicate to the house or dwelling. In other words, such arson was a threat to the habitation. It will be subsequently shown that many state statutes have now included the phrase, "dwelling, place of habitation, or parcel thereof," which is intended to protect human life from the ravages or criminal acts of the arsonist. The scope includes hotels, apartment houses, house trailers, and tents, regardless of whether or not any person is actually residing in the space at the time.

Arson has always been classified as a "heinous and aggravated offense." The courts have repeatedly stated, "Not only does it endanger human life and the security of the habitation, it evidences a moral recklessness and depravity of the perpetrator." (People v. Caiazza, 61 Cal. App. 505, 215, Pac. 80) Sir William Blackstone stated, "This offense is of very real malignity and much more pernicious to the public than theft because of the terror and confusion as well as by the law of society; and, lastly, because in theft the thing stolen only changes its master but still remains in use for the benefit of the public whereas, by burning, the very substance is destroyed. It is also more destructive than murder itself of which it is too often the cause; since murder, atrocious as it is, seldom extends beyond the felonious act designed whereas fire too frequently involves in the common calamity persons unknown to the incendiary and not intended to be hurt by him, and friends, as well as enemies. For which reasons the civil law punishes with death such as maliciously set fire to houses in towns, and contiguous to others; but is more merciful to such as only fire a cottage or house standing to itself." *(Blackstone's Commentaries,* Book IV, Chapter XVI.)

Blackstone's comments about the "common calamity and terror" caused by the incendiary were obviously applicable to his time, as they were in Nero's when Rome burned. Perhaps his commentary is even more appropriate to modern times, particularly in our distressed urban areas, when vandalism, crime, civil strife, and common terrorism by arson and bombings are frequent items of news coverage today that are often relegated, after a few hours, to the back pages.

In practically any week in any year, one can read of dwelling, apartment, and hotel fire losses and multiple deaths with news commentary, "The cause is undetermined but investigation continues," or "Arson is suspected but no suspects are identified." The news coverage usually fades in accordance with the glow of the next emergency of the moment and relegates the former tragedy and unsolved crime to the back seat of the vehicle of neglect in the continuing parade of current crisis.

Many states began adopting what was described as a "Model Arson Law" which was designed to provide a more uniform standard of statutes dealing with the willful and felonious setting of fires. This Model Arson Law was intended to help clarify some of the then current legislative neglect and the uncertainties manifested in the laws then in existence in most of the United States and state jurisdictions. Of importance was the suggested principle that passage or acceptance of the Model Arson Law, by all jurisdictions, would create a foundation for better understanding by fire and law enforcement officials and the judiciary, and certainly more uniformity in the laws of the penal system governing fire safety and security.

The Model Arson Laws, in one form or another, have been in effect in the majority of our states for the past forty years; some states having adopted the Model Law as far back as 1929. Up through the years, such laws or codes have been updated and supplemented depending upon the trends in the areas. For example, during the periods of civil and social unrest of the 1960's, amendments and supplements were made in various jurisdictions to cover possession and use of explosives and explosive devices, of incendiary devices, etc.

The following sample codes are a current part of the Penal Code System in one state and are illustrative of the Model Arson Laws from which they evolved since their adoption in 1929. They are similar, in greater or lesser degrees, to the laws governing arson and incendiarism in most of the more progressive states today. The reader should study the sections and compare them with those in his own jurisdiction.

ARSON DEFINED — PUNISHMENT

Any person who willfully and maliciously sets fire to or burns or causes to be burned or who aids, counsels, or procures the burning of any trailer coach, as defined in Section 635 of the Vehicle Code, or any dwelling house, or any kitchen, shop, barn, stable or other outhouse that is parcel thereof, or belonging to or adjoining thereto, whether the property of himself or of another, shall be guilty of arson, and upon conviction thereof, be sentenced to the penitentiary for not less than two years or more than twenty years.

(In respect to the above, it should be noted the statute covers a considerably wider spectrum of property than that covered under common law arson; additionally, the statute makes the willful and malicious burning a felony whether the "property of himself or of another." Under the older common law, such burning of one's own house charged no offense.)

Further, as to what constitutes a burning, it has been repeatedly held, in a charge of arson, "if an attempt is made to burn a house by lighting a fire, and the wood of the house is charred in a single place so as to destroy its fibre, the crime of arson is complete, even if the fire is extinguished." (People v. Haggerty (1873) 46 C 354.) Evidence that a wooden partition to a building was charred by fire and that one place burned through is sufficient under the law, in most jurisdictions, to constitute a burning. So long as

other elements of the *corpus delicti* are present, it is within the intent of the statutes to constitute fire damage; in other words, that a criminal element or agency was the cause of the fire. Under the statute, the burning must have been willful and malicious "and it is up to the jury to determine whether the act of burning one's own house is both willful and malicious." (People v. George (1941) 42 CA 2d 568 109 P2d 404.)

BURNING OR AIDING AND ABETTING BURNING OF A BUILDING NOT A PARCEL OF A DWELLING HOUSE OR NOT USED AS A DWELLING — PUNISHMENT.

Any person who willfully and maliciously sets fire to or burns or causes to be burned or who aids, counsels or procures the burning of any barn, stable, garage or other building, whether the property of himself or of another, *not a parcel of a dwelling house;* or any shop, storehouse, warehouse, factory, mill or other building, whether the property of himself or of another; or any church, meeting house, courthouse, workhouse, school, jail or other public building or any public bridge; shall, upon conviction thereof, be sentenced to the penetentiary for not less than one nor more than ten years.

(It should be noted that this section covers property "not a parcel of a dwelling house," thereby expanding the spectrum originally covered under the common law. There is considerable legal precedent upholding the above section, embracing acts in the field of arson in the sense it is applied today.) See People v. Chavez (1958) 50 C2d, 778, 329 P2d 907.

BURNING PERSONAL PROPERTY — PUNISHMENT.

Any person who willfully and maliciously sets fire to or burns or causes to be burned or who aids, counsels, or procures the burning of any barrack, cock, crib, rick or stack of hay, corn, wheat, oats, barley or other grain or vegetable product of any kind, or any field of standing hay or grain of any kind; or any pile of coal, wood or other fuel; or any pile of planks, boards, posts, rails or other lumber; or any streetcar, railway car, ship, boat or other watercraft, automobile or other vehicle; or any other personal property not herein specifically named except a trailer coach, as defined in Section 635 of the Vehicle Code; (such property being of the value of twenty-five dollars *and the property of another per-*

son) shall upon conviction thereof, be sentenced to the penitentiary for not less than one nor more than three years.

(The above is another example of the legislative extension of penal laws governing incendiarism and arson.)

BURNING OR AIDING AND ABETTING BURNING OF PERSONAL PROPERTY WITH INTENT TO DEFRAUD INSURER — PUNISHMENT.

Any person who willfully and with intent to injure or defraud the insurer sets fire to or burns or causes to be burned or who aids, counsels or procures the burning of any goods, wares, merchandise or other chattels or personal property of any kind, *whether the property of himself or of another,* which shall at the time be insured by any person or corporation against loss or damage by fire, shall upon conviction thereof, be sentenced to the penitentiary for not less than one nor more than five years.

(It is noted that not only is this statute limited to the burning of personal property, but also that an essence is the requirement of a specific intent, i.e. "to injure or defraud an insurer." It has been held, in this type of charged offense of burning insured property, that an acquittal on a charge of burning insured property is *not* inconsistent with a conviction of Arson.) See People v. Miller, 1940-41 CA2d 252, 106 P2d 239.

ATTEMPT TO BURN PROPERTY — PUNISHMENT — WHAT CONSTITUTES AN ATTEMPT.

Any person who willfully and maliciously *attempts* to set fire to or attempts to burn or to aid, counsel, or procure the burning of any of the buildings or property mentioned in the foregoing sections, or who commits *any act preliminary thereto,* or in furtherance thereof, shall upon conviction thereto, be sentenced to the penitentiary for not less than one nor more than two years or fined not to exceed one thousand dollars. The placing or distributing of any flammable, explosive, or combustible material or substance, or any device in or about any building or property mentioned in the foregoing sections in *an arrangement or preparation with intent to eventually willfully and maliciously set fire to or burn same,* or to procure the setting fire to or burning of the same shall, for the purposes of this act,

constitute an *attempt to burn such building or property.*

(It should be noted that the legislature, in considering this section, elected to impose either a severe felony type sentence (imprisonment in the penitentiary) or an alternate fine *without* prison sentence which would render the act, upon sentencing, of misdemeanor class. The sentencing, upon conviction, would probably depend upon the gravity of the offense and surrounding circumstances — in other words, "let the punishment fit the crime." The "attempt" section is extremely useful where the act of arson falls short of completion regardless of the particular circumstances. Especially in conspiracy and insurance fraud cases, very often the preparation may be elaborate with the chain of activities of the criminal or conspirators falling just short of the goal of arson through interruption but with sufficient evidence to sustain conviction for attempt.)

The difference between "preparation, the attempt, and the completed act of arson" may be touch and go and one of legal as well as investigative and physical interpretation. It should be recalled that, earlier in this chapter, it was suggested that investigators are the fact finders. Get the facts and consult with your legal or prosecuting officer for guidance as to where you are in the investigation and the legal progress in the inquiry your evidence suggests. Our comments on the above statutes are to illustrate some of the legal complexities that may be encountered and emphasize the importance of competent legal guidance as the evidence develops.

A penal code section of a western state provides as follows: "Every person who willfully and maliciously burns any bridge exceeding in value fifty dollars, or any structure, snow shed, vessel, or boat, not the subject of arson, is punishable by imprisonment in the state prison for not less than one year, nor more than ten years.

"Every person who willfully and maliciously burns any growing or standing grain, grass or tree, or any grass, forest, woods, timber, brush-covered land, or slashing, cut over land, not the property of such person, is punishable by imprisonment in the state prison for not less than one year nor more than ten years."

(The above appears to be an extension of the laws governing incendiarism but it should be noted the law states that the property covered is that "not the subject of arson." It would also appear that the legislature intended the property have a minimum value of fifty dollars where said property be of personal property category. The second paragraph was obviously designed to cover real property "not the subject of arson" thus including forests and wildlands.)

It is well known that arson has often resulted in death. This is recognized in legislative acts identifying murder. For example, Section 189, California Penal Code, states:

"All murder which is perpetrated by means of poison, or lying in wait, torture, or by any other kind of willful, deliberate, and premeditated killing, or which is committed in the preparation or attempt to perpetrate arson, rape, robbery, burglary, mayhem, or any act punishable under Section 288, is murder of the first degree; and all other kinds of murders are of the second degree."

It should be mentioned that arson is one of the crimes which may, upon conviction thereof, lead to a person's being designated as a habitual criminal and confined as such in a number of jurisdictions. In this context, the debate as to the modern definition of arson continues: whether, within the habitual criminal context, the old common law definition of arson will prevail or whether arson now includes the property spelled out in the Model Codes which have been adopted in so many jurisdictions. The controversy concerning what acts shall be construed as arson in the habitual criminal context is illustrated in such cases as the Bramble Decision, 31 Cal (2d) 43, 187 Pac. (2d) 411 (1947); People v. Angelopoulos, 30 Cal. App. (2d) 538 86 Pac. (2d) 873 (1939); People v. Miller, 41 Cal. App. (2d) 252, 106 Pac. (2d) 239 (1940); People v. George, 42 Cal. App. (2d) 568, 109 Pac. (2d) 404 (1941).

During the past two decades, escalation of loss of life and property from fire has again increased interest in the crime of arson, and much has been written concerning legal aspects as well as the sociological and scientific phases as well as the need for increased scientific detection. Much has been written about the psychological profile of the arsonist. Numerous studies with various conflicting reports, but no convincing definitive answers, are available.

On the more practical and constructive side, the American Law Institute has, as late as 1960, attempted to upgrade a Model Arson Code dealing with arson. Perhaps a step in the right direction would include updating and standardizing *all* penal codes across the nation. This applies even more specifically to the criminal who now goes "where the action is." This includes the arsonist who works for profit and the arsonist who is retained to get a job done regardless of the specific motive for the fire. The movement of this type of arsonist from New York to Arizona or California, or from Florida to Alaska, or from Texas to Washington, is only limited to the availability of air fare and the length of air travel. While his psychological profile may be of interest and, ultimately meaningful, investigative know-how in dealing with him and uniformity of the law in its application are of more practical concern at the moment.

CHAPTER III

MOTIVES FOR ARSON

The word motive grows out of *motivus,* meaning "moving" or "to move." Webster defines motive as "some inner drive, impulse, intention," etc., that causes some person to do something or "act in a certain way, incentive, or goal." All the definitions are relevant to motivation as it applies to arson and incendiarism. Although Webster utilizes impulse and intent in dealing with motive, the law and the courts distinguish between the terms, as will be shown throughout this chapter. The investigator should understand and distinguish between motive and intent in his evaluation of the investigative picture and the suspect.

At the moment, motive (the reason for the act) is not an essential ingredient of the proof of a crime; although, if relevant in the proper measure, it may be used, either by the prosecution or the defense. Intent, on the other hand, is a necessary element of proof in a felony matter, such as arson, and connotes the essence of willfulness of the act. The distinction may appear to be a fine one from the investigator's point of view, but it must be recognized.

Numerous studies (and reports) by experts on human behavior over the past one hundred years indicate one answer for certain: The psychology or thought processes of criminals in general and, perhaps, arsonists in particular, are often bewildering. The records of the courts are abundant with contradictions between eminent psychiatrists and experts on human behavior as to the state of mind and real or fancied motivations that triggered particular crimes. With the admitted conflicts and uncertainties expressed, of record, by such eminent authorities, it would appear the street level arson investigator has his work cut out for him in identifying a suspect and evaluating the motivations leading up to some of our more serious conflagrations.

The courts will generally accept proof of motive if they can be shown that motive has some legal and logical relevancy to the criminal act according to known rules of human conduct. The admissibility of such evidence is, in essence, for identification of the suspect rather than proof that the fire was of incendiary origin. If it has no such relation, or points in one direction as well as another, it cannot be conered a legitimate part of the proof. "If the motive is common to a large number of individuals, it loses its power of selecting the single guilty individual." (Curtis, Law of Arson Par. 341.)

Investigators occasionally assume that because a person is over-insured this fact is a circumstance supporting evidence that the fire was incendiary in nature; or, because the accused was seen leaving the building shortly before discovery of the fire, that the fire was of incendiary nature. For this purpose, such evidence is not acceptable under the law. While overinsurance, for example, may be a circumstance suggesting motive, it is by no means an item in the proof that arson or incendiarism had been committed. The fact that a person was observed leaving the premises shortly prior to the fire is not acceptable in showing that a crime had been committed. Simply connecting a person to the scene is not adequate.

While the absence of apparent motive for setting a fire is not a defense in itself, it has been held that it is a very favorable circumstance for the accused. This is interesting in light of the fact that the courts have repeatedly held that motive is not an essential ingredient in a prosecution for arson. As we have already indicated, evidence of motive, if relevant and competent, may be admitted on behalf of the people or the defendant. The courts have said, "Should the defendant be deprived of his rights to show he had no reason for committing the crime, or his right to rebut any evidence tending to show motive, the conviction cannot stand." (People v. Hurst, 57 Cal. App. 473, 207 Pac. 499; Regina v. Grant, 4 F&F (Eng.) 322; State v. Isensee, 64 N. Dakota 1, 249 N.W. 898; Commonwealth v. Connelly, 7 PA, Supr. 77, 43 WKly; N.C. 34; Dunlap v. State, 50 Tex. Crim. 504, 98 S.W. 845.)

There are numerous cases holding that the State can introduce evidence showing animosity between the defendant and the owner, occupant, or victim of a fire, and the relations between the accused and injured person are open to inquiry and proof in this manner. (Curtis—Law of Arson 343.)

The courts are apparently generally agreed, when considering motive, that its credibility be carefully weighed; further, the values of such evidence diminishes as time passes without any known effect on the part of the accused to seek revenge. Another factor is consideration of the seriousness of the original motivational provocation in reference to the psychology of the accused and the subsequent relationships, following the provoking incident, between the accused and the victim. For example, according to the courts, "The wrong may have been righted or condoned; or, new fuel may have been added continuing the unfriendly relations. Unless it can be clearly said that the difficulty was too remote, the evidence is generally received and the jury is permitted to weigh the evidence of motive along with the other evidence presented." (Hudson v. State, 61, Ala. 333.)

Authorities on human behavior consider motivation as a major and sometimes vital factor in human conduct. This conduct may appear to be rational or irrational, depending upon many behavioral factors. Some authorities suggest that the line of demarcation between the rational and irrational is often obscure. They emphasize events in history and of record as examples: individual acts, group acts, community acts, and even national acts. Some acts considered irrational today were acceptable 200 years ago; certain acts we accept as rational or commonplace today would have been unacceptable in societies 100 years ago.

It is axiomatic, however, that motivation is a key factor in human behavior with a strong effect on our society. In the lives of the obviously increasing and alarming percentage of our society who engage in serious crime, including the acts of arson and incendiarism, the motivational spectrums have obviously broadened in proportion to the sophistication of our lifestyle. This may be illustrated later in the chapter in the discussion of classes of motivation and specific motive.

Motivation is a key factor, objectively and subjectively, in the lives and operating efficiency of the investigators in solving crimes, including fires, regardless of real or fancied motives of the criminal.

Again, in dealing with motivation for arson or incendiarism, motive must be distinguished from intent, which is a necessary element in any action in the prosecution of arson. In the earlier discussion of the definition of arson, it will be recalled that the fire must have been set willfully and maliciously in order to place the act within the purview of arson and related felony fire crimes.

The perpetrator must commit the act "knowingly, willfully, and with guilty mind" as the courts have so often stated. It is for this reason that they insist on real or constructive proof of intent. Malice can then be inferred from this proof of intent. One of the reasons why the courts insist on proof that a fire was set willfully is to insure that it did not result from some negligent, careless, or unintentional act or cause.

Motive, on the other hand, connotes "why." What prompted the person to set the fire? Perhaps his reason was completely logical to *him* although it may not appear so to a jury of his peers; for example, a reformed alcoholic may torch a cocktail lounge because he believes he can thereby prevent other persons from becoming alcoholics. Or, a discharged employee may willfully drop a match into his boss's waste basket as he departs the premises. Logical? It all depends upon one's point of view. Perhaps the suspect was a merchant in financial distress and with a fat fire insurance policy. He thinks the situation over and decides to liquidate his stock to the insurance carrier by means of fire. His motive is obvious: financial self preservation. This may appear logical to him; it may even appear logical to his associates, the community in which he resides, and even to the average person in today's society, although it is not acceptable as a rule of conduct in our society or under the law for a number of historical reasons.

Although motivation is a key factor in the "why" and often essential to the investigator in pursuing his investigative leads and understanding his suspect, it is not a necessary element of the offense in a prosecution for arson. The average experienced investigator and prosecutor knows that the Court and Jury not only want to know if the defendant set the fire, they also must be convinced, beyond a reasonable doubt, that the defendant did set the fire.

They also must be convinced, by acceptable evidence, how the defendant set the fire. If they cannot be shown why he did it, however, the outcome may be subject to considerable question. It is true, of course, that cases occur where direct testimony of reliable eyewitnesses are produced, establishing that he was seen actually setting the fire. In such cases, even though the defendant declined to say a word or to discuss a motive, he may be convicted since the evidence is considered convincing. On the other hand, the majority of arson cases, growing out of acts of unobserved stealth, are dependent upon an unbroken chain of circumstantial evidence. In such cases, the investigator will find it well to be able to produce reliable evidence of motive for the act— evidence that a jury can believe.

Regardless of what some modern cynics would have us believe, the courts and juries have shown, time and again, the basic fairness and intelligence of the American judicial system.

Motive is further important in that, if we are to reasonably control arson and incendiarism, we must know why people set fires. Although many studies have been conducted and much has been written about incendiarists and pathological fire setters, during the past fifty years, according to a report of Bernard Levin, Center for Fire Research, National Bureau of Standards, Washington D.C., our knowledge about the psychopathology of fire setters is limited to those arsonists who are caught or give themselves up. Mr. Levin pointed out the lack of our present knowledge in this field very eloquently when he stated: "In short, we know the most about the least successful arsonists," (*The Fire and Arson Investigator,* Volume 27, #3, January, 1977.)

There is little productive research in the field of motivation for incendiarism and there are few reliable answers in many critical sectors, including the pathological fire setter and the juvenile who sets fires and may or may not continue the pattern into adulthood. We know why fires are set less than 10 percent of the time. There is no reliable statistical data, on a national basis, for percentages of arson or incendiary fires by specific categories such as insurance or fraud; fires to cover other crimes such as murder, burglary, and larceny; the "psycho" or "pyro" fires; juvenile fires; or fires set as a result of domestic quarrels, such as between husband and wife.

As a matter of fact, according to the most recent study of the President's Fire Prevention and Control Commission of Fire Causes, approximately 20 percent of the nation's fires are classified as unknown or undetermined. This, of course, further prevents the possibility of identifying motivation for arson. It would reasonably follow that, if we do not know the cause, we cannot identify the motive for the act. Even more obviously, we cannot take realistic steps to prevent recurrence.

Very little constructive information has been produced concerning the motivation behind the fires resulting from social and urban unrest in many inner

city and urban areas during the past two decades. We know, of course, that these fires are exacting an enormous economic toll in addition to the human suffering and loss of life that invariably accompanies congested urban area fires, particularly those of incendiary origin. It is not for the fire investigator, of course, to attempt to diagnose the motive behind such fires. He has his work cut out in identifying the cause of the fire and following the investigative leads to the person or persons responsible.

The fire investigator may have contact with those intimately acquainted with the environment, scene, or specific situation and who may be able to put him in touch with the motive for the fire. It is the street level fire investigator who will probably be the first to talk to the suspect and who, within the legal framework of interview and discussion with the suspect, will be in a position to pick up the investigative thread which will lead to the real motive for the fire (not necessarily the same motive the defendant later relates to his probation officer in striving for a lessening of probation, nor what he may later lay out for a psychiatrist in the form of self justification). Although circumstances alter cases, an investigator, properly cognizant of his job and with his feet squarely on the ground, is in a position to provide constructive assistance in the field of motivation and its relation to fire causes as well as to utilize the factor in rationalizing the fire and identifying the suspect.

THE MORE COMMON MOTIVES FOR ARSON — CLASSIFIED

1. *Fires for financial gain*
   A. Burning insured property
      According to a public statement by Mr. Howard Swift, Vice President, American Insurance Association, "More than 20 percent of all fire losses and 40 percent to 50 percent of all resulting dollar damage are caused by intentionally set fires. From 1973 to 1975, losses from incendiary or suspicious fires in the nation rose from $800 million to $1.3 billion." (Los Angeles Times, 5/2/77, as quoted from Chicago Sun-Times)

   This class of fires embraces all classes of property, real and personal—industrial, manufacturing, commercial, agricultural, and habitational—including hotels, resorts, and apartments. The personal property includes distressed wholesale and retail inventories, as well as commercial and private watercraft.

Loose underwriting practices, including inadequate inspection and supervision, often set the stage for the insurance fraud fire. Inducement for repetition is indirectly encouraged by inadequate and incompetent investigation and mass production-oriented claim settlements. The investigation of the possible insurance fraud oriented fire requires objective thorough analysis of all relevant factors. Too often, these factors are ignored or overlooked, either by the authorities examining the circumstances of origin (and cause) of the fire, or by the claims representatives in "closing another file." There continues to be an information and communications gap between the representatives of the insurance carriers and the investigating personnel at the fire scene level. This fault is often compounded by lack of knowledge and understanding of legal complexities and responsibilities, including the use of confidential official and private information.

The fire or arson investigator must be familiar with general underwriting practices and claims adjusting procedures. He must know what he is looking for and where to look. Although "overinsurance" may be an inducement to the insurance fire, other circumstances can provide the necessary motivation: the need for remodeling or decoration, distressed real property or inventory, or a change in zoning that outdates further practical use of existing structures and improvements. These examples are merely illustrative of the wide and increasing range of motives, other than mere overinsurance, that can lead to arson for fraud.

By their very nature, fires in this category require that the investigator contact the insurance claims representatives early in the investigation and continue this liaison until the financial picture is clearly established. Impetuous conclusions, unwarranted by the evidence, too often lead to serious investigative errors difficult to rectify. For example, fraudulent inventory claims may grow out of fires of clearly accidental origin; on the other side of the coin, accidental fires can and do occur where financial distress or overinsurance are quickly apparent. Yet, the insured may be completely innocent of wrongdoing. The investigator must refrain from being stampeded into false conclusions which can result in injustice to the innocent and success for the criminal. Since this chapter is intended to be limited to motive rather than investigative practices and procedures, the latter will be dealt with in detail elsewhere in this text.

B. Arson by creditors to liquidate investment.

This category is often closely related to the common insurance motivated fire. In certain aspects, this class of fire may be more "sophisticated" in planning and execution. It appears to have been in more frequent use during recent years of extended credit and elaborate promotional procedures. The means by which this type of fire can be utilized are only limited by the ingenuity of the people involved in the planning. This category is commonly utilized by organized crime and loan shark operators, including gaining control of various types of business operations—distressed and otherwise.

For example, A is a merchant who may be overextended or overstocked. Credible loan or banking sources may decline the loan. Shortly thereafter, A may be approached by B who represents a group who accepts such loan risks at a lower rate than usual if A relinquishes certain controls on the business. Such conditions do not always appear on the record but A understands those informal arrangements and is made aware of the implications if he chooses to ignore them. After A is securely "hooked," suitable arrangements are made to insure the property. Sometimes the insurance remains with the original broker and carrier; occasionally, the property is insured through a selected broker or agent. The loan sharks may or may not be named on the loss payables of the policy—again, depending upon the hold upon A by B.

The fire may be arranged with or without the specific knowledge of A—again, depending upon the particular circumstances of the setup. The loan sharks often prefer to insure ignorance on the part of A in order for him to emerge "clean" in the insurance investigation, including his inventory and proof of loss, and a very probable examination under oath which may, by insurance contract requirements, be demanded by the insurance carrier. In the meanwhile, the "beneficiaries" of record, or *not* of record, depending again upon the arrangements, wait in the wings until the settlement is made. They are usually adept in collecting from A once the settlement is completed.

Unscrupulous loan hustlers often resort to the use of professional "mechanics" or torches to produce the fire or explosion. The package may include the services of unscrupulous appraisers and adjusters who will prepare and expedite the claim for the insured.

The fire mechanic who may be retained to arrange the fire, if competent, will produce a fire which may appear to the investigators as strictly accidental and be classified as such. Or, he may produce one which will appear to have been set by vandals or burglars, as circumstances demand. Such a fire will remove suspicion from the insured. He will be "home free" except in his obligations to his creditors who arranged the fire. Loan sharking is a tool of the underworld, whether it be considered organized crime or not. It is well recognized and its presence is felt in most metropolitan areas of the United States. There is nothing really new or unique about their fires except that they are obviously on the increase.

Businessmen are subject to human frailties and weaknesses as much as anyone. They are usually subject to the same temptations and desires—all well known to hoods and fixers. They may become overextended financially because of perfectly reasonable and logical business trends or they may become involved, a little at a time, through personal indulgences beyond their means and, ultimately, beyond their control, thereby becoming fair game for the sophisticated sharks swimming in the vicinity.

Unscrupulous operators often prey upon the apparently healthy business operations, acquire control, then manipulate the physical or paper inventories; such as substituting distressed or false inventories for more expensive ones, then insuring and burning.

The detailed coverage of this category of motive is beyond the scope of this text. The arson investigator has his work cut out for him in the investigation of this type of fire and should seek all the help he can get.

C. Burning to break a lease

This category of motive is not uncommon and involves most occupancy types—industrial, commercial, agricultural, resort, and multiple and individual occupancy types. Financial depreciation, deterioration of the area, rezoning, or other changes restricting occupational use, along with financial distress, are some of the principal reasons why further use of the property may not appear feasible to the tenant. He may consider the fire clause in his lease to be the only financial escape hatch available by which he may emerge financially whole; his lease obligation may be terminated under the wording of the particular lease. In the process, he may liquidate his merchandise or other insured assets in the process of vacating his lease by fire. He is home free with a reasonable profit, depending upon the vulnerability of the investigators and insurance claims people and the astuteness of his own representatives. If he doesn't benefit by the insurance coverage, he may come out, indirectly, through the tunnel of tax write-off.

During recent years, this type of fire has also been predominant in areas being cleared for urban renewal, rezoning, freeway and highway development, and a number of other conditions developed in our increasingly changing society. This class of "fire for convenience" often negates the necessity of expensive litigation between concerned parties.

D. Burning to cover embezzlement and theft of inventory.

This category is more or less self-explanatory and, again, only limited to the ingenuity of the perpetrator. The evidence of the motive is often destroyed in the fire or it may be entirely overlooked by incompetent or incomplete investigation.

For example, A, a company official, in a continuing fraud on the stockholders, has been disposing of valuable liquor stock through B, who is a friend and confederate. The "sale" does not appear on the company records and the merchandise is disposed of through a discount, insuring a profit for all concerned. No sales taxes appear since the transaction is off the record. Those involved in the transaction are "off the hook" with the state and federal income tax people since the illicit income does not appear as a matter of record.

The time for company inventory approaches and this is when the physical inventory shortage will be discovered. The fire occurs before the inventory and the warehouse is destroyed. The cause is undetermined and the insurance carrier, knowing the insured company to be financially sound and beyond reproach, quickly accepts the book records of inventory and pays the loss. After all, they say, the lengthy investigation would have been expensive, the cause was undetermined, and any attempt to establish the physical inventory, considering the demolition of the fire, would have been practically hopeless.

A not uncommon device in arranging this arson category is the substitution of distressed or less valuable inventory at some conveniently acceptable interval preceding the fire. Another example of arson in this category is destruction of records which are incriminating or fraudulent, such as situations where the subject may be under impending audit by creditors or tax agencies.

E. Intimidation

This category has been common in periods of labor strife. The record, over the years, is abundant with coincidence of known incendiary fires involving buildings, yards, vehicles, and trucks during strikes. The responsibility of either side is seldom established, each faction attributing the fires to irresponsible and unauthorized individuals on the opposite side. The investigation of such fires is too often dismissed on the basis that the fires and other acts of vandalism will invariably cease with settlement of the dispute.

Adequate investigation is a practical fire and crime prevention tool which should supplement lawful and equitable negotiations. Where such investigations have been utilized by competent, appropriately informed law enforcement officials, this type of loss has been minimized in many cases of record. This is particularly true where law enforcement agencies have details assigned to work with labor and management during such crises.

Arson is utilized as an intimidation tool in numerous other situations including ethnic-oriented neighborhood and school problems. It is utilized by hoodlums and gangs in various urban "protection" scams.

F. Arson to cover evidence of another crime

This category embraces arson to cover other crimes such as murder, burglary, and other property related offenses. The murderer desiring to destroy the identity of his victim or to destroy the evidence of cause of the victim's death is one example. Careful fire scene examination and/or autopsy may disclose the precise cause of death even though most of the body is incinerated by the fire. (See Snyder, LeMoyne, Homicide Investigation: Practical Information for Coroners, Police Officers, and Other Investigators, 2nd ed., C.C. Thomas, 1973.) The murderer may also seek to destroy the scene of the crime, thereby negating evidence of his *modus operandi* and also evidence of his presence at the scene.

The burglar may set a fire to cover evidence of his presence; for example, his fingerprints or evidence of entry and/or missing property. If the stolen property is deemed lost in the fire, the burglar/arsonist will have less of a problem in disposal of the property since it will not be covered or described on a stolen property or crime report.

G. The revenge and spite fires

Malicious fires in this category cover a wide spectrum of situations often overlapping with other passion oriented grievances, be they real or fancied. These include the so-called neighborhood fires involving strife between juveniles or adults; they also include the domestic fires. It is occasionally stated that women resort to setting closet fires involving clothing of the other person; that lovers of either sex will often put the torch to the bed; that homosexuals

often put the torch to personal items of the victim, and so on. Some theories and teachings are as varied as the Freudian hypotheses collected and expounded over the years. The arson investigator may become confused in the clouds which emerge, in some circles, regarding such fires, to the extent that he gets lost in the maze and the case continues unsolved. Here again, the investigator must keep his feet on the ground. He must make his own evaluation of what he reads and hears about the numerous theories and so-called "complexes." He must only use that evidence and information upon which he can rely and refrain from placing too much credence upon folklore and superstition. He must investigate the case upon its merits.

H. Politically-motivated fires

In the late 1960's and early 1970's, fires were set to dramatize political issues. Such acts were fairly common and exacted a considerable economic toll. There is reason to believe that such fires may continue, although possibly on a diminishing scale. Individuals and groups engaged in setting fires to banks, public buildings, churches, university properties, and schools did so with the stated purpose of embarrassing public officials who were in opposition to social and educational systems, and to publicize particular grievances. Such fires may be in connection with meetings or public gatherings, marches, protests, etc., or apart from them.

Vandalism and arson are occasionally accompanied by the use of explosives and portable incendiary devices such as have been utilized against public utility improvements in certain areas of the nation. These are usually selected as targets with political or civil dissidents taking credit for the destruction and damage.

Investigation of such fires and related incidents requires investigative skills, organizational knowledge, and tact. Experience has shown that an irresponsible investigative approach to this type of problem often triggers further violence and property loss without identification of the individuals responsible. Progressive agencies increasingly recognize the need for an educated, intelligent, and organized approach to this increasing problem geared to preventing recurrence, and dealing with them in the manner prescribed by law.

Group action fires, sometimes classified as riot fires, were prevalent in certain areas during the late 1960's. Various authorities have categorized these fires as evolving out of urban and social unrest. They are in some disagreement about whether the so-called rioting was spontaneous or whether it was fostered by extremists. There is very little reliable evidence to provide a solid answer. It is a well established fact that such fires were often accompanied by looting and attacks on law enforcement and fire personnel, and emergency equipment. This is similar, in many respects, to riot and organized resistance to established authority in many other parts of the civilized world today.

Progressive public safety authorities have devised means of coping with this type of unrest which has proved effective when in the hands of thoroughly trained and oriented personnel. The preventative handling of these areas is highly sophisticated and requires intelligence, patience, and tact. The investigation of incidents in this category usually requires more than the efforts of individual arson investigators.

Although the importance of identification and prosecution of suspects or groups in the above category should not be minimized, civil authorities must learn to cope with the problem on a broader and more realistic basis; this includes the organization and assignment of carefully selected law enforcement, fire, and investigative personnel to establish communication and understanding with dissidents at the community and street level. This is a modest price to pay in terms of prevention of loss of life and property damage that may continue in the foreseeable future.

There is no simple answer to arson loss in this category, but neither can the problem be ignored.

I. Psychological and mental disorders and the apparently motiveless fires

Common usage seems to have characterized fires in this general class as pyromania. Pyromania, of course, is only a word. It is defined by Webster as "a morbid propensity to set things on fire." Others have described the "pyro" as one who suffers from the irresistible impulse or compulsion to set fires. One of the possible general misconceptions, of course, is that the "pyro" or pathological fire setter is identified by the "gleam in his eye" or by his disheveled or unbalanced appearance. Experienced detectives and arson investigators recognize that they cannot rely upon this theory. Even with the modern scientific and medical technological advances, medical authorities on human behavior are in disagreement on appearances, causes, and effects of human behavior in the field of violent acts such as incendiarism.

Neither this chapter nor this text is intended to cover the medicolegal aspects of fire setting. However, a look at the investigative picture may assist in orienting the arson investigator to his place in identification of the arsonist and possibly assist in producing factual answers to *why* these fires occur and, last but not least, what practical steps can be taken to prevent their recurrence.

Questions have been raised throughout the past, and continue to be raised: "What type of person would set a fire just for the hell of it? Does his act always suggest a personality disorder?" As most experienced fire investigators have long since learned, incendiarists (arsonists if you will) come in all sizes, ages, condition of appearance, educational, environmental, religious, ethnic, and occupational backgrounds. Yes, unfortunately, even firemen and law enforcement officers are not excluded. Incendiarists include both sexes and, more often than not, do not manifest the wildeyed appearances described in novels and characterized on television series. They do not necessarily conform to categorization too often placed on them by some medical experts and amateur investigators. Experience has shown that they are not necessarily bed wetters or frustrated homosexuals.

Certainly, most admitted incendiarists in this category may be found to have departed from the traditional norm in one or more obvious respects. Some very respected medical authorities would then ask, "But what *is* traditional?" This is one area in which some prominent authorities in the field of human behavior disagree.

Experienced medical authorities and arson investigators generally agree that "fire bugs" cannot always be recognized on sight. Neither are they always predictable. Their reasons for setting fires may appear almost reasonable when learned or the reasoning may appear to be illogical or even disgusting to the average individual. The reason may be one of compulsion — unpredictable even to the suspect. In some cases, such as in certain types of recognized illness, or under the influence of alcohol or narcotics, the arsonist may have no recollection of what he did. These are merely samples of situations the investigator may encounter in dealing with this class of fire.

One respected author recently stated, "Most arsonists as well as other felons can be characterized as psychopaths, or as having psychopathic personalities." There are numerous medical and legal authorities as well as experienced investigators who would respectfully disagree with this generality. If his conclusions were true, it might be difficult, if not impossible, to convict a criminal, including an arsonist for profit (or other objective motives), of his charged offense once the defense, as above categorized, was raised. It is well stated that because all horses are animals, it does not follow that all animals are horses. Perhaps the above author's quoted comments are, in a sense, illustrative of the confusion and uncertainty confronting the medicolegal aspects of incendiarism even today.

According to an excellent report by Bernard Levin, Center of Research, National Bureau of Standards (as published in the International Association of Arson Investigators, Vol. 27, January-March 1977), "Our knowledge of psychopathology of fire setters is limited to those arsonists who are caught or who give themselves up. In short, we know the most about the least successful arsonists." In my opinion Mr. Levin couldn't have stated the problem better.

A wide variety of publications have appeared, over the years, dealing with the psychopathology of incendiarism, including many excellent writings on mental disorders such as pyromania. A careful review of the publications will illustrate the contradictions in the conclusions of many respected authorities. These contradictions often appear graphically in criminal cases, including prosecutions of arson cases, when the testimony of eminent medical experts differ categorically as to the basic points of diagnosis, state of mind, and knowledge and understanding of the act in the mind of the accused: whether he recognized what he was doing, whether he could avoid doing the act, and whether or not he knew the difference between "right" and "wrong."

The responsibility of seeking out the incendiarist continues to rest with the public safety departments, police and fire, and with the trained arson investigator. These people must seek out information and advice from the medical experts in identifying patterns in fires and suspects. This is particularly necessary in the so-called "repeater" fires. Once the suspect is identified, apprehended, and moved into the justice system, the medicolegal aspects of the inquiry may proceed. But until the suspect is identified and brought into the system, the investigator must utilize all of his knowledge, training, and back-up resources. He must *think*.

In the field of identification and apprehension of the pathological fire setter, the picture may be a continuously changing one. This class of arsonist usually operates alone, often in the dead of night, in the absence of witnesses, and with little rational concern for lives and property. He often selects the entrances or exits of multilevel apartments and hotels in congested areas or other targets of the required combustion and attention potential. Numerous examples of fatal conflagrations appear in the news and record indexes each year, frequently with unsuccessful investigative results. The unidentified arsonist remains at large to select his next victim at a time and place subject to his impulse.

An example of a successful investigative solution to an incendiary series occurred when fires plagued a Southern California industrial and commercial area several years ago.

Patterns developed slowly. For example, most of the fires occurred along railroad sidings or rights of way. Railroad car journal box waste was identified at origins of most of the fires which usually occurred late at night when there was limited activity in the areas. Because of delayed discovery, many of the fires gained major proportions. The final toll was several millions in property losses not including lost production and employment in a number of plants. The losses included plants, warehouses, yard storage, and packing sheds.

The suspect was finally apprehended setting a fire while another fire in the same neighborhood was in progress. He was an average appearing laborer identified as a section hand in his mid-twenties; calm and pleasant to talk to and with no apparent hostilities or hang-ups. His co-workers spoke well of him other than that he was a "loner."

Because of intelligent handling by investigators, the suspect, throughout the closing days of the inquiry, directed them to the scenes of dozens of major fires he had set during the several previous months. His recollection of how and where he set the fires corresponded in detail with known and recorded facts concerning the origin of the fires. In addition, the suspect directed the investigators to several properties not destroyed by fire and where he had set fires which were unsuccessful—most of which had been discovered and extinguished by owners, occupants, or employees without material damage and without report to the authorities. (In some instances, owners and occupants were questioned, and stated that they did not report the incidents to the authorities fearing their insurance would have been cancelled or, at best, the premiums raised.)

Not only did the suspect factually identify with over $16 million in fire losses, but he also identified with several other fires which he had set and which were *not* reported.

Why did the suspect set these fires? He stated that he usually returned to the scene of each fire after the fire department arrived on scene and was engaged in combatting the fire. Because the fires were large and spectacular, the press was usually on hand. He stated he would "stand around listening to the fire officers telling the press about how the fire must have started and where it started" and he always got a kick out of it because "they were usually dead wrong." He added, "I was the only one who really knew." He commented that this fact always gave him a great deal of satisfaction.

The defendant was found to be sane, within the meaning of the law, and was convicted on multiple arson charges and sentenced to the State prison for the term prescribed by law.

As experienced investigators well know, not even the major percentage of costly series of incendiarism are successfully solved. An example of a somewhat less than successful conclusion is illustrated by the following series that occurred encompassing several communities, approximating a 40-mile radius across residential areas. Again, a common denominator appeared to be the suspect's *modus operandi*. For example: (1) the suspect selected occupied modern apartment complexes; (2) he set his fires either in the vehicles parked in the open end car ports or spaces under the building or in the wooden storage cabinets at the rear of each parking space; (3) he utilized combustibles available at the scene as kindling to get his fire going; (4) all of his fires were set where he could return to a freeway within less than one minute; (5) he made it a point, after setting his fires, to call the dispatcher in the particular community where he happened to be operating and stated that he had set another fire; (6) he became known to the authorities and the press as the "Thursday Night Firebug" because this appeared to be his favorite evening of operation; (7) recordings of the voice of the suspect suggested certain idioms and word pronunciations that suggested he was from another part of the United States and that the mannerisms were not affected; and (8) his *modus operandi* suggested he had considerable knowledge of emergency dispatching procedures as well as of investigative techniques. He did not appear to be excited, as he usually addressed the particular dispatcher in a matter-of-fact tone.

On the basis of available information, it appeared that the suspect was using some type of motor vehicle to move around and that he apparently operated alone.

During the several months these fires continued, neighboring fire and law enforcement agencies cooperated closely, utilizing all known criminal suspect and *modus operandi* files and full investigative, technical, and operational procedures in attempts to identify the suspect. Select investigation and surveillance teams were assigned, employing night observation techniques and helicopters. All units were radio coordinated.

Hundreds of witnesses, suspects, and informants were interviewed with information disseminated and coordinated by all concerned agencies. Legally authorized measures were taken to identify or trace the suspect when he made his periodic telephone calls.

Although the elaborate investigation resulted in the apprehension of numerous criminals involved in other crimes, such as burglary and crimes unrelated to arson, the arsonist in this major series was never identified. Despite hundreds of thousands of dollars in property damage, fortunately there was no loss of life with these fires.

It is unknown whether the arsonist moved to another area of the nation, perhaps because of investigative pressure; whether he was arrested on an unrelated crime and maintained his silence as to these crimes; or whether he is deceased, grew bored with the activity, or reformed. The latter, in our experience with other arsonists of this category, would appear the most unlikely.

JUVENILE AND ADOLESCENT ARSON

Reliable data on juvenile and adolescent fire setters is limited. This applies to motivation as well as to what percentage may continue fire-setting activities into adulthood. There are no reliable statistics on those who are repeaters. There are differences of opinion between experienced law enforcement officials, field investigators, juvenile probation authorities, and medical authorities on human behavior in the field of fire-setting behavior in this class. In view of the present lack of data, each group should be afforded the consideration deserved although they may come from opposite ends of the environmental, educational, and experiential spectrums.

As stated earlier in this chapter, useful and revealing studies have been made, based upon limited groups with a limited access to all background information. As in the case of adult impulse and repeated fire setting, it is suggested among most specialists in fire setting and human behavior that more than random, occasional study of *all* facets of the problem and treatment might be the best practical approach to fire prevention and crime prevention over the long haul.

From information provided by numerous experienced fire and law enforcement people over the years, the majority of juveniles apprehended for willfully setting fires usually provide reasons for grievances which, when worked out, are seldom repeated. This applies to such acts as school firesetting, neighborhood fires, "boredom" fires, etc. This applies to fires set by the juvenile to get attention and also to "gang fires," which are becoming more common.

Juveniles almost invariably go through a period, usually when quite young (and curious) where they inspect, examine, and, if possible, experiment with everything within reach. This includes electric lights, water faucets, television, matches, the stove, and the fireplace. Fire, by some primitive instinct that remains a mystery to us, is nearly always of particular interest to a small child. Children have and will continue to play with matches and experiment with fire. Common sense tells most parents and fire investigators that there is nothing abnormal about this. These fires are *not* arson although the damage can be great. These fires are not malicious but they can cause loss of life, and frequently do. The process with the growing juvenile, in such fires, is attention, training, and education.

As the average juvenile grows, his curiosity about fire usually diminishes in proportion to his progress towards maturity. Throughout these stages, the juvenile develops varying psychological and behavioral patterns that, as they emerge, fit him into particular motivational patterns and regulates his association patterns in society and with the so-called "making a living" process. The study and analysis of these growth and behavioral patterns are very properly the field of competent medical and psychological experts. It is probably outside the scope of the field fire investigator, other than through the process of everyday experience in observing juvenile fire setters, their acts, and attempting to help them, along with their associates and families, at the street and neighborhood level.

Children (juveniles), depending upon their environment and development, may be expected to manifest the same attitudes, responses, and impulses, in varying degrees, as adults. These manifestations may include distrust, jealousy, insecurity, desire for attention, lust, hate, and so on. They may respond in terms of acts of violence, including incendiarism and arson.

Where emotional problems exist, juveniles may be expected to continue acts as long as that problem, real or fancied, exists. It is not for the arson investigator to attempt to classify these emotional problems, but he must be aware of the more common patterns in order that he will be able to identify the responsible juvenile and deal with him on that basis. He must be practically familiar with juvenile (and adult) behavior to understand the reasons a suspect may advance for doing what he does. Once the juvenile is identified with the cause of a fire, the matter should properly be referred to the court and the juvenile and probation system designated to handle such matters. The procedures vary, depending upon jurisdiction, and the fire investigator should be familiar with the procedures in his area.

It is a matter of record that juvenile incendiarism has increased significantly during the past decade. This increase is apparent in school fire losses in particular.

According to a Senate Subcommittee recently impaneled to investigate juvenile delinquency and crime, juvenile arson destroyed over $600 million worth of school property during 1975. (This doesn't include other types of juvenile vandalism such as theft, broken windows, and damaged school vehicles and general maintenance equipment.) In one Southern California city, a recent school fire of definite incendiary origin cost $250,000 in damages; in that particular area, juvenile school vandalism leaped from $302,109 in 1975 to $800,000 in 1976.

This increase in vandalism (most of it arson) cannot be attributed to urban decline alone nor can it be attributed to poverty because the areas of the most extensive vandalism were in what is generally termed middle-class to affluent neighborhoods. The bulk of the vandalism is directly traced to juveniles from average to upper-middle-class families. While it is true that schools and public properties in areas of neglect and urban decline also account for a high order of incendiarism and vandalism, they are by no means unique in this respect. A definite incendiary fire recently caused extensive damage in an elementary school building in a major Southern California city. Investigation disclosed that the building was in the process of refurbishing and repainting. The evidence indicated that an incendiary device had been thrown through a window during the early morning hours. The matter remains under investigation.

On the motives for juvenile arson and incendiarism, one psychiatrist was asked, "What kind of sick mind is involved here? Why do they do it?" The psychiatrist replied that motives could be as numerous and varied as the leaves on the tree. Most authorities on juvenile behavior agree that the questions as to "why" are not easy to answer. One commented, "There may be as many reasons juveniles set fires as there are juveniles who are setting fires." The expert was not discussing the class of very small children who have rather common tendencies of cuiosity about fire and who, like most small children, play with matches and cause fires until they either grow out of the habit or are corrected, in one manner or another, by their parents or by the authorities.

To the question "What are juvenile arsonists like?" one psychiatrist experienced in the field of juvenile antisocial behavior replied, "Well, perhaps the juvenile is not in the mainstream of social activities at school or he may feel alienated or he may believe in his own mind that the school is confining or punitive. His anger may be directed toward a specific teacher or it may be directed to the school authorities. He expresses that anger with a fire." It should be noted that school fires occur in affluent neighborhoods as well as in depressed ones. Why? Some of the arsonists are from upper-middle-class environments with the traditional conveniences and privileges. So, what about this juvenile? He didn't burn the school because of hunger, deprivation, or social inferiority. He didn't break in to steal, break up the furniture, and burn the place simply to cover his tracks. He wasn't a narcotics addict and his father was not languishing in the county jail or the State prison. So why?

One seasoned investigator remarked, "Perhaps it comes to a breakdown of the family system in our society today. Where is the stability and parental guidance and control?" The officer continued, "For example, what about the answers we get from the kids like when they come home and Dad doesn't get in until very late, often staggering, and Mom sometimes not till later! The kid says, 'What the hell else is there to do?' He says his dad never talks to him, his mother seldom. He wants some attention, *any* attention, even if it's me, the cop."

Another experienced investigator stated, "Parents don't have time to raise their kids anymore. To get by, they both gotta work and the kids are on their own most of the time. They don't have time for their kids." An investigator commented that the problem is not unique to the working neighborhoods. It was present in the more affluent areas as well. "Parents don't take the time to be with their kids anymore; they're concerned with status situations, entertaining, and touring the right spots. They build a swimming pool for the kids when an hour's attention a day is what the kids really wanted. That's the real nut of the problem with most of the ones I deal with when they cop out to me. I know damn well it ain't just a cop out when I get around to talk to the parents if and when they will ever take the time to sit down long enough to talk to me." The officer continued, "How do you blame a kid like this for setting a few fires to get some attention when all he hears at home is how to cheat the guy next door before he cheats you? The way I see it, kids are impressionable and adaptable: give them a chance and they'll usually do the right thing, but that chance has gotta start at home. We can help down here at the precinct but we can't do it all."

With the lack of integrity and uniformity of fire statistics, including the low percentage of successful fire investigations, precise figures on a nationwide basis are presently unavailable. However, reliable authorities in areas where accurate and complete investigations are conducted produce records to support the contention that the majority of juvenile fires are most certainly *not* the acts of compulsive or psychopathic types. In most instances, juvenile incendiarism results from deliberate acts of individuals and groups. As the expert stated, motives, real and fancied, are as numerous as leaves on the trees.

Whether the stated grievances in a particular situation would have merit is not within the province of the fire investigator. The point is that it motivated the act or acts resulting in the burning of the school or other property that may have been involved.

Techniques of investigation, including interview and handling of juvenile and adolescent witnesses and suspects are discussed elsewhere in this text. Suffice it to say that at the moment, dealing with juveniles and adolescents requires compassion and tact. Additionally, special procedures establish guidelines in most jurisdictions. The arson investigator must be familiar with such procedures.

Most experienced investigators and detectives have found it practical and rewarding, when dealing with juveniles, to think back upon their own thought processes and behavior patterns when they were the age of the suspect. Regardless of the heinousness of the particular offense under inquiry, most juveniles, and even adolescents, including the abnormal, are quick to sense insincerity in others and accordingly are more inclined to "clam up" and face it out regardless of the consequences. Regardless of what emphasis should or should not be attached to the Freudian theories of motivation, response, and behavior, most experienced investigators have found that common sense, human kindness, and *knowledge* of all available facts will go a long way toward eliciting the truth from juveniles and adolescents. It is usually just a matter of taking the time and care to find out what really happened and then lay it out to the juvenile. Time, understanding, patience, firmness, and knowledge of the circumstances are of great importance.

Summarizing this chapter, it should now be apparent that there are all kinds of people, young and old, from every ethnic and social background, every size and shape as well as condition of appearance, who set fires for material reasons and at random, as well as without apparent motive. Not all arsonists are psychopathic, regardless of what may be said by some of the authorities on human behavior. The record is abundant with examples of cold, calculated arson committed for material reasons as well as for economic and political reasons. These are not wild-eyed deviate types.

Although motive is not a legally essential element, it should never be disregarded by any investigator desiring to conduct a complete and factual investigation. The key to motive often opens the door which leads down the hall to the suspect. The key to motive in certain classes of fires which are plaguing communities today, may reasonably provide a useful avenue toward a better understanding of individuals, gangs, and groups; whereupon adequate preventative and corrective action can be taken along fire and crime prevention lines.

It has been well stated that, "The best fought fire is the one that never occurred." It is equally true that the best solved crime is the one that "never came off." In this regard, the arson investigator stands in a unique position as a fact finder. He is "where it is," and "sees it like it is." If he really knows what is happening and "tells it like it is," and if people at the decision level will take the time to listen, we may be making just a start in lowering our incidence of incendiarism in our communities and in the country.

CHAPTER IV

INTENT

Intent is quite different from motive and is defined as the purpose to use a particular means to effect a certain result. Motive is the *reason* which leads the mind to *desire* the result (*Ballentine's Law Dictionary;* also, Baker v. State, 120 Wisc. 135 97 NW Rep. 566). Intent is ordinarily an inference of law from acts proved (State v. LaPage, 57 N.H. 245 24 Am. Ref. 69).

Investigators occasionally confuse motive with intent, assuming that because an individual has motive to commit an act, and that incident occurs, such as a fire, that person with apparent motive intended that the incident occur. Finding the apparent motive, they overlook the necessity of seeking out and proving intent.

Motive, as discussed in Chapter III, is not a necessary element of proof in a crime. Intent *is* a necessary element. It must be shown that the defendant intended to commit the act (State v. Shell, 184 Ark. 248, 42 S.W. 2d 19; People v. Maciel, Cal. App. 234 Pac. 877).

In investigating and proving a case of arson, the intent to set the fire must be shown, whether the crime alleged is arson of one's own house or of another's. Direct proof of an intent to commit the crime is never required. The criminal intent may be inferred from the circumstances (Luke v. State, 49 Ala. 30, 20 Am. Rep. 269; People v. Lepkojes, 48 Cal. App. 654, 192 Pac. 160; People v. Schneider, 154 App. Div. 203, 139 N.Y.S. 104). It may be proved by evidence of hostility of the accused to the owner (Massachusetts Commonwealth v. Hudson, 97 Mass. 565). It can also be proved by showing that the defendant was financially embarrassed or that he had overvalued or overinsured his property (People v. Sevine, 85 Cal. 39, 22 Pac. 969; Commonwealth v. Hudson, 97 Mass. 565; People v. Kelley, 11 App. Div. 495, 42 N.Y.S. 756).

It cannot be proved, however, against an accused who is charged with having committed arson for the purpose of securing insurance money, that he has had fires in buildings other than the one mentioned in the indictment; and, generally, where the accused is charged with arson for the purpose of securing insurance money, evidence showing or tending to show that he was interested in preserving the building that has been burned is competent (People v. Rose 38 Cal. App. 493, 176 Pac. 694; Dunlap v. State 50 Tex. Cr. 504, 98 S.W. 845).

If the accused is charged with setting fire to the property of another, evidence to show his familiarity with the premises, and that goods which were in the house shortly before it was burned were subsequently found in his possession, is admissible in showing intent (State v. Vatter, 71 Iowa 556, 32 N.W. 506).

The intent may reasonably be inferred from the act itself if the inevitable consequence of the act is the burning of a building or if the particular purpose cannot be effected without the burning of the property. It has been repeatedly held that every person is responsible for the reasonable or natural consequences of his actions. For example, in a case where the defendants placed matches in unginned cotton in a warehouse with the expectation that they would be ignited in the handling of the cotton, and they were ignited and the building burned, it was held that the crime of arson was committed (Overstreet v. State, 46 Ala. 30).

Neither under common law nor under existing statutes in this country can a defendant be convicted of arson or related statutes merely upon proof that his negligence, even gross negligence, resulted in the burning. The intent to burn is lacking. Any evidence that the fire was unintentional requires that the issue be submitted to the jury (Jones v. Commonwealth, 239, Ky. 110 38 S.W. (2d) 971; Wigfall v. State, 57 Tex. Crim. 639, 124 S.W. 649d).

However, it is well established that if a person sets fire to a building while he is engaged in the commission of another felony, it is arson even though there was no specific intent to set the fire or to burn the building (People v. Fanshawe, 137 N.Y. 68, 32 N.E. 1102).

Intent to defraud an insurer may be formed *after* a fire has occurred even though the origin of the fire may have been accidental and without fault of the insured, and following which the insured willfully permits the spread of the fire with the design of collecting on an insurance policy (Commonwealth v. Cali, 247 Mass. 20, 141 N.E. 510).

The intent again comes into play when one sets fire to a haystack or other personal property so that the fire may reasonably or likely extend to a nearby building and such building is then burned (State v. Roberts, 15 Oregon 187, 13 Pac. 896; Rex v. Cooper, 5 C & P (Eng) 535, 24 E.C.L. 694; Turner and Readers Case, 1 Lew. C.C. (Eng.) 9).

It has been repeatedly held that the means or device used in setting an incendiary blaze is unimportant except that the means be shown. If one sets fire to one building or contents adjacent to or therein, with the intent that the fire shall communicate to another building and the fire extends to that building, the person can be prosecuted for the arson of the latter building. The jury may infer the intent from the acts of the accused in the starting of the initial fire (Commonwealth v. Harney, 10 Metc. (51 Mass.) 422). The intent to burn the latter building may be inferred since one is presumed to intend the natural consequences of his wrongful acts (State v. Colgate, 31 Kan. 511, 3 Pac. 346, 47 Am. Rep. 507).

From what has been said, we may conclude that while criminal intent is a state of mind of the person committing the act at the time the crime is being committed and essential to criminality in this type of case, that intent must again be carefully distinguished from motive and the belief by the perpetrator in the "righteousness or wicked character" of the act. Criminal intent consists of one or another of the following states of mind: (1) direct intent to do the act, such as setting a fire, and (2) intent to do some other felonious act from which the crime charged (for example, arson) resulted as a natural consequence, even though it may not have been contemplated or foreseen by the defendant.

Direct general intent is the common example of criminal intent; namely, the intention to commit the act.

Intent to commit some other serious crime which incidentally results in a fire, produces the situation wherein item (2), constructive intent, comes into play. For example, the suspect breaks into a commercial occupancy and is busy opening the safe with his speed torch and a fire results. He intended to break into the space, and to hit the safe and remove the "loot." This is the specific intent. He didn't really intend that the place burn. However, the law has supplied that intent and he may also be charged with arson.

On the other hand, mere carelessness or recklessness in one's behavior in the handling or use of fire will not supply the necessary intent, nor guilty mind, to support a charge of arson unless, as described above, the suspect just happens to be engaged in the commission of some other felony.

No crime of arson is committed unless the act and the intent exist at the same time. If the intention exists at one time and, later, the act is unintentionally done, there is no arson even though there may be a fire. The two must coexist.

The intent, being a state of mind, is not open to observation like substantial things but can be shown by the evidence of the conduct of the person; what a man thinks and intends is usually manifested in what he does. Acts performed even some time before, or thereafter, may throw light upon the intent existing at the time of the crime. The best proof of intention at the time may be the action at the time.

What a person in possession of his faculties does, he is presumed to have intended to do. Where the crime consists of three elements, the act done, the intent to do it, and the criminal purpose to be accomplished by committing the act, no conviction can be had by proof of the act done without proof of the particular criminal design to be accomplished thereby which supplies the specific intent essential to that particular crime. In *constructive* specific intent, the criminal design may be supplied by inference from the act. For example, where the defendant is shown to have willfully thrown an ignited incendiary device into the hallway of an occupied building in the late hours of the night, he is presumed to have intended the consequences of his act: the involvement of the premises in a fire and the injuries and loss of life resulting therefrom. Further, one who set fire to his own house to obtain the insurance was held liable for arson because the fire spread and a burning shingle fell on the house of his neighbor long enough to set fire to a shingle on that roof (Commonwealth v. Tucker, 110 Mass. 403). In a case where a prisoner set fire to the floor of a cell, with intent to control the flames with some water he had for washing and drinking, until a hole would be made in the floor and through which he might escape, it was held to be arson though he had no design at the time he set the fire to burn the jail (Luke v. State, 49 Ala. 30).

MALICE AS DISTINGUISHED FROM INTENT

Under the common law and under our statutes, malice is an element of the offense of arson although, if the other elements are proved, it may be inferred from acts and statements of the suspect, the method of setting the fire as well as other circumstances. In the investigation of the fire and collateral acts, possible evidence showing presence of malice or lack if it cannot be overlooked or disregarded. This again points out the need for conducting a complete investigation. Even though a particular arson statute may have eliminated the word "maliciously," the element of malice is generally considered essential. It is generally held that malice may be shown by direct evidence or it may be inferred from surrounding conduct and circumstance. It may be implied from evidence presented pointing to the deliberation of the act.

Malice has been defined as a "condition of the mind which shows a heart regardless of social duty and fatally bent on mischief, the existence of which is inferred from the acts committed or words spoken" *(Ballentine's Law Dictionary).* In its legal sense, malice has been held to mean a wrongful act, done intentionally, or with evil intent, without just cause or excuse, or as the result of ill will. It does not necessarily imply spite against any particular individual but rather, in many circumstances, merely a wanton disposition grossly negligent of the rights of others.

Malice is *not* synonymous with intent or willfulness. A statutory definition of "malice" or "maliciously" in California describes the terms as "importing a wish to vex, annoy, or injure another person, or an intent to do a wrongful act, established either by proof or presumption of law" (People v. Wilkinson, 30 Cal. App. 473, 158 Pac. 1067). Under this ruling and definition, the Court may instruct the jury that malice, within the meaning of the law, includes not only anger, hatred, and revenge, but every other unlawful and unjustifiable motive (People v. Daniels, 4 Cal. Unrep. Cas. 248, 34 Pac. 233).

In an arson case, the Court held, "The malice which is a necessary element need not be expressed, but may be implied. It need not take the form of malevolence or ill will but it is sufficient if one 'deliberately and without justification or excuse' sets out to burn the dwelling house of another." (State v. Pisano, 107 Conn. 630, 141 Atl. 660.)

In another arson case, the Court said, "A malicious burning would be such an act done with a condition of mind that shows a heart regardless of social duty and bent on mischief, evidencing a design to do an intentional wrongful act toward another, or toward the public, without any legal justification or excuse." (Love v. State, 107 Fla. 376, 144 So. 843.)

Like the element of "intent," malice may be implied or inferred from the deliberate character of the act (State v. Lockwood, 1 Boyce (24 Del.) 28, 74 Atl. 2). In the quoted case, the Court instructed the jury: "With respect to malice, being the remaining element in the crime charged against the prisoner, the Court says to you that malice indicated in the law signifies not general malevolence, but rather the intent from which flows an unlawful act, committed without legal justification. An attempt to burn a house in which human beings dwell is a cruel act, and the law holds that malice of this kind is implied from every deliberate, cruel act committed by one person against another. The law considers that he who does a cruel act voluntarily does it maliciously. In the crime of attempted arson, the law holds that when the act constituting the attempt is proved to have been done, and to have been done willfully, it is then inferred to have been done maliciously." (State v. Lockwood, 1 Boyce (24 Del.) 28, 74 Atl. 2.)

CHAPTER V

FIRE AND THE INVESTIGATOR

The phenomena of fire has the capability of distorting and, in some cases, obliterating the evidence of its cause. Arson investigators are particularly confronted with this problem because, not only must they attempt to factually determine the point of origin, but they must also attempt to produce reliable evidence, of a direct or indirect nature, as to cause. They must be able to show that the cause did not result from accidental means. In other words, they must prove the fire resulted from willful and incendiary means.

In felony crimes, of which arson is one, a willful and malicious act must be shown. For example, in a homicide case in a prosecution for murder, a mere showing or producing of a dead body is insufficient, if there was no identified cause, other than natural cause of death. On the other hand, if autopsy disclosed multiple stab wounds to the heart and resulting hemorrhage, garrotting, or non-self-inflicted bullet wounds, this or these factors would be acceptable to provide the *corpus delicti* (body of the crime) in the prosecution for murder or manslaughter depending upon the state of mind of the perpetrator. It is not the purpose of this chapter to cover the legal or probative aspects of *corpus delicti* in the crime of arson but merely to emphasize the relationship between the destructive aspects of fire and developing a reliable cause of a fire, including proof of the *corpus delicti* in the offense of arson.

Knowledge of the principles of ignition, combustion, including fire growth and its relation to fuels, ventilation, and fire loading, for example, is vital in arson investigation.

All too often, if the fire has not destroyed the evidence of cause, residue at the origin will have been altered or discarded by firemen during overhaul. Briefly, three factors may irrevocably alter the fire scene to the point of negation of reliable evidence of origin or cause: (1) The consuming process of combustion and resulting demolition; (2) The destruction or overhaul by firemen, salvage personnel, and, occasionally, by the investigators themselves; and

(3) Premature abandonment of the fire scene leaving it unattended or unsupervised prior to arrival of competent authorized personnel, thereby, regardless of the legal implications (which will be discussed elsewhere), rendering subsequently recovered physical evidence subject to question because of either accuracy or integrity. The aspects of systematic fire scene examination will be dealt with elsewhere in this text.

Experience has shown that nearly everyone is impressed with the magnitude and occasional spectacular violence of fire. This is repeatedly evidenced by crowds attracted to fires and the usual news coverage. The tendency is not unique to the public. Supposedly experienced fire fighters often classify fast-growing or spectacular fires as incendiary because of their rapid growth. While accelerated spread or explosive characteristics may be a factor, depending upon the structure involved (fuel load, ventilation, and other specific variables), rapid growth or explosive characteristics, *per se,* are not conclusive. Many experienced firemen have been quoted in the press over the years, saying, for example, "That fire had to be set—it was too fast." Or, "She's a boomer—probably a gasoline job."

Such comments are "choice meat" for early editions but of little practical assistance to the investigator who should be more conservative in his evaluation. He may be confronted with the necessity of producing a more convincing quality of evidence in a court of law at some future time.

The tendency to jump to conclusions is not unique to firemen. Too often, there is a tendency by insurance claims personnel, including investigators, to advance conclusions, unwarranted by reliable evidence, particularly in cases of large fires where cause remains under investigation.

While consideration of the early stages, ultimate size, and final demolition of a fire are important, preoccupation with these factors should not be permitted to submerge calm, systematic analysis of origin and cause. Preoccupation with the ultimate size of a fire, including extensive demolition, often leads to hopeless confusion. Certainly, the perimeter and entire fire area should be considered. Origin and cause, not extent, is the primary concern of the arson investigator.

There is another unfortunate and occasionally expensive tendency common to the investigation of fires; this is the manifestation of an apparent bias to a particular cause. For some, it is "electrical;" others, "careless smoking," without sufficient factual investigation for identification of any reliable cause. There are numerous examples, of record, where fire causes, initially identified as "electrical," "careless smoking," or "faulty equipment" were later proved to have been willfully caused.

There is a tendency in recent years, because of product fault or liability, to assign a cause through subjective investigation, slanted toward plaintiff- or defense-oriented factors, with the true cause being overlooked or deemphasized in the exigency of the moment.

In one such case, a major industrial plant was destroyed in a fire which was classified as undetermined by the authorities. A subsequent insurance company investigation, subrogation-oriented, classified the cause as "electrical." Meanwhile, the owners of the plant, faced with production contracts to fulfill, leased a building in a neighboring area, equipped the plant, and continued production.

Within days of initiation of production at the new location, a late night fire caused extensive damage in the plant. A more intensive official investigation established forced entry through a rear cargo door and a probable incendiary origin to the fire. While the investigation continued, the manufacturer retooled and continued production. Several days later, a late night fire totally destroyed the plant, again putting the manufacturer out of production. Further official investigation disclosed the third fire resulted from arson with strong evidence of internal personnel problems. More factual investigation of the first fire may well have prevented the costly second and third fires.

It is unfortunate that prejudgment is an occupational disease in the investigation of fires. Understanding and factual application of principles of combustion are essential to constructive results in arson investigation.

CHAPTER VI

BASICS OF COMBUSTION AND FIRE SPREAD

It is well known that one of the principle reasons for neglect of arson investigation is lack of understanding of the anatomy of fire origin and behavior.

Our legal system requires, in the investigation of all major crimes that, first and foremost, a crime was, in fact, committed. In arson cases, this happens to be true although this fact is commonly misunderstood. As has been stated in this text, under discussion of the law of arson, it is necessary to prove not only that a fire occurred but also that the fire resulted from a criminal agency. This simply means showing that the fire was willfully and intentionally set or in some jurisdictions, "that the fire was intentionally set with human hands." The criminal agency (willful and intentional act) may be shown by direct or indirect (circumstantial) evidence, but there must be a factual showing of (1) *where* the fire started, and (2) *how* the fire started—again, that the "cause" was other than accidental and with some reliable showing of incendiary means.

Now, what has all of the above to do with combustion and fire spread?

It is well known that fire and the resulting demolition not only can destroy the evidence of where it started but also of how it started. This is unfortunate but it is one of the facts of life. It must be squarely faced when such conditions do exist. Conversely, alleged fire damage and demolition are too often utilized as alibis for false, undetermined, and unfactual causes. False conclusions can lead to escape of the incendiarist from detection and punishment. They can also lead to unjust accusation of the innocent.

It is well known in competent investigative circles that the more prevalent reasons for failure in arson investigations are lack of knowledge of the principles of fire origin and behavior and how to apply competent knowledge. This investigative "void" is too often further compounded by indifferent fire overhaul and salvage procedures.

It is difficult and occasionally impossible to reha-
bilitate a fire scene and its evidence when the integrity of the scene and evidence has been disintegrated by indifferent, ignorant, or even on occasion, willful mishandling procedures.

Finally, it is unlikely that a reliable cause, incendiary or otherwise, will be established without the active participation of an investigator qualified in the origin and behavior of fires and who, furthermore, is qualified to appear and testify as an expert witness as to origin and cause of the fire. (This phase will be discussed in detail elsewhere in the text.)

This chapter is not intended as a complete thesis on the chemistry and physics of fire. Fundamentals of the phenomena of fire, with the more common and basic fuels, are set out in nontechnical language with the thought that the investigator may desire further study and research as he progresses in experience. The arson investigator must keep up to date on such subjects as fire-causing factors, equipment, and reaction of industrial compounds and structure materials to heat and fire. This is a continually expanding area of technical development and particularly relevant to fire cause and fire investigation.

COMBUSTION DEFINED

Webster's College Edition Dictionary defines combustion as: "(1) the act or process of burning; (2) rapid oxidation accompanied by heat and, usually, by light; (3) slow oxidation accompanied by relatively little heat and no light; and (4) violent excitement or agitation—tumult."

As we shall later see, this is somewhat of an oversimplification. The term "burning," as defined by Webster, is too broad in its present usage to be of constructive use other than, as accepted in the chemical sense, burning to undergo combustion. Again, this doesn't really tell us much.

It may come as a surprise to many, but it wasn't until the middle of the seventeenth century that researchers of the time really began to understand the basic chemical principles of fire. We know, of course, that fire was accepted as friend or foe, depending upon its circumstance and size, as far back as man has been able to communicate. During the middle ages, the notion prevailed that fire was an element. There were various theories, up through the ages, evolutionary, religious, etc., all varying but none understanding. Some authorities on human behavior continue to attach significance to the fact that most people are attracted to large fires, appreciate fireworks displays, and are attracted to watching the logs in the fireplace, climatic conditions notwithstanding. As some psychiatrists put it, "The magnetism of fire is strong regardless of man's civilized stature or educational background."

Francis Bacon classed the "superstitions of fire" as one of the "phantoms of the marketplace." Relatively speaking, this wasn't too long ago. In the middle of the seventeenth century, Robert Doyle proved that atmospheric oxygen was essential to combustion during his experimentation with charcoal and sulphur. He also proved that saltpeter ignited when heated in a vacuum and only continued to burn so long as air was present (it wasn't identified as oxygen at that time). Also in the middle seventeenth century, Robert Hook, another scientist, continued Doyle's experiments. Varying theories were advanced with greater or lesser accuracy during the same general period, all concerning the possible chemistry and identity of fire. For example, John Mayow, a student of Boyle, experimented with candles and other combustibles in a jar of air enclosed over water, and observed that air is diminished in bulk when the flame continues in the enclosure. The residual air will no longer support combustion. At this time, of course, the experiments were insufficiently sophisticated to identify oxygen loss and displacement of gases (carbon dioxide, carbon monoxide, etc.) by combustion.

He also observed the respiration of animals in limited atmospheres, noting how respiration ceased, as did fires, when the atmosphere available to the breathing (or fire) process was no longer available. He theorized that the respiratory and burning processes were probably analogous. Subsequent studies, of course, found his studies and theories basically correct. Historical records of the chemistry of combustion show that this life and fire supporting "gas," later named "oxygen," was so named in the late eighteenth century by L. Lavoisier whose experiments and scientific conclusions disproved much of the ignorance about combustion that had prevailed up to

his time. It was Lavoisier's work that established oxygen as the active constituent of "air" and that it is necessary to the combustion process which is a chemical evolution. His methods of quantitative experimentation and reasoning opened the door to the era of modern chemistry. After his findings, the process of combustion was no longer a mystery to the scientific world although much experimentation continued to refine the knowledge of the physical and chemical process of combustion.

The experimentation continues even today because of newly developed materials and fuels. This research includes the spectrum of gases and explosive reactions resulting from critical combustion which will be discussed below.

Returning to the definition of combustion, Von Schwartz, in his studies of fires and explosions, describes combustion as "the process whereby substances or individual constituents of the same combine with oxygen with the liberation of heat." (Von Schwartz, *Fire and Explosion Risks,* translated by Charles T.C. Salter. Chas. Griffin & Co., London, England. 3rd Edition, 1926.)

According to the most reliable authorities, based upon field and laboratory studies, combustion proceeds in a uniform manner given the same fuels, fireloading, oxygen supply, and ventilation. (Byrd-Docking, *Fire In Buildings,* Adams & Charles Black, London, 1949.) This work is based upon British fire studies mainly during the German "Blitz" and the Battle of Britain.

It is a platitude among most firemen that no two structures burn alike and no two fires are alike. From the fireman's point of view, of course, this is a fairly correct premise despite the theory propounded by Byrd-Docking that fire growth and behavior follow known chemical and physical laws. Neither premise can be disregarded and, perhaps, common sense and experience come into play. The differences in the behavior of fires are due merely to the varying conditions in which these laws operate. For example, the fire loading of an occupancy or space, the separations, the oxygen supply, initial and continuing ventilation, and method of attack of the fire by fire department or other control measures are all affected by temperature rise, and the undeniable factors including conduction, radiation, and convection. More on these factors later.

Basically, organic compounds and certain mineral substances, when heated, produce combustible gases or vapors. If uninterrupted, this process of heat and gas production proceeds through the mass (substance to be consumed), accompanied by continuing disengagement of heat and, in most circumstances, apparent in its physical effects such as distortion, char, cracking, displacement, etc., depending upon the available fuels, oxygen, and rate of temperature rise, which may be compounded as area and volume increase.

For our purposes, it may be fairly stated that combustion is essentially a simple chemical reaction of oxidation which proceeds with development of heat and is exothermic.

Fire authorities were probably afforded one of the most comprehensive opportunities for fire study during the bombing of London in World War II. John Bryan covered the subject of heat balance in relating to fuel load in *Fire Protection and Air Raid Precautions Review,* London, August, 1940. The report indicated that the progress of a fire is dependent on the relation between the rate at which heat is liberated and the rate at which it is dissipated. Heat balance was defined as "the difference between the rate of heat production and the rate of heat dissipation." For example, in the case of a "growing" fire, the heat balance is positive until the fire reaches its peak intensity. There is probable temperature rise within this spectrum. From the peak on down, the heat balance becomes negative.

For example, a waste basket is filled with wadded or loose sheets of paper and ignited. Ignition is quickly followed by visible flame pattern and temperature rise. During this brief burning cycle, radiated and convected heat is physically apparent, then dies quickly as the tinder-like fuel is consumed. The phenomenon is also easily demonstrated (and apparent to the senses) in somewhat greater scale when low flash point fuels, such as gasoline or acetone, are poured onto a flat concrete surface and immediately ignited. There is an accelerated temperature rise followed by equally sharp temperature decline as the volatile fuels are quickly consumed. If the poured fuel is permitted to vaporize, thereby providing an appreciable explosive mixture in the atmosphere above the poured material, ignition will then be explosive with a quicker temperature rise and drop, the sequence being in pattern with the ignition lag.

On the other hand, a kerosene lamp, for example, would illustrate a condition of equilibrium in heat balance. The rate of heat production in the lamp flame equals the heat loss, and combustion at the tip of the wick proceeds at a steady rate (neither increasing nor decreasing in intensity); in short, a steady flame.

Whether firemen recognize it or not, heat balance is an important factor in determining the progress of a fire and the reduction of this balance is a fundamental objective in the process of fire control. The heat balance can be reduced by (1) removal of fuel; (2) removal of the oxygen; (3) reducing the burning temperature; or (4) a combination of all three.

There are three factors essential to the process of combustion, namely, the substance or material to be consumed; the available oxygen; and, the disseminating factor: heat. At this point, it might be well to explain that atmospheric oxygen is composed principally of 20 percent actual oxygen with the remaining 80 percent being incombustible nitrogen. Nitrogen, in its pure state, is fatal to all combustion. It is the oxygen, in appropriate proportion, that acts as the chemical bellows. Without oxygen, the fire could not continue. A corresponding influence is exerted by oxygen in explosions which will be dealt with elsewhere. Suffice to say, at the moment, that the percentage of oxygen in certain gases renders them explosive, as does its presence in certain solids. Certain compounds may be self-oxidizing, unstable, and therefore dangerous.

Of course, the technical treatment of the process of combustion may be extremely sophisticated in that the structure of some compounds and their reactions must be considered. Some are simple; others are complex. Tables of dangerous compounds are listed in certain technical bulletins including publications by the U.S. Departments of Transportation, Commerce, and Treasury, along with various state and municipal codes. The National Fire Protection Association publishes volumes and pamphlets describing and identifying gases, combustible solids, dust, and explosives; and handling, use, storage, and reactions in the atmosphere and environment.

Utilization of National Fire Protection Association Codes, Standards, and pamphlets must be appreciated by the fire scene and arson investigator.

Hydrocarbons, of course, are well known to us as material and industrial fuels as well as fertilizer sources. Gasoline, one of the more widely used hydrocarbon fuels (including incendiary and arson fires), routinely contains close to thirty compounds which are all hydrocarbons in liquid mixture.

Perhaps the most common and important type of organic compounds in our daily fire investigation activity are the carbohydrates which comprise the bulk of wood. The carbohydrates differ from the hydrocarbons in very significant ways in that the carbohydrates, being already partially oxidized, have a high oxygen content. The process of burning wood is, very simply, a completion of the natural oxidation that started in the synthesis of the wood. Wood products may be one of the most common fuels with which the fire investigator will probably deal; however, without delving too deeply into the complexities of compounds, it is a fact that modern science is continually providing new combinations in plastics, synthetics, metal combinations, structures, industry, furnishings, clothing, utilities, aircraft equipment, and materials used in transportation.

Many of the construction, industrial, and commercial procedures materially alter the fire investigation picture from that which existed even thirty years ago. For example, plastic plumbing can and has served as a communication vehicle of fire through walls and vertical levels, often misleading fire investigators to interpret burned out spaces as "separate and distinct" areas or points of origin.

For example, a recent major fire in a modern, three-level apartment complex, when discovered during late hours of the night, was burning on all three levels and the garage spaces under the rear. The fire was controlled after extensive damage on all levels, including the attic and roof.

Because of apparent, separate burn-outs at various locations on all levels, the fire was initially classified as arson. Investigation, in depth, disclosed beyond any doubt that the origin of the fire was inside a wall behind a heating unit of an apartment on the second level. The cause was an improperly installed, spring-loaded gas fuel valve. The fire followed plastic plumbing lines into various spaces and all levels until the flames broke into the attic. The fire was discovered shortly thereafter.

Construction was such that occupants did not smell smoke until shortly before the flames were discovered. With the extensive demolition, witnesses suspected arson which was disproven by cool, deliberate investigation by the Fire Department authorities. This is the type of situation that emphasizes the importance of taking the time to conduct a full, accurate investigation. It also emphasizes the importance of analysis of certain synthetics commonly used in the construction industry and their relationship to origin and spread.

Modern motor vehicles may be at least partially constructed of synthetics. These may well alter ignition, burning characteristics, and burn patterns relied upon by some fire investigators as recently as twenty years ago. Some fire investigators continue to rely upon information concerning ignition and spread patterns in motor vehicles that may have been reasonably factual until the introduction of synthetics and engineering exhaust design specifications in today's motor vehicles.

Furnishings, carpeting, and decorations in office spaces and dwellings react differently in addition to producing toxic, combustible, and even explosive vapors.

The production of toxic halogen compounds may be present when a halogen containing plastic is burning. Ammonia and cyanides may be present if nitrogen-containing plastics are involved. (Halogens include any of the four very active nonmetallic chemical elements: bromine, fluorine, chlorine, and iodine. The members of this salt-producing group are very active; they are not, in themselves, combustible, but will support combustion of certain substances including turpentine, phorphorus, finely divided metals, etc., which ignite spontaneously in the presence of halogens. Additionally, the fumes are poisonous and corrosive.)

Plastics may be generally classified as either thermoplastic or thermosetting. This grows out of their behavior when subjected to heat and fire in appropriate quantity. The thermoplastic compounds will soften in the presence of sufficient heat, whereas the thermosetting plastics tend to harden and become brittle. Many of these synthetics behave quite differently in the presence of heat and fire: some will ignite readily and some surfaces will burn slowly under laboratory or test conditions. Others ignite readily and burn with near explosive velocity. It has been found that plastics, tested and reported as having fire resistance and slow flame spread characteristics, have been found to ignite and burn rapidly and, in fact, with near-explosive velocity when exposed to accelerated or elevated temperatures of an ongoing fire. This phenomenon has been repeatedly demonstrated in fires involving carpeting, paneled walls, and even tunnel lining.

Returning to the basic topic of this chapter, combustion may result from (1) direct ignition from a flaming or glowing substance or material; (2) faint but constant and prolonged heat (this deals with pyrolysis which will be discussed in detail later in the text); (3) spontaneous heating or spontaneous ignition (commonly called spontaneous combustion); (4) electric sparks, arcs, lightning, and natural atmospheric phenomena; (5) focused rays of the sun under precise conditions; (6) pressure, friction, and shock; (7) chemical reactions; and (8) explosions.

Ignition sources may lead to combustion and continuing fires provided the necessary supporting factors are present: heat, fuel, and oxygen. If the oxygen supply is removed, combustion ceases. If the temperature is reduced below the combustion and rekindling point, combustion ceases. If the fuel is removed, combustion also ceases.

Now, let's think about oxygen supply for a moment. All other things being equal, the speed of burning varies with the rate and volume of oxygen supply. Therefore, the presence of air in a burning space is important to the presence and progress of the fire. Draft, or air movement, is also important to fire growth—for example, the location of openings such as windows, doors, and shafts. This draft factor is also important in forest and wildland fires. The draft factor in forest, brush, and wildland fires may also be influenced by relative humidity, slope, general topography, and wind. Ultimately, in forest and wildland fires, given certain environmental, topographical, fuel, and weather conditions, the so-called fire storm may develop. The fire then creates its own weather as it moves along, again compounding the spread of the fire. In a sense, this is true in the case of structure fires (one of scale) of conflagration proportions under certain urbanized construction conditions.

Such structural fire storms have commonly occurred throughout history in urban areas and continue to do so even today. Recent conflagration examples are the fires in the Southern California Bel Air and San Clemente areas during the past twenty years.

The importance of atmospheric oxygen and air movement cannot be discounted in judging temperature rise and the resulting fire growth.

It is fairly stated that oxygen is an essential ingredient in the chemical process or reaction of burning. All other factors being equal, the speed of combustion or burning varies directly with the rate and volume of atmospheric oxygen supply at the seat of the fire. According to studies on fire growth, an enclosed space containing 1,000 cubic feet of space contains 210 cubic feet of atmospheric oxygen of which only 60 cubic feet is available for flame combustion. This amount of available oxygen is only sufficient for the burning of approximately 3½ lbs. of ordinary wood. If the oxygen supply is completely shut off at that point, the fire goes out. If, however, there are cracks under the door, or other limited air access at low exposures, enough

atmospheric oxygen may seep in to permit continued limited combustion or smoldering. The elevated temperatures may remain in a closed room for some time whereupon a suddenly opened door or window can cause a flaming combustion to return. But without the air the fire merely succumbs and expires. This is why some "smoker" fires in closed rooms asphyxiate air-breathing animal life (including humans) on so many occasions where relatively limited heat or flame damage is apparent. The products of combustion may not, in themselves, be poisonous gases, but they use up all the life-giving oxygen needed by the fire to continue, and by living victims caught inside the space.

Lack of sufficient atmospheric oxygen also happens to be why some of the so-called arson jobs fail. It is also one of the reasons why residue of accelerants, such as gasoline or acetone, may be found after the fire is extinguished. The initial flame-up of the fire may have utilized or exhausted the available oxygen. Following this, the fire became "lazy" and dormant. Smoke may have been observed seeping from windows or through ventilators; if care was exercised to prevent flash-over upon reopening the space, the seat of the fire and the accelerants may have been recovered.

Briefly, this is also one of the basic reasons why residue of low flash point accelerants so often utilized in arson may be found under floor and wall molding, under carpeting, chair legs, etc. This is due to the limited oxygen supply and protection afforded by the molding or furniture. Search-and-examine procedures will be covered in detail elsewhere in this text.

In further reference to oxygen supply, the gases of combustion occupy many times the bulk of the burned fuels. This results in interior pressure which normally prevents intake of oxygen from outside spaces. The fire may remain "sluggish" but will continue sufficiently to build pressure with limited air, again, drawn in at low levels, beneath doors, through grates, etc. The heat in the involved space may reach levels which, accompanied by interior pressures, may be sufficient to displace window glass. The interior pressure released, oxygen is then admitted and the phenomenon known as flash-over may occur. This phenomenon may also result when a window is broken or a door opened. The person opening the door or window may be injured by escaping pressurized combustion products and flame.

The process of combustion and flame spread is not always understood by firemen; it is often misunderstood by investigators. Ignition and combustion proceeds through an evolution which may be almost instantaneous or slow moving with only gradual temperature rise.

In the first place, the fuel, for example, a log in the fireplace, must be raised to a certain temperature before it will burn. This temperature must be sufficient to cause the subjected fuel, liquid or solid, to produce vapors. These vapors, in appropriate mixture with oxygen, will burn. More commonly, when dealing with liquid fuels, we should say that the material has reached its flash point when it produces flammable vapors.

Flash point is generally described as the lowest temperature of a substance or compound at which it may produce a vapor sufficient to form an ignitable mixture with the air near the surface of the substance or in immediate vicinity of the body of the fuel concerned.

Ignitable mixture is that mixture within the flammable range, between upper and lower limits, that is capable of the propagation of flame away from the source of ignition.

Flame propagation is the spread of flame, from layer to layer, independent of the ignition source. A gas or vapor mixed with air in proportions below the lower limit of flammability may burn at the source of ignition, that is, in the zone immediately surrounding the source of ignition, without advancing *from* the source of ignition. Combustion is not necessarily continuous at the flash point. According to the considerable amount of information supplied by the National Fire Protection Association and other respectable research organizations, the term flash point applies mostly to flammable liquids although there are certain solids that sublime at ordinary temperatures and, therefore, have flash points even though in solid state.

In discussing flash point, Von Schwartz states that with materials subject to combustion, it would be perfectly justifiable to also speak of flash point in connection with paper, wood, straw and other solid substances which, likewise, produce vapor upon being subjected to certain temperatures during the process of burning.

Even at the flash point, the substance may not have reached the stage of continuing combustion, although the introduced temperature may have been sufficient to cause the material or substance to produce flammable vapors. When the heat source is removed, the reaction may terminate. Again, observe the log burning in the fireplace. Upon closer

scrutiny, it will be noted that it is the gases emitted from the log that are providing the visible phenomenon of flame. During the early stages of the fireplace fire, the flame propagation from the gases is usually more noticeable; as the logs deteriorate to coals, the phenomenon is less noticeable but the process remains the same.

The introduction of a burning match above a partially filled container of gasoline will ignite the vapors which will continue to burn above the surface of the liquid so long as the liquid continues to provide vapor. Place a cover over the top of the container, excluding oxygen supply, and the fire will go out. Immerse the burning match in the liquid gasoline and the match flame is extinguished. Again, at this level of the combustion process, it is the gasoline vapor that burns.

The *ignition temperature* of gasoline, for example, is approximately 825° F. The flash point of gasoline, on the other hand, is –45° F. If gasoline were stored in an open container in a room where ambient temperatures were below zero, the liquid would produce flammable vapors. If the liquid is stored in closed containers in spaces where temperatures reached 825° F., instantaneous ignition could be reasonably expected throughout the mass.

The flammability of a material depends upon (1) the gas it contains, and (2) its capacity for liberating (volatilizing) that gas.

The *burning point* of a substance or material is the temperature to which it must be raised before it will ignite.

We have already mentioned flash point. If the flash point is below 50° F., a substance is considered universally dangerous. According to Von Schwartz, substances "flashing" between 77° F. and 140° F. are only considered directly dangerous if the usual precautionary measures in the handling, transport, storage, etc., are ignored. By comparison, until approximately ten years ago, National Fire Protection Association Standards classified flammable liquids as follows:

Class
1 A — Flash Point below 73° F and boiling point below 100° F.
1 B — Flash Point below 73° F and boiling point above 100° F.
1 C — Flash Point above 73° F and below 100° F.
II — Flash Point above 100° F and below 140° F.
III — Flash Point above 140° F and below 200° F.

Most jurisdictions accept either of the above and others have slightly different standards for classifying flammable and combustible liquids. For example, the U.S. Coast Guard classifies them as follows:

Combustible liquids are those which flash above 80° F.
Group D combustible liquids are those which flash above 80° F. and below 150° F.
Group E combustible liquids are those which flash above 150° F.

Group A — Those which flash at 80° F. or below with Reid vapor pressure 14 lbs. or more
Group B — Those which flash below 80° F. with Reid vapor pressure under 14 lbs. and over 8½ lbs.
Group C — Those which flash below 80° F. with Reid vapor pressure under 8½ lbs.

Usually, the burning point is higher than the flash point within the general classes of fuels of concern to arson investigators. The exceptions may be found in rapidly volatizing, explosive compounds. Reliable authorities have determined that substances with low flash point and high burning point are more dangerous than those with high flash point and low burning point. Low flash point suggests explosive tendencies, as with acetone or gasoline. A low burning point, on the other hand, suggests composition subject to the production and extension of flame, such as Grade A crude oil, wood, coal, etc.

In addition to flash point, ignition temperature, and burning temperature, we must consider the spontaneous ignition temperature (spontaneous ignition point). This is a term expressing the temperature at which solids, vapors, and gases will ignite and continue to burn without outside heat or flame. They will ignite under the influence of heat alone. This may be long-term heating and slow temperature rise depending upon the actual environment, structure, or composition of the substance; for example, decayed vegetable matter, fertilizers, oils, and fats. Conversely, the ignition may be rapid and violent, manifesting explosive characteristics, such as in oxidizers, chemical compounds, and related unstable materials.

There are many compounds which will ignite spontaneously at ordinary room temperatures. There are also compounds which will ignite spontaneously when introduced into a water environment such as metallic sodium or potassium. Knowledge of these factors is extremely important to the investigator when dealing with storage, transportation, or use of cargos, including their presence in fires of suspicious origin. The working knowledge is also important to the investigator when he is dealing with some classes of industrial as well as agricultural fires.

Combustion, in the chemical sense, is accompanied by either (1) flaming phenomena; (2) incandescence or glowing phenomena; or (3) the absence of either flaming or glowing appearance. All of the above, however, manifest one common denominator—heat—which may proceed slowly or rapidly depending upon composition, storage, environment, and ventilation. The phenomena may proceed with or without smoke, again depending upon the above described factors.

The most common type of fire is, of course, flaming combustion and it is important for the investigator to remember that there cannot be flaming combustion unless a gas is burning. This is true whether the gas is produced from atmospheric mixtures or pyrolized from the so-called solid, such as timber, plastics, hay, coal, liquid fuel, etc. The flame is the apparent reaction. With the flammable or combustible liquids, only the burning evolution can result since these liquids, in themselves, do not burn. Again, as we have heretofore indicated, this phenomenon is the result of the combination of the fire triangle: heat, fuel, and oxygen, each essential to the process.

The structure fire, for example, may be preceded by glowing combustion, followed by flaming combustion and, finally terminating the cycle with glowing combustion in the form of the charcoal debris prior to or in the process of final extinguishment or final burn-out, as the case may be.

On the other hand, the fire may be initiated with instantaneous explosion or flaming combustion. For example, in the presence of highly combustible bulk or liquid fuels and accompanied by rapid temperature rise, flame propagation proceeds rapidly through the entire mass or the involved spaces and is accompanied by displacement or separations.

Circumstances of fire behavior are as varied as the nature, quantity, packaging, and condition of fuels, ventilation, and structural environment. All of these factors *must be* understood and considered by the investigator in evaluating the origin and cause of a fire. *Emphasis is too often placed upon the ultimate destruction of a fire rather than the known fuels and their behavior in the environment and structural circumstances involved.* Well-grounded knowledge of the basic chemistry and behavior of fire is as essential to fire scene investigators as to firemen. One of the more common causes of fire scene investigative delinquency is ignorance of the behavior of fire.

We have discussed fuels as a necessary part of the combustion triangle and their relationship to two other considerations: heat and oxygen. Fuels are vital factors in the behavior of the fire—from ignition right on through temperature rise and spread of the fire. Fuels, in this context, include every combustible that may happen to be in any occupancy and also the materials used in construction, decorations, furnishings, or stock. In this context, fuels include parts of aircraft, motor vehicles, transportation facilities, cargo, stock, and supplies including liquids, gases, and solids. Their effect, during combustion, is evidenced in the energy they produce.

The heat energy production of fuels is extremely important to any competent fire investigator in determining fire load in the premises or equipment under investigation, again in respect to its potential in affecting temperature rise and spread and the time spectrum.

Calorific (heat-producing) values of fuels have a direct impact as can be seen in comparing the difference between wood and petroleum products. The calorific or thermal properties of nearly all materials in use today may be obtained from reliable technical references published by the National Bureau of Standards, National Fire Protection Association, American Gas Association, American Standards Association, American Society for Testing Materials, American Petroleum Institute, Bureau of Mines, and other organizations and agencies.

Calorific values may be measured and evaluated in British thermal units per pound (Btu's per lb.). For example, acetone is rated at 13,228 Btu's per lb. Toluene is rated at 18,252 Btu's per lb.; gasoline, 19,710 Btu's per lb. Wood varies from 7,000 Btu's per lb. to 9,000 Btu's per lb., depending upon the type of wood, porousness, etc. Cotton, air-dried, produces 7,170 Btu's per lb. while ordinary newspaper produces from 6,700 to 7,800 per lb.

Coal products vary in their heat-producing qualities. For example, lignite coal produces from 5,000 to 8,000 Btu's per lb.; while anthracite may produce as high as 13,800 Btu's per lb.

Animal fats, waxes, oleomargarine, tallows, stearic acid, butter fats, lard, etc., produce from 16,000 to 17,000 Btu's per lb. (It should be noted this is much more than coal.) Gas heat producing potential is generally measured in Btu's per cubic foot (Btu's per cu. ft.). For example, coal gas varies from 450 to 670 Btu's per cu. ft. Natural gas varies from 710 to 2,250 Btu's per cu. ft. Oil gas varies from 510 to 880 Btu's per cu. ft. Ether, by contrast, produces 22,000 Btu's per *lb*.

Methane gas produces 23,861 Btu's per lb. Butane gas produces 21,293 Btu's per lb., in contrast to hydrogen gas which produces 60,000 Btu's per lb.

It is well known to experienced firemen and investigators that, following control of a fire, large or small, rekindling (restarting) may occur because, although the control process may have reduced the temperature below the combustion level, or removed the oxygen or apparent burning fuel, there may remain a combination of heated fuel or ignition source environment sufficient to reestablish the burning cycle long after the firemen have departed from the scene. It is human nature to resist the implication of error. This is occasionally true with firemen. It is also true in the case of some investigators. There are examples of record where rekindling has been misinterpreted as a separate fire with the resulting implication of arson where arson, in fact, did not exist. The investigator must be able to assess all factors before arriving at a conclusion of origin or cause where rekindling is a reasonable possibility.

A classic example of ignorance or disregard of rekindling occurred when a Fire Department responded to a living room fire in a southwestern city during late evening and wherein the owner/occupants reportedly departed for the theater after banking and screening the fireplace. Fire Department investigators, responding to the scene, after brief investigation, determined that the fire originated in the wall framing immediately adjacent to the fireplace from a crack in the fireplace masonry and from which location the fire extended inside the wall and into the attic area. Overhaul was limited, as was inspection, either in the attic or in the unopened wall spaces. Fire Department returned to quarters.

Approximately two hours later, neighbors reported smelling smoke. By the time the Fire Department had arrived, the interior of the dwelling was again involved, the flames extending through the roof. The fire was controlled after near total destruction of the dwelling and contents and extensive exposure damage to adjacent premises.

Because of the alleged "second" fire, an arson unit was assigned and, without thorough consideration of either origin or cause of the initial fire, assigned the cause of the fire as incendiary, based upon multiple points of origin. The following investigation attached suspicion to the owners, who had returned from the theater after the first fire, found the power turned off and the interior too cold and smokey for occupancy, packed some temporary clothing, and moved to a hotel as temporary quarters.

Evidence presented in a subsequent action in the

Superior Court clearly disclosed beyond any question that the origin of the first fire was inside the wall framing adjacent to the fireplace. The cause of this fire was clearly ignition of combustible wall framing from deteriorated fireplace masonry. Due to limited overhaul, following control of the first fire, of interior wall and subfloor, progress of the fire had not been completely exposed for total extinguishment of the fire. These areas had continued to smolder, penetrating the interior and attic areas and, finally, breaking into flaming combustion involving the entire interior and attic spaces. The deep-seated floor frame areas were identified by relatively inexperienced insurance and fire investigators as separate and distinct points of origin, upon which they based the premise of arson. Fortunately for the innocent persons involved, the Court very sensibly concluded otherwise.

Determination of fireloading is useful in evaluating the behavior of fire under some circumstances. There is reliable authority indicating that the original conception was by Ingberg in the United States, with the evaluation process more fully developed by the Building Research Station in Great Britain.

Briefly, if the calorific value of combustible contents, their weight, and the floor areas are known, a figure may be obtained which provides a measure to evaluate the fire problem that may reasonably be expected, including temperature rise, temperatures to be expected, and the ultimate spread, again depending upon separations, partitions, and ventilation. Fireload of a given space may be established by knowing the type of combustibles in storage, their calorific heat-producing capacity in Btu's per lb., the total weight of the combustibles in storage, and the square foot capacity of the space.

The formula is as follows: Multiply the calorific value of the contents in Btu's per lb. by the total weight of the contents or materials in pounds. Then, divide the result by the area in square feet. The answer is the fireload per square feet.

National Bureau of Standards and American Standards as well as National Fire Protection Association and British Time/Temperature curves are in general agreement as to what temperature rise may be expected in various occupancies, with known fire loads, particularly during the first two hours of combustion.

For example, with sufficient oxygen to support continuing combustion, fires in buildings may be expected to attain 1,000 to 1,200° F. during the first five to ten minutes, accelerating on the curve to ap-

proximately 1,550° F. in the first half hour and with temperatures reaching the order of 1,700° F. at one hour. British and American time/temperature curves are in agreement that there is a general diminishment or levelling out in the temperature rise from that point on. The curve may reach approximately 1,850° F. after two hours, 2,050° F. after four hours, and 2,200° F. after six hours in major building fires.

In fires where accelerants are present, legitimately or otherwise, the initial temperature rise may be much sharper on the scale. Again, the variable may be governed by the quantity of accelerants, storage, and ventilation. For example, in a storage room with all doors and windows closed, ignited accelerants may cause a sharp temperature rise so long as oxygen remains available. With the exhaustion of available oxygen, further combustion ceases. From this point, the fire may "lay down" subject to ventilation of the fire or other means, whereupon fire progress continues in accordance with continuing fuel and atmospheric environment if temperature for rekindling or reignition remains.

It will be noted, in reference to the accepted time/temperature curves, that the temperature rise figures beyond a one hour spectrum are probably more applicable to major commercial/industrial fires since dwelling fires are usually controlled well under one hour.

Fire loading in building and space evaluation is generally categorized as low, moderate, and high. All are defined in the measure of British thermal units per square foot. These categories may be used as a guide to the fire investigator, principally in major fires where temperature rise and time spectrum may be a factor. The fire load of a space is considered low if it doesn't exceed 100,000 Btu's per square foot of net floor area of any compartment, or an average of 200,000 Btu's per square foot in limited, isolated areas. Examples of the latter occupancies are offices, restaurants, hospitals, schools, and institutional and administrative buildings.

Occupancies of moderate fire load may exceed 100,000 square feet of net floor area if any compartment does not exceed 200,000 Btu's per square foot or an average of 400,000 Btu's per square foot of isolated area. Examples are factories, work and retail shops, and repair shops.

Occupancies of high fire load are those which exceed an average of 200,000 Btu's per square foot of net floor area of any compartment but does not exceed an average of 400,000 Btu's per square foot net floor area, or an average of 800,000 Btu's per square

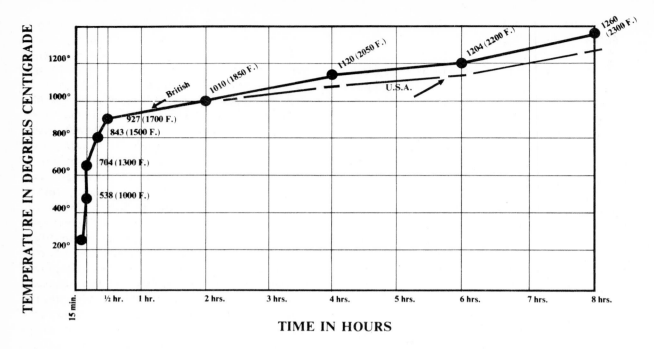

The above illustrates the time/temperature curve generally accepted in the U.S.A. and Great Britain to gauge averages that may be expected in building fires. It should be remembered, however, that there is a wide variation in the intensity rates in building fires, depending upon fire load, ventilation, density, etc.

foot in limited isolated areas. Examples are warehouses and other buildings used for storage of combustibles of a recognized nonhazardous nature.

The subject of fireloading is covered in excellent detail in the National Fire Protection Handbook and other NFPA publications and includes temperature values that may be expected of given combustibles in various occupancies from single space dwellings to apartments and commercial, storage, industrial, and institutional occupancies. The competent arson investigator will familiarize himself with the above publications since frequent reference is required in practical and factual evaluation of the fire scene, particularly in the case of major fires where origin and cause may be subject to question.

British studies, which in most cases coincide with American studies, indicate that hospital ward occupancies usually carry a fire load under 8,000 Btu's per square foot; office occupancies, with light files, may carry a fire load of 58,400 Btu's per square foot, while school classrooms may carry 29,600 Btu's per square foot. A residential occupancy may be expected to produce in excess of 21,000 Btu's per square foot. At the high end of the spectrum, a textile factory may carry 200,000 Btu's per square foot and a rubber warehouse may exceed 2,000,000 Btu's

per square foot. As one can see, the burning of a rubber warehouse may be a very "hot" proposition.

In the evaluation of the heat-producing potential of various fuels, the investigator should refer to tables of the Bureau of Standards, National Fire Protection Association, American Gas Association, American Petroleum Institute, American Society for Testing and Materials, British Department of Scientific and Industrial Research; numerous Federal Agencies also supply factual data in this field. For example, average wood and timber products produce approximately 8,000 Btu's per lb.; wool, 9,800; sulphur, 4,000; naphthalene, 17,300; and petroleum ether, 22,000 Btu's per pound. (See Tables.)

The investigator may make certain evaluations of temperatures produced in a given fire by examination of metals exposed to the fire at various locations; for example, near the origin, near areas of initial spread, and in areas of ventilation such as windows or through skylights or roof. The condition of the metals after the fire may tell at least part of the temperature story.

Wrought iron melts at approximately	2,750° F.
Cast iron melts at approximately	2,102° F.
Mild steel melts at approximately	2,460° F.
Brass melts at approximately	1,724° F.

Aluminum melts at approximately	1,220° F.
Zinc melts at approximately	786° F.
Lead melts at approximately	617° F.
Ordinary glass melts at approximately	1,472° F.

Generally speaking, glass may melt around the above figure or as low as 1,220° F. but extreme caution must be used when gauging temperatures by melted glass because of differences in the processing. Further, investigative misconceptions can result from emphasis placed upon the so-called "crazing" or "scarring" of glass by heat and fire since these manifestations may vary depending upon the production process of the glass.

During the past thirty years, aluminum has come into general use as a structural material; it is increasingly utilized in electrical installations including conductors. The relatively low melting point of aluminum and its alloys is relevant to its integrity in resistance to fire as well as its reaction to electrical energy produced in the form of heat. Aluminum's reaction to electrical heat has been the cause of concern and is presently the subject of intensive study by various fire protection and engineering agencies. This concern has grown out of fires which have been attributed to aluminum conductors and connections in structural fires. One theory entails the improper use of aluminum fittings in electrical circuits by connecting to metals with different coefficients of expansion — for example, copper. This will be dealt with elsewhere in the text but is mentioned, in passing, as an example of the importance of knowledge of melting temperatures of metals in the factual investigation of fire causes.

Again, the investigator should refer to the Bureau of Standards, National Fire Protection Association, Bureau of Mines, Department of Commerce, and other authorities for specifications on above materials concerning their reaction to high temperatures.

EXPLOSIVE COMBUSTION

We are not dealing with the true high velocity explosion in this context since we are considering fire and arson investigation in the general sense.

Explosive combustion may occur when vapors, true gases, and fire residues are introduced into an environment of atmospheric or pure oxygen in appropriate mixtures with an ignition source. Upon ignition, rapid burning may extend through the mass accompanied by disengagement of heat and possible displacement of exposures. The time spectrum is dependent upon the fuels, placement, and mixture, and the phenomenon, for all practical purposes, is generally termed an explosion.

As indicated, displacement of low velocity order may result in the form of walls moving outward and displaced windows; and generated heat may ignite low density exposures such as cellotex, curtains, furnishings, clothing, etc. Bulk fuels such as beams and framing are not usually ignited, the flame and heat not being present for sufficient time to raise bulk fuels to their burning point. The tinder type fuels ignited, however, may in turn remain burning sufficiently in time to cause ignition of furniture, carpeting, and, ultimately, the heavier fuels in the space or structure; tinder type fire brands, ignited in the initial explosion, may be propelled from the immediate scene and with resulting ignition of lower density fuels or tinder type fuels of adjacent exposures. Such is the case with shingle and shake roofs, dry annuals, and brush and forest cover.

This type of explosion may be experienced with dust explosions in grain elevators and industrial operations. It is not uncommon in coal mines and certain classes of warehousing, cargo storage, and handling. The phenomenon may occur in heavier than air gas explosions such as vaporized hydrocarbon fumes, liquid petroleum gases, pit gas, mine gas, and sewer gases. It may also occur in the lighter than air industrial gases and vapors.

If the explosion precedes the fire, its source should be of initial importance. How was the explosive atmosphere introduced? What was the source of ignition? If the explosion follows the fire, the key answers are of equal importance. Was the explosive atmosphere accidentally or intentionally introduced? What is its identity? What was its source? What was its condition and means of confinement while the fire was in initial progress and how was it released?

Another process of combustion, mentioned very early in this chapter, is nonluminous combustion which is usually a characteristic of certain chemical reactions which may proceed slowly and quietly without external manifestation or appreciable liberation of heat. The process occurs mainly in the interior of organic substances. Studies have shown that the general course of these reactions is similar to those of flaming and incandescent combustion and furnish the same final products. They differ, however, in the extreme slowness and without the more external and obvious manifestations such as flame and rapid temperature rise. Thus, nonluminous combustion may result from decay or organic reaction. In acid, compounds under certain conditions may also develop through a graduating or escalating process to the stage where flaming combustion will follow.

SPONTANEOUS IGNITION

Under this heading, we must consider cases of slow or rapid reaction by the process of oxidation resulting from biological, chemical, electrical, or physical processes, each acting without outside assistance or independent ignition source.

Authorities on the subject have indicated spontaneous ignition may be preceded by heating inside the substance or pile. Certain types may occur suddenly and explosively and, in the context, they might be classified as spontaneous explosions. Dr. Von Schwartz, in *Fire and Explosion Risks,* has classified the latter type as acute and the former, slower ones, as chronic. Examples of compounds subject to acute spontaneous ignition are ethyl, methyl, and propyl compounds; pyrophorous substances when mixed with air, hydrogen gas, or coal gas; unstable compounds when brought into contact with spongy metals; explosive vapors when exposed to electrical arcs or sparks; and explosive detonating compounds when exposed to pressure, friction, shock, or spark. Examples of the compounds subject to chronic spontaneous ignition include agricultural products, oleaginous substances, and coal when stored in large unventilated piles; organic substances, such as wood, when exposed to protracted drying; coal or lampblack when mixed with sulphur; potassium, sodium, and carbides when exposed to moisture. These are only a few samples of materials wherein the possibilities of spontaneous ignition exist. In areas where questions may arise, qualified laboratory assistance should be obtained.

A recent explosion and fire in a major industrial area totally destroyed a large warehouse and damaged exposed buildings surrounding the property. Some of the investigating authorities classified the explosion as resulting from a bomb or bombs and proceeded with thousands of man hours of investigation on that basis. More careful and factual investigation disclosed that unstable compounds, such as aluminum trimethyl and aluminum tripropyl, had been improperly packed and stored. Chemical action, including exposure to the air, caused the explosive reaction which, in turn, triggered other unstable compounds stored on the premises. The records are abundant with authenticated examples where unstable compounds, improperly packaged, transported, or stored, decompose or transform into explosive or flammable condition. Often the explosion or fire is incorrectly faulted as an act of arson or bombing by persons unknown. This, of course, diverts law enforcement manpower from investigation of matters where bombings and arson have, in fact, occurred.

Initial factual investigation by qualified personnel can prevent the waste of countless man hours pursuing the "will-o'-the-wisp."

Spontaneous ignition may occur under certain conditions such as storing coal and carbon, or drying and heating wood, fertilizers, and other organic substances. It may occur in finely divided metallic sulphides; with occlusion of moisture in materials such as quicklime, potassium, sodium, and the carbides; and by exposure to the sun's rays with materials such as phosphorus and hydrogen gas. The phenomenon has been found in materials such as phosphuretted hydrogen and pyrophoric materials merely exposed to the atmosphere. Spontaneous ignition is more common in the improper storage and handling of certain vegetable fats and oils; it has been repeatedly established that this type of heating can occur where organic decay or ripening is an active chain and where the heat production is faster than the heat dissipation from the pile. This causes prohibitive temperature rise and, finally, flaming combustion. As had already been stated, the improper packaging, transportation, usage, or storage of numerous chemical combinations commonly used in commerce and industry today can result in spontaneous heating and, in process, explosion and/or fire.

While drop cloths, paint rags, and other wastes saturated with vegetable paints and compounds, such as linseed oil and turpentine, will heat spontaneously, it is fairly well established that cloths, rags, and debris saturated with hydrocarbons will normally not spontaneously heat.

Occasionally, firemen and investigators, finding a pile of carbonized oily rags near the seat of a fire, such as in a service station or garage, automatically proclaim the cause as "spontaneous combustion." Experienced authorities would have been more careful in determining the true cause of the fire. For example, "Was it a cigarette or a match?" After all, oily rags are often utilized by an arsonist to accomplish his mission. The rags may have been "handy." Experienced in setting fires, he may well know that firemen and investigators are often inclined to jump at conclusions or select the quick and, often, too obvious cause. Admittedly, if the fire were caused by an arsonist with designs to cover his tracks, the *corpus delicti* may be tough to prove. Nevertheless, the problem won't go away. We have to live with it.

Tests have shown that spontaneous ignition in vegetable compounds, microorganic activity, is in the temperature frame of 160° F. with the heat confined in the pile. A temperature rise continues until the pile temperature reaches approximately 550° F. This, of course, is above the ignition temperature of materials such as wood, paper, cotton, wool, plastics, and normal household furniture items. In hay piles and bales, experience has shown fires commonly occur from ten days to five or six weeks after the hay is stacked, or after it has been baled and warehoused. The experienced fire investigator will look for deep-seated smoldering or tunneling of fire resulting from spontaneous ignition—he will look for caverned areas extending deep in the pile. This tunneling can also be found, in smaller scale, with spontaneous ignition in paint cloths particularly where the pile has been covered with protective tarpaulin or drop cloths, such as on construction projects. On such jobs, brushes are often cleaned and placed in the perimeter along with the tarps, cloths, and other materials common to that type of operation.

Fires occurring under such conditions are often labelled "careless smoking." Sometimes they do result from careless smoking. Occasionally, they may well be dressed up cases of arson. Recognition of the symptoms of spontaneous ignition and its usually apparent characteristics is a necessary part of fire investigative skill. There will be occasions when specialized skills and expertise, including the assistance of laboratory people, will be essential to the production of accurate answers.

A recent fire caused extensive damage to the new library building of a west coast city college at a time when construction was nearing completion. The fire occurred in the early morning hours. Because of other known incendiary fires in the area, including schools and public buildings, insurance carriers assumed the cause of this fire to be incendiary and assigned their own investigators to inquire. The insurance investigators classified the cause as "highly suspicious" and proceeded with a long investigation.

The fact subsequently resolved in court was that the origin of the fire was in a paint storage area. The painters, in the process of completing their work painting the interior, had covered the paint cans and supplies with tarpaulins when they finished work the previous evening. The paintbrushes, paint

clothes, etc., had been stored under the tarps, along with turpentine and other vegetable oil based materials. The building was tightly closed. The weather was warm and muggy.

The pattern of spread of the initial burning was directly from the pile and the synthetic floor tile under the pile was totally carbonized in pattern with the pile. The carbon deposit on ceiling, walls, and window glass indicated very gradual temperature rise and heat build-up from ceiling down and with the most pronounced ceiling heat damage, in spall form, directly above the storage pile. Soot deposit in separated spaces of the building was consistent with long term heating and smoldering combustion. No evidence was found that was compatible with incendiary origin or with forced entry to the building via either doors or windows, except the point of entry made by responding fire department officers.

The above was finally corroborated by the hand position of an electric clock, which was completely overlooked by the insurance "sleuths." The clock circuit was energized from a set of conductors in the ceiling directly over the storage area. The clock hands had stopped one and one-half hours after the painters secured for the day—seven hours before the discovery of the fire.

In this case, the fire department authorities had very properly diagnosed the origin and cause of this fire as accidental. They were not influenced by the panic of other incendiary fires in the area. Their correct diagnosis of the origin of the library fire provided them with more man hours to devote to investigation of the actual incendiary and criminal fires.

PYROLYSIS

Generally, it may be said that pyrolysis is the process of heat reaction and decomposition which occurs within solid fuels as a result of heat communicated from surrounding environment or adjacent environment. The phenomenon of pyrolysis has been known for a very long time but the process is not clearly understood in connection with many compounds and materials in use today. With the exception of chemically pure materials, its behavior is not precisely evaluated according to authorities such as B.L. Browning in *Chemistry of Wood;* H.W. Eickner in *Basic Research on Pyrolysis and Combustion of Wood;* and the comments of Paul Kirk in his work *Fire Investigation.*

To completely understand what occurs during the process of pyrolysis in a given fuel, it is necessary to consider that all practical fuels are organic in nature and often consist of complex mixtures. It is not the intent of this text to get into technical aspects of atomic structure, carbon content, or formation of bonds and molecular structure. That is the job of the physicist, the chemist, and the qualified laboratory technician.

In plain language, the arson investigator's interest in pyrolysis is in the cycle from incipient heating of a particular fuel through the stages of its internal temperature rise and to and through flaming combustion and then to the production of charcoal. Sometimes, in areas of limited ventilation (sealed wall spaces, for example), the complete evolution may occur, from initial heating, up to and including the production of charcoal or ash, *without* flaming combustion or production of visible smoke. (It has been found by careful questioning of occupants or witnesses who are familiar with the premises, that they have smelled "odors" from time to time, sometimes investigating but never finding the source of the odor. It is always well to question people familiar with the premises. Invaluable information may be turned up. Too often, today's investigator is either too sophisticated, too self satisfied, or too lazy to bother talking to witnesses who may be able to provide key information.)

Where a wood beam in a wall is heated by a pressurized steam pipe or where structural framing encloses a fireplace, such framing or supports may be heated gradually and dried over periods of months and even years. The beam may ultimately carbonize and the shape of the framing, joint, or beam, where carbonized, may remain. If there is no structural stress at this point, it may even remain intact.

Since the arson investigator is dealing with wood products in much of his investigative work and, since wood is a fairly well known material, structurally, he will use wood illustratively in explaining the pyrolysis phenomenon. Normally, wood is stable towards heat except for the loss of water and certain gaseous constituents up to 212° F. Over extended periods at this temperature, water and other aromatic constituents are expelled in a gradual process. With sufficient time, the wood structure becomes skeletonized or deteriorated. If the temperature is increased to the order of 300° F., eventual external darkening or browning of the wood appears and carbon monoxide, carbon dioxide, hydrogen, and other products of combustion are expelled, further deteriorating the remaining mass in its transformation to charcoal.

As the temperature mounts to around 450° F., the wood rapidly darkens and loses its strength although the apparent structure may remain. If the temperature builds to around 900° F., carbonization increases more rapidly and additional remaining volatile constituents are lost to the surrounding environment. The pyrolytic reaction is mostly complete at temperatures between 900 and 1,000° F. In the absence of oxygen, such as in confined or enclosed wall spaces, the wood may deteriorate to charcoal and, as previously indicated, nearly retain its original form. On the other hand, with sufficient oxygen available, flaming combustion may take over with accelerating temperature rise, again depending upon the quantity and type of bulk fuels available in that particular environment.

Experience has shown that wood, cloth, plastics, and other organic compounds, subjected to heating, will deteriorate in their slow process of heat decomposition to where ignition will result at lower temperatures than normally classified for that particular material. For example, certain wood products carry "rated" ignition temperatures varying from 450° F. to 550° F. However, the same fuels, after long-term gradual heating, may readily ignite at temperatures far below the above; for example, at 300° F. Some authorities report pyrolytic heating ignition after long-term process as low as 250° F.

Numerous serious fires have resulted from pyrolysis of wood framing by steam pipes. Pressured steam pipes with gauge pressure of 50 PSI develop approximately 300° F. of temperature. Placed against wood beams in brick and masonry walls, they have been known to cause long-term heating, resulting in deterioration of the wood beams to charcoal.

Improperly insulated fireplaces are not infrequent examples of such ignition. The fireplace may serve for months or even years before the wood framing or supports deteriorate in the long-term atmosphere of communicated heat and result in ignition; again, the framing may merely turn to charcoal without flaming combustion until the process reaches an attic or open seam where available oxygen produces the vehicle for accelerated and more apparent flaming combustion.

Examples of pyrolytic action are fires which result from heat lamps improperly insulated from combustible walls and ceilings, or electric bulbs too close to shelves or other bulk fuels. Such conditions have resulted in pyrolytic action and, ultimately, flaming combustion. Electric heating lamps develop bulb surface temperatures in the order of 400° F. 300–500 watt bulbs produce surface temperatures in excess of 400° F. These temperatures are sufficient to initiate the process in most wood and fibrous products in use today. Common examples of pyrolytic action are restaurant kitchen ranges with improperly placed or insulated walls, or with hooded stacks or vents improperly insulated from the appliance/equipment, and the wood framing improperly protected.

THE PHYSICAL PROCESS OF FIRE GROWTH

Earlier, we discussed ignition temperatures, the combustion process, the dependence of fire growth on available fuels, ventilation, and temperature rise. The effects of the production of heat by the original burning are pronounced so long as the heat balance is positive. There are three generally accepted processes of heat propagation affecting fire growth from its incipient stage and continuing throughout the spread. This is so regardless of whether the fire is in a structure, forest, brush, or grain field. These three factors must *always* be carefully considered in evaluation of a fire scene.

(There is some contention that a fourth factor, "slope," should be considered. As a practical matter, however, where slope is involved, it can be considered as being included under the subject of convection which will be explained below.)

Basically, a burning object or pile loses heat to its surroundings by the processes of (1) Radiation, (2) Conduction, and (3) Convection.

Radiation consists of electromagnetic waves activated by temperature differences. The temperature is merely an expression, in measurable terms, of the relative amount of heat energy. Radiation may be said to travel at the speed of light.

Conduction is heat passing from a burning object, heated substance, or source, through an exposed object or mass which is heated and through the exposed conducting mass. For example, a kitchen range may, appropriately positioned in relation to a wall, produce heat which will be conducted through the wall to the opposite side where tinder-like combustibles may be stored and which, in turn, may be ignited without presence of visible flame in the intervening sections.

Convection is the process by which heated portions of air are conveyed and may, for example, be noted in air rising as it becomes heated. Convection currents may be created by the heat source or by combination of condition of ventilation of the space and by the influence of the heat source. It has been simply stated, for example, that it is convection air movement which fills the hot air balloon—the heated gases produced by the gas burner rising, expanding, and trapped by the envelope of the balloon. It is convection that plays a major part in moving the warm air over a stove, up and into the hood and out the stack. It is mainly convection that moves a fire from a lower space through a door into a vertical shaft, quickly involving higher level exposures.

In structure fires, the three processes of fire growth—radiation, conduction, and convection—move simultaneously. However, depending upon the fuel, temperature, wind condition, slope, and position of exposure, one or the other of the three factors may predominate. In major fires—structure, forest, brush, or grain—the upward convection currents communicating hot gases may become so great as to create what is occasionally called a fire storm. In large scale conflagrations, the phenomenon may be manifested in whirlwind or semi-tornado effect.

In test fires on inside structures, this fire storm effect has been observed and photographed in smaller scale and therefore may be present in even smaller degree. The fire investigator should bear in mind that, when considering fire growth, the differences are principally in scale but this knowledge is essential to factual evaluation of "where" the fire started—whether there was a single area of origin or multiple points. The trial record of arson cases is abundant with examples of unfamiliarity with the subject of fire growth by so-called "expert" witnesses. Errors in fire evaluation may result in accusation of innocent persons in situations where fires of obvious accidental origin were classified as incendiary; conversely, ignorance of the principles of fire growth all too often results in the escape of the guilty party where fires classified as accidental were, in fact, of criminal origin.

In conclusion to this chapter, it is reiterated that we have only attempted to cover the basics of combustion and fire spread. The competent and successful arson investigator recognizes the necessity of continuing study and research. Without accurate knowledge of where the fire started and precisely how it started, the investigation is practically meaningless.

Fire cause investigators, including arson investigators, should reconize that, during the past thirty years, the techniques of construction, industry, and general commerce have emerged from the purely empirical into the scientific. Again, bear in mind the new construction materials and building designs, emphasizing glass and synthetics, use of sophisticated ventilation systems, etc. Consider the modern use of plastics in interior furnishings as well as in electrical, mechanical, and plumbing systems. Consider that the sophisticated arsonist for hire can and does take advantage of these advanced techniques and materials not only in concealing the evidence of his criminal act but also in insuring the desired damage from his fire.

Fire, perhaps more than ever before, is a destructive force to be reckoned with in our increasingly crowded and complicated environment. Waste from fire, arson or accidental, is a "luxury" we can less and less afford. All of this is relevant to the importance of seeking out where the fire started and why. To seek out the cause and where that cause is criminal, to deal with the problem promptly and effectively in the case and manner prescribed by law is what public safety and security is all about.

Recognizing the increasingly technical aspects involving fire cause, the arson investigator must not only study, he must also know when to seek out technical assistance whenever factual answers to the problems presented by the fire are not abundantly clear.

CHAPTER VII

JUSTIFYING SPECIFIC DEPARTMENT RESPONSIBILITY FOR ARSON INVESTIGATION

One of the basic reasons for neglect of the arson and incendiary problem is the failure of most city and county governments to assign investigative responsibility and accountability for arson investigation to a particular department. Without definite accountability, the function becomes the unwanted child that is disclaimed by all department heads when the going gets tough and the chips are down.

It is not the intent of this chapter or this text to suggest Law Enforcement or Peace Officer departments as more suitably staffed or equipped than Fire Control or Fire Departments. There are numerous examples where arson investigation (and arson control) has been and is being accomplished. in police-oriented systems and other equally good examples where the job is getting done in fire-oriented departments. Some cities and counties have selected officers from police and fire—working as a team—and have accomplished excellent results and continue to do so. State Fire Marshals' offices have staffed their arson bureaus with selected qualified personnel from Federal, State, and local police and investigative agencies as well as from fire departments. Experience has shown that, carefully selected, these people can and do work together and get the job done as it should be done. The old, old prejudice that fire-oriented people and police- or law enforcement-oriented officers don't blend is neither relevant nor true. While the separation of basic fire and police functions may continue to be practical, both functions are essential to the public safety and the functions merge at the criminal investigation level, and arson and incendiarism *are in the category of major crime*. The importance of the investigative aspects must be brought into focus. So long as accountability is not required for arson investigation in a community or jurisdiction, the problem will continue to exact its disgusting toll on loss of life, injury, suffering, and irrecoverable property loss.

For example, Uniform Crime Reports covering major crime throughout the United States for 1975 (published in August, 1976) stated, "Serious crime is increasing faster in rural America and the smaller towns than it is in the big cities." There was an overall increase during 1975 of 10 percent. The report stated that there were 11.3 million serious crimes in 1975 but that only one in five ended in arrest. This broke down nationally to an average of 21 serious crimes committed every minute during the past year including a violent crime every 31 seconds. The report stated that the 1975 analysis of reported crimes disclosed that the biggest volume of crime is in "the mass of middle America, the average size American cities." Again, "only one-fifth of the major crimes are solved by arrest."

Now, stipulating that the above picture is not a pleasant one, let us compare them with the figures currently available on arson which, of course, also happens to be one of the most heinous crimes in the book. Recalling the one-in-five major crimes solved by arrest, the only reliable figures presented concerning arson arrests disclose that only one in one hundred reported arson cases are solved by arrest.

It should also be noted that the Uniform Crime Reports do not list arson in the major crime reporting category analysis, and never have. The author has been reliably advised that this is because of the lack of investigative and reporting uniformity by the local jurisdictions who should have this investigative responsibility.

It should also be noted that most jurisdictions consider major crimes as solved by arrest. This doesn't really tell us much, particularly when the above-described arrest vs. conviction rate is considered. Close analysis suggests that most jurisdictions and communities have a "long way to go" in the process of improving our criminal investigation procedures, including those involving incendiarism and arson.

One of the very probable basic reasons for the particularly poor record in the prevention of arson and its investigation may well grow out of the fact that fire often destroys the evidence of the cause. Regardless of what the inexperienced and some of the theorists who have seldom been in a dark alley might say, fire cause is a difficult and often complex investigative task. Physically, it is a dirty and exhausting business, often fraught with danger. A task all too often assigned to "tip toe" investigators who hover about the scene until news interest fades.

The investigator must determine the cause before proceeding to a conclusion of arson. This is a legal requirement as well as an ethical and moral one. Legal, because society demands it and has so legislated. Legal, because of the requirements that society be protected from the acts of the criminal. Legal, in the further sense that the law and the courts require that evidence of crime must be shown in the cause of a fire before a person may be charged and held for feloniously setting a fire. Legal and moral in the sense that in our system of government, the accused is entitled to the presumption of innocence at every step of the way. This is a presumption too often neglected by the amateur, overzealous in his zest to get the job done and get on to the next.

Regardless of jurisdictional level—Federal, State, County, Municipal, or District—the assignment of carefully screened and trained investigators is required. The effectiveness depends principally upon identification of the arson unit with specialized equipment and personnel, regardless of whether they are assigned to a fire-oriented or police-oriented agency.

In either case, the importance of arson investigation must be recognized and supervised with adequate priorities to accomplish the investigative task in a meaningful manner, case by case. The personnel must be assigned in a manner designed to realistically handle the case load. Anything short of this leads to frustration of intelligent personnel and a continuation of the statistical charade.

Experience and the record clearly show that arson cases, in all categories of motivation, have been solved where assignment of competent personnel was implemented. Organized and so-called "white collar" crime involving arson cases have been solved by Federal agencies cooperating with local authorities. During very recent months, State-level arson

squads have been staffed to supplement the efforts of local jurisdictions and cooperate with them on request. The initiate is usually retained at the local level with the assistance provided from the State level.

Police Detective Bureaus are often staffed with personnel comprising arson, bomb, and explosives details. These units have worked effectively with Fire Department personnel in the successful conclusion of major arson and fraud cases, relying upon fire department expertise in examination and preservation of the evidence of origin and cause.

Sheriffs' offices are increasingly staffed with detectives specializing in arson and explosion investigation expertise who work closely with other law enforcement jurisdictions and assist fire departments and districts upon request. Excellent crime laboratory facilities supplement this type of operation.

Many of the larger fire departments, including Federal, State, and some county forestry and rural departments, staff arson units. These generally contain firemen/investigators who have indicated aptitude and motivation for investigative work and are carefully trained in fire investigation as well as law enforcement procedures including rules of evidence, searches and seizures, law of arrest, civil rights, and other knowledge required of the modern law enforcement officer.

In California, for example, fire investigators working full time for an organized department are designated peace officers by statutory enactment and are required to attend and complete a state-approved peace officers' training course before they are deemed peace officers. Under this system, the fire department arson investigator works closely with his opposite number in the police department or sheriff's office as the case may be.

Another system proven successful is the arson unit which may be assigned to either fire or police department but which is staffed by teams from both departments.

The success of any system depends upon the understanding and support of the administrators, permitting the units to accomplish their missions without pulling them off active assignments where the priority actually exists.

One of the long-term, outstanding examples of arson investigative efficiency is the City of Los Angeles Fire Department Arson Unit which operates out of the Bureau of Fire Prevention and Public Safety. This unit is currently manned with 21 full-time arson investigators supervised by three captains. Assigned personnel work in plain clothes and are equipped with unmarked, radio-equipped vehicles. The unit is equipped with a special mobile laboratory for detailed fire scene examination. The investigator teams are equipped with kits for scene examination and photography as well as proper marking and preservation of physical evidence.

The City of Los Angeles Fire Department has long recognized its responsibility in fire safety and considers fire and arson investigation an integral part of the fire safety program. The Fire Department maintains primary responsibility for arson investigation within the city; at the same time, a close investigative liaison is maintained with the police and other departments. For example, in surveillance and "stake-out" situations and where manpower and/or equipment may be required beyond fire department resources, police assistance may be required and is received. Additionally, police officers make arrests where circumstances require—always notifying and working closely with the fire department where the arrests are relevant.

The arson unit maintains a close liaison with the Los Angeles County District Attorney's office and with other public agencies as the circumstances require.

The selection of its arson unit personnel illustrates the department's recognition of the importance of factual and efficient arson investigation. First, the selection of an investigator trainee must be from the ranks of assigned fire department personnel. It is required that an investigator trainee will already have completed a probationary period as a fire fighter before being assigned as a regular fireman. During this period, he will have received additional training and experience in fire fighting and related duties.

If the fire fighter indicates interest in becoming an arson investigator, he must first have served satisfactorily as a fire fighter for at least three years. If the fireman's application to the arson unit is considered, he will be interviewed by officers from the arson section. The Chief Engineer of the Fire Department may designate other supervisory personnel to assist in this rather detailed, initial evaluation of the applicant. The emphasis is to select the best employees available, bearing in mind such qualities as intelligence, education, motivation, aptitude, personality, and integrity.

If selected as an arson investigator trainee, the fireman must then serve a period of one year in the trainee capacity. During that period, he will receive eight weeks' training in the headquarters' office,

learning office and basic procedures, files, records, report writing, basic investigative training and peace officer training. The peace officer training is necessary since, under the California law, he is required to measure up to peace officers' training standards. The trainee will be carefully scrutinized and supervised during this basic training period in the arson unit. If his performance is satisfactory, he will then be placed in the field with an experienced arson investigator assigned to the section. He will be indoctrinated in approved investigative procedures in the field. During this stage, he will be moved from area to area in the city, always working with an experienced investigator, to acquaint him with the widely varying conditions, environments, and problems that may be found in most metropolitan areas; for example, industrial, commercial, harbor, and vast residential areas including mountain brush and watershed areas. Unlike arson investigators in some metropolitan areas, a member of the Los Angeles Fire Department arson section must know how to investigate incendiarism in brush, forest, and watershed areas.

If the arson investigator trainee's performance has fulfilled the standards required during this year's training assignment, he is again evaluated by supervisors of the arson section and by other supervisory personnel as the Chief Engineer may designate. If the evaluation finds him satisfactory, the investigator trainee is assigned as a regular member of the arson section with a substantial increase in salary.

All arson investigators of the section are closely supervised. They are assigned to areas according to the case demand and are also assigned special cases as priorities and abilities may require.

Primary responsibility for explosive and bomb investigation rests with the City of Los Angeles Police Department. An especially selected, trained, and equipped unit of the police department handles all such assignments.

Arson section investigators currently average a case load of twenty four assignments per month. The City of Los Angeles Fire Department experienced approximately 30,000 fires in 1975 of which approximately 3,000 were regarded as suspicious. The arson section classified 2,400 of the total as definitely incendiary. Investigative attention must, of necessity, be based upon available personnel and priorities in respect to particular incendiary fires. Fire companies, through their officers, may handle certain classes of neighborhood and juvenile fires; in such circumstances, however, the arson section is informed and may provide assistance and advice as required.

Major fire losses known to be arson are handled by the arson section. Special attention is being devoted to a reported substantial increase in fraud-arson and arson believed to be perpetrated by organized groups regardless of what the objectives or motivations of these groups may be. Such investigations are often coordinated with specialized units of the Los Angeles Police Department, the District Attorney's office and other agencies with common interest.

In 1975, there were 150 adult arson arrests. Ninety-six of these developed into arson felony complaints out of which 72 were held for trial. Because of the current plea bargaining process, there are no reliable figures on the number of actual arson convictions. The available statistics, however, place this department in the highest category of investigative efficiency in the investigation and prosecution of incendiarism and arson in the United States today.

In Seattle, Washington, the arson loss figures increased from $621,000 in 1971 to $3,000,000 in 1973. Seattle authorities reported, in 1974, that incendiarism accounted for over 50 percent of the dollar loss figure; they projected arson losses to escalate to more than $4,000,000 in 1975 if the trend continued. A fire investigation task force concept was introduced which included redefining investigative responsibilities in the Seattle area with various law enforcement agencies cooperating with the establishment of guidelines for interdepartmental cooperation.

The task force includes the Seattle Fire Department, Police Department, Mayor's office, Prosecutor's office, the Public Safety Committee, City Council, Kings County Sheriff's office, and the insurance industry. Each department or agency assigns at least one man with the understanding and authority to act. For example, in addition to qualified investigative personnel, assigned in arson teams, the prosecutor has assigned a special arson prosecutor. Special problems may be taken to designated individuals in any of the cooperating agencies.

Analysis systems may coordinate investigations and identify related crimes. For example, burglary/arson, fraud arson, and other forms of arson where police and fire have a common problem. Police-oriented investigators will attend fire-oriented training sessions and fire-oriented investigators will attend police training sessions. Police/fire investi-

gating teams will be assigned cases as circumstances require.

One of the earliest organized, specifically assigned arson units in the police-oriented spectrum is the Los Angeles County Sheriff's Office Arson-Explosive Detail which, until 1977, was staffed with 18 highly trained and specialized arson-explosive investigators. (In 1977, approximately twenty additional investigators were added to the staff.) All investigators on the staff have the benefit of original basic training received by all County Sheriff's Department officers which includes intensive training and screening at the training academy. This is followed by field experience in the patrol division. Additionally, each member of the unit has completed at least two years in the detective bureau as an investigator.

Applicants to the arson-explosive detail receive further screening before acceptance into the unit. If accepted, they undergo further specialized training in fire and explosion investigation. This covers evaluation of the more conventional arson and explosion scenes as well as recognition and evaluation, handling, etc., of the more sophisticated explosives and devices including incendiaries and bombs. The unit's functions are supplemented by one of the finest crime laboratories in the nation.

In addition to intradepartmental assignments, the unit cooperates closely with the Los Angeles Fire Department, which is one of the largest and most highly regarded in the country. Fires and explosions of suspicious or known criminal origin are assigned by the Fire Department to the Sheriff's Office for handling to conclusion. Representatives of the Fire Department Fire Prevention Bureau and Investigative Detail provide informational and technical assistance as circumstances require.

The Arson-Explosives Detail also provides expert assistance to police and fire departments throughout the area with assistance upon request, depending upon availability of personnel. The long-term record of the Los Angeles County Sheriff's Arson-Explosives detail is a classic example of the investigative efficiency of a law enforcement agency in the field of criminal investigation of fires and explosions and of the close cooperation that may be developed between the fire and law enforcement (police-oriented) agencies when higher administrative understanding and support prevails. This, and numerous other examples, such as those previously related, discount the "myth" that police and firemen cannot work in close harmony. Nothing is further from the truth if they are given the chance and the support to show what they can do.

The City of Santa Ana, California Fire Department has a nationally recognized, long standing record of fire prevention and fire cause investigation. A number of major arson cases have been solved in this community over the past decade, including one investigation which identified an arsonist who had been setting fires over a number of years throughout the nation and which included one major southern California conflagration which took the lives of several firemen. The unit has also successfully prosecuted perpetrators of major industrial and commercial fires which were motivated by insurance fraud. The record of this unit is exemplary of what can be accomplished in a medium-sized, modern city when there is investigative cooperation between fire and police departments supplemented by meaningful support of the prosecutor's office. The record is also illustrative of constructive results in actual reduction of fire and arson losses in the city and the reduction of other major categories of crime at a time when losses and crime continue to escalate in too many other areas.

Perhaps it would be pointless to specify each department, police or fire, that is successfully coping with the incendiary problem. There are numerous examples where such progress can be cited in every area of the country. It is interesting to note that wherever progress is evident, the same common denominators are observed: the careful selection of investigative personnel; thorough training; administrative understanding of the complexities of the investigative problem; interagency cooperation; and last but not least, community support. Without community support, there cannot be budget support.

It is significant that most of the communities wherein progress has been made in the reduction of incendiary related crime, encompass the basic factors in common: for example, depressed areas, urban decay, sociocultural differences, and the usual industrial-economical conditions that occasionally contribute to arson related crime. Yet, with these same handicaps, they are making progress in the form of reduction of fire-related crime. Perhaps this suggests that when investigators and administrators are willing to work together and meet the members of the community more than half way, the community is willing and ready to respond in the terms of reduced property damage and crime, regardless of the diversity of urban problems.

THE RURAL AND SUBURBAN AREAS

Until recent years, rural areas were generally considered as agricultural, grazing, forest, watershed, and wildland areas, depending upon their location in relation to thickly populated areas. Fire protection was highly organized in some rural areas and practically nonexistent in others. Fire investigation was equally spotty, depending upon administrative jurisdiction and law enforcement responsibility. Increasing attention has been focused on these so-called nonincorporated or rural areas. Much of this attention grows directly out of movement of industrial and commercial development out of the cities. This is accompanied by mass population movement from the inner cities and with inner city cultural patterns often following the population flow. A fact of life is that some of these cultural patterns included fire setting and crime.

The need for increased fire protection was apparent to traditional authorities and administrative bodies as was the need for traditional law enforcement facilities. Unfortunately, the need for emphasis on fire prevention and crime prevention efforts, including the investigation of incendiarism, was tragically overlooked in most respects. The results of this general oversight have been apparent in the increased incendiary and crime losses in these areas.

The increasing awareness of the ecological and economical value of forest, agricultural, and wildland protection has evidenced the necessity for more practical public attention to the protection of our natural resources in the form of fire protection and law enforcement, particularly in the field of incendiary fire investigation. The necessity of fire protection is emphasized in the obviously uninterrupted, continuing depletion of our natural resources from the ravages of fire. Incendiary fires continue their increase in this loss spectrum.

The serious investigation of incendiarism has been tragically neglected in most of our rural and forest areas over the past years and continues to be neglected in too many areas today.

During the 1960's and 1970's, there has been increased attention on the problems of arson and incendiarism in the suburban and rural areas. This attention has principally resulted from the staggering increase of incendiarism along with other major crime in these areas. The attention is evidenced, in part, by the assignment of arson squads at the state level in a number of states and by Sheriff's arson units as well as County Fire Department and District

Arson Investigation units. Much of the impetus in the increased emphasis on arson investigation is the direct result of the research and efforts of such organizations as the International Association of Arson Investigators, International Association of Fire Chiefs, California Conference of Arson Investigators, and the National Fire Protection Association. Private industry has, in some areas, provided substantial, meaningful support to problems dealing directly with fire and crime prevention including studies of our arson problem and what can be done about it. An excellent example of meaningful assistance in studying the problem and seeking out an answer to what can be done about it is the Survey and Assessment of Arson and Arson Investigation (Law Enforcement Group) by the Aerospace Corporation. The report was prepared for the National Institute of Law Enforcement and Criminal Justice, Law Enforcement Assistance Administration, U.S. Department of Justice (October, 1976).

Fire and arson investigation seminars are regularly conducted in many states; many of these seminars are supported and/or sponsored by state educational systems. By and large, the seminars have raised the standards of fire investigation and law enforcement training but they have also pointed up the need for further scientific research in fire cause and fire behavior as well as improving the qualifications of instructors. Some of the educational facilities have made considerable progress in upgrading investigative techniques and investigative equipment but, again, emphasized the need for more exact investigative education. Governmental support, from Federal on down through the local level, has been decidedly limited in these areas in the practical sense.

The United States Forest Service has long recognized and attempted to deal with arson and incendiarism through the fielding of trained investigators over the past forty years as well as through research and forest product laboratory efforts. These investigators are specialists in the investigation of incendiarism as well as in general criminal procedures and work closely with other federal agencies as well as with state and local authorities in inquiries of common interest.

The California Division of Forestry is an example of leadership in the field of forest and wildland fire investigation. The department was one of the pioneers in establishing a criminal investigation division to investigate incendiarism and arson on state protected forest and wildlands. The investigation section is staffed by highly trained and experienced criminal fire investigators who are assigned throughout the state and who cooperate closely with other agencies where their interests are in common.

Because of the fact that the California Division of Forestry, by virtue of law, contracts with various counties throughout the state for all rural fire protection, including structural, the investigators also investigate structure fires in most of those areas of interest. The California Division of Forestry Investigative Staff and its record of accomplishment is exemplary of what can be accomplished in the rural fire investigation field.

Because of the increase in arson and incendiarism during the past decade, including in and throughout the school system, and because of the shortage of competent fire investigation personnel in many of the smaller communities, a State Arson Squad was established to work under the administration of the California State Fire Marshal. Again, this unit was staffed with carefully selected civil service appointed personnel who have the powers of peace officers and who are assigned, on a rather limited basis, throughout the State of California, to assist the local authorities in the investigation of fires of incendiary or suspicious origin.

Many states have excellent fire investigation units under the administration of State Police, State Fire Marshals' offices, or under appropriate public safety departments.

Many County Sheriffs' offices have established arson and explosives details. An excellent example has been previously set out. It is interesting to note that, once the detective is assigned to such a unit, he usually remains throughout the balance of his career. As earlier indicated, Sheriffs' investigators work closely with their counterparts in county fire departments and fire districts as well as with fire department volunteers which are prevalent in some areas of the country.

The success of any investigative system depends upon key factors including careful selection and training of personnel, supplemented by the understanding of fire investigation problems by supervisors; meaningful support by administrators; accomplishment of investigative missions by assignment of a practical time; and making available support facilities essential to the case, when necessary.

CHAPTER VIII

FIRE SCENE EXAMINATION

Much has been written about the various aspects of fire investigation. Some of the information published emphasizes the legal aspects which, of course, are important; others indicate preoccupation with fringe issues and repetitious narrative avoiding the grass roots and technical problems that must be faced in arson investigation if a constructive purpose is to be served. It is the field investigator who is ultimately faced with assembling the information, including that produced by the fire scene, and it is up to him to produce factual answers to where, when, and how the fire started. Next, if the cause is shown to have been incendiary, the investigator has further work cut out for him. For example, "Who did it?" and "Why?" This is what it is all about. It is hoped that this chapter will provide some general guidelines and some specific suggestions useful to the field investigator "where the action is."

It was once stated that the investigator burns his bridges behind him, that once burned, they stay burned. Whether this should be taken literally or not depends, to some extent, upon the investigator, his training, and the particular circumstances at hand. The first bridge, in the arson investigation field, might well be the destruction of key physical evidence of fire cause during fire department overhaul. In this circumstance, such evidence may be distorted beyond value or totally destroyed. It is up to the arson investigator to prevent this from happening. He can do this, as a rule, through liaison with department heads, training officers, and the officers and firemen at company level.

The second "bridge" may be destroyed by the investigator or his aides during improper or indifferent fire scene examination. Key information or evidence may go unrecognized, overlooked, or its integrity may simply be destroyed.

A relatively small fire may require more investigative attention than a major fire. For example, there may be a fatality or serious injuries in the small fire requiring investigative teams from both arson and homicide. It is recognized that most modern fire and police departments have regulations for response to fire and crime scenes which include procedures for securing fire scenes and follow-up investigation. In many cases, administrative orders spell out subsequent practices and investigating procedures, including consultation and advice from the prosecutor's office when circumstances require. Some departments provide company officers and firemen with checklists that must be completed and filed for each fire scene. Such lists are often valuable to the investigator in subsequent interview of responding firemen as well as reminders to the investigator of what to cover or supplement, as circumstances demand, when he examines the scene.

Such checklists may include:

1. Condition of external openings, doors, windows, hatches, on arrival.
   Describe 'unusual' such as forced entry.
2. Means of Fire Department entry.
   Each entrance and by whom.
3. List any persons on premises at time of arrival.
   Name. _____
   Address. _____
   Duty or reason for presence.
   (This is mainly appropriate for industrial-commercial fires during non-business hours)
4. Watchman or Security Patrol Service.
   Name. _____
   Address. _____
5. Sprinkler valve.
   Position and condition.
6. Who cut utilities?
   Position of primary switches, circuit breakers, disconnects.
   Position of secondary or space switches and circuit breakers.
7. Electric clocks stopped? Time?
   (As to each unit found)
8. Who turned in Alarm?
   Name _____
   Address _____
   Phone _____
9. Who was on premises when F. D. arrived?
   Name _____
   Address _____
   Phone _____
10. Possible area or space of origin.

11. Possible cause.
12. Premises released to:
    Name _____
    Address _____
    Phone _____
    Time & Date _____
13. Physical evidence removed.
    Describe:
14. Utility representatives called to scene.
    Name _____
    Address _____
    Phone _____
15. Narrative comments as to any unusual conditions found.

Signed,

Officer or Fireman

A third "bridge" may be inadvertently burned when recovered evidence is improperly identified, transported, packaged, or stored.

A fourth "bridge," not necessarily in this order of priority, may collapse if the investigator has violated, willfully or not, fourth amendment guarantees of those under investigation by means of observation, search, and/or seizure without due process when due process is required. For example, the law has described and the courts have defined when fire departments and emergency officials can enter private property on an emergency basis and in the interest of the public safety without due process; they have defined when that emergency ceases to exist and when reentry without clear consent or without previously authorized court order is prohibited.

These "bridges" appear, sometimes at unpredictable intervals, and must be dealt with as they appear because fire scenes are varied and often complex. The arson investigator who claims to have "seen it all" and who professes he knows all the answers deludes himself and his associates.

It is the intent of this chapter to provide the field investigator with practical and workable suggestions that are designed to get the job done in a legal and practical manner. General procedural rules concerning fire scene examination are flexible and can be adjusted to fit the requirements and personnel of any investigative jurisdiction. For example, the same scale of fire scene examination and techniques, such as gridding, plotting, etc., that might be used on a major industrial fire scene would not necessarily be applied to a fire scene limited to a single occupancy store space. Investigative teams might be dis-

patched to a fire scene by one jurisdiction whereas a neighboring jurisdiction might dispatch a single team or merely one investigator.

It is well known that fire, by its nature, is capable of destroying the evidence of its cause. Some theorists and *de facto* investigators have written that no fire obliterates the evidence of its cause. They occasionally add, "Fire merely changes the appearance of the evidence and it is then up to the qualified arson investigator to identify it in its changed form and recognize it for what it is." While this may well be correct in some cases, any practical, experienced, and truthful field investigator knows that major fires can and do totally obliterate the evidence of cause. This does not imply that the investigator should cease to search or neglect his examination of the scene. It is suggested, however, that the destructiveness of fire is a fact of life and must be faced honestly and squarely by the investigator. Even so, it is also true that important clues to the origin and cause of a fire are all too frequently overlooked or destroyed by untrained or indifferent firemen during overhaul and salvage operations. With proper training, supervision, and liaison, this investigative gap can be materially reduced.

Properly trained and coordinated firemen, responding to a fire, can be utilized to advantage and there are numerous examples on record where alert firemen discovered and preserved essential physical evidence that later made the difference between winning and losing an arson case. Actually, who has better opportunity to discover and preserve key evidence? Treated properly, the vast majority of firemen are invaluable assets to arson investigators. On the other hand, indifferent or condescending treatment usually encourages response in kind. There are numerous examples, throughout the nation, where lack of rapport between fire fighters and investigators negates chances of the successful conclusion to an investigation. It is under such circumstances that the physical evidence at the fire scene goes "sailing out the window" during fire department overhaul.

THE ENGINE COMPANY'S RESPONSIBILITIES IN ARSON DETECTION

Modern fire departments recognize and encourage teamwork in suppressing fire. It is a *must*. Firemen are trained that their basic function is fire control and saving life and property in this order of priority. This is as it should be. They are trained to respond to the fire as quickly and safely as circumstances permit; once on the scene, their entire attention is directed toward saving and protecting life and, next, extinguishing the fire as quickly as possible. Now, while this may be stated in a number of different ways, this is where the fireman's attention and immediate activities are directed. It is occasionally difficult to convince the fire officer or fireman that at least some of his attention should be directed toward factors which may later be of assistance in determining the origin and cause of the fire. This *can* be accomplished and experience tells us that it is being accomplished without diminishing the efficiency of the fire control operation. The effort merely requires planning, tact, training, and cooperation.

Teamwork, traditionally understood and accepted by all firemen in the fire control and rescue operations, is not so readily understood by them where fire investigators are concerned. Frequently, his teamwork or cooperation is not forthcoming because he feels he is left out of the picture. This cooperation and communications gap can be closed by the investigator who properly understands his job and the value of investigative cooperation from every fireman who responds to a fire scene.

It is frequently the case that circumstances and evidence suggesting a suspicious fire are observed by "first-in" firemen or by the firemen conducting the overhaul. A common tactical error of investigators is to charge headlong into a fire investigation without carefully interviewing the firemen first on the scene. Examples can be cited by experienced prosecutors and investigators where investigations and prosecutable actions failed because firemen had not been interviewed in detail as to their observations. These discrepancies were subsequently discovered and introduced by the defense.

For example, in one classic case of the arson of a gambling club, the Fire Marshal testified that he had made an examination of the fire scene and that he found three separate and distinct areas of origin. He identified these origins by the intense, low fire and the burn-through of the floor at each location. He found no residue of flammable liquids at any of the three points but testified that, based upon the burn pattern at each location, he was certain flammable liquids had been used as accelerants. He further testified, on direct examination, that the burn pattern and the pattern of collapse of the floor were identical at each location. (The club was on the second floor.) On cross-examination, the defense attorney asked the Fire Marshal if he had taken the trouble to consult with the officers who first responded to the fire and who first entered the club during control activi-

ties. The Fire Marshal, a man of considerable background and experience, responded that he had talked to "some of them" but not "all of them" and that it was not necessary for him to do so since he made his own independent evaluation of the physical evidence as he found it. Asked if, as a matter of fact, he had taken the trouble to talk to the Battalion Chief who was "first-in" at the involved area, the Fire Marshal's reply was "No."

When the defense put up their case, the "first-in" Battalion Chief was called to the stand as a defense witness. His attention was called to a photograph of the interior of the gambling club which showed the three areas of origin including the hole in the floor testified to by the Fire Marshal. Pointing to the large, impressive-looking hole, the defense attorney stated "Chief, calling your attention to people's exhibit X and, particularly, to this large hole in the floor, do you personally know how that hole came to be in the floor?" The Chief replied that he did recognize the hole and did know how the hole came to be in the floor. Defense questioned, "How did the hole get in the floor, if you know." The Chief replied, "As I was walking through that area, I fell through that hole. There was no fire on the surface of the floor in that area. I later determined that the fire had been burning in the attic under the floor at that location and had weakened the floor. I simply fell through."

The credibility of the *corpus delicti* was questioned and the case was dismissed. Had the Fire Marshal bothered to visit the scene with the Battalion Chief, he would have learned how the hole got in the floor. Whether or not he would have been able to prove a *corpus delicti* without the third point of origin becomes moot.

Over 25 years ago, the Arson Committee of the International Association of Fire Chiefs recommended that each Fire Chief designate at least one man from first-in companies whose principal duty shall be to examine the scene for evidence of incendiarism, to protect and preserve the evidence of any suspicious circumstance he might find, and to make his findings known to his superior officer who would notify the appropriate investigator in accordance with the administrative chain of command. It was recommended that such firemen receive special training in recognition, collection, and preservation of evidence. Unfortunately, this intelligent and necessary recommendation seems to have been neglected in many departments across the nation, at least during the more recent years, and continues to be overlooked by many fire and arson investigators who continue to lament about "how firemen continue to throw the evidence out of the window."

Fire companies should be provided with the basics of fire cause investigation as a part of their training curriculum. A responsible member of each company should receive further specialized training in arson detection.

Fire companies should be alerted to make observations upon approach to the fire scene. These observations should include weather, wind, etc. As the company approaches the scene, they should be alert for vehicles and persons leaving the scene as well as those on the scene. It is recognized that the above may not be applicable in heavily congested urban areas under certain conditions, and that the fireman's first duty is to get to the fire as quickly and safely as possible. On the other hand, experience tells that firemen responding to fires often make key observations of extreme value to investigators.

Most fire company officers carry notebooks and many have recorded license numbers, vehicle, and people descriptions which subsequently lead to successful apprehension of the suspect. This type of information is particularly useful in incendiary fire 'series' situations where a suspect 'pattern' situation may be developed.

As the fire company approaches the scene, the color of the flame and smoke should be noted; this may be suggestive of the fuels and type of fire they will encounter. Conditions of ventilation are important in respect to the term, behavior, and spread pattern of the fire.

The visible space involvement of the premises may be significant as the companies approach the scene and may also be relevant in point of rapidity of spread. This information may be valuable to the investigators when considered along with origin and subsequent progress of the fire. In some major conflagrations, where demolition is complete, it is often difficult, if not impossible, for even the most experienced investigators to determine even the occupancy or space of origin from the remaining physical evidence. He must rely, at least in part, upon the observations of early witnesses including first-in firemen if he is to progress to searching for the cause with any degree of accuracy. This was graphically illustrated in a recent major fire which destroyed several commercial occupancies. The fire was in extended progress when reported during the dark, early morning hours of a weekend. Following control, all supporting columns, separation walls, and most of the exterior walls were down; the roof caved into the center of the building early in the fire and roof and supporting beams and framing were totally incinerated by the time the fire was controlled.

No factual determination of the space of origin could be made upon physical evidence alone. Careful interview of early witnesses, including civilians, police, and firemen, plus early helicopter photos of the fire, shortly following discovery, permitted factual determination of the point of origin and subsequent progress of the fire.

In another recent late night shopping center fire, again, because of delayed discovery and report, the fire was in extended progress through three occupancies and through a common attic by the time the first fire units arrived on the scene. The fire was confined to the shopping center with total demolition of the multispace building of origin. It was impossible to determine the precise space of origin from physical evidence. However, information provided by one of the first-in firemen led to identification of a witness who, alerted by what sounded like an explosion, produced a camera in her apartment which was across the street and took photographs of the scene. The first shot placed the fire in a single identifiable space in the shopping center; subsequent shots recorded the progress of the fire into adjacent spaces and into the attic area.

The space of origin identified, the cause was accurately determined.

First-in firemen should be alert to possible separate fires and the location of the apparently heaviest involved areas or spaces, inside or out. Again, the color and intensity of smoke and flame and the direction of spread of the fire must be considered. They should be alert to any explosions, bearing in mind their locations and their possible relationship to the venting of the fire or flashover. Firemen may observe odors or fire behavior which may be consistent with the presence of flammable or explosive compounds. They may identify and preserve containers, broken glass, or other physical evidence which might be otherwise obliterated during further fire control activities or overhaul.

First-in firemen are invaluable in identifying their own means of entry and their progress through the spaces which may later have been destroyed in the extinguishing of the fire. This information, if unknown to the investigator, may result in a completely unrealistic evaluation of origin in the final investigative analysis. For example, in one dwelling fire, the Fire Department responded in the early morning hours and extinguished the fire. The occupants had escaped without injury but with loss of most of their personal possessions. During overhaul, the firemen removed certain items from the living room to the yard. Included was an upholstered divan which suffered moderate damage. Applying considerable water to the divan after it was removed to the yard, firemen believed it was extinguished. Shortly thereafter, the companies returned to quarters. The Chief planned to return the following morning, during daylight hours, and complete his investigation.

About two hours after the Fire Department returned to headquarters, they were again summoned to the scene. The divan had rekindled. This time it was totally demolished by the flames that had been hidden inside the upholstery.

Returning to the scene the following day, the Chief completed his investigation which placed the origin in a wall circuit in the opposite end of the house, which was consistent with his preliminary findings of the previous evening. He had eliminated the divan because of the relatively moderate damage when it was moved into the yard for overhaul.

Several days later, the scene was visited by an insurance investigator. Examining the extensively damaged divan (still lying out in the yard), he "opinioned" it as "the lowest, heaviest, and longest burn" and therefore the point of origin of the fire. He attributed the cause of the fire to careless smoking. Of course he hadn't bothered to check with the Chief and learn that the heaviest and longest burn he observed in the divan actually occurred out in the yard and that it was due to rekindling. Further, he had neglected to ascertain that the occupants of the premises did not smoke.

Firemen can often supply factual information as to which exterior doors or hatches were open, closed, or locked on arrival; whether windows were open or closed; the possibility of outsiders having gained or attempted entrance to the building prior to the arrival of firemen. The observer fireman should note whether the occupant is present and his manner of dress and demeanor. Circumstances vary, of course, with type of occupancy and time of day. The occupant or person present may volunteer comments which may be useful and relevant at a later time; for example, the circumstances of his presence, what he observed, anything unusual concerning his clothing, shoes, hands, or general condition or appearance.

Suspects, regardless of their motivation for the fire, are often inclined to converse freely with firemen when they would avoid contact with an investigator or police officer. First-in firemen have proven invaluable in obtaining key information leading to the cause of the fire and identity of the person responsible.

Provided with proper training and supervision, firemen will exercise care in the application of hose streams during overhaul. He will conduct the overhaul and salvage work, carefully preserving the suspected area of origin. He will avoid unnecessary activity and traverse in areas where further fire scene examination is required and, if necessary, isolate an area by posting a suitable barricade or guard until investigators take over the scene.

The observer fireman should request another fireman to observe discoveries of items of suspicion which require further investigative attention, making note of description, location, time, and date. If it becomes necessary to remove the evidence or items before the investigators arrive, the items should be first photographed, in position, with tie points, then tagged, properly packaged, and removed to a locked location. Such preliminary precautions are occasionally required when, for example, there is danger of walls coming down, falling beams, or circumstances indicating that the area may be unattended between the time of fire department departure and the arrival of investigators.

As we have emphasized in this chapter, so far, alert, properly trained, first-in firemen and overhaul personnel are some of the most valuable investigative resources in the investigative picture. The scope of their potential assistance is probably broader in rural areas, especially in forest and wildland fires. For example, the fireman has the first opportunity to observe and record persons and vehicles in the vicinity of fires which may occur in remote or isolated areas. In such circumstances, he may have an unusually favorable opportunity to observe and preserve tire tracks, foot prints, and other evidence of presence at a fire scene. The preservation of such evidence may make the difference between apprehension of the suspect and "losing" him.

While the origin of forest and wildland fires may be established from physical evidence and features such as exposure surfaces, burn and spread patterns, etc., under certain rather limited conditions, experience has shown that, when major conflagrations occur, behavior patterns may be seriously altered by topography and changing wind conditions, including retraverse of a burned area by the fire. Physical evidence of forest and wildland fires can be deceiving. Therefore, the investigator should be particularly careful to evaluate the information supplied by responding firemen or fire fighters and other early witnesses before he goes off the "deep end" as to precisely where the fire started and how. He may be able to coordinate this information with information that may be available from forest fire lookouts, again depending upon topography, weather, wind and cover conditions, and degree of visibility from the particular observation point.

In summary, the arson investigator, whether assigned to fires in congested urban areas, suburban districts, or rural spaces, will do very well indeed if he seeks out the responding firemen. The investigator should solicit his cooperation, observations, and assistance just as successful police detectives have always sought out the patrolmen and patrol units who are usually the first-in on report of a crime and who observe and hear things that would usually be lost forever to the detective, regardless of the circumstances of his arrival on scene.

CHAPTER IX

PROCEDURAL FIRE SCENE EXAMINATION

As a general rule, the earlier the investigator can be on the scene, the better.

If the fire companies have departed, the investigator should be certain that his entry on the premises and examination is not conducted under trespass circumstances that would subsequently preclude the admission of evidence discovered on the scene. This section is not intended as a discourse on the law of searches and seizures or the exclusionary rule. Suffice it to say that the official investigator must be familiar with the law and the rules of procedure in his jurisdiction regarding authority and when and under what conditions a fire scene may be examined.

When there is any doubt in the investigator's mind about whether he can enter a fire scene, in reference to any particular locked or closed space of that scene, and under what conditions and with whom after control of the fire, he should contact his City Attorney, District Attorney, or other appropriate legal authority before proceeding. Meanwhile, if circumstances justify, he may leave a representative to observe from the outside and monitor what is removed from the scene. Again, this 'monitoring' is also subject to the limits of searches and seizures and may therefore be limited to what is removed in plain sight of the observer.

Briefly, the law, including the Fourth Amendment of the Constitution, protects citizens and their property from unlawful intrusions and searches and seizures by officials except under due process as specifically defined in the law. The Courts have generally acknowledged the right of Fire Emergency and Safety personnel to go on private property to extinguish fires and to make what intrusions are reasonably necessary, including forced entry, to extinguish the fire and to prevent spread of the fire. In plain language, this includes the entry of exposed spaces where, in the opinion of the fire officials, the fire may be reasonably expected to have spread. This can reasonably include adjacent exposed occu-

pancies where conducted, convected, or radiated heat may be apparent on the walls or separations to the exposed occupancy. In apartments and hotels, for example, forced entry by the fire officials may not only be necessary into the primarily involved spaces but may also be required to gain access to adjoining spaces not only in insuring control of the fire but also in the interest of the even higher priority function of saving life.

The emergency nature of the control of the fire embraces the common knowledge of the destructive nature of uncontrolled fire and its hazard to life and the general public safety. This is the essence of the authority granted under the law for emergency access to all classes of private property and the grant continues so long as the emergency exists. The Courts have generally held that Fire Departments may take such steps as may be reasonably necessary to control the fire, to "seek it out" in all its possible avenues of spread, and to take such measures as are necessary to completely extinguish the fire in order that it will not recur. (This includes all reasonable overhaul efforts.) The Courts have also said that fire and public safety officials may take such steps as may be reasonably necessary to protect the public from collapsing walls, cornices, beams, and other conditions caused by the demolition of the fire; such efforts may reasonably extend after control of the fire. The conditions vary with the circumstances and what is reasonable in the interest of public safety may become a question of fact.

Such precautions may include the installation of barricades, and posting against entrance to the property—except as may be specifically authorized by the authorities—so long as the emergency conditions continue. Questions are continually raised concerning how long and under what conditions the emergency authorities may restrict or regulate reentry of lawful owners or occupants; for example, to return and salvage their belongings, inspect the loss with their insurance representatives, or investigate the cause of the fire on their own behalf. Generally, the Courts take a dim view of restricting reentry of lawful owners or occupants on the pretext of the interest of public safety when the facts indicate that the hazard does not exist. However, they have traditionally approved fire cause investigation proceeding in conjunction with the emergency presence of fire and safety officers during control of the fire and also during reasonable periods of fire overhaul.

Once the premises are turned over to the representatives of the owner or occupant and firemen leave the scene, it is generally held that the emergency ceases. The question of fire scene investigation, by the authorities, following the release, becomes a much more involved problem. From this point on, the continued search of the scene, or reentry and search, may well be in violation of due process if accomplished without the clear consent of the lawful owner or occupant (whosoever has the first right of occupancy) or a lawful court order such as a search warrant. Such circumstances raise interesting and sometimes very complicated questions (with even the eminent legal profession disagreeing) such as "Was the consent voluntarily given to the Fire Marshal by the occupant or was it given under duress?" Or, "Was the occupant fully informed by the officer when he obtained the consent?" And, "What did the consent imply? How far did he say the officers could go?" And on, and on.

The additional question is often raised, "Was the emergency really still in effect or were the fire authorities merely holding the premises to stall until they could complete their investigation?" Or, "Were they holding the premises until they found something that they could utilize for probable cause upon which a court-issued search warrant might then be founded?" Did the leaning wall or the loose overhanging beam really constitute such a hazard that the authorities had a right to keep the occupant or owner or his insurance representatives from entering the premises? Or, on the other hand, did the fact that the insurance adjuster had a right to enter the premises excuse the Fire Marshal from obtaining a search warrant when they returned to the premises, three days after the fire, and found incriminating evidence involving the insured occupant?

The above are briefly illustrative of the complex problems that may grow out of post-fire search of the fire scene. A fire scene examination *is* a search. Suffice it to say that the investigator should remem-

ber the old-fashioned railroad crossing signs: "Stop—Look—Listen!" This applies to any fire investigator approaching any fire scene. The burden is on him, at all times, to know the law and observe it. Indifference or ignorance, regardless of the heinousness of the particular offense or the convincing nature of the evidence, may result in the exclusion of that evidence by the Court simply because of the tainted nature of the evidence from illegal search.

For example, a city Fire Marshal responds to a mercantile fire during the early hours before dawn. During overhaul, firemen have discovered several partially burned plastic containers evidencing a residue of gasoline.

The Fire Marshal decides to leave the containers at the scene when he is suddenly called to another early morning blaze in another section of the city. By the time he leaves the second fire, and returns to the original scene, he finds that the fire companies have turned the premises back to the owner and returned to their quarters. The owner has locked the premises and departed.

The following day, instead of either contacting the owner for permission to reenter or applying to the Court for a search warrant, the Fire Marshal advises an insurance adjuster of his earlier findings at the scene and his suspicions concerning the cause of the fire and involvement of the owner. The Fire Marshal asks the adjuster to pick up the containers since the adjuster has a key to the premises. The key was provided to the adjuster by a real estate firm which carried the involved property on its listing. The adjuster unlocked and entered the premises, found the containers, and photographed them as found. He then removed the containers, along with other debris from the origin, which evidenced the strong odor of gasoline, and delivered them to the Fire Marshal at Fire Department headquarters. The items were tagged and the Fire Marshal provided the adjuster with an official written receipt listing each and every item.

Regardless of the good faith of the adjuster and the Fire Marshal in seeking out and delivering the physical evidence at the instructions of the Fire Marshal, the adjuster was acting in an agency capacity for the officer and the evidence was therefore picked up (seized) without due process and would probably not be permitted into evidence in a criminal prosecution.

It should be apparent, as initially stated, that the sooner the investigator can get on the scene, the better. How *long* he can maintain control of the scene after the fire companies depart will depend upon the particular circumstances at that scene. Common sense and reasonability must be exercised and, if there is any doubt concerning leaving and returning to the scene; length of time on the premises; or about excluding owners, occupants or their representatives from the scene; the investigator should be considering whether he has sufficient probable cause for a search warrant and he should consult with the appropriate officials in order to obtain a search warrant before continuing.

Continuing with the procedural aspects of fire scene examination by the investigator, the size of the fire may or may not have a bearing on the length of time, complexity of the investigation, and personnel that may be required. Too often, inexperienced investigators are confused by the size and demolition of a fire and lose track of the fact that most fires start as small ones. In most cases, early witnesses or initial "size up" of the scene will save countless man hours of unnecessary and often confusing activity at the fire scene. Initial size up and planning by experienced and competent fire investigators can spell out the difference between a successful inquiry and an investigation that failed to produce any reliable factual information as to origin or cause. This may be likened to a diagnosis of engine trouble by an experienced mechanic. If he knows his business, he recognizes and understands symptoms: He knows how to look and where to look. This is also true with the competent fire scene investigator. The symptoms may be apparent, though not always, in the remaining physical evidence. Some of these symptoms in the area of lowest and severest burn are char patterns, spread patterns, initial ventilation, and areas of initial structural failure and roof collapse. These and numerous other symptoms may enable the experienced investigator to eliminate major areas from the search simply because they are not relevant to origin or cause.

The initial diagnosis may include careful interview of early witnesses, particularly the first fire officers on the scene and the first-in firemen. The investigator may find the need to return and re-interview these witnesses after he has completed his fire scene examination. Good investigators consider all available evidence. This is particularly significant and applicable to fire scene examination.

The order in which an investigator approaches the investigative procedures depends, again, upon circumstances. These circumstances include the size of the fire, the type of structure, and the circumstances of discovery and report. He must cover the following itemized procedures in his investigative journey although not necessarily in the order set out:

1. Early preliminary conference with the company officer or Chief. This may lead to individual preliminary interviews of first-in firemen and any other personnel. The interview should include such information as has been described in our earlier treatment of firemen witnesses responding to the scene.

2. Preliminary interview of witnesses who discovered the fire if they are available. If not available, identification and briefing of information provided by them should be noted for follow-up interview at the earliest possible moment. The investigator might elect to assign this task to other investigative personnel and for utilization while he is conducting fire scene examination.

3. At major structural fire scenes, it is well to make a preliminary tour of the perimeter and interior for initial size-up and orientation; familiarizing oneself with exposures; means of access and egress; general pattern or patterns of spread; ventilation; apparent initial structural collapse, if any; secondary collapse; and last, but not least, the area of heaviest flame concentration, although this may not necessarily be the area of earliest fire.

The above suggested detail is not necessarily required in limited space fires, such as one-room fires in dwellings or shops; nevertheless, a careful preliminary "look-around" before moving in detail is never a bad idea. It always pays to be oriented. This may be particularly true when the investigator begins to listen to what the witnesses have to say and it becomes even more relevant if and when the investigator reaches the point where he is evaluating what the suspect has to say.

In the instance of many structural fires, it is possible, during the preliminary survey, for the investigator to identify the general area or space of origin and the spread pattern. The area of origin may be manifested in the degree of incineration in that space if the fire was ventilated, or it may be indicated in the lack of total incineration if ventilation in that space was limited. The general origin and behavior of the fire may be evident in the collapse of combustible exposures such as shelves and ceiling over the area of origin and supplemented by the flame pattern as the fire progressed into other spaces. The progress of the flame spread is often evident in flame penetration of door panels and partitions, high or low depending upon the distance from the actual point of origin; the patterns are also expressed in the progress of the flames through windows, skylights, and interconnecting spaces.

During this preliminary survey, the experienced investigator may be able to form a reasonably accurate evaluation of the time spectrum of the fire as it progressed from space to space. In this regard, he takes into consideration the fire-loading in each space, the types of walls and separations, and the flame resistance of those separations and walls. For example, the walls may have been "one hour" walls which were not penetrated, whereas one half-hour rated separations near the area of origin were penetrated.

Backtracking to the room of origin, he may observe that, while the origin appears to be near floor level, the plaster ceiling is penetrated and the fire has extended into the attic at that point. His further examination of the attic area may show him that the fire spread in the attic is relatively limited although there was plenty of ventilation for continued flame progress. Such factors are relevant in the evaluation of the time spectrum of the fire.

His initial survey of the premises may also provide him with basic information concerning the fire's early behavior. This is particularly relevant in the room or space of origin. For example, regardless of the fact that the point of origin is not at this time established, was this a fire producing an abnormally rapid temperature rise considering the fire loading and exposures? Rapid temperature rise might be characterized in wide lateral, low level (near the floor) involvement where materials such as low flash point accelerants were present—along with heavy char at low levels—on contents of the room such as merchandise or furniture. On the other hand, a very slow temperature rise might be evidenced by deep charring of a single furniture or stock item with a corresponding heat pattern on the ceiling above that location, with penetration of the plaster immediately adjacent to that location. The general space would indicate gradual heat or temperature build-up from the ceiling down, and windows covered with glaze from incomplete products of combustion. Damage to furniture or other combustible items might be limited to char pattern, from top down, and to radiated heat damage from the direction of the originating source of heat.

During this preliminary survey of the scene, the investigator will determine the location of the main electric and gas service entrance, main switch panels, meters, and the gas regulators and meters.

It is a good practice to photograph the perimeter

if this is a major fire area such as a burned-out shopping center. Aerial photographs are often helpful where an extensive shopping or industrial area is involved. If the fire is confined to one structure, photographs showing all sides are desirable. It is good practice to photograph power and gas service panels, including drip loops, if any, and to show the position of main switches and valves.

During the preliminary survey, again depending upon circumstances, the investigator might check exterior doors, hatches, and openings for evidence of forced entry, meanwhile identifying Fire Department entry. All forced entry evidence should be photographed. If skylights or hatches are relevant, these should also be examined and photographed where frames and locking mechanisms indicate that they have been forced prior to the fire. It is always good practice to verify all forced openings with fire department responding personnel. It may be too late for them to recall several weeks later.

It is acknowledged that the detail suggested in the above size-up might not be required in an apartment or hotel room type of fire. The competent fire investigator learns to tailor his preliminary survey to the scene. For example, certain factors or conditions may catch his eye on his first trip through or around the scene; or, they may be called to his attention by firemen on the scene.

For example:

A. In a men's haberdashery, are the clothing racks full? Are the items consistent with the location and type of shop involved? What is the situation in the storeroom?

B. In a dwelling, are personal items that would normally be found present? How about closets, drawers, and personal items such as insurance papers and records?

C. In a furniture warehouse, what about the inventory records as compared to items in the premises? Record model, make, and condition of items in storage, apart from fire damage.

D. In a beauty parlor, several secondary circuit breakers are taped closed and the hair dryer lamp units are all connected with switches on, even though the premises have been closed over the weekend.

E. In a restaurant fire occurring several hours after closing time, the kitchen range and oven burners are found on. An explosion blew out the windows of the premises and the fire followed. The flash pattern extends from the water heater located in a closet off the kitchen entrance.

4. Following the preliminary survey, the investigator should find some quiet location where he can sit down, rest his feet, and decide on how he wants to proceed from this point. He should produce his working note pad which should be at least 8" x 12" with lined and graphed pages. These lines and spaces certainly do not interfere with detailed note taking. They do facilitate sketching, where necessary, including measurements that should be set down to scale.

The investigator will outline the jobs to be done as contemplated at this time. This is particularly important to the investigator who may be called to another scene, interrupting this investigation, and who may have several other investigations on his mind at the same time. Careful notes and outline of contemplated and necessary procedures, in respect to this fire, may prevent costly mistakes or oversights at a future time. Again, in this particular situation, the size, condition, and circumstances of this particular fire scene should govern the detail necessary in the jobs that should be done.

In the search for the point of origin, we must continually reflect on known factors governing the behavior and chemistry of fire and its effect on exposures. These subjects were covered in some detail in earlier chapters of this text. Given the same environment, ignition sources, fuel load, and structural and ventilation conditions, fire growth from a given source will follow identifiable and often definitely predictable patterns. In fire tests, it has been demonstrated that fire growth patterns and flame spread conditions are repeated again and again. Study and experience in identifying and interpreting these fire patterns is essential in any factual analysis of fire origin.

Fire spread or fire growth manifests itself in a number of ways. The principal fingerprints of fire growth in wood, for example, are indicated in the transformation of wood from its structural state into carbon. This is manifested in what is generally known in the fire investigation profession as "alligatoring" and/or charring, the latter term being common to nearly all combustible materials whereas alligatoring is more unique to fibrous wood products and even more particularly to cut smooth surfaces. Alligatoring and charring proceed in accordance with the severity of the fire and are variable, as to surface appearance, depending upon not only the heat generated by the fire but also by the particular structure of the wood and its moisture content.

Due to limited scientific experimental study on these particular phenomena in relation to wood and fire, there is no present reliable data tending to identify the size of the alligatoring (its coarseness or fineness), its gloss, or other visual appearance with either rapid temperature rise or with the presence or use of flammable accelerants such as gasoline, acetone, thinner, or other volatile liquids or incendiary materials.

For example:

A. Should the utility company experts be called to assist and, if so, what areas should they be asked to cover? Should other specialists be called in at this time? If so, in what fields?

B. What preliminary building plans or investigative scene sketches will be necessary? Should a grid system be utilized for the area of origin? Such systems are desirable in explosion scenes where displacement of objects and exposures may be apparent and where precise detail in area examination and item location is desired.

C. If this is not a major scene, what investigative assistance will be required from this point and who will assist?

D. What legal and practical steps can be taken to preserve the integrity of the fire scene until it is released? This includes limiting access to critical areas.

Once the preliminary survey and evaluation of the fire scene is completed, the general area or space of origin may have been ascertained. From this point, the investigator must, if possible, narrow the focus to the point of origin.

In the earlier chapters dealing with the chemistry and behavior of fire, it was stressed that, regardless of the ultimate extent and damage, the origin of most fires was probably confined to one ignition source. More simply stated, most big fires start as little ones and under normal conditions, from a single source, at a single location. Examples include a match; an electrical arc; a spark; a heat source without flame, spark, or arc (such as an electric iron or stove); or spontaneous chemical, biological, or physical ignition. From such heat sources, ignition of exposed combustible materials may follow, forming in pattern, accompanied by fire growth from that ignition source.

From that heat source and initial ignition of the conventional combustible materials, a cone-shaped pattern of spread emerges on exposures such as walls, doors, and partitions. The apex of the cone is found at the ignition source, with the pattern widening as the continued burning extends, usually upward, from the source. The pattern is often graphically exemplified when waste baskets beneath desks or against walls burn out, leaving the pattern extending up the wall from the position of the basket.

This pattern, although usually identifiable at the origin, and corroborated by depth of char at the seat of the fire, may be altered by furniture, shelves, merchandise, and other obstructions; it may be further altered by the presence of vertical openings, stairways, and other structural features affecting draft. The normal progress of heat is upward and this is evidenced in the cone pattern. This can be considerably altered as the fire gains in intensity and volume and moves away from the point of origin.

The distortion of the fire cone may also appear, if flammable liquids, such as gasoline, are spread over a floor surface and ignited. The sharp cone effect is lost because of the wide base ignition of the vapors over the floor surface. The evidence of laterally-radiated initial temperature rise is significantly greater and often manifested in flash pattern on other floor-level, exposed items in the room. Once the gasoline vapors are consumed, the cone pattern may appear on exposures but in wider base scale since the heat-producing capabilities of the gasoline vapors were greater in the period immediately following ignition and distributed over a wider base area, again depending upon the quantity of fuel distributed.

Alligatoring is one manifestation of the process of thermal decomposition of wood products. The internal structure expands and reacts to heat and produces gases that make up the conventional combustion process. As those gases are released from the compound, they harmonize with atmospheric oxygen and the combustion process continues. The wood surfaces crack and open in various sizes and patterns, depending upon the wood's structure, the temperatures within the so-called cracks, and the dryness of the wood. The depth and size of the cracks and individual alligator pattern sections also depend upon the time spectrum of the particular fire.

Experimental observations have repeatedly demonstrated that alligatoring not only varies according to the above described conditions but may also be altered by weathering as well as painting, processing, or artificial treatment for a particular utilization of the product.

Experiments have demonstrated that large scale alligator patterns commonly appear early on many flat grain wood surfaces from smoldering as well as from semi-explosive, rapid temperature rise types of fires; that as the combustion process continues, these large and occasionally glossy surface patterns break up in the process, disintegrating in a continuing reduction of the wood fiber structure down to the charcoal stage. The alligator pattern becomes less and less pronounced until it is indistinguishable because of the total carbonization of the fibrous wood surface. As the combustion/oxidation chain continues into the deeper recesses of the wood body, the patterns are no longer distinguishable as the alligator pattern initially observed.

While it is correctly stated that, although there is no presently acceptable means of visual identification of slow or rapid temperature rise fire based upon alligator pattern, flat wood surface alligator pattern may be of some limited value in determining the spread pattern of a fire over very limited areas.

Some fire investigators have offered theories that the size and appearance of alligatoring may, in itself, indicate that flammable hydrocarbons or other volatile compounds were present at the location. Such theories should be accepted with extreme caution.

Charring is manifested in most compounds susceptible to the combustion process. It is evident in the most common construction fuel with which the fire investigator will deal—wood. Charring is also evident, in one form or another, in all compounds where oxidation and the heat decomposition process occur, including vegetable matter, synthetics from various mineral matter, animal fats, etc. Charring is a result of the combustion process as the compound is reduced to charcoal.

Char patterns and depth of char are useful to the investigator in tracing the course of a fire. In following char pattern, the investigator may backtrack, tracing the fire from its ultimate end or control point back to the seat or origin of the process. Depending upon the size and complexity of the scene, this may be a tedious, frustrating procedure. Or, it may be a simple one such as tracing a fire from a hot stove surface to a combustible wall to a ceiling, or from a ceiling exposure to a certain and back to a burned-out wastepaper receptacle.

Char patterns can be misleading, even to the most experienced fire investigator. Such patterns may be secondary such as separate patterns created by falling burning curtains or drapes which, when ignited by the original or "main" fire, burn off, drop to the floor surface and thereupon create their separate char patterns and fire cones which may ultimately be mistaken for the original fire source or, even more seriously, for separate and distinct points of origin, creating the illusion of a fire that has been willfully set at separate and distinct locations.

Char patterns can be misleading because of conditions such as chain reaction ignition of combustibles, each separate reaction being triggered as the combustible reaches its ignition, burning, or combustion temperatures, as the fire advances from the true point of origin. Such conditions are common in warehouse and storage areas; the phenomenon is also present in modern construction projects where synthetic construction materials are commonly and extensively utilized. The phenomenon is also common in forest and wildland fires under conditions of extremely low humidity and where flaming brands and embers are produced in the original conflagration, again often mistaken by amateur investigators and the news media as indications that the fires are occurring independently and are therefore of incendiary origin.

Char patterns can be misleading where there is a major conflagration with the fire "venting" at several locations and where these openings may alter the behavior of the fire through a material change in the ventilation process of the fire. The patterns can be hidden by collapsing floors, ceilings, roofs and walls; in such circumstances, it may be necessary for the investigator to conduct his examination "layer by layer," removing, in a tedious step-by-step process, the roof right on down through the various collapsed levels and to the ultimate origin level of the fire. This process may require the utilization of heavy equipment and much carefully supervised hand labor. The process may require a step-by-step and level-by-level removal of structural members and merchandise in the reverse order of collapse, until the seat of the fire is reached. This is identifiable from the continuous char in the fire path to the origin which may be deep-seated incineration of the wall, for example.

The origin might be evident from the deep-seated char in the studs on each side of the header plate of a gas fueled wall furnace where the furnace was improperly and inadequately insulated from the wall framing; from this point, the char pattern might be traced in continuous char pattern up through the wall, between the studs, through the fire stops, and finally extending into the attic spaces. The burned-out fire stops in the wall might provide the investigator with additional information supporting the time of origin of the fire in the wall.

On the other hand, the investigator might have traced the char pattern through layer after layer of debris, following the char pattern along a wall surface into an office space and from that point to the surface of an office desk. The waste basket may remain virtually intact under the desk, protected by the top and sides of the desk. The heavy alligatoring and/or char might be on the desk surface—possibly extending from a heat-broken ashtray—with deep alligatoring on the top of the desk that is consistent with the position of the remains of the glass ashtray and with the point of origin of the fire.

Conversely, the char pattern might *not* extend from the ashtray on top of the desk. Perhaps the top surface of the desk was intact except for moderate, even surface burn from reflected or radiated heat, whereas, under the desk, the carpet is burned out "in pattern" from the waste basket location. The waste basket is completely consumed except for the circular plastic bottom which is glued to the carpeting immediately beneath the waste basket and the desk drawers are penetrated by fire from the position of the waste basket location. The carpet section immediately beneath the waste basket is not incinerated because the plastic bottom protected the carpet. There was insufficient oxygen available to the area beneath the basket to afford combustion of that section of the carpet. (Bear in mind that we are talking about char patterns and points of origin, *not* about cause.) All of the above conditions are consistent with a waste basket fire with origin in or at the waste basket.

Now, let us change the picture again. Assume, after digging down through the collapsed roof, attic, ceiling, and debris, and following the char pattern down the wall and down into the office, we again find the office desk. Again, we find no alligator pattern or deep char on the top side of the desk although it is damaged from exposure heat in an even, "top down" pattern but with heavier charring on the side closest to a set of file cabinets next to the wall. We find that the heaviest char is in a cone-shaped pattern up the wall in front of the file cabinets. The file drawers are open and the contents are badly charred. A section of the shag synthetic carpet is burned out, along with the matting, at the base of the fire cone. The char pattern up the wall from this point extends along what is left of the ceiling and with the pattern extending into the attic, showing that this is where the office fire penetrated the attic. Investigation discloses that nothing could have fallen from the ceiling, wall, cabinets, or desk that would have caused this fire cone as a secondary fire. Further, there is a similar burn pattern and fire cone in a separate office and, again, in front of the file cabinet. The file drawers of this file cabinet are also open and must have been open during the fire because of the fire damage inside the cabinet and the flame pattern evident on the exposed drawer sections. The file contents were incinerated in the fire. Again, the shag carpet is consumed at the base of a fire cone extending from the floor adjacent to the cabinet and the fire from this location has penetrated the ceiling and extends into the attic. Further, a long, irregular, deep burn pattern in the carpeting extends from the location of the fire cone in office number one and to the fire cone in office number two.

The oblong and irregular fire pattern in the carpeting connecting the two points of origin is a char pattern that is indicative of the presence of a flammable accelerant. Samples of the carpeting and matting should be preserved for laboratory analysis. Samples of the molding should be removed at the wall section at each fire cone for analysis. Again, it should be remembered that this section of the discussion deals with *origin* rather than *cause*. The char pattern, in the last hypothetical case, followed the fire from the roof down through the various levels of debris to the fire cone in office number one to the carpet char pattern in office number two, and connecting the second fire cone. It was then possible to identify that fire cone with a separate and distinct pattern of spread up the wall, involving the file cabinets, penetrating the ceiling into the attic where that fire merged with the blaze that extended from office number one.

Some fire investigators, often as a result of incompetence and, occasionally, in the interest of biased expedience or in the 'saving' of time, select an electrical or apparent mechanical fault and, without further factual analysis of the fire scene, attempt to build that apparent fault into a specific or probable cause and with complete disregard for the fact there is no evidence to connect that cause with the factual area or point of origin of the fire.

True char patterns are most commonly apparent where combustible exposures such as wood are involved. However, similar procedures may be utilized where exposures that are not readily combustible are present and may, again, provide fingerprints or clues to the origin and path of the fire. For example, these may appear in spalling which is a condition of displacement or deterioration of cement or concrete in ceilings, walls, and floors. Some experts in fire investigation have stated that spalling in a concrete floor indicates that a flammable liquid type of accelerant was present at that location during at least the early stages of the fire.

There is no reliable scientific basis for the contention that spalling in concrete or any mineral base, surface, floor, wall, bulkhead, or ceiling denotes either the presence of hydrocarbon flammables or any other volatile accelerant, or that spalling indicates criminal or incendiary origin. On the contrary, spalling can reasonably occur as a result of poor cement or concrete surfacing techniques and with deteriorative spalling resulting from use and weathering rather than from heat. Spalling is common where concrete surfaces are exposed to heat generated in a fire, regardless of the cause of the fire, and when water is applied to the hot surfaces during extinguishment causing rapid temperature change and cooling.

While char patterns do not appear on noncombustible surfaces, heat patterns *do*. Other manifestations of heat may also be apparent and utilized to identify the path of the fire and even to track the fire back to the source of ignition. For example, a broken or leaking high pressure gas line is often identified by the heat scarring at the point of fracture or leak, with the high pressure heat pattern extending along a wall, boiler face, or bulkhead surface. This may not, however, have been the point of origin. For example, the fracture or leak in the line may occur with the gas escaping from this opening, but where no ignition immediately occurs because there is no ignition source at that point, such as spark, flame, or arc. The gas may mix with the atmospheric oxygen, at low or high levels, depending upon its relative weight, until it reaches an ignition agent and is in flammable or explosive mixture. This will be where the "action" will begin. The pattern left by ignition and the following chain reaction may be reasonably evident when the ignition point is identified. The pattern of heat or chain displacement may be evident from the ignition point right back to the leak, with the pattern being pronounced on the exposures until the flow of gas ceases. This pattern may appear in the form of char on combustible exposures, as discoloration along metal surfaces, or in the form of disfiguration or displacement. Heat patterns may be indicated in the form of fused, lower temperature metals such as aluminum, plastics, or melted glass.

Fire pattern may be indicated in soot or carbon deposit on ceilings, walls, and door and window glass. The original smoldering or flash characteristics may be significant in the locations and quantity of carbon deposit, not only on exposed hard surfaces but in soft items such as furniture and clothing. Heavy soot deposit is common to unventilated, smoldering fires and incomplete combustion and is also common in cases where victims may not survive the fire because of asphyxia.

The origin or ignition point, in addition to being traceable by char, heat, or carbon patterns, can be distinguished in certain types of fires by fused metallic substances resulting from electrical fires and, occasionally, from mechanical malfunction such as fracture, pressure, friction and shock, or impact. The fingerprints become apparent in the form of a welded conduit at the service entrance, usually near main power panels, fused metal, or melted conductors. Similar conditions may be found at electric motor installations and, occasionally, where there is bearing or other relevant electrical or mechanical fault.

Such electrical and mechanical clues do not necessarily attest to the origin of the fire. They may reasonably be secondary in sequence and resultant from conditions imposed on the equipment or environment of the fire. These secondary possibilities simply must not be ignored or overlooked. They must be evaluated in context with specialized expertise in the area of question: The reason for the fault must be reconciled with the origin.

Frequently, fire and char patterns can be readily traced by an experienced investigator in situations where there is little structural damage. For example, the fire cone may appear in the living room, extending from the base of a wall receptacle and upon removal of the wall covering, it is found that the stud or wall framing to which the receptacle is affixed is heavily carbonized and the char pattern extends up and inside the wall, through the fire stops, and into the attic. For example, the receptacle may have been one designed for use with copper wiring and examination disclosed that aluminum conductors had been improperly attached with fusing or melting around the connections. On the other hand, the char pattern might extend from a point in the attic where the Romex or nonmetallic cable extended along the rafters and where examination disclosed that the ca-

ble was improperly stapled to the attic framing so that the staple penetrated the insulation, thereby destroying the integrity of that insulation with resulting heating of the conductors, ignition of the destroyed insulation, and final spread and involvement in the attic.

Or the char pattern may extend from an improperly collared furnace vent with the pattern of char extending from the point of contact of the vent with the combustible roof framing—a precise point of origin only confirmed by detailed inquiry and further examination of the furnace.

Fire investigators occasionally identify deep floor surface charring as indicative of the presence of a flammable accelerant—again, with implications of the incendiary character of the fire. Deep, localized floor surfaces should always be carefully scrutinized. Experience has shown that this type of char is commonly consistent with a longer burning fire at this location or the presence of accumulated papers, clothing, fallen curtains, or drapes. On the contrary, low flashpoint, volatile liquids, such as gasoline or thinner, poured over a tight floor surface, whether hardwood or soft wood, vaporizes and burns off quickly, seldom leaving deep charring or burn patterns. Actually, it is the vapors of the liquid that burn, the liquid protecting the surface until it is consumed. Unless the liquid was given time to soak into or penetrate the floor surface, deep charring could not be expected. Further, if a time lag between the application and ignition was allowed, sufficient to permit penetration of the floor, liquids such as gasoline, acetone, thinner, and even kerosene would vaporize and, with delayed ignition, an explosion would normally follow. In short, deeply charred, localized floor surfaces are more inconsistent with the presence of flammable liquids than not.

On the other hand, if a flammable, volatile liquid is applied on the surface of a wood floor where there are cracks, holes, or defects in the floor surface, the effects of a flammable liquid char pattern might be found deep between the cracks or even beneath the floor, with a resulting char pattern in the subflooring. In some cases, identifiable flammable liquid or accelerant residue has been recovered from the relatively unburned subflooring defect points and also from the dirt beneath the flooring in the foundation spaces.

In the investigation of a fire involving the offices of a real estate developer, initial fire investigation placed the origin of the fire at a gas fueled floor furnace. The cause was attributed to a defective floor furnace. An insurance investigator removed the floor furnace for preservation in anticipation of subrogation against the furnace installers and landlord. After removal of the floor furnace, arson investigators noted there was no char pattern consistent with ignition of the floor framing or walls from conducted heat from the furnace. A check with office personnel indicated no history of furnace trouble and examination indicated that the wall thermostat control had been turned off at the time the office closed at the beginning of the weekend, two days before the fire.

Further examination of the space under the office disclosed that the char pattern was extensive under the building and consistent with origin under the office rather than inside the office. Laboratory experts called to the scene extracted samples of dirt from under the furnace location which disclosed residues of gasoline. A gasoline container, subsequently recovered, was traced to a young associate of the real estate developer. One pair of his shoes and a pair of his trousers produced traces of gasoline residue as well as traces of the soil from beneath the office.

In summary, the associate confessed to setting the fire at the request of his friend, the real estate developer. The real estate developer had been under investigation by Federal, State, and local authorities and his files and records were the subject of inquiry. He hired his friend to set the fire to destroy the office and its records, advising him, "Be sure and make it look like an accident because I already got more trouble than I need." The intentions of the young man who set the fire were "good." He planned to make the fire look like it started from the floor furnace. He nearly succeeded. He *did* succeed in convincing the insurance investigator who had his heart set on subrogation. He did not anticipate the arson investigator's interest in char patterns, gasoline containers, and residue in his shoes and clothing.

Perhaps the above illustrated case suggests the need for careful examination and understanding of char and burn patterns—a vital link in the orderly process of moving from origin to cause.

In Chapter X, we will progress from establishing *where* the fire started to the process of determining how it started. Once the origin is established, the cause, of course, may be obvious. This may have been established by eyewitnesses, with the observed events and circumstances obvious. It is not with such circumstances we are presently concerned, assuming that the eyewitnesses correctly observed what they reported to have seen.

Again, the purpose of this chapter is to assist the investigator in identification of the cause, where the cause is questioned or undefined. Is the cause accidental? Or is it incendiary? The following chapter will deal with the more common accidental causes of fires, first in order since, in identifying the cause of some fires, it is necessary to eliminate the reasonable and logical common causes in a factual manner in order to show that the true cause is other than accidental and, therefore, of incendiary origin. To consider such possible accidental causes, the investigator must understand them.

CHAPTER X

COMMON ACCIDENTAL CAUSES OF FIRE

It will be recalled from our discussion of the Law of Arson that the Courts require proof of the *corpus delicti* in a prosecution for arson—showing that the fire resulted from "other than accidental or natural means" or, dependent upon the requirements of the particular jurisdiction, "that the fire was willfully set with human hands," and as others put it, "an affirmative showing that a criminal agency was involved with the origin of the fire."

This may be shown by affirmative evidence but it is also well settled in the law that the presumption of accidental origin must be overcome with reasonable certainty. Historically, and up to the present time, the law presumes that all fires are accidental in origin. This presumption may be overcome by identification and elimination of the usual accidental causes by factual means. (People v. Sherman, 97 Cal. App. 2nd, 245, 217 P 2nd 715-1950.)

At the same time, the prosecution is not required to rule out "every conceivable cause." (People v. Andrews, 234 Cal. App. 2nd '69, 44 Cal. Rpts. 1965.) The Court will consider that which is reasonable and sensible. In the above case, the prosecution negated "spontaneous ignition, electrical, gas, and ordinary carelessness" within reasonable probability. However, in State v. Duboit, 514 P 2nd Hawaii, 1973, the Court said that circumstantial evidence of *corpus delicti* must reasonably dispose of any theory except guilt. And, in People v. Trippoda, 341 NYS 2d, 66, 1973, the Court said that "expert testimony must point to incendiary origin—this is insufficient if they fail to eliminate an electric lead wire as the cause of fire." Interestingly, the court also remarked that "circumstantial evidence should not be a snare to trap the innocent."

This is what this chapter is all about: accurately identifying the cause, be it criminal or accidental. The establishment of the area of origin will be followed by seeking out the cause. There may be apparent indications of specific cause, or said "cause" may be suggested by witnesses. The features or factors may point to either incendiary or accidental origin.

This may be manifested in the presence of an incendiary device or residue thereof; at the other end of the spectrum, the cause may be evident as accidental such as a burned-out electric motor bearing, a welded electrical service entrance, or the accidental ignition of a cleaning compound in a factory process—in the presence of eyewitnesses.

If the cause is not apparent, the investigator must proceed, systematically, to determine what caused the fire. He will examine the physical fire-causing agencies which should reasonably be present, such as electrical, mechanical, heat causing, storage, and yes, even the human conduct that might have been expected on the premises involved. The examination must include physical scrutiny as well as interview of witnesses—probably including firemen. In this process, the competent investigator will consider each cause factor in order and eliminate or include it as the evidence demands.

If he eliminates all reasonable accidental cause factors, he may then be considered to be dealing with a fire of probable criminal origin. In order to reasonably eliminate accidental cause, the arson investigator must conduct something more than a tip-toe examination; further, he must be familiar with the basics of the more common accidental causes.

The arson investigator cannot be expected to be conversant with *all* possible accidental causes since they embrace a vast and continually increasing field. In our technical/industrial society, we experience heating and ignition problems that make the investigative task ever more complicated.

The experienced investigator knows of this ever-changing picture and meets the problem by personal research and study and by the practice of calling in experts when he encounters problems he does not personally understand. This again emphasizes the importance of care in the examination of the fire scene and amplifies the necessity for expert- and laboratory-related assistance where the cause may be cloudy. The arson investigator must remember, at *all* times, that the Court is going to expect him to explain why he eliminates each accidental cause or why the evidence found points affirmatively to willful and incendiary origin. Further, the Court will expect the explanation in language and logic that is reasonable and understandable.

In the discussion of the process of combustion, we have already emphasized that the primary source of fire is heat in some form. For this to be true, the attendant materials must be present: the fuel to sustain combustion and the supporting factor, oxygen. As previously stated, the heat sources may include friction, chemical reaction, radiation, conduction, and convection. We may be dealing with electrical equipment; heating equipment; mechanical, natural, or biological phenomena; chemical reaction; sparks; or open flame.

All reasonable possibilities must be considered in the absence of an outstanding, *logical* cause.

The majority of our fires result from ignition of common materials such as wood, fabric, plastics, and combinations thereof and it follows that we are dealing with ignition temperatures generally in the 400° F.–600° F. spectrum for the more common furnishing, commercial, and industrial materials. In consideration of accidental cause, electrical sources in the form of conductors, appliances, and equipment cannot be disregarded. While it has been fairly stated that proper use of electrical energy has actually decreased the fire dangers in our society, it is equally correct to state that the misunderstanding, neglect, and misuse, deliberate or otherwise, continues to be a major fire-causing category of considerable magnitude.

Electricity is one of the most common and most powerful heat sources. The effect of electrical energy may be manifested by three general classes of phenomena:

1. Incandescence of an electrical conductor or current-carrying object or vehicle.
2. Sparks from circuit interruption or overload.
3. Luminous arcs.

Electrical energy is encountered in nearly every aspect of modern society. Pause and think for a moment. In view of its potential, as will be discussed later, it is a small wonder that electricity appears as a fire cause. We are dependent upon electricity and we have learned to live with it, yet we have much more

to learn in living with it *safely*. Like the tiger, treated with carelessness or indifference, it can strike with alarming speed and often devastating results.

No one ever invented electricity. The phenomenon had been around for billions of years before man came into the picture and "discovered" it. From the time of man's discovery of electrical energy, he has been in the process of learning how to harness it. Regardless of what some would have you believe, there is much about electrical energy that man still has to learn. Obviously, he is making progress. He produced his first light bulb about 1879; the electric fan came along about 1882. It is estimated that more than one billion electrical appliances are in use in the United States today. Since World War II, the consumption of electric power in the United States *has doubled every ten years.* In 1950, the average home was built with capacity that could, in effect, light seventy 100-watt light bulbs simultaneously. In the 1970s, we have multiplied the home capacity for electric use by four times. The same relative increase may be accurately applied to commerce, agriculture, and industry. Wisely and safely used, electrical energy is our friend. Ignorantly, indifferently, or negligently used, it is a quick and efficient destroyer of life and property.

Electrical arcs are capable of developing temperatures in the order of 7,000° F. (Compare this, for a moment, with the ignition temperatures of common construction materials such as wood, plastic, fabrics, etc.) Copper wire, commonly utilized in conductors and electrical equipment, melts at approximately 2,000° F. Aluminum, increasingly utilized in electrical conductors and installation equipment, melts at 1,200° F. Although modern engineering specifications and code standards minimize the probabilities of electrical fault and resulting fire from electrical sources, misuse, poor maintenance, faulty installation, fatigue of materials, and unforeseen contingencies, such as structural settling and earth movement, have set out repeated examples of causes of serious electrical fires. Again, electrical energy is an absolute necessity in our modern society. The exercise of reasonable caution and observance of strict standards of care in its use are essential to its safe use. This is why we have the National Electrical Code and other standards based upon scientific research as well as practical experience in dealing with the safe and efficient use of electrical energy.

Briefly, the most common cause for fires from electrical fault is the short circuit. This may occur when any element of the conducting vehicles are at different potentials and may come in contact with each other. To utilize the electrical energy in the context of this chapter, it must be conveyed through the conductors to a lamp, motor, or other appliance. The work done, the current flows away through a return wire in much the same manner steam is conveyed to and exhausted from a steam engine.

In much the same manner as the steam engine piston offers resistance that must be overcome by steam, so does the light bulb, motor, or other appliance offer resistance to the passage of electrical current. It may be said that as steam or water pressure builds up in a pipe, so does current, passing through the wire, build up pressure in the conductor. The load required by the light bulb, motor, or other appliance may exceed the carrying capacity of the conductor. Consequently, if the current, in passing through the wire, encounters a location where the wire is defective or weak, or the insulation is defective or absent, therefore opposing a lower resistance to the escape in the pre-designed direction, the current naturally chooses the easier and usually shorter path. Since the line and return conductors are usually close and possibly thinly separated, the short circuit is facilitated. As the current has not performed its assigned task, it is able to exert its intensity in the object traversed (such as the shortcut area conductor) and because of its obvious heat producing factor, this conductor is raised to incandescence, often sufficient to fuse the conductor and ignite the adjacent environment such as insulation, house framing, carpet, furniture, window curtains, etc.

Fire and arson investigators, as a rule, are not electrical engineers or master electricians. It is emphasized that, when electrical cause is suspect, unless the answer is factually obvious and supportable without further inquiry, a qualified expert should be called in. Electrical experts and engineers do not profess to be expert fire investigators. Most fire investigators are certainly not electrical experts either.

The following basics are set out to assist the fire investigator in primary evaluation of a fire scene where electrical fault may be relevant.

The average residential structure is supplied by a 60 cycle alternating current for inside distribution. The voltage leaves the power station and is transmitted through appropriate lines to the substation. From the substation, the electricity is communicated through step-down transformers on poles or in vaults. The power from the step-down transformer is carried into the house under voltage which may be 120 or 240 volts. (In larger operations requiring more power, such as commercial/industrial, we would be talking about larger appropriate voltages.)

The service connection on the house may be 60, 100, or 200 amps or even more depending, again, on the requirements of the user. For the usual residential occupancy, requirements would be 110 to 120 volts for small appliances, lights, television, radio, etc. A 220- or 240-volt circuit would be required for use of heavier appliances such as air conditioning and electric stoves. The breakdown of these units would be at the distribution board or panel. In many of the newer installations, the distribution panels and meter are installed outside.

The main circuits through the service entrance are provided with main disconnect switches which normally include the rated fusing for the service load assigned to the occupancy. For example, the service load may be 100 or 200 amps. It will have the main disconnect rated for that value.

A line will be distributed through this main disconnect switch to a box which will contain the fuses for the secondary circuits which normally are 15 or 20 amps; these secondaries will be supplying lights, small appliances, and wall sockets. The appliances requiring 220–240 volts will be in a separate box with higher fuse ratings, again depending upon expected and tolerable load.

Where interior electrical fault is suspect, inspection of secondary fuses should be made to determine if they are blown and, if so, why. For example, if a fuse is black and appears burned, this might indicate a full or dead short in the circuit. On the other hand, if the metallic strip is burned through with no blackening of the face, this might indicate an overload or partial short with more gradual conductor heating.

Fuses are generally constructed in two ways. The older type is equipped with a transparent isinglass window which reacts faster than the more recent glass-base type fuse. Fuses, although expected to open the circuit at or below the rated value, may not react because the circuit is over-fused or because the temperatures at the fault ignited combustibles before reaching temperatures sufficient to burn out the fuse strip and open the circuit. For example, less than 5 amps may ignite combustibles whereas the 15 amp fuse will not open the circuit much below 12 amps.

Rather than over-fusing a circuit which may have been consistently blowing the desirably rated fuse, users have been known to place the ground strap of the fuse on the center contact to complete the circuit and thereby "cheating" the circuit opening or safety factor of the fuse. There are other common devices used to circumvent or cheat the fuse. The cheating devices may result from ignorance or willful action where a fire is expected or desired.

Loose panel connections and improper grounding can result in heating of conductors with resulting fire. Corrosion, moisture, debris accumulation, and oxidation may reasonably result in electrical fault and fire. Circuit breakers are a more modern innovation during recent years. The theory of the circuit breaker or "trip" is that the circuit cannot be overfused or cheated. Fuses and circuit breakers approved and authorized for specific use are classified and marked approved by Underwriters Laboratories and described in detail in the National Electrical Code. The investigator may find it necessary to establish whether the fuse or circuit breaker was designed and approved for use in the particular circuit environment considering use load and conductors involved.

A circuit breaker also operates on the principle of heat and is designed as a form of heat disconnect switch. In examining suspect circuits and circuit breakers, it is important to note the exact location of the breakers and environment; a breaker located in a wet or damp area may be affected due to corrosion or dirt or grease. Users may tamper with loose connection breakers and impede their disconnect efficiency. The circuit breaker may be located in a much colder environment such as on a wall outside the building which may further delay its activation due to increased time for the heat build-up which is necessary to activate the mechanism. During this delay, ignition of combustible exposures along the heated circuit may have occurred well inside the building.

The fire investigator should have a general understanding of wire gauge or size and, in general, how it should be utilized in its distribution and tolerance. For example:

    #18 wire will handle   5 amps
    #16 wire will handle   7 amps
    #14 wire will handle 15 amps
    #12 wire will handle 20 amps
    #10 wire will handle 30 amps
    # 8 wire will handle 45 amps

Outer jacket insulation usually identifies wire size and the number of conductors. For example, Romex 12/2 would indicate this is Romex cable, 12 gauge with 20 amps capacity and that there are two conductors in the jacket. BX (Armored cable) also carries identification, size, and number of conduc-

ALLOWABLE CURRENT-CARRYING CAPACITIES (Amperes) OF INSULATED CONDUCTORS. Not More Than Three Conductors in Raceway or Direct Burial, based on 30°C, 86°F ambient. Condensed from National Electrical Code) COPPER

Max Oper Temp	60°C TYPES	75°C TYPES	85-90°C TYPES	110°C TYPES	125°C TYPES	200°C TYPES
Size AWG or MCM	RUW (14-2), T, TW	RH, RHW, RUH (14-2), THW, THWN, XHHW, THW-MTW	V, MI, TA, TBS, SA, AVB, SIS, FEP, FEPB, RHH, THHN, XHHW	AVA, AVL	AI (14-8), AIA	A (14-8), AA, FEP, FEPB
14	15	15	25	30	30	30
12	20	20	30	35	40	40
10	30	30	40	45	50	55
8	40	45	50	60	65	70
6	55	65	70	80	85	95
4	70	85	90	105	115	120
3	80	100	105	120	130	145
2	95	115	120	135	145	165
1	110	130	140	160	170	190
0	125	150	155	190	200	225

ALLOWABLE CURRENT-CARRYING CAPACITIES (Amperes) OF INSULATED CONDUCTORS. Not More Than Three Conductors in Raceway or Direct Burial, based on 30°C, 86°F ambient. (Condensed from National Electrical Code) ALUMINUM

Max Oper Temp	60°C TYPES	75°C TYPES	85-90°C TYPES	110°C TYPES	125°C TYPES	200°C TYPES
Size AWG or MCM	RUW (12-2), T, TW	RH, RHW, RUH (12-2), THW, THWN, XHHW	V, MI, TA, TBS, SA, AVB, SIS, RHH, THHN, XHHW	AVA, AVL	AI (12-8), AIA	A (12-8), AA
12	15	15	25	25	30	30
10	25	25	30	35	40	45
8	30	40	40	45	50	55
6	40	50	55	60	65	75
4	55	65	70	80	90	95
3	65	75	80	95	100	115
2	75	90	95	105	115	130
1	85	100	110	125	135	150
0	100	120	125	150	160	180

tors. Again, the investigator should familiarize himself with identification procedures and this can be done by reference to the National Electrical Code as well as manufacturer's and wholesaler's advertising and installation specifications. The identification means is not complicated.

Where electrical fault is suspected, all wiring should be checked and determination of correct conductor size and code compliance completed, if reasonably possible. What was the load on the suspect circuit and was the load within the tolerated spectrum? A check of the unburned sections of the building might establish if there were other possible code or violations relevant to the cause of this fire.

It can be stated that an overload will occur when a given circuit is required to deliver more current than the carrying capacity of the conductor; for example, where a group of appliances are united into one receptacle with a #14 gauge conductor designed for 15 amps, the appliance demand exceeds 15 amps and the circuit is protected by a 30-amp fuse because the 15 amp fuses kept blowing. Heating may then occur along the conductor and this heating may ignite combustible exposures such as insulation, furniture, carpeting, or structural framing or paneling. A short circuit can be much more pronounced. As previously indicated, this is the communication of the energy from or through conductors of two different potentials; an example might be a contact of bare conduction against the armored cable or a staple or nail carelessly driven into NM (nonmetallic) cable for the purpose of securing it to the framing, where the staple has destroyed the integrity of the conductor separation or insulation. While a current protection device (fuse) should react, there may be sufficient heat at the fault to ignite exposed combustibles, without opening the circuit at the protection device, in time to have prevented the fire.

It should be remembered that heat and a subsequent fire can only result from a closed circuit; therefore, a closure that is not normal to the function of the facility must be sought. In this respect, it may be said that the current in every part of the circuit is a part of the total circuit.

Electricity, though not improperly installed or overloaded, may be an indirect cause of fire. For example, we must recognize the heat producing characteristics of electric lamps, bulbs, etc. which produce surface bulb temperatures from 200° F. in 40–100-watt lamps to 400–500° F. for 250-watt lamps. We must again remember that some forms of wood and other materials, when exposed over a period of time to temperatures as low as 250° F., may ignite spontaneously.

Tests have shown that so-called "low wattage" light bulbs in confined locations, such as storage areas with paper or fabrics in proximity, will produce temperatures of 700°–800° F., which is clearly above the ignition temperature of the material and whereupon combustion of the material is probable. If the area of the electric bulb is the apparent origin, then would it be reasonable to presume the bulb heat as the cause?

Was the bulb in the "on" position? Was the bulb in "normal" position? In cases where the bulb surface touched the materials and was suspected as the heat source, charred materials might be found adhered to the surface of the bulb. It is not implied, however, that charred residue would adhere in all types of materials. Possible corroborative evidence may be found in the fusing at the lamp socket and further substantiated by a blown fuse or tripped circuit breaker. These conditions may be subject to the question of which came first: the so-called short (overcurrent condition) or the fire? A tracing of the circuit may disclose a clock on that system or in the same secondary breaker system which may provide a guide to the sequence of events. All evidence and circumstance must be considered with credence extended, or not, in the link and chain circumstance of the events.

Some investigators rely heavily upon the condition of fuses and circuit breakers to establish or negate electrical fault as a fire cause. Authorities have pointed out, however, that the condition or position of the circuit protection device, in itself, does not tell the entire story. Neither does the condition of the conductors. Recent studies by the University Engineering Research Division, Washington State University, concerning electrical wiring in building fires, disclose that there is no basic difference in the grain pattern of the copper conductor subjected to flame heating as opposed to electrical heating. In this respect, it has long been the teaching of some fire investigators that they can examine an electrical conductor and visually distinguish between fusing or arcing that *preceded* the fire and such conditions that *succeeded* the fire. To date, there is no known scientific basis or known engineering support for such conclusions. A number of experienced fire investigators, aware of the problems and current disagreement in this area, have recommended further study by qualified laboratories and, hopefully, more specific answers.

We do know that an electrical arc, as previously indicated, can generate temperatures in the order of 7,000° F. If arcing is found in the area of origin, it must be considered as a reasonably possible cause and with further investigation to define the failure at that location. Again the question: which came first? The arc or the fire?

Copper conductors will burn without fusing at 1,981° F. Depending upon the composition, brass melts at temperatures varying between 1,625 and 1,780° F. These metals are commonly used in electrical circuits. More recently, aluminum has been introduced in electrical equipment and conductors. Aluminum melts at a much *lower* temperature than copper—1,220° F. Therefore, it has a different heat reaction coefficient than copper or brass and, where improperly used in interconnections with other metals, conductors can be expected to expand and contract with the variations of heat produced by the current flow through the circuits. This can ultimately result in loosening of the interconnections which will, in turn, cause heating, imperfect current flow, possible creeping, which all result in heating. In turn, this all creates electrical fault sufficient to cause fire.

According to reliable official reports and studies, including Fire Departments and State and Federal Agencies, fires resulting from 'improper' use of aluminum conductors and connectors have been a cause of major concern during the past fifteen years. Such factors must be fairly considered where origin is apparent at an improper connection or splice.

While it has been written that "internal heating" of electrical conductors, such as from overload, tends to burn away the insulation next to the conductor rendering the insulation "loose on the sleeve," there is no present scientific support for this theory and it should only be considered with caution. The same condition of interior heating inside the insulation can be found where fires have started in other areas of a building and have, in turn, caused electrical failures in remote sections of the spaces and circuits. The so-called "loose sleeve" condition has also been found to have been artificially produced under test conditions not consistent with electrical origin or fault.

Fluorescent lamp fixtures are a common cause of fire, particularly those with transformers having no contained automatic thermal disconnect switch and where installed against low density combustibles such as cellotex ceiling or fiber walls. The heat source is usually a progressive deterioration in the windings of the ballast transformers which commonly contain combustible pitch blend. This material, when heated, expands, breaking the casing which may result in flaming combustion when the heated contents are exposed to atmospheric oxygen.

Normally, the ballasts start with a load pull of about 700–900 volts and then drop to approximately 400 volts. This process can be a wearing and heating process. Although these ballasts are designed to last from 12 to 15 years, the actual life efficiency is more directly related to the starting function and related use factors. The so-called automatic thermal disconnect switches have been introduced in recent years and have, no doubt, prevented many fires; however, studies by laboratories have not suggested the improvement as foolproof and transformers with thermal disconnects have been faulted on numerous occasions in connection with fluorescent fixture fires.

A study and report of fires in buildings occupied by a federal agency during the late 1960s showed that ballast transformers were a continuing source of fire and eliminated the use of all transformers except those specifically equipped with approved thermal disconnect switches and installed in a strict, code-approved fashion. (See National Electrical Code regarding installation of fluorescent fixtures.)

Electric motors can and do cause fires. These motors are normally protected with an overload tolerance for starting. However, according to some reliable authorities, they cause more fires than any other single electrical component. They accumulate dust and debris and this, in turn, may deteriorate or damage insulation; conditions resulting in short circuit, arcing, sparking, and fire may result in motors of home appliances and in offices, heating systems, and industrial operations. Basically, lack of proper maintenance resulting in accumulation of debris, oil, etc., may be a factor. The arc or heating may cause ignition *before* the circuit disconnects activate. Fires may result from thrown or frozen bearings or friction ignition of motor belts.

Bedroom fires, involving fatality, are almost invariably quickly categorized as smoker fires. Investigative embarrassment is often encountered when it is later established that the victim did not smoke. Was the victim alive or dead at the time of the fire? This type of fire requires careful evaluation regardless of the extent of the flame damage. Were faulty extension cords extended under the mattress or under the carpet where it could have been damaged by heavy furniture or continued walking over? Often, the vinyl or other synthetic protector has been damaged thereby permitting short circuiting or heating within the insulation sufficient to ignite combustibles such as bedding, carpeting, curtains, etc., before tripping the circuit breaker. The smoldering combustion may continue, with very slow temperature rise and little or no actual flaming combustion. This may be particularly true where certain types of plastics or synthetics are involved such as in furnishings, decorations, or clothing. The phenomenon, in the end process, may result in asphyxiation of the victim. Flaming combustion may occur only AFTER the fire penetrates adjoining spaces, breaks a window, or otherwise provides itself with sufficient oxygen to raise the tempo of the fire from smoldering to flaming combustion.

Similar electrical causes are common to receptacles and fixtures; such conditions commonly grow out of misuse, ordinary part fatigue, or overload of the circuit. These conditions may also be found in any type of space where a receptacle and/or cord may be loaded with "added" appliances such as heat lamps, heating pads, etc. The conductors may heat and cause ignition *before* the fuses activate or the circuit breakers trip, whichever the case may be.

Continuing with bedroom fires, the careless cigarette or match may be blamed for an electric blanket fire. Electric blankets and pads are in increasing use and, by the record, a continuing problem. According to available information, the majority of fire-causing problems with this type of comfort equipment grows out of misuse and improper maintenance or wear. The origin of this type of fire is usually in a bed or wherever the item may have been in use, such as on an upholstered chair or a couch. Misuse includes the improper cleaning practices of electric blankets and pads or leaving the appliance or blanket switch in the "on" position while the blanket is folded over on the bed, the covering on top, thereby "trapping" the heat in the fold. The approved blankets are normally equipped with main bimetal thermal control switches which are activated by ambient room temperature, not blanket temperature. The blankets are usually equipped with internal bimetal controls in the heating circuits with the number and circuitry depending upon the manufacturer of the blanket. These controls are usually sealed in plastic and theoretically disconnect through the grid if the blanket is overheated. Whether they operate or disconnect depends on the location of the fold or the extra blanket, pillow, or other item which may have been inadvertently left

on the bed or, as previously indicated, the circuitry may deteriorate because of fatigue or abuse.

If the blanket control switch is left on "high," with the room continuing to cool, the system will continue to function heat input to the blanket, regardless of the temperature already inside the blanket. The blanket control switch, permitting the continued flow of energy, is dependent upon the environmental room temperature. If that environment is cool, then that is what the temperature control is telling the service source. Fires have originated in the "tucking" areas at the foot of the bed as well as in fold-over areas or areas covered by personal items thrown on the blanket, thereby trapping the heat.

Certain types of recliner chairs with internal heating/vibrator circuits have caused fires. Experience has shown that, regardless of initially careful design, assembly errors and mass production mistakes can result in electrical problems such as poor placement or damaged insulation of circuits such as between the switch controls on the arm or side of the chair and the interior circuits inside the pad or upholstery. Occasionally, wearing and/or pinching of the circuits in the moveable frame parts of the chair causes insulation damage, electrical fault inside the chair, resulting in fire. These fires usually originate in the form of smoldering combustion which may or may not progress to flaming combustion depending upon conditions of ventilation in the space or origin and/or conditions of discovery and report of the fire.

An example of this class of fire occurred recently and caused extensive damage to a dwelling owned and occupied by an elderly retired couple in a desert resort area. We shall call them Mr. and Mrs. A. They had purchased an expensive recliner chair equipped with electric heating and vibrator components. Mrs. A liked to sit in the chair in the evenings and watch her favorite television programs. On the night of the fire, Mrs. A was alone in the house because Mr. A was away on a hunting trip. The night was very cold and the house was tightly closed. Mrs. A sat in the recliner chair and watched television until shortly before midnight at which time she straightened up the chair, turned off the television, and retired to her bedroom which was at the opposite end of the rambling, one-story dwelling. About 3:00 a.m. the first alarm of the fire was received by the Fire Department from Mrs. A's neighbors who subsequently stated that they had been awakened by a noise at their door. Investigating, they found Mrs. A burned and in shock; they then observed the flames in her residence across the street. They reported the fire and called an ambulance. Mrs. A was quickly removed to a hospital. Fortunately, although badly burned, she survived.

Meanwhile, the Fire Department responded and extinguished the fire after heavy damage in the living room and extensive smoke and heat damage in the other spaces in the dwelling. An examination of Mrs. A's bedroom disclosed she had been in bed during the early, long smoldering stages of the fire; this was indicated by the soot deposit around her body print in the bedding. Her hand prints in the soot deposit on the bedroom walls and the hallway walls, as she had risen and felt her way out of the smoke-filled house, supported her later narrations of her awakening, discovery of the smoke- and heat-filled house, and her escape therefrom.

The origin of the fire was at the location of the recliner chair in the living room. The chair was the most heavily damaged object in the room. This was supported by the spread pattern on the carpet, the burn pattern on other objects in the room, and also by the condition of the ceiling directly over the chair.

Laboratory analysis of recovered parts and electrical circuits from the chair disclosed that the circuits from the arm control switch to the heating pad had been installed in a manner such that the recliner frame pinched the electrical conductor insulation each time the recliner position was changed. Framing damage indicated that initial ignition occurred at this point. Exemplary chairs were examined with the result that the same construction fault and fire causing conditions were observed and could be duplicated in testing process. With limited ventilation, the chair smoldered without breaking into flaming combustion until the flamespread broke through the plastic and synthetic chair covering. The subject fire, of course, was a long-term, smoldering fire. The house had been tightly closed and oxygen was limited. Mrs. A's life had been undoubtedly saved by the fact that she closed her bedroom door upon retiring. Another indisputable factor in her survival, of course, was her calmness in feeling her way to escape down the hall despite the intense pain and discomfort she encountered.

It is of possible interest that some officials initially classified the cause of this fire as careless smoking. Mrs. A did not smoke. When it was learned she did not smoke, others conjectured that it was probably arson. This was concluded in the absence of any reliable information or evidence in any form whatsoever. The correct answer came only after careful consideration of all the evidence by investigators qualified to conduct the inquiry and evaluate the facts.

Perhaps the above incident is illustrative of the care an arson investigator must exercise in evaluating a possible accidental cause when affirmative evidence of arson is not apparent.

Electric irons produce temperatures in the order of 800° F. beneath the iron. Combustion may be expected quickly or over a long period, depending upon the position of the iron when the switch is left in an "on" position and the iron is exposed to ignitable materials. It should be added that electric irons have been utilized to simulate accidental fires. An example was where the proprietor of a clothing and alteration shop later admitted he had caused the fire by this means, after he had made several "test runs" to perfect his alibi. There was a further interesting sidelight to this case. The clothier was also a bookie who ran into financial problems with some of the "lay off" people; this condition suggested he had better have a fire and move. He was on very friendly terms with his insurance company claims representative who, after the fire, came galloping onto the scene with words of condolence and encouragement, assuring that the company would settle quickly and without question.

Soldering irons neglected in an "on" position are recorded, known causes of fire. These are not normally equipped with thermal control switches. A classic example was a soldering iron left on in a construction project during a coffee break which ignited construction paper adjacent to a workbench.

Construction project fires occur, not infrequently, when plumbing is sweated where sawdust and other waste in wall, attic, and floor areas is ignited, smolders and is not readily visible to the worker. Sweating in joints is accomplished, as a rule, with open flame torches. Workers "highballing" to get the job done often neglect to clean up the area before the job or to check it later. There have been numerous examples where fires have occurred in construction projects after the employees have gone for the day. Inquiry usually discloses scorched areas at numerous locations in the uninvolved spaces and buildings where sweating with open flame has been accomplished. A check of the uninvolved areas usually discloses the caution exercised by the plumbers. Frequently, in construction projects, because of separate fires occurring shortly after the crews leave for the day, the incidents are mistakenly classified as incendiary. While it is certainly true that incendiary fires can and do occur on construction projects, the competent investigator will check all factors, including what the plumbers were doing in the area or areas of origin on the day the fire occurred.

Molten metals are a less common source of ignition but must also be considered in repair and industrial operations. Accidental fires from this source include welding, cutting, sweating joints, and certain types of fabrication and construction projects. It should be borne in mind that some alloys, including certain solders, will not usually retain sufficient heat to ignite combustibles upon which they fall. Again, attention to detail cannot be ignored in factual consideration of reasonable accidental cause.

Ferrous alloys from welding and cutting operations *will* ignite combustible materials under molten conditions.

GAS APPLIANCES AS A CAUSE OF FIRES AND EXPLOSIONS

Within the framework of this subject, we are concerned with the gases commonly used in commercial, industrial, and domestic occupancies. As indicated elsewhere in the text, experience has shown that arsonists *do* utilize gas as a tool or device of property destruction. More commonly, however, it is misuse of gas through careless ignorance or neglect, including equipment fatigue and failure, that most often results in fires and explosions. No attempt is made in this treatment of the subject to cover all phases or bases concerning the properties and uses of gas. Detailed treatment may be found in American Gas Association, National Fire Protection Association, and industrial and governmental data.

Gas may be accurately defined as an aeriform matter lacking in independent shape or volume which may expand or mix with the atmospheric environment. It is different from liquids and solids in respect to identifying it as to its precise size and shape—its minute particles are constantly in motion. Usually, the higher the temperature is, the more violent the motion.

We are concerned with the more commonly used flammable gases and these are only flammable when introduced into an oxygen environment in approximate proportion commonly described as flammable or explosive limits. Perhaps this is a good place to mention that our environmental atmosphere is not pure oxygen as we generally refer to it. Our atmosphere consists of 21 percent oxygen which is the

supporter of the conventional forms of combustion. The remaining 79 percent of our atmosphere consists of incombustible nitrogen. Conversely, it is the oxygen percentage in any gas mixture which decides the question of whether fire or explosion will occur.

Oxygen percentage in gases has an equally corresponding influence in any continuing fire. Before dealing with the flammable or explosive gases most commonly identified with the industry, we should consider oxygen and its place in the picture. This is why industrial use, transportation, and storage of such gases requires careful standards including the presence or lack of an oxygen environment and temperature control. This may also include consideration of the presence of substances that are chemically charged with oxygen which may be described as carriers of oxygen since these compounds may contain a portion of their oxygen in a loosely combined state and will part with this oxygen under certain conditions. It may be said that the carriers of oxygen behave like the element oxygen and, therefore, will exhibit the same dangerous properties. The peroxides and their classes of acids which are supersaturated with oxygen (peracids) are examples of such oxygen carriers. Other examples are barium peroxide, lead peroxide, manganese, perox, sodium peroxide, hydrogen peroxide, permanganic acid, iodic acid, and chloric acid.

According to reliable authorities such as the AGA or the NFPA, any material in a gaseous state that will burn in normal, atmospheric concentrations of oxygen at atmospheric pressure and temperature is considered a *flammable gas*. It can be generally stated that all fuel gases fall into this category because they are composed of hydrogen and carbon. Some of the flammable gases commonly encountered are natural, liquified petroleums (LPG) such as propane and butane. The common fuel gases are methane and ethane, with acetylene occasionally used. Various utilities may mix other gases according to the particular needs or conditions of use.

The gases that will not support combustion are generally classified as inert and include helium, argon, carbon dioxide, sulphur dioxide, and, as previously stated, nitrogen.

Where fire or explosions investigation requires analysis of diffusion rates, leaks, or line or equipment failure, the investigator would be wise to engage qualified laboratory or technical assistance. Fires and explosions where gas is suspected often pose complicated questions that can only be answered by careful scene examination and evaluation of *all* the facts. The scene may be complicated by fire or explosion demolition and further compounded by careless or indifferent fire department overhaul.

As indicated earlier, natural gas is the more common type of so-called "city" gas presently in use and it is lighter than air. It consists principally of methane with varying mixtures of ethane, butane, propane, and relatively small amounts of carbon dioxide and nitrogen, the differences varying in actual source or process. The term "manufactured gas" includes coke, carburized water gas, coal gas, and oil gases, all manufactured by various industrial processes. Manufactured gas contains carbon monoxide which is toxic and also combustible.

Natural gas does not contain carbon monoxide but is suffocating in sufficient quantity. It should be remembered, however, that natural gas, in incomplete combustion process, will *produce* carbon monoxide. The investigator, when examining a suspected gas-caused fire or explosion, should determine if the lines, appliances, and accessories are AGA (American Gas Association) labelled and installed in accordance with code requirements. AGA publishes a list of laboratory-approved appliances and equipment. For example, some equipment is listed for limited pressures and circumstances. Gas or installation may be exceeded over the listed pressures or conditions or burner orifices or parts approved for the LPG gases would not be adequate for the gas actually in use.

In certain distribution lines, pressure exceeds 60 lbs. per square inch. Lesser capacity city mains may carry between 10 and 20 lbs. pressure per square inch. In residential space, pressure is usually reduced to $\frac{1}{8}$–$\frac{1}{3}$ lbs. per square inch.

Fuel gases are evaluated according to their heat producing capacities in values of British thermal units per cubic foot (Btu's), as to their limits of flammability in percent of air by volume, as to specific gravity by comparison to air with air valued at 1.0, and as to ignition temperature of the vapor when in flammable or explosive mixture. These are the principal guiding values the average fire investigator must consider in this type of inquiry. While there are additional evaluating factors, the problem very obviously requires laboratory and more specialized expertise.

In considering the basics of evaluation of some of the common characteristics, natural gas, methane type, produces 960 Btu's per cubic foot gross; its lower flammable range is 4.7 percent and the upper is 15 percent. This means that when the gas mixture is lower or higher than the above percentages, respectively, no fire or explosion may be expected. The specific gravity of methane, compared to air, is .56. The number of cubic feet of air required to burn a cubic foot of methane is 10.2. The ignition temperature of methane is 999° F.

The hazard properties of materials, including liquids and gases, may be found in detail in tables listed in National Fire Protection Association publications including the *Handbook on Fire Protection*. This includes flash point; ignition temperature; flammable limits; specific gravity with water; vapor density with air; boiling point; and, where applicable, water solubility and methods of extinguishment. The hazard properties may also be found in dangerous chemical and material codes published by various municipalities and Federal and State agencies.

As a further example, the parameters for oil gas are 575 Btu's per cubic foot, lower flammable range—4.3 percent, upper flammable limit—32.5 percent, specific gravity—.47, cubic feet of oxygen required to burn 1 cubic foot of this gas—4.9, ignition temperature—850° F. By contrast, Butane produces 3,261 Btu's per cubic foot, flammable range—from 1.9 to 8.5 percent, specific gravity—2.07 (much heavier than air), and ignition temperature—864° F.

When dealing with gases, the investigator must consider how the gases were confined or transported and how they are used in specific applications since the principal hazard may be associated with the constant possibility of the gas escaping and forming a flammable or explosive environment. He must consider the possibility of leaks, misuse, or willful release, all of which introduce some interesting possibilities and some of which require careful scrutiny from the very outset.

The common reasons for escape of gas may include leakage due to inadequate seals, corrosion, or fatigue; chemical reaction in the lines or equipment; mechanical fracture, either accidental or willful; and failure from communicated heat from an adjacent heat source such as a torch or an independent fire causing fusing or melting of connections, seals, or components. This can result from trash and exterior fires—impact or displacement. Leakage can occur from automatic controls or valves that causes unignited gas to escape from pilot or burner and extends into the environment, to ducts and vent systems. The gas can then reach an ignition source, in flammable or explosive mixture. Gas may be released by manual manipulation or misuse of burner controls without ignition, thereby permitting the gas to communicate to an ignition source. The willful opening of a gas valve may result from an intent to commit suicide. The use of gas by means of opening valves in order to ultimately introduce the vapor to ignition sources in remote areas has also been utilized in other types of crimes against persons and property.

It is a matter of record that both negligent and willful misuse of gas installations and appliances causes fires and occasionally serious explosions. It is also true, however, that firemen and investigators often mistakenly identify gas and gas appliances as the cause when further careful inquiry discloses otherwise.

For example, brooms, mops, and household materials are commonly placed in furnace and water heater closets in proximity to burner areas where ignition frequently follows. Housewives commonly utilize such spaces for storage of cleaning compounds which react to heat. This, of course, is a bad practice and is discouraged by fire prevention bureaus. Nevertheless, housekeepers seem to keep right on doing it. When fires occur in such spaces, firemen and investigators frequently, on the record, fault the appliance for the fire when, factually, the appliance was properly installed and insulated from combustibles. It worked efficiently when examined at the laboratory and the *real* cause was placing combustible housekeeping materials in spaces not suitable for storage. It is also a matter of record that arsonists have utilized the procedure of placing brooms, mops, and other combustibles in heater or furnace spaces in such a manner that combustion and spreading fire could reasonably be expected (and usually happens), thereby "covering" the crime of arson.

In fires, particularly those resulting in extensive damage such as above, firemen and investigators are prone to select the quick and obvious cause thereby closing the door to what really happened. Too often, the question "Did the gas line leak or did appliance failure precede the fire or did the fire cause the leak or apparent failure of the appliance?" is never asked.

The gases commonly used by the utility companies are basically odorless and various odorants are therefore introduced prior to distribution into the systems. Leaking unignited gas is usually detected by its odor. There are occasions, of course, where, regardless of odor, detection does not occur until too late. This can happen in industrial areas and on projects where other odors are present. It can and does happen where persons have no capability of detecting or differentiating such odors; for example, sleeping persons, persons with certain physical handicaps, and intoxicated persons.

The person who attempts suicide may or may not be aware of the odor as he opens the gas valve and waits for things to happen. He is often greeted with explosion and fire when "nothing happens" after he has opened the gas valves. Becoming bored, he lights up a cigarette. His lighted match triggers the explosion. He hadn't contemplated the explosion and fire: all he wanted was to quietly go to sleep.

A classic example of incomplete and unfactual fire scene examination occurred recently in a western city when the Fire Department responded to a report of a fire and explosion in a residential area of the city. First-in officers found a severely burned, middle-aged lady in the front yard of the burning dwelling. She was immediately removed to emergency where she expired without being able to relate what had happened other than that she was the sole occupant of the involved premises.

The fire was extinguished after flash fire damage to the kitchen and limited displacement of the kitchen windows from explosive force; there was extensive flash fire damage in the bedroom and residual heat and smoke damage throughout the balance of the one-story dwelling.

The investigating authorities classified the kitchen as the area of origin and the ignition point was designated as probably the pilot or water heater burner. The cause was identified as probable gas leak from stove or oven pilot. The investigation was closed.

Further detailed investigation, by outside investigators, disclosed evidence of gas accumulation in the kitchen, hall, bedroom, and attic spaces and that the oven burner had been in a full, on position at the time of explosion and fire. No food materials were in the oven or on the stove. It was noted that all windows and exterior doors had been tightly closed at the time of the explosion and fire, although the outdoor temperature was 75° on the morning of the fire. Further examination of the kitchen area disclosed that some of the victim's undergarments and a nightgown had been wadded and placed in the kitchen range vent.

The flash pattern indicated that free gas from the oven burner had accumulated throughout high levels of the kitchen and seeped slightly into the attic space despite the wadded garments placed in the vent. The flash pattern also extended through the hall and into the bedroom at high levels. The shadow area on the turned-down bed indicated where the victim had been lying at the time of explosion. The burn pattern indicated that the point of ignition was near the head position on the bed. Discarded, partially burned cigarettes and matches were found in a tray alongside the bed and a burned match was found near the head position on the bed. An unlighted cigarette, partially scorched, was found on the carpet alongside the bed near the head. No suicide note was found.

However, about two weeks after the incident, the authorities were advised that a relative had received a letter from the victim announcing poor health and that she contemplated ending it all. The letter had been mailed by the victim the morning before the fire.

Leaking or released unignited gas may accumulate too gradually for detection even by sensitive noses and spread or disperse into ducts and ventilation systems until it reaches an ignition source in explosive mixture with the atmosphere. In such cases, a diffuse type of explosion may be expected with the scorch or flame line apparent and, occasionally, traceable to the ignition source. Tinder type fuels such as drapes, towels, paper items, and wallpaper may be ignited and continue to burn; these fuels may be sufficient to sustain burning temperatures long enough to ignite the bulk fuels such as furniture and framing. The phenomenon may be accompanied by partition displacement or blown glass, depending upon the energy generated by quantity and mixture of the vapor in proportion to the resistance exerted by the partitions, objects, or glass.

In gases lighter than air, the normal initial scorching and displacement, if any, is high. This is true in most utility gases presently in use. In gases heavier than air, such as the LPG groups, initial displacement and flame pattern may be low. It must be remembered, however, that the low or high displacement is *not* a hard and fast rule because of definite variables in structural resistance, circumstances involving the source of the gas, and conditions of interior air movement preceding the explosion.

Explosive force usually suggests the "lean" end of the flammable-explosive range with little continuing fire unless, as indicated, tinder type fuels are present. If the mixture builds to the "rich" end before reaching ignition source, the flash over will generate proportionately less actual displacement force and may produce more continuing flame, igniting such items

as attic framing, studs, and light furniture. In such a case a continuing fire may reasonably be expected. In most cases where the ignition point is at the source of the leak, the explosion does not occur because combustion of the escaping gas progresses with the leak, *at* the leak. The flame production, under such circumstances, is proportionate to the pressures and volume behind the leak and may be manifested, following control, by the burn pattern on adjacent objects.

Gas lines are joined by various means including threaded joints and low melting alloys. The failure of a gas line from the melting of an alloy from an independent heat source will usually limit the gas-fed fire to the area of failure and which may or may not appear as an independent flame pattern depending upon the line pressure, magnitude of the fire, structural collapse and, last but not least, circumstances of post fire overhaul. All too often, the answers to the fires and explosions are permanently obliterated because of the on-scene actions during fire overhaul by indifferent or unskilled personnel, including investigators.

In major structure fires, it is not uncommon for temperatures to exceed the melting temperatures of solders, aluminum, and alloy fittings, and those utilized in connections. It may be expected that post-fire, gas fitting leaks may occur, in pattern, with the progress of the fire, unless the gas service has been interrupted at the service end. As earlier indicated, a blow torch pattern may be found at a broken line or fitting and this should not be confused with an origin of the fire; the leaking gas may reasonably have ignited and burned as it emerged from the fracture when subjected to an ignition source. Again, such separate burn patterns must be carefully scrutinized to determine their correct place in the investigative picture.

As indicated elsewhere in this text, arsonists occasionally plan their fires to simulate accidental gas leaks and accidental gas explosions. For example, in a recent "arson for insurance" fire, the hired torch introduced gasoline into a theater at various locations. He then "thoughtfully" extended the trails through the air conditioning ducts while carefully extinguishing the heater unit pilots and opening the gas burners. He then ignited the gasoline plants via trailers extending across the roof and down into the alley. The behavior of the explosion and resulting fire clearly defined the presence of gasoline vapors heavier than air. This was further corroborated by the presence of gasoline residue in the carpeting and baseboards inside the theater. Further alerted, the investigators detected the tampered gas burners and lines and the presence of gasoline and trailers in the ventilating system and across the roof.

In a major shopping center fire, gasoline was introduced at several locations in a laundry with the expectation that the authorities would fault the gas dryers and diagnose the explosion as a gas leak. The initial low burn pattern at the seat of the fire alerted the investigators to the actual cause although the "torch" had set the stage by tampering with the gas lines at the rear of the premises.

In another major shopping center fire, the authorities suspected arson in a coin operated laundry because an explosion had accompanied the fire. Extended investigation disclosed a fatigued line and pilot control in one of the dryers, with solid evidence of a history of trouble with the pilot prior to the fire. The day before the fire, an employee had attempted to force the tightening to a copper fitting and had cracked the fitting, further aggravating the leak. He also removed the bi-metal automatic burner control. The explosion occurred when the leaking gas had reached an ignition source which, according to the flame pattern, was another dryer which had been activated.

The suspected gas fire or explosion should be investigated carefully, utilizing unbiased, qualified experts when circumstances require.

One of the more common causes of gas appliance fire and explosion is the failure of the thermostat and the high-level control which is a second thermostat sometimes located in the circulating air ducts. As a rule, the second thermostat is connected in series with the basic thermostat and adjusted to open the circuit at a given maximum temperature usually somewhere between 200° F. and 240° F. If both thermostats should malfunction, the furnace burners will continue pouring heat into the system; this can result in prohibitive plenum or duct temperatures and ignition of wall or attic framing may reasonably be expected. Failure of the fan controls can result in prohibitive duct temperatures and ignition of exposures.

Flame-out in furnace closets can result in ignition of unprotected or improperly installed walls and doors. This phenomenon is often misclassified as gas leak by firemen and impatient investigators when, actually, the cause may well have been a result of improper ventilation of the closet or enclosure, thereby denying the furnace sufficient combustion air for appropriate draft. Engineering standards require that furnace cabinets and closets be provided with prescribed quantities of outside air for determined quantities (in Btu's) produced by the heat-producing unit. This factor can quickly be determined by an investigator who will take the trouble to read the capacity mounted on the gas burning unit and measure the vents upon which the unit depends for outside air. These standards are prescribed by the American Gas Association and set down in the Uniform Mechanical Code and Uniform Plumbing Codes.

In conclusion, where gas or gas appliances may be suspect, either as to willful manipulation or accidental cause, the investigator should make every reasonable effort to protect the integrity of the fire scene and all equipment therein and call for expert assistance if he is in over his own depth as to what really happened and why.

Careless disposal of smoking materials must be considered as a commonly accepted fire cause.

Although disposal of smoking materials is undoubtedly faulted for the cause of more fires than the investigative record can substantiate, this classification must be considered by the Arson Investigator where other specified cause is not abundantly clear. On the other hand, there have been numerous, well documented examples wherein the careless smoker theory has been totally incompatible with the physical evidence on scene. There are also cases of record where the arsonist has used the careless cigarette stall to hide his act of arson. For example, careful investigation of a cocktail lounge fire disclosed that the bartender had been hired to torch the lounge in such a manner that it would appear to be an accidental fire.

Investigation by the Fire Department of the gutted lounge disclosed origin in a waste basket under the end of the back bar. The fire had been discovered and reported nearly four hours after closing time. Investigating officers classified the cause as careless cigarettes dumped in the waste basket by the bartender when he closed. Experienced fire investigators concluded that the burn-out around the back bar was insufficient for a four-hour, smoldering fire, even granting limited ventilation. Their interviews with the bartender disclosed that he dumped lighted cigarettes into the waste basket on numerous occasions shortly prior to closing time; that, on some occasions, the waste would burn out without igniting the bar. When his bosses started leaning on him to "get the damned job done," he selected an evening, locked up as usual, filled the waste basket with wadded paper, and departed. Returning, about two hours later, he found the interior filled with smoke but, no fire. He obtained two cans of charcoal lighter fluid from his own "pad" and returned and poured the fluid around the burned out waste receptacle, reignited it and again departed. As he later stated, "Man, that lighter fluid sure did the job, huh?" Samples from the floor molding and mop board disclosed residue of lighter fluid and confirmed the bartender's story, much to the discomfort, financially and otherwise, of the owners.

All fires in waste baskets and upholstered furniture are not accidental smoking fires just as certainly as all rapid temperature rise fires (flash fires) are not incendiary. The investigator must examine and evaluate *all* of the available evidence.

A glowing cigarette will occasionally ignite dry combustibles such as upholstery, piled merchandise, vegetable matter, and dry grass. Ambient temperatures, relative humidity, fuel moisture content, and wind are important factors, particularly in reference to forest and wildland fires. Tests have shown that, as a general rule, lighted cigarettes and cigars, merely placed on top of upholstered items, only burn out, leaving the ash along the linear scorch line and rarely producing sufficient heat to induce combustion of the exposed item.

On the other hand, if the cigarette or glowing tobacco form is placed between the end of the cushion and the side of the chair, or between the cushions, enough confined heat may develop to initiate smoldering combustion with resultant penetration and ultimate production of flaming combustion. Tests conducted with lighted cigarettes and various plastics have indicated continued combustion is unlikely either during the smoldering term of the cigarette or thereafter. Similar tests with sponge rubber, also used in furniture items, have most frequently resulted merely in the melting away of the rubber along the glow path of the cigarette until it is consumed along its length, with no following combustion of the rubber. Sponge rubber, admittedly, is extremely flammable once ignited and burns very hot. It is emphasized that ignition from a cigarette is unlikely, *not* impossible. The hazards of lighted cigarettes and tobaccos in bedding should never be discounted although some authorities have written that this type of hazard is "less than commonly supposed." Tests have shown that cigarettes and other forms of smoking materials, placed upon cotton sheets, pillows, and some blanket materials, may easily create smoldering combustion situations be-

cause of the very context of the materials and the usual ventilation afforded in the bedding once it is unmade. Kapok, used in pillows, is easily ignitible.

Fires resulting from smoking in bed can appear as short-term flaming combustion fires or long-term smoldering depending upon the bedding material, point of origin in the bedding, proximity of flash type exposures such as curtains and some types of carpeting and, last but not least, ventilation.

Fatalities have been experienced in smoker fires in living room spaces and bedroom areas where long-term smoldering combustion, producing gaseous products of combustion and exhausting the oxygen supply, has caused asphyxia with relatively limited evidence of flame damage to contents or victim. Conversely, smoker fires have developed quickly into flash type conflagrations with extensive flame damage to contents and victim. In some cases, the victim, although severely burned, survives the fire.

The human hazards from exposure to heat and the products of combustion are varied and often complex. These subjects are capably handled in various texts on homicide investigation. The investigator should also refer to Gettler and Freimuth, *Carbon Monoxide in the Blood;* Stolman and Stewart, *Toxicology; Mechanisms and Analytical Methods;* Le Moyne Snyder, *Homicide Investigation;* Golovina & Khaustovich, *8th Symposium on Combustion,* 1960.

There is a general misconception that glowing cigarettes, cigar ends, and pipe heels will ignite volatile, flammable liquids. Numerous reliable authorities have conducted tests for the purpose of attempting to induce explosions by introducing such materials into an explosive vapor. The results have been negative. While it cannot be positively stated that ignition of vapor in exposure mixture *cannot* be so induced, the authorities who have conducted the tests indicated that, so far, this does not happen. On the other hand, there is no question but that an "open flame" introduced into explosive vapor environment will cause ignition. An electrical spark or arc into such an atmosphere will act as an ignition source. This, of course, is why fire and safety codes require vapor proof cables, switches, conduits, etc., in explosive environments. Friction in certain forms and static electricity may also be an ignition source.

The National Electrical Code dwells upon the subject of electrical circuits and spark sources in areas where explosive vapors may be present and in eliminating and handling static electricity and proper grounding. Again, the investigator must be familiar with these subjects if he is to trace and eliminate electrical sources as causes of fires.

An abused cause of ignition is the subject of rodents chewing matches. This has been cited as the cause of numerous fires throughout history. Although it is known that rodents have packed matches to their nests and it is remotely possible that, while carrying certain limited types of friction matches, one may be ignited by scratching it along an abrasive surface, most present day matches cannot be ignited in this fashion. Certainly, the moist process of chewing the head of a match can be eliminated as a reasonable possible cause. In a series of studies by Underwriters' Laboratories and by the Diamond Match Company, as reported in the *NFPA Quarterly,* it was shown that rats, placed in cages with matches, will starve to death without gnawing the match heads. A search through the research division of the U.S. Department of Agriculture, and U.S. Public Health Service disclosed not one single authenticated case of fire resulting from rats gnawing on matches either in urban or rural areas.

Spontaneous ignition cannot be disregarded by the arson investigator as a possible accidental cause in numerous situations, such as in paint storage; warehouses; coal, hay, grain, and vegetable and animal fat storage; cargo holds; and numerous areas of use and storage of unstable chemical compounds.

One of the more common forms of spontaneous ignition is activity of microorganisms in curing alfalfa, hay, and other compounds which may occur in initiating temperatures of approximately 140 to 160° F. and, when insulated or confined in pile or mass, develop temperatures exceeding 450° F. which is in the order of ignition temperature for alfalfa and other vegetable materials as well as wood products.

The gradual spontaneous heating phenomenon may be detected along the exterior surfaces when such heating is deep in the pile; it has been reliably stated that spontaneous ignition, in improperly cured hay, may occur within a week or two after stacking or baling and may evolve over an even longer period extending from ten to fourteen weeks. This type of fire may be traced to its source deep within the pile and working its way to the outside, heating and carbonizing the fuel in process. The unburned interior areas adjacent to the "tunneling" may be dark in color and acidic in odor. If a suspect stack is torn apart, these unburned but heated areas will usually burst into flame because of increased ventilation by the opening. Similar caverned areas may be found in improperly ventilated cargo, coal, and slag piles; fertilizer piles; and rag bins.

There have been authenticated examples of spontaneous ignition in tightly piled building materials including fiber board and shingles; however, such cases should be viewed with extreme caution when not showing evidence of vegetable reaction in the presence of heat-generating or unstable compounds.

In summarizing this chapter, the reader will recall that emphasizing the Law of Arson and our system of jurisprudence requires that reasonable accidental cause be eliminated before an arson charge can be sustained or supported. The significance of this should be apparent after considering only a few of the more common causes we have set out and how ignition can occur in these categories.

As indicated, we have only covered the more common accidental categories. We could add, for example, the mechanical causes in motor vehicles, watercraft, and aircraft in commerce and the industrial spectrum, which are widening as methods and materials multiply.

The arson investigator must fully utilize his data and assistance resources if he is to do his job properly. He must not permit himself to be stampeded into "quickie" decisions because of interest pressures or exigencies of the particular moment. Factual analysis of the fire scene is in the public interest. Anything short of that merely compounds the fire prevention and law enforcement problem.

CHAPTER XI

CORPUS DELICTI IN ARSON

Corpus delicti, the body of the crime, is made up of two elements: First, that a certain result has been produced, as when a man has died or a building has been burned; second, that someone is criminally responsible for the result. *(Ballentine's Law Dictionary.)* The body of the offense or the substance of the crime, in a homicide, would include the fact of death and that a criminal act of another was responsible for that death; in larceny, the *corpus delicti* would be composed of two elements: First, that the property was lost from the possession of the owner; and second, that it was lost by the willful and malicious taking by another.

It is a well established fact that a fire, regardless of its spectacular appearance, spread or ultimate size, creates no presumption of criminal origin; on the contrary, the law attaches a definite presumption that the fire resulted from natural or accidental means.

It is well known that fires often cause speculation, particularly those of magnitude attracting public interest. Fire authorities as well as lay witnesses occasionally confuse evidence with the circumstance of spectacular behavior of a fire without factual and supportable investigation.

The Law of Arson very correctly demands considerably more in proving a criminal origin of a fire. Overinsurance, poor business prognosis, revenge, malice, or other motive factor may be a possible reason why a fire may have been set (*if* it was set) but is never acceptable as a part of the *corpus delicti*. For example, a person may have been heard to state, "I will burn the place." Or, he may have been observed at the scene shortly before the fire. Such evidence, suspicious as it may be deemed by the investigators, is not a part of the *corpus delicti* though all of the above may be important in showing motive, opportunity, intent, and even presence at the scene but it is not a part of the *corpus delicti*.

As the courts have said since the very beginning of our federal and state judicial system and continue to say today, "There is no presumption that a burning building has been set on fire; on the contrary, the presumption of innocence which is accorded the accused, carries with it a presumption that a fire is *accidental* or providential in origin." (So held by appellate decisions in states including Alabama, California, Georgia, Kentucky, Massachusetts, Minnesota, Mississippi, Missouri, New Jersey, Oklahoma, Pennsylvania, West Virginia, Nevada, Virginia, and many others including New York.)

The Courts have always recognized the serious nature of the crime of arson and have historically and repeatedly classified it as one of the most "heinous and devastating crimes known to man" because of its inherent destructiveness and hazards to life and the public safety. Yet, in their calmness and wisdom, the Courts have always insisted upon the protection of the innocent in our judicial system by installing evidenciary and procedural safeguards to insure that innocent persons will not be unjustly convicted or, in fact, convicted of a crime that was not, in fact, committed. For example, the Courts have always held that, before a person may be convicted in the case of any felony, there must be a reasonable showing, by independent credible evidence, that a crime was, in fact, committed. In a charge of murder, the state must show the victim died of other than natural cause; for example, the autopsy may show a bullet in the brain or a knife wound in the heart with resulting fatal hemorrhage. And so it is with a charge of arson.

First, it must be shown that a fire did, in fact, occur. In this regard, it need not be a large or devastating fire. The showing may be satisfied if a char of the wood fiber or fabric of the structural member occurred. Anything less would be construed as an attempt.

Second, there must be a reasonable and credible showing that the fire was willfully and intentionally caused, usually by some affirmative act. (This evidence might be a production of residue of accelerant, incendiary trailer or device, explosive, or it might even be manipulation of electrical or mechanical equipment in such a manner that a fire or explosion could only reasonably be expected.) The willful and intentional fire may also be shown by circumstantial evidence or showing by elimination of all reasonable mechanical and natural sources of ignition.

Third, it must be shown independently of any admissions, statements, or confessions by the defendant. Even a complete and detailed voluntary confession does not negate the necessity imposed by law to first prove the criminal cause before the admissions or the confession be admitted in evidence against the accused.

As the best authorities have repeatedly stated, "This is as it should be, otherwise it might be possible, in our system, to convict defendants of a charge of arson when, in fact, the cause of the fire may have reasonably resulted from accidental or natural means." This necessary legal safeguard, built into our legal system, requires particular investigative knowledge and integrity in the examination of the fire scene. Here is the area of the greatest administrative neglect and investigative misunderstanding, both in the Fire Service and the Law Enforcement system. Here is where the majority of arson investigations and prosecutions fail: at the bridge of the *corpus delicti*. The failure most frequently occurs in inappropriate examination at the fire scene and in the identification and preservation of the evidence of cause. The probable second failure, in order of priority, is failure of the investigators (and experts) to factually support their findings concerning proof of the *corpus delicti* when the case gets into court.

In the absence of proof of *corpus delicti* to the satisfaction of the Court, the case collapses since there is no evidence a crime was committed. This is irrespective of how incriminating other evidence may appear to be such as motive, opportunity, presence at the scene, confessions, etc.

The examination of fire scene and search for evidence has been discussed in some detail in other chapters. It will be recalled that the examination of the fire scene may be compared to a crossing of bridges. The crossing of the bridge of *corpus delicti* occurs at at least two locations:

(1) The fire scene. Once the integrity of the scene is destroyed, that bridge is crossed. The evidence is missed, and the bridge is burned.

(2) The witness stand. Here is where the officer or expert who will testify must describe and interpret what he found in the form of evidence that goes to prove the *corpus delicti*. If he is ill-equipped in

knowledge, training, or ability, or the case preparation is otherwise lacking in competency or integrity, this will probably become abundantly apparent during the cross examination by the defense. The bridge will have been burned and it cannot be recrossed. The damage is done. The case will be dismissed on the grounds that the *corpus delicti* has not been proved. The defendant will be discharged.

"One cannot be convicted of arson unless the presumption of innocence is rebutted, and the incendiary origin of the fire is shown beyond a reasonable doubt." (Wash., State v. Pfeuller, 167 Wash. 485, 9 Pac. 2d 785; People v. Lee, 231 Mich. 607 204 N.W. 742. and in many other states including California and New York.)

"It is an elementary proposition of criminal law that, to be entitled to a conviction, the state must first establish the *corpus delicti,* the fact that a crime as alleged has been committed by someone. This being established, the guilty connection of the accused with such offense must also be established, both beyond a reasonable doubt." (State v. Cristani, 192, Iowa 615, 185 N.W. 111.)

"The *corpus delicti* may be proved, with other elements of the offense, by circumstantial evidence." (People v. Roganovich, 77 Cal. App. 158, 246 Pac. 132. There are numerous other leading cases in various states supporting this position.)

These circumstances include indicating the presence of flammable materials, accelerants, incendiary devices, and explosive residues not in natural presence on the premises; that the fire started at two or more separate and distinct points in the premises; the isolation of the premises and absence of any natural cause, including precautions taken to avoid fire.

While *corpus delicti* cannot be proved solely by the confession of the accused, if sufficient evidence of the *corpus delicti* has been presented so that a confession of the accused is admissible, such confession can then be considered as additional evidence of the crime. (People v. Jones, 123 Cal. 65, 55 Pac. 698; People v. Saunders, 13 Cal. App. 743, 110 Pac. 825; People v. Jenkins, 67 Cal. App. 631, 228 Pac. 405. There are similar rulings in most other states including Illinois, Michigan, Kentucky, Tennessee and New York.)

"At common law the actual burning of the whole or some part of the house must be proved, though proof of the actual burning of the smallest part is sufficient. It need not be shown that the wood 'blazed' but proof that the wood or other flammable material was charred (i.e., reduced to charcoal), and its identity destroyed, is always required. A mere discoloration or scorching black by smoke or heat is not enough. (Commonwealth v. Hayden, Mass. 332, 23 N.E. 51; People v. Handley, 93 Mich. 46, 52, N.W. 1032; Woolsey v. State, 30 Tex. App. 346, 17 S.W. 546; and others.)

Traditionally, the basic destructive characteristics of fire has impeded investigation of cause and, in process, the establishment of *corpus delicti* from actual reliable remaining physical evidence. Fire demolishing the area of origin often discourages the exercise of care and investigative expertise that circumstances usually demand. Police and law enforcement officials are frequently reluctant to become too deeply involved in a type of inquiry they do not fully understand; for example, the fact that it may be required to rely upon opinionated evidence that a crime was or was not committed.

In an era of case load emphasis and increasing demands continually being placed upon investigative personnel by increasing incidence of other major crime, fire investigation (and arson investigation) is often relegated to secondary investigative priority. Again, this neglect has been compounded by the official awareness of the hazards of unreliable physical evidence of the cause of fire. This has resulted in considerable skepticism in some very respectable law enforcement and police oriented areas toward certain technical and procedural data and techniques used in fire investigation, particularly where such information may decide whether or not a felony prosecution will follow.

Increasing professionalism in our law enforcement and investigative system demands the highest degree of skill in the investigation of all classes of major crime, including arson and incendiarism. It is clear we have barely scratched the surface in the approach to scientific fire scene investigation. Laboratory science and scientific fire research has opened the door to improved investigative techniques. However, the record is abundant with examples where public and private investigators have not utilized the scientific resources currently available to

their full potential, including fire and arson investigation.

It is also well established that further qualified laboratory and scientific research is needed in the fire investigation field to eliminate the guesswork too often associated with the investigation of fires.

Again, the proof of the criminal agency in connection with the cause is an essential ingredient of the crime. As the Courts have repeatedly said, "In order to prove *corpus delicti* of arson, it is not sufficient merely to show a burning, which may have been the result of an accident. It must be proved, beyond a reasonable doubt, that the burning was *not* accidental, but was willfully and maliciously caused by some person who was morally responsible for his actions." (Winslow v. State, 76 Ala. 42; Daniels v. State, 12 Ala. App. 119, 68 So. 499; State v. Pienick, 46 Wash. 522 90 Pac. 645, 11 L.R.A. 41; 16 L.R.A. (N.S.) 285; and Brown v. Commonwealth 87 Va. 215, 12, S.E. 472.)

"A voluntary confession or admission of the accused is not sufficient to prove the *corpus delicti* unless there is other evidence tending to support the same, either direct or circumstantial, or, in other words, a confession or admission by the accused to prove the *corpus delicti* must be corroborated." (Martin v. United States, 264 Fed. 950; Boland v. United States, 238 Fed.; People v. De Martini, 50 Cal. App. 109, 194 Pac. 506; Moon v. State, 12 Ga. App. 614, 77 S.E. 1088—arson; Sims v. State, 14 Ga. App. 28, 79 S.E. 1133—arson; Collins v. Commonwealth, 123 Va. 815, 96 S.E. 826.)

"Defendant's confession in *open court* will establish *corpus delicti* and will sustain a conviction." (Wall v. State, Ga. App. 305 63 S.E. 27.)

"Where the evidence is sufficient to show that the crime has been committed or where there is any evidence to show the confession in proof of the *corpus delicti*, the confession or admission is admissible." (Berman v. State, 35 Ohio Cir. Ct. 386; Murry v. United States, 288 Fed. 1008, certiorari denied in 262 U.S. 757, 67 L.ed. 1218, 43 Sup. Ct. 703.)

CHAPTER XII

RECOGNITION OF EVIDENCE OF ARSON AT THE FIRE SCENE

Previous chapters have dealt with the practical and legal necessity of establishing the origin of a fire and eliminating accidental cause and natural cause. It should be recalled that, in *all* jurisdictions, the law requires proving *corpus delicti* before a conviction will be sustained. This means that it must be shown not only that a fire did, in fact occur, but further that the fire was willfully and maliciously set. (People v. Clagg (1961) CA 2d 209, 17 Cal. Rptr. 60.) As has previously been set out in some detail, this means that a criminal agency must be involved in the cause of the fire. As courts have stated in every jurisdiction in the nation, the mere showing that a building burned, regardless of the size and outward manifestations, does not establish the fact the fire resulted from arson. (People v. Holman (1945) 72 CA2d, 164 P. 2d 297.) On the other hand, *corpus delicti* is established by evidence of separate and unrelated fires and connection of the defendant to the scene is not part of the *corpus delicti*. (1945 72 CA2d, 164 P. 2d 297.) Authorities often make the mistake of premature arrest of a defendant simply because he allegedly departed a scene shortly before a fire was discovered. While his presence might well be a suspicious circumstance and while such evidence is relevant in placing the defendant at the scene, it is not a part of the *corpus delicti*. (People v. Hayes (1950) 101 CA 2d 305.)

The Courts have held that the proof necessary to show the *corpus delicti* need *not* have convincing force which establishes guilt and a *prima facie* showing suffices. (People v. Andrews (1963) 35 Cal. Rptr. 118.)

Proof of the defendant's identity is not a part of the *corpus delicti* and need not be shown in proving a fire was of incendiary origin. (People v. Andrews (1963) 35 Ca. Rptr. 118; People v. Mass, (1956) 145 CA 2d 69, 301 P. 2d 894.) The investigator should confer with the prosecutor in his jurisdiction and familiarize himself with the current attitude and re-quirements of the Courts in his jurisdiction in reference to the type and sufficiency of evidence which will be required in "holding a defendant to answer" on a charge of arson and in sustaining a conviction on such a charge.

It must be remembered that proof of the *corpus delicti* within the requirements of the law must be met; otherwise, no admissions or confessions of the defendant may be admitted regardless of how incriminating those statements or admissions might be. The defendant's statements, admissions, or confessions are not a part of the *corpus delicti*. Investigators often assume that because a suspect may be placed at the scene of a fire and that he made conflicting or otherwise damaging statements, this is sufficient in showing the criminal agency in connection with the cause of the fire. This is simply not the case.

To get on with the topic of physical evidence of arson or incendiarism and "what it is all about," such evidence may be of a very obvious and direct visible nature. Some examples are a fire bomb or "Molotov cocktail," thrown through a window or against the side of a building with the fragments and gasoline residue recovered from the debris, or flammable accelerants and combustible trailers in the form of rope or plastic bags extending through exposed spaces on an involved premises. The evidence may be visible in the form of a shattered locker at the seat of an explosion and fragmented concrete and slivered window glass common to the detonation of high explosives.

On the other hand, the fire may have been set in such a manner to make it appear that the fire resulted from purely natural, mechanical, electrical, or other accidental means. This more sophisticated criminal approach is often utilized by those engaged in the setting of carefully planned, organizational fires related to intimidation and fraud. This *modus operandi* is extremely effective in defeating the investigative efforts of insurance oriented claims personnel and their investigative staffs who occasionally accept the visible evidence at its face value as the basis for insurance subrogation action. The surface appearance of accidental origin also defeats official investigation where such investigation is inexperienced, indifferent, or is simply not permitted to take the time necessary to investigate the scene to completion.

Illustrative of arrangement of incendiary fires to appear as accidental, is the manipulation of mechanical, electrical, and normally present materials as igniting agents: stoves, ranges, heaters, electrical circuits, light bulbs strategically located against combustibles, and arranged waste basket fires, for example. Tavern owners commonly utilize waste baskets conveniently filled with wadded toweling and placed in appropriate locations. Ignition is usually blamed upon a "carelessly placed match or cigarette" attributed to the bartender who secured for the night and who is quick to hang his head in an embarrassed manner explaining how he just happened to clean the ashtrays off the bar after closing time and probably forgot to insure that those nasty old cigarettes were out before dumping them in the trash. This tactic taxes the patience and skills of the most experienced and thoughtful investigators.

In an apartment fire, a careful investigation disclosed the suspect, in order to collect his insurance, had made several attempts to produce an accidental fire but without success. Finally, after experimenting with his wall furnace thermostat control, he learned that by opening a window near the control location, the wintry breeze would blow into the room with the result that the environment around the thermostat would remain cold. The gas wall furnace at the opposite end of the room would operate continually because the open window would maintain the low temperatures at the thermostat. It would keep right on telling the furnace, "It's cold in here." An upholstered chair was placed close to the furnace face. The burners, controlled by the thermostat, operated continually, causing extended temperatures at the furnace location ultimately igniting the piece of furniture near the furnace face as well as the wall framing at the furnace header plates.

Although the cause of the fire was very understandably classified as accidental by the fire authorities, a police officer, curious as to why the hall window had been wide open on a cold, cold night, conducted further inquiry which included questioning a domestic. This, in turn, led to further questioning of the pleasant faced young executive who had so carefully arranged to burn his own apartment. Briefly, confronted with certain hard evidence concerning his movements prior to the fire, and motive, the suspect admitted arranging the fire to collect his insurance.

A lady burned her dress shop utilizing a bowl-shaped electric radiant heater. The Fire Department had extinguished the early morning fire after it had caused extensive damage to the contents of the shop. The portable electric heater was found plugged into a wall socket and the switch of the appliance was full "on." The fire cone and burn pattern extended from the heater location. The proprietor advised the officers she must have inadvertently left the heater on and too close to a dress rack when she locked up at 9:00 p.m. that evening. (The fire was discovered and reported at 3:30 a.m.)

An inquisitive deputy Fire Marshal, visiting the scene the following morning, observed that the carpet and matting were totally incinerated around the base of the heater; he also observed residue of what appeared to have been burned fabric down inside the face and grill of the heater, although the heater was at a location where no fabrics would have fallen on the heater in the process of the fire.

Samples taken from the carpeting and matting around the base of the heater disclosed residue of a compound similar to charcoal lighter fluid. There was no reason for the presence of this type of compound in the premises, particularly at the location of the heater. Examination of a similar electric heater disclosed it would not ignite combustibles such as linens, cottons, or synthetics further than 18 inches from its face or two feet above the top side with the heater full on; however, radiant and conducted heat would ignite such fabrics placed in close proximity to the face or immediately above the heater.

A door-to-door canvass of the neighborhood disclosed a janitor who knew the proprietor of the dress shop by sight and who observed her enter the shop at 3:00 a.m. the morning of the fire. He observed her enter the shop but only the night lights remained on. He observed the lady depart via the back door at 3:15 a.m. At 3:30 a.m., a police patrol unit observed heavy smoke pouring out of the dress shop into the alley. The unit radioed the alarm.

The officer tried rear and front doors and found them locked. Although signs on the doors indicated the premises were protected with a burglar alarm system, there was no response by the system. Subsequent inquiry disclosed that the proprietor of the shop had ordered the system discontinued on the first of the month preceding the fire.

The lady's initial comments to the Fire Department and her insurance adjustor were that she had visited a restaurant with a friend until 1:30 a.m., at which time they returned to her apartment where they remained until she was notified of the fire at about 4:30 a.m. Confronted with evidence on the probable cause and the information provided by the janitor, the lady admitted she had set the fire. She had "set up" the scene at closing time. At about 3:00 a.m., she drove to the scene, applied the charcoal lighter fluid she obtained from her barbecue, placed some garments immediately over the top of the radiant heater, turned it on full and departed.

The fire was initially classified as accidental by the responding fire companies; this was confirmed by the watch investigator. The true cause was established only because a deputy Fire Marshal took the time and made the effort to look at the "cause behind the cause."

Several cafes and cocktail lounges have been destroyed by professional torches who utilize liberal quantities of shredded packing paper which they spread through the attic of the target occupancy. These fires usually cause sufficient damage (depending upon time of discovery and control) to require insurance subsidized redecorating and remodeling. The cause is usually classified as electrical by the fire departments because, after all, the attics are where the electrical circuits are found. The "ear marks" of the fires are attic fires and, therefore, the cause "must be" electrical.

The shredded paper is easily ignited and ignition may be arranged to suit the convenience of the perpetrator. Attics, as a rule, are dry and usually well ventilated. The incriminating shredded paper is usually totally consumed or, if not, ignored since its purpose is not usually recognized. There is, of course, no affirmative evidence of criminal origin of the fire and the case is quickly forgotten.

As another example of the *modus operandi* in covering the criminal cause, a series of labor jurisdictional disputes involved laundries and dry cleaning establishments, during which advocates utilized persuasive tactics to bring the non-negotiators to their knees: first bombings, then fires. The "goons" quickly learned that the bombings (usually a stick or two of dynamite at the front door) were attracting too much attention from the law enforcement authorities and the press. So they decided on a more subtle approach but one which would be just as

quickly appreciated by the target personnel. Their new M/O (*modus operandi*) was changed to sewing capsules of metallic sodium into the padding of garments. Identifying information was then removed from the garments which were then sent to the selected laundry or cleaners for servicing. The capsules activated upon exposure to moisture. Most of these tumbler fires were classified by the authorities as accidental, resulting from sparks and explosions in cleaning materials.

The extent and ingenuity of covering incendiarism and arson with the cloak of accidental cause is only limited by the knowledge and ability of the arsonist, regardless of his particular motive. His success is only limited by the thoroughness, knowledge, and integrity of his opposite number—the fire scene investigator. If the investigation is the usual "routine response and investigation," the chances of discovery of the carefully planned incendiary fire is minimal. This is unquestionably verified in the presently dismal apprehension-conviction statistics as reported by the National Fire Protection Association and the Department of Justice statistics on major crime. (See U.S. Department of Commerce Final Report of the National Fire Prevention and Control Administration, National Academy for Fire Prevention and Control dated September, 1976, and Aerospace Corporation Systems Equipment Improvement Program Law Enforcement Development Group Survey and Assessment of Arson and Arson Investigation Report to National Institute of Law Enforcement and Criminal Justice, U.S. Department of Justice dated October, 1976.) Although there is some slight variance in the statistics on arson, arrests, and convictions, depending upon reporting procedures and practices, the most optimistic figures available indicate that there is only one person arrested and convicted for each 100 known arson or incendiary fires. The arrest and conviction record is much better than this where jurisdictions provide appropriate investigative attention to the problem, but the one percent arrest-conviction applies to the national picture *as of 1977*.

While it may be reasonably conceded that arrest and conviction is not the ultimate criterion of arson and fire prevention, these functions continue to be a vital part of our justice system in the control of major crime, including arson which is the most devastating single crime in our society today. It is undoubtedly true that sociological-economical problems have as much impact on arson as on other crime. However, neglect of investigation of the cause of arson and fires in general only further impedes the psychological and sociological approach to correcting the problems.

Now, to get on with the physical aspects of searching for affirmative evidence of incendiary origin of a fire, as earlier indicated, the signs may include separate and distinct points of origin which, in turn, may be manifested in separate and distinct burn patterns either unconnected or originating in separate spaces. We have previously discussed separate cones or spread patterns in Chapter VI. For example, the placement of tinder type combustible fuels at separate locations illustrates chain reacting heat sources. Trailers may or may not be utilized in the communication of fire from an initial ignition source to boosters in separate locations.

Accelerants, such as gasoline, alcohol, kerosene, charcoal lighter fluid, acetone, and thinner, may be utilized in a connecting process. Low flash point fuels such as acetone and gasoline may be very effective in the hands of the careful or experienced arsonist. In the hands of the careless, indifferent, or ignorant arsonist, it may ignite prematurely, in which case the arsonist may be trapped or seriously injured. He or she is frequently identified in this manner.

Where the use of boosters or trailers is suspected, the investigator should proceed with caution when removing samples of residue from the suspected location whether an identifiable odor remains or not. The use of some of the more reliable hydrocarbon vapor detectors may be of value in checking this type of fire scene. These detectors should be relied upon only for preliminary evaluation and not for final determination of the identity of the residue.

Although low flash point accelerants are rapidly dissipated in the presence of heat and flame, experience has shown that identifiable traces may be recovered from fire scene residues particularly in wood compounds, and from certain classes of fabrics, baled and piled goods, and certain classes of upholstery not entirely consumed in flame.

The removed samples should be placed in tightly sealed, absolutely pre-examined, clean metal or glass containers which are plainly marked as to the precise location from which it was removed. The containers should be tightly sealed and promptly transported to the laboratory in accordance with procedures set out by the examining laboratory. Identification of accelerants or boosters may then be made by the laboratory through use of gas chromatography or other reliable procedures.

The sense of smell of the investigator has often made preliminary identification of residue of accelerants where they have been placed upon a floor covered with carpeting, matting, and even synthetic tile. On carpeting, for example, liquid patterns may be recognized by the deep liquid-type flow patterns manifested in the deep char on down into the nap and weave of the carpeting, corresponding, in pattern, to the way in which the liquid was applied to the carpet, matting, or in some classes of synthetic tile. The reason the char pattern is pronounced and identifiable is because the flammable liquid penetrates the material *before* ignition thereby permitting the saturated depth into the fabrics to become impregnated for deep burn. The harder or tighter the surface, the less likely this pattern is to be found. Where the suspected patterns appear, photographs should record the condition and the entire surface should be retained if reasonably possible. In any event, burned and unburned samples should be removed for laboratory analysis. The same pattern phenomenon may be found in upholstered furniture surfaces, bedding, tabletops, and on some types of wall surfaces. The pattern is often easily apparent where accelerants containing fire bombs have been used.

The above described accelerant or flammable liquid patterns are not normally found on hard floor surfaces; the reason is because the liquid does not penetrate sufficiently to provide the deep seated "wick" effect so pronounced in softer surfaces such as carpeting and synthetics. For example, on a wood floor surface, most notably on hardwood types, materials such as gasoline and thinner actually tend to protect the surface since the liquid does not truly burn—it is the vapor above the fuel surface that is burning. The more volatile fuels quickly vaporize and the vapor is consumed throughout the combustion process, leaving little or no character on the wood surface and most certainly none on asphalt or concrete.

Where accelerants are suspected as having been used on hard floor surfaces, the investigator should look for lateral burn or char on floor to wall baseboards or molding and heavy low level char on lateral exposures such as furniture around the perimeter of the suspected area. This relatively low level char may be produced by the wide area application of the accelerant accompanied by the extremely rapid temperature rise introduced into the environment by the booster or accelerant at relatively low levels as well as in the higher reaches of the involved space.

In further regard to the areas of hard floor surfaces where use of accelerants is suspected, the investigator should open the tongue and groove or seams of the flooring; the presence of residues of the accelerants may be detected where the liquids have penetrated into the tongue and groove or seams. Unopened sections of the suspected floor should be taken promptly to a qualified laboratory for further, more specific analysis.

Where suspected flammable liquids may have been present on floor surfaces, analysis of the spaces *beneath* the flooring should be carried out; for example, soil from the foundation areas where flooring is old and cracked and where liquid may have penetrated to the areas beneath the suspect floor. Soil may preserve accelerant residues for extended periods particularly where water has been applied to extinguish the fire and has dampened the areas beneath the floor. There are numerous examples where soil samples from beneath suspect floors have produced identifiable accelerant residues several days after the fire. Such examples include fires where the incineration of the interior of the premises has been extensive.

It is not uncommon for calculating arsonists to apply accelerants from a sub-floor area around a floor furnace to make the fire appear to have resulted from a malfunction of the furnace. Where ignition is beneath the floor, whether utilizing liquid accelerants or not, the char pattern will usually point to this fact by the pronounced alligatoring on the underside of the planking or flooring. In this case, the liquid is below the floor level with the heat pattern extending vertically and directly attacking the exposed undersurfaces of the planking or flooring. In such cases, traces of the accelerant may be identified by appropriate preservation of sections of the floor followed by qualified laboratory analysis.

When accelerants are suspected on a hard floor surface, even though the surface pattern may tell very little, the investigator should remove the wood molding and/or baseboard surrounding the suspected area; residue of the booster or accelerant may have penetrated beneath the molding or baseboard, in which case there may reasonably have been insufficient oxygen in the tight fit to permit complete combustion.

Where the suspected area is not close to a wall but where physical items such as furniture and stock bound the perimeter, the investigator should look for samples beneath the floor surface area protected by such furniture (the table legs, for example) or cartons. This search should include spaces under protective matting, carpet, garments, or other items which may have fallen and formed a smothering, protective obstruction to complete combustion.

In major arson projects such as warehouses, department stores, cafes, and cocktail lounges where accelerants may have been utilized in quantity to insure the desired damage from fire, explosions have often accompanied the fire because some of the vapors accumulated in explosive mixture *prior* to ignition. This effect often occurs where timing or delayed action devices are used; it also occurs where the job doesn't go off according to plans. In such cases, ceiling sections may be displaced, lodging on the floor, smothering the floor fire and protecting the telltale traces of the accelerant (including even gasoline) for appropriate analysis and identification. This phenomenon can occur *without* explosion. It can be caused by rapid temperature rise from the presence of accelerants and the early collapse of ceiling tile or sections and, again, smothering and protecting the accelerants for identification. The same results can occur from falling drapes, again smothering the fire and collapsing interior partitions.

Collapsing ceiling panels and partitions protected areas of ignition where accelerants were utilized to destroy a gambling casino. The proprietors retained the services of an imported torch who used alcohol in generous quantities in several storage spaces including one where the lottery and keno tickets were stored. He used alcohol not only because it was a good booster but also because it was available in quantity on the premises and he reasoned that discovery of its presence in the fire debris would excite no particular suspicion.

Following ignition, early displacement of wood shelving caused packaged tickets to collapse onto one of the areas of origin thus preserving the evidence of the accelerant. The collapse of second-level partitions preserved at least two other separate and distinct points of origin and also one ignition device.

The investigator must be alert for the containers used to transport the booster or accelerants to the premises. Arsonists fully recognize that there is always an element of 'risk' in the moving of the necessary fuels into a projected fire scene, particularly the type of premises where such materials might not normally be found. For example, the arsonist may bring in his materials early or he may move them in shortly before the fire. In any event, it is seldom that he wants to take the chance of carrying the containers away from the scene *after* he has prepared the scene and sets the fire. As a rule, he relies upon the fire to obliterate identification of the containers if it does not indeed totally consume them. He usually trusts there will be little other than the usual tiptoe investigation.

In some cases, of course, plastic containers or even plastic bags are utilized and, under such circumstances, they may be destroyed beyond identification in the fire. In many cases, however, a container may be discovered in a collapsed area or in an area of the building where incineration was not complete. This occasionally happens where boosters are used in several locations and where ventilation is insufficient for total sustained combustion in one or more of the spaces.

The container may be metal or glass. It should never be assumed because it has been through a fire that it cannot be identified, traces of its contents cannot be identified or, last but not least, that latent fingerprints cannot be raised. Such possibilities should never be discarded without consulting with the appropriate experts in the crime lab. This is particularly true in reference to glass containers including fragments from incendiary devices thrown into or against premises. In such circumstances, the party throwing the device usually assumes it will be shattered on impact or destroyed in the fire. While he may be safe in this assumption in most cases, the record produces evidence to the contrary. Latent prints may be recovered from remaining glass and metal fragments including some from the bottom of the container and the lid.

The investigator should be alert for the incendiary device, including apparent *modus operandi*, designed to stand out to the extent that it appears obvious to the investigator that the arson resulted from vandalism, burglary, or another outside source. "Too obvious" evidence may be just that—*too* obvious. The investigator should keep his feet firmly on the ground. This type of stacked deck appears in occasional business fraud fires. Some business people, faced with financial difficulty or tax problems, for example, occasionally ransack their own files, along with simulated evidence of forced entry and with the evidence of actual cause of the fire unmistakenly incendiary. While some burglars and vandals happen to be crude or obvious, most burglars are usually somewhat more subtle. In cases of suspected forced entry, burglary, and arson, it is good practice to call in an experienced burglary detective to check out the apparent means of entry.

If it really is the work of a burglar, the burglary expert may recognize the M/O and be instrumental in identifying the burglar. After all, it is important to identify the burglar, particularly if he is incorporating incendiarism into his M/O. Experienced investigators on forced entry are often able to recognize a simulated forced entry for what it is—a phoney. This is also important in identifying the arsonist. Further, if the involved premises are protected by intrusion devices of any kind (and there are many in the sophisticated and unsophisticated class), experts in this field should be consulted. Was the system operating at the time of the fire? Or was it cheated? Fire alarm systems, if present, should also be examined with equal care. Monitoring stations and logs should also be carefully scrutinized.

Plastic containers of rigid and nonrigid construction are frequently utilized not only to transport flammable accelerants to a projected scene but are also used at separate locations, placed over floor furnaces or adjacent to wall furnaces or open flame heat sources where the plastic will react to the heat and ultimately release the accelerant which, when heated, will quickly vaporize and react in the form of flaming or explosive combustion. Under such circumstances, the melted plastic residue may be identifiable on the grill or the floor adjacent to the heat source. Experience has shown that where the container residue may not be identifiable as such, the container cap or portions of the base may be recoverable. In circumstances where thin plastic wrapping bags are used, such as by hanging over or near an ignition source, the problem becomes more complex and residue of the envelope may not remain for identification. Only the local intense peripheral temperature rise may be apparent and it will be evident in the otherwise unexplained deep char on exposed combustibles surrounding the suspected area.

This may be apparent in warehouses and storerooms where localized flash type fires have occurred, with the usual significant pattern of rapid temperature rise, and where flash type combustibles had no reason to be present; the phenomenon may also be accompanied in the form of displacement of glass, lamps, and partitions. Residue from the perimeter as well as the suspected seat of fire should be retained for laboratory analysis; this includes displaced glass. Residue from the perimeter and spaces some distance from the seat of ignition should be carefully scrutinized since it may have been propelled from the origin by explosive force or convection currents developed in the fire.

It is generally recognized that gasoline is probably the most commonly used booster or accelerant. Perhaps this is because of its availability and common domestic use. Its low flash point (-45° F.) and explosive tendencies are well known and respected by experienced arsonists who, although utilizing these qualities when necessary for their purposes, prefer other safer fuels such as kerosene which, of course, have a much higher (and safer) flash point and is therefore more stable for casual distribution throughout a premises where multiple "sets" may be desired and, also, for the utilization of trails (lines of communication) between the sets. Some arsonists have been known to use the more explosive gasoline at the individual sets with kerosene trailers connecting the sets and extending from a preselected igniting station, usually outside the building. Because of the relatively low volatility of kerosene, it burns evenly and dependably along the trails to the sets. Kerosene, in normal atmospheres, is unlikely to explode. Being less volatile, kerosene leaves more distinguishable residue, usually in the form of carbonized trails and carbon patterns where it has been applied; evidence of this can often be photographed and should always be recovered and preserved for laboratory analysis.

Arsonists occasionally utilize kerosene saturated or charcoal lighter fluid saturated cotton or even synthetic rope—usually about clothesline size—as wicks for trailers. Such wicks are sometimes used where timing is desired. The timing depends upon predetermined tests with the particular liquid selected and the wick utilized. The trailers are reliable and have been utilized to connect separate spaces by passing the trailer through holes in windows, partitions, transoms, and air conditioning and duct systems. The investigator should be alert for this type of wick or trailer where widely separate origins are suspected and where heating, air conditioning, shafts, and stair casings may have been utilized. For example, in a recent commercial fire, a booster in the form of gasoline was utilized in a storage space. Kerosene saturated, rope type trailers connected the sets to the main water heater burners. When the water cooled sufficiently, the automatically controlled burners came on, igniting the trailer communicating the fire to the boosters.

Some arsonists occasionally utilize alcohol because its presence may be reasonably explained on a particular premises such as some types of warehouses, restaurants, and cocktail lounges. There is also a general belief that alcohol vapors are more difficult to detect. Alcohol is even more volatile than gasoline and therefore provides considerable risk to the arsonist unless he knows what he is doing. Liquors of ninety to one hundred proof are successfully used as accelerants; alcohol is occasionally diluted with water to reduce its volatility and resulting explosive tendencies. Unlike gasoline or other petro fuels, alcohol *can* be diluted with water and, up to a certain percent, it will continue to burn. Fire investigators should be alert to the possible use of alcohol, particularly where it is normally present. For example, in one case, the owners, finding that ordinary waste baskets, though completely filled with scrap paper and ignited, usually burned out without igniting the premises simply because the contents did not produce high enough temperatures for a long enough period to ignite the furniture and walls at the location and under the conditions desired. They learned that by adding alcohol to the mix in the waste basket, the fire would produce enough heat for a sufficient length of time to create the environment for a continuing fire. In that particular case, the proprietors wanted it to appear that the origin of the fire was accidentally caused by disposal of unextinguished cigarettes in a waste receptacle located under the rear end of a service bar. The test waste baskets simply burned out without igniting the underside or wall behind the bar. The added alcohol did the trick. The details of their M/O, learned from a bartender who "talked," were verified in further investigation and duplicated by experiments in a mock-up re-creation of the environment.

The investigator should be alert to the use of other commonly available accelerants—for example, paint thinner and charcoal lighter fuel. Hydrocarbon thinners are usually of the naphtha group and may contain less volatile fractions than gasoline but somewhat more than that of kerosene. Since naphthas are widely used and easily available, especially in cleaning and industrial establishments, arsonists like to use them. Their presence in unusual locations should be carefully scrutinized.

Historically, candles have been utilized by arsonists as reliable delayed ignition devices. Their availability is well known. Their reliability as delayed ignition devices depends upon the ingenuity or expertise of the arsonist; they are not used by experienced arsonists where explosive hydrocarbon compounds are present. They may be used as igniters where gases are systematically released into an environment. The candle is positioned high or low depending upon whether the type of gas to be used is lighter or heavier than air and further depending upon the rate of introduction into the target environment, the condition of ventilation, and the air capacity of that space. In such cases, ignition occurs when the gas reaches the candle flame position or level in explosive mixture with available atmospheric oxygen.

The timing depends upon the expertise of the arsonist. The candle is also utilized as a timer by arrangement of combustibles around its base, the candle gradually burning down until the flame reaches the prearranged combustible materials such as tissue, oil saturated shavings, and powder trails. The predictability of the fire may be gauged in the burning time of the candle. Most commercial candles are stearin, tallow, paraffin, or wax; the average rate of burning is approximately one inch per hour although the time may be speeded in the small diameter decorative candles. The arsonist may select the candle best suited to his timing after he conducts his own experiments.

The use of candles in incendiarism continues, particularly where timing is desired; there are fairly current examples of its use in commercial *and* domestic fires in dwellings. It has been utilized in the setting of forest, brush, and grain fires. While a match or matchbook, or delayed action cigarette placed in a matchbook may be totally incinerated and, therefore, unidentified in a fire, this is frequently *not* the case where candles are used. Melted wax will often persist through a fire at the point of origin. For example, the candle ignites the "kindling" at its base which, in turn, ignites the combustible exposures as the fire builds in volume. Soon, the occupancy or space may become a roaring inferno. However, the fire and heat goes up and away from the ignition point, leaving it to burn out in its own manner; or the burning walls, ceiling, or objects above the set may fall, smother, and otherwise protect the residue. This, in turn, may be found by the investigator when he comes along if he knows what to look for and if he takes the time and makes the necessary effort to search it out. The wax residue may be clearly identifiable, even at the base of the wick, and further identifiable for laboratory analysis.

While some investigators (and authors) discount the continuing use of the candle as a delayed action device, this is apparently because they haven't really been "where it is" or because they neglected to look. It is true, of course, that more sophisticated methods are now available such as mechanical and electrical devices. It is equally true, however, that arsonists occasionally like to keep things as simple as possible.

It should be apparent from the above described, more obvious indications of arson that fire scene investigation cannot be considered lightly. Fire scenes require more than a casual glance and fire scene investigators must know what they are looking for and how to interpret it, meanwhile keeping their feet firmly on the ground until all the facts are in.

ARSON 'APPEARING' AS ACCIDENTAL

This section is intended to alert the investigator to some of the more common devices used to produce the illusion of natural or accidental cause. In earlier sections, we discussed preliminary "size up" or survey of the fire scene and determination of the security of the involved premises *prior* to the fire. We have discussed methods of determining the areas of origin and point or points of origin and reading fire patterns. We have discussed the more common accidental and natural causes of fires. In the preceding section, we discussed some of the more obvious signs of arson that are apparent to the investigator who is willing to take the time to carefully examine the scene.

Now, we arrive at the next plateau. This is the arson designed to deceive the investigator. This type of fire has become more common during the past decade. There are a number of reasons for this, including the availability of intrusion and alarm devices and equipment; the widening range of industrial and construction procedures; the increase in fraud oriented crime where fire destruction is a necessary part of the criminal fraud picture; and the increase in criminal sophistication in setting fires that has clearly outdistanced the efforts of fire and law enforcement agencies. (See Final Report of the National Fire Prevention & Control Administration, National Academy for Fire Prevention & Control, U.S. Department of Commerce, September, 1976. Also see Survey & Assessment of Arson and Arson Investigation, prepared by Aerospace Corporation, Report to U.S. Department of Justice, October, 1976.)

For example, the incidence of arson increased 325 percent in the decade ending 1975—more than any other indexed major crime such as murder, rape, aggravated assault, robbery, burglary, larceny, or vehicle theft. The records reflect (and the reports note) the lack of trained arson investigators and up-to-date scientific investigative data and equipment. The report noted that arson arrests and conviction rates are lower than any other major crime. For every 100 fires classified as incendiary, about nine persons were arrested, two convicted, and 0.7 incarcerated. This compares with 21 arrests, 6 convictions, and 3 incarcerations for every 100 persons of the non-arson related major crimes.

The reports reflect the lack of adequate, sophisticated analysis and research equipment dealing with fire and explosion cause.

Experience indicates that some of the more ingenious arsonists, whatever their specific motives, plan the cause of the fire to appear accidental to the investigator. They often attempt and occasionally succeed in introducing the "red herring" to the fire scene with increasing success. For example, large quantities of shredded packing paper may be placed throughout an attic space, and the fire may then be triggered by any ignition source or type, at a time selected by the torch. The result is the usual total consumption of the shredded packing paper regardless of the ultimate destructiveness of the fire. The origin of the fire is usually correctly attributed to the attic space and the cause is usually evaluated as "electrical" since, after all, most of the circuits extend through the attic space and, after such a fire, conductors and boxes are usually extensively damaged. This *modus operandi* has been commonly utilized in restaurant and cocktail lounge fires. The "mechanic" retained to set up the job knows well that the average fire investigators seek out the lowest and heaviest burn and, in the absence of solid evidence of accelerants or other affirmative evidence, the inquiry is closed.

In a recent school fire, painters had been painting the interiors of several classrooms in one building. At the end of the day, the painters cleaned their brushes, covered the equipment with drop cloths and locked up the premises. Some time after 3:00 a.m. the following morning, the Fire Department was summoned to the scene. The interior was heavily involved. The doors were locked and forced entry was made whereupon the flames were extinguished. Fire Department investigators classified the cause as spontaneous combustion. This was principally based upon the fact that painting had been in process on the previous day and that the origin was inside one of the spaces where paints and brushes had been stored. They neglected to ascertain that the paints were water base; that the origin was on the opposite side of a partition from where the brushes, paints,

and canvas were stored; and that, although the doors were locked upon arrival of the Fire Department, a window had been broken, from outside in, prior to the fire. They further overlooked the residue of an incendiary device inside the broken window and at the seat of the fire.

Ingenious methods are utilized by some arsonists for hire whereby sparks may be produced when a motor is activated or when a selected electric circuit is closed. The environment for ignition of combustibles, including volatile or explosive fuels, can be created and an ignition source may be introduced in the form of reduced electrical conductor size incapable of carrying the electrical load. This may cause heating along the conductors with resulting ignition of the insulation or of kindling or tinder type fuels placed alongside the selected conductors; ignition may also occur from short circuit arcing or sparking when the conductors come in contact, thereby igniting a gas or vapor environment. This type of fault may be introduced into a conductor system in the form of one or two wires of a multiwire cable; this is a condition which may be easily overlooked even by experienced electricians. The discovery of this type of cover-up can only be expected where the origin of the fire is carefully and accurately noted and then the environment of the origin is carefully analyzed for specific cause, usually with the assistance of a competent laboratory.

Clock mechanisms can be used to channel electrical current into selected conductors (to close certain circuits and to open others) which, in turn, heat deliberately undersized conductors, creating sparking or arcing which ignites the desired fuel. Clock mechanisms are more commonly utilized in improvised, high velocity, explosive devices (bombs). Electric light bulb filaments have been used to achieve extremely high temperatures for planned ignition of an explosive environment. They are energized by a time switch such as a clock-activated display sign and mechanism. The investigator should be alert to the position of extension and service cords, particularly where the bulb or "use" end is found in a location that really doesn't make much sense.

Air-conditioning systems have been utilized in clouding the scene with apparent accidental cause. The systems can be used to communicate hydrocarbon vapors through the premises from a predetermined source and ignited by a gas pilot or other selected flame source; this, again, can be regulated by a pre-selected thermostat. The natural gas in a heating system may be released into the system or into the general occupancy spaces, again, to be ignited by a selected ignition source. The use of the system by the arsonist is only limited by his technical knowledge and abilities; his continued success depends upon how well he can adapt the equipment at hand in a manner that will be accepted by the investigator as reasonable accidental cause.

The professional torch is usually well versed in the doctrine of reasonable doubt and the judicial presumption that the fire was accidental rather than incendiary. He is also well aware that the burden of proof rests squarely upon the shoulders of the investigator.

The fire investigator should be alert for fresh tool marks on connections; for unscrewed or loosened fittings; and for the presence of residue of trailers or wicks in plenums, ducts, and at other equipment or structural locations. He should request the assistance of experts in plumbing, mechanical, or electrical fields where he does not clearly understand what he sees.

Chemical ignition may be utilized by arsonists and when it is stated that this method of operation is unique, this is somewhat less than factual. One respected author has indicated that the use of chemicals in incendiary fires would only occasionally be found. The record, during the past decade, indicates that chemical incendiaries are more commonly used by arsonists, including those involved in civil disturbance fires, and not only in urban but suburban and rural areas. So-called instructional manuals, carefully indexed and covering the construction and use of incendiary and explosive chemicals, were published and placed in circulation in the late 1960s and early 1970s. One of the more widely circulated was *The Anarchist Cookbook.*

This "text," available in some public and campus bookshops across the country, covered such widely divergent subjects as the use of firearms silencers; chemicals and gases; how to make tear gas in your basement; how to make nitroglycerin, mercury fulminate, blasting gelatin, ammonium nitrate compounds, gelatin dynamites, pictric acid, nitrogen tri-iodide; and so on, along with how to improvise substitutes for incendiaries and explosives from common household materials. The text also covered the use of the more common detonators: walk traps and time delay devices, as well as homemade hand grenades, bangalore torpedoes, Molotov cocktails, book traps, door traps, and lamp traps. In brief, there is no shortage of detailed and illustrated instructions to the arson or sabotage minded person if

he is willing to search out the information in some of the bookshops across the nation. Further illustrative was the publication and circulation of *The Militant's Formulary,* copyrighted in 1970. This also dealt with, among other things, how to procure and compound the ingredients of explosives such as potassium chlorate, dynamite, gunpowder, igniters, chemical delay igniters, and bombs, including match head bombs and pipe bombs. An example of one of the paragraphs dealing with special types of bombs is quoted as follows: "Flower pot shape charge—This is a real crowd pleaser. When it explodes, the flower pot disintegrates but for some reason the junk goes where the thing is aimed. The theory of the shape of charge is explained in Lenz's *Explosives and Bomb Disposal Guide.* Potassium chlorate, TNT, or dynamite is needed as the device doesn't provide the confinement gunpowder must have for a proper explosion. The hole in the bottom of the pot is covered with a round piece of tin with a hole only large enough for a fuse. An aluminum TV dinner tray is first flattened and then shaped into a shallow cone. Fill the cone with nuts, bolts, and nails and cover them with heavy paper. The device is usually put in a paper sack and armed with a chemical delay. The best place to put it is in the gutter under a car."

The investigator who ignores the availability of incendiary and explosive data to the criminal is a very gullible person indeed.

One of the "hotter" compounds commonly available is thermite, which is a mixture of iron oxide and aluminum. This compound produces an extremely hot fire resulting, after ignition, from the marked difference in the heats of combustion of iron and aluminum. When this is used, the investigator may find that the burning compound has produced sufficient heat to melt such materials as iron, eating its way quickly through floors and exposures and igniting every lesser combustible in its path. The investigator should be alert for deep-pitted or deep-seated burn where penetration is outside the norm. The pattern may produce a residue of aluminum oxide, iron, or its oxide, which should identify its presence.

There are numerous chemical combinations susceptible to spontaneous ignition and these can be controlled by the arsonist for a predetermined time spectrum from a desired ignition time. Properly introduced into the target spaces, the combination and device may be destroyed if the fire is extensive, or scattered in the demolition from explosion. On the other hand, the telltale residue may go undiscovered in a quickly extinguished fire, the fire being classified as "careless smoking," "electrical," "spontaneous combustion," or the cause most commonly utilized—"undetermined."

Such compounds are numerous and varied; they include hydrogen peroxide, phosphorus, and a great variety of oxidizing compounds and chemical gelatins. When the ignition point is identified at a fire scene but the cause is not clearly apparent, laboratory assistance should be requested; preferably, the assistant should visit the scene for he may recognize the symptoms in the fire residue that are unrecognized or misunderstood by the fire investigator. The laboratory may then be able to come up with a factual analysis of the precise cause.

Today's arsonists often improvise, knowing that investigators' suspicions may be aroused by the presence of unusual residues in the debris such as gasoline or acetone in a furniture store display area or the living room of a dwelling. The arsonist may select a booster which will provide the initial heat to involve the desired space yet which will leave no definite, identifiable trace.

Today's commercial, artificial fireplace log is such an example. When used according to the package instructions, and in a conventional fireplace, it is an even burning, safe commodity. The average artificial fireplace log weighs about six pounds. Lighted without breaking open, it will burn steadily for between 1½ and 3 hours, radiating a nice even flame. One log produces an average of 60,000 to 100,000 Btu's and the more common products are made up of oil treated sawdust (sometimes cedar), with a copper based coloring compound which may be apparent in the ash residue if a very careful search is made. The arsonist has utilized it by breaking open the package, placing it at the desired location, and igniting it. The broken package produces a very hot fire over a much shorter period and burns out completely in the process.

The enterprising arsonist likes it because of its heat producing capability. It can be purchased practically anywhere; is compact, clean, and easy to transport, place, and ignite as desired; and leaves little identifiable residue.

Summarizing this section, the planned arson may, at first, appear as a perfectly natural or accidental fire. The illusion created by the enterprising criminal for the investigating authorities may only be penetrated by training, experience, and a considerable amount of understanding and patience. The old wives' tale that arsonists are the traditionally wild eyed misfits, sexual deviates, or mental incompetents is not compatible with the record that is available today. There *are* skillful, intelligent, and calculating people who set fires for a various number of reasons. They will continue to do so only as long as the percentages, as the gamblers like to say, are in their favor. This is well known to experienced fire and law enforcement authorities who have been where it is and who have looked the problem squarely in the eye.

CHAPTER XIII

EXPLOSIONS

Explosions were briefly discussed in Chapter VI, in the context of combustion of solids, gases, vapors, and flame spread. The phenomenon of explosion, in an appropriate environment, can cause fires; conversely, it can result *from* fires. It is relevant to fire cause investigation. Perhaps, before we move too far along, it should be emphasized that there is a difference between the subject of explosion investigation and bomb investigation. Some laymen and even a few fire investigators confuse the terms and investigative activities. Explosions may result from bombs or other deliberately or criminally designed devices or environments or they can result from compounds or environments through purely accidental means. Bombings are characterized as part of many explosions when, factually, this is not the case. It is with the phenomenon of explosion and its cause that we are mainly concerned in this chapter. To identify the criminally designed explosion, we must understand the accidental one.

This chapter is not intended to cover the entire spectrum of explosions and bombings, but rather to sufficiently introduce the subject of explosion, emphasize its place in the arson scene and, hopefully, to suggest the need for calling in qualified experts for analysis of the scene as the circumstances require.

Although we will discuss high velocity explosives and bombings later in this chapter, perhaps it is appropriate to state at this time that arson investigators, unless specially trained, are not bomb experts or bomb disposal specialists. Conversely, bomb disposal experts are not necessarily specially qualified to evaluate a fire or explosion scene. In appropriate circumstances, each may be of invaluable assistance to the other.

Perhaps this chapter will suggest the importance of further research and study in the field of explosions, explosive devices and compounds, and reactions that may be expected. There are numerous excellent texts and reference data available in public and university libraries as well as specialized manufacture, use, and identification data available from

manufacturers on explosive compounds, blasting compounds, detonators, caps, fuses, igniters, fuse and prima cords, squibs, delaying devices, and boosters. Hundreds of pages of descriptive literature has been published identifying and describing the availability and use of these materials through manufacturer's sources. Additional data is available through the U.S. Departments of Commerce and Transportation concerning the transportation and storage of unstable compounds, including explosives. Some of the suggested reliable reference tests dealing with the phenomenon of explosions, explosive and unstable compounds, liquids and gases, and explosive atmospheres are: *National Fire Protection Association Handbook on Fire Control* (Fire Protection Handbook); *National Fire Protection National Fire Code, Vol. 3,* dealing with combustible solids, dusts, and explosives; *City of Los Angeles Dangerous Chemical Code; Explosives,* by Dr. H. Brunswig, translated and annotated by Drs. Charles E. Monroe and Allan Kibler of George Washington University; and *Explosions: Their Anatomy and Destructiveness,* by Robinson.

The Institute of Makers of Explosives (IME) maintains offices at 420 Lexington Avenue, New York, N.Y. Most major explosive manufacturers are members of the Institute which publishes safety data concerning the handling, use, hazards, and identification of explosives.

At the moment, suffice it to say that the availability and use of explosive compounds has become more sophisticated in recent decades and has introduced more potentially explosive hazards into our everyday environment. It is also fair to state that the development and utilization of high velocity explosives has advanced considerably during the past twenty years. Continued advance is only limited by man's ingenuity and this is evident in the present wide range of devices from the tiny electric squib right up to the fission bomb. The so-called old fashioned powder, dynamite, and nitro explosives are being replaced by the plastics, which are safer to store, transport, and mold to the particular need. In 1974, the major explosive manufacturer in the country announced it would probably discontinue production of dynamite over the next few years and replace it with the new water gel called Tovex which may make dynamite obsolete. The use of gelatins and plastics is becoming increasingly common for a number of very practical reasons.

It must always be remembered that some criminals keep abreast of technical developments, including the availability and use of sophisticated explosives; they know how to obtain what is needed, how to improvise the substitutes for the materials not readily available, and adapt them to their particular criminal designs.

During the past decade, the nation has experienced thousands of bombings in this category; the statistics for the latest reported year indicate there were 2,074 such bombings involving all types of property which resulted in 22 deaths and 136 personal injuries, with property loss from such bombings reported at $27,003,981.

Property attacked in the bombings includes law enforcement facilities, public utilities, banks, public buildings (Federal, State, and local), commercial establishments, churches, and private dwellings. Records indicate that explosions and bombings can result from individual acts or group acts such as civil disobedience dissidents and quasi-revoutionary individuals and groups. At the other end of the spectrum, the explosion or bomb job is occasionally utilized by individual criminals for insurance, fraud, or intimidation; it is also utilized by criminally syndicated factions for persuasion or intimidation tactics as occasionally evidenced in warehouse, dock, truck, and transportation facility explosions. Explosions are also criminally utilized to cover evidence of other crimes.

Explosive technique is often successfully utilized by the more sophisticated criminal to screen the evidence of another crime such as arson or fraud. The reason he is successful is because the device is not suspected and accordingly not recovered. Of course, the bomb device placed in an airport locker and detonated is usually quickly recognized for what it is and adequately investigated. On the other hand, explosive compounds placed in a warehouse or truck are often sufficiently destroyed in the demolition and fire that follows so that no productive investigation follows. The first day's headline "Mysterious Explosion Rocks Warehouse" is quickly forgotten. Or, "Ruptured Gas Lines Cause Explosion and Fire in Downtown Office Building" didn't tell the story of how the gas lines became ruptured in the first place because the investigators did not make sufficient examination as to what really caused the gas lines to rupture. They were trapped by the effects rather than concerned for the cause.

EXPLOSION DEFINED

Webster has defined explosion as "an exploding, especially blowing up; bursting with a loud noise; detonation." Now, while this may well be correct, it doesn't really tell the investigator much.

In its chemical sense, the phenomenon of explosion is the sudden and usually enormous expansion of liberated gases from a solid or liquid combination. The term explosive, when applied in the chemical sense to such solid and liquid substances that possess the facility will, under certain circumstances, undergo instantaneous decomposition and extend throughout the entire mass. This is accompanied by disengagement of heat. The substance in the process is thus converted into the gaseous products of decomposition.

According to authorities on the subject, solid or liquid explosives generally represent gases or vapors condensed into the smallest mass either in liquid or solid form. These include materials used in the general explosives and blasting fields as well as Liquid Petroleum (LPG) and Liquid Natural (LNG) fuels under appropriate conditions.

Although certain uncompressed gases and vapors are generally termed explosive, this is not basically true so long as they are pure and under ordinary pressures. Their flammability or explosibility is contingent on mixture with oxygen or other gas combinations in appropriate percentages and with the introduction of an ignition source. We have discussed flammable liquids, vapors, and natural gases elsewhere in the text in connection with the accidental and intentional causes of fires.

Although certain agricultural and industrial dusts are also commonly discussed in connection with explosions, these, like vapors and gases in a normal atmospheric environment, are not basically explosive *per se*. They are only explosive in appropriate mixture with oxygen and in the presence of an ignition source such as static electricity, spark, or flame. Dust explosions may occur in improperly vented elevators, bins, industrial operations where organic or chemical dusts may be present with atmospheric oxygen in proper mixture, or in other improperly ventilated environments.

The phenomenon of explosion is usually accompanied by displacement of windows, bulkheads, stationary objects, and structural members depending upon the velocity of the explosion. Velocity will be discussed later in the chapter. The explosion may be accompanied by heat or flame depending upon the involved compounds; again, there may be resultant ignition of exposures depending upon location and composition of those exposures and the explosion environment. For example, high velocity explosions, such as those involving some of the nitro compounds, may shatter exposures without igniting them whereas lower velocity explosions, such as those involving petroleum vapors, may ignite contents, walls, and framing over a wide area. Dust explosions may ignite low density walls, building framing, and accumulated debris. Natural gases, the lighter than air group, occasionally ignite tinder like exposures such as wallpaper, curtains, drapes, and hanging garments. Again, it is emphasized that the capability of all explosives and explosive environments to ignite combustibles must be considered very carefully in the context of the particular environment, time spectrum, and condition of combustibles. Quick, expedient answers to all questions posed by an explosion scene should be regarded with suspicion.

Explosions capable of moving or displacing fixed walls and objects must be considered capable of loosening or fracturing gas and fuel service lines, thereby releasing flammable and explosive fuels into the environment which may cause secondary fires and explosions. They may damage framing or structural support of electrical conductors and appliances, thereby creating the environment for electrical arcing and further secondary damage.

Explosions are characterized by release of energy, often so rapid as to appear instantaneous. According to the *National Fire Protection Association Fire Protection Handbook,* Vol. 12, "An explosion is an effect—not a cause." The very excellent section on explosions continues that explosions may be categorized in four general groups:

1. Energy release generated by rapid oxidation such as gasoline vapor (air explosion).

2. Energy release generated by rapid decomposition such as in a dynamite explosion.

3. Release of energy such as that caused by excessive confined pressure in a boiler, drum or other container such as an LPG or compressed gas cylinder under expanding pressure. (Other authorities do not classify this type of phenomenon as a true explosion since it is a result of failure by internal pressure rather than of the chemical reaction order. Of course, it is true that internal pressure can shatter a steam boiler and cause extensive peripheral damage. Also, the pressure release of compressed gas chambers can release compounds under considerable force, and the immediate dispersal of the compounds, quickly mixing with surrounding atmospheric oxygen, can cause further explosive damage upon reaching an ignition source.)

4. The release of energy created by nuclear fission or fusion. (Uranium or hydrogen bomb explosion.)

The NFPA Handbook offers an additional, infrequent cause of explosions not included in the above four categories: uncontrolled polymerization with rapid release of energy. (See NFPA Sections 6 and 7, Chapter IV.)

The rapid oxidation type of explosion, categorized above in NFPA group 1 is not uncommon regardless of extreme safety and engineering standards concerning transportation, installation, maintenance, and use of facilities and equipment. As indicated in the chapters dealing with causes of fire, this type of explosion can result in accidental leak. Unfortunately, it can also be deliberately contrived or manipulated.

Heavier than air and lighter than air gases are common in domestic and industrial/commercial use today. It has already been pointed out how ignition can occur and under what conditions explosion and fire may be expected. The hazardous properties of these gases and compounds are set out in detail in Table 6-126 of the *NFPA Fire Control Handbook.* Additionally, tables are available from the U.S. Department of Commerce, the U.S. Bureau of Mines, the American Society of Testing Materials, and the American Gas Association.

The explosions generated by this class of fuels are generally categorized as diffuse which is actually an extremely rapid combustion resulting from a favorable mixture with oxygen. This is simply a rapid extension of flame through the mass of the explosive environment. Although there may be explosive pressure generated, the phenomenon is not in the category of high velocity. The shock wave is about 3,000 feet per second as compared to a shock wave of 25,000 feet per second in the case of the true explosive compounds which will be discussed later.

The diffuse explosion in the average structural environment moves walls and other items or forces of resistance depending, in part, on volume. It may displace glass and, under the right conditions, ignite combustible exposures. This type of explosion seldom produces the brisance encountered in high velocity explosions that are created by the true explosive compounds.

The initial displacement may be high or low depending upon whether the gas or vapor is heavier or lighter than air. The initial source of the leak and, often, the ignition source may be identified by tracing the flash or scorch pattern along exposures on the periphery of the explosion. The flash/scorch pattern may be evident although a fire did not occur because there was insufficient sustained heat to raise the temperature of exposures to their burning temperature. In other words, the explosion produced high temperature for only a brief period. The high or low initial displacement is *not* a hard and fast rule of whether the vapor or gas was heavier or lighter than air.

Variables influence displacement. For example, was the initial leak high or low? Ventilation, as exhibited by modern air-conditioning systems, affects air movement and, accordingly, leaking vapor dissipation. The position of doors, windows, and halls can be factors influencing explosive vapor location and the resulting displacement and heat manifestations on the remaining exposures. The patterns must be carefully considered before any attempt is made to definitely classify the vapor involved.

For example, an explosion and fire caused extensive damage to a resort hotel at a mountain ski area. The seat of the explosion was determined to be the hotel basement. The resulting fire spread from the basement, to the stairwell, through the lobby, and up the stairs, thus involving upper floors.

Investigators found what they believed to be a gasoline trail extending from the basement, across the back yard, and about 100 feet down a ravine to a trash burner where they conjectured the fire had been triggered by human hands. They classified the cause as arson. More detailed investigation disclosed that a liquified petroleum gas supply tank was located outside the rear of the hotel. The LPG fuel was utilized for certain hotel kitchen and domestic purposes. The line entered the premises just outside a staircase to the basement. Approximately two hours before the explosion, a delivery truck had inadvertently backed into the regulator and damaged the system. They had driven off without reporting the incident. The weather was extremely cold— below zero. The heavier than air LPG vapors escaped from the damaged coupling and seeped down

the stairwell into the basement. They also followed the descending contour down the ravine in back of the hotel until they reached the trash burner where they were ignited by the open flame of the burner. From this point they flashed back up the gully and into the basement where the confined explosion occurred. Here was an example of premature evaluation of an explosion scene before all the evidence was in.

Explosives are compounds capable of rapid decomposition which is usually accompanied by exerted pressure on adjacent surroundings. This is the result of an extremely rapid conversion of the material into hot gases or volatile substances that have a larger volume at the surrounding pressure than the volume of the original compound. Since at the instant of formation the gases occupy only the volume of the explosive, their pressure is relatively higher than the normal pressure. Their pressure is raised by the generation of heat in the course of the explosion and overbalances the restraining order of the surrounding matter. Rapid expansion in the form of explosion follows.

Thermochemistry tells us that most chemical change is accompanied by either evolution or absorption of heat. If the exchange between a reacting environment and substance is delayed, the temperature of the reacting substance either increases or decreases—the former is exothermic and the latter is endothermic. In general, only the former (exothermic) includes fast explosion processes because chemical reactions are usually accelerated by heating and decelerated by cooling.

It is generally stated that an explosion must:

1. Contain a substance or mixture which remains unchanged in ordinary conditions and environment but reacts rapidly on proper stimulation such as from an igniter, friction, shock, or heat. For example, drop tests indicate conditions of explosion on the following compounds:

EXPLOSIVE	RELATIVE HEIGHT IN INCHES FOR A 5 LB. WEIGHT
Mercury fulminate	2
Nitroglycerin	4
Tetryl	8
Picric acid	14
TNT	20
Black powder	30

However, it is well known that thin films of many explosive substances are much more reactive chemically than larger masses of the same material. A thin film of molten explosive caught between solid walls in such a way that it cannot move when struck, not only must absorb all the kinetic energy of the impact but must also do so under unusual conditions of reactivity making it more sensitive to impact or pressure than usual. Under such conditions, TNT, an ordinarily insensitive explosive, may become nearly as sensitive as lead azide. A coarse, granular mass of explosives contains voids and openings between the crystals. The solid may move into these voids when pressed or impacted and this, to some extent, cushions and absorbs the blow. An explosive that is a mixture of crystals and liquid should have intermediate sensitivity between that of the straight liquid and that of the crystals alone.

One of the most well known, early, highly explosive materials was amatol. This was used in World War II and was a mixture of TNT and ammonium nitrate. Less sensitive explosives, such as TNT, may be detonated by more sensitive ones, such as tetryl. Tetryl, in turn, may be detonated readily by mercury fulminate which is much less powerful but extremely sensitive.

2. Yield gases whose volume under normal pressure but at the high temperature resulting from explosion is much greater than that of the original substance.

3. Be exothermic in order to heat the products of reaction and thus to increase their pressure. All types of chemical reactions may produce an explosion. Acetylene decomposes explosively into its constituent elements of carbon and hydrogen. These elements, in the form of charcoal saturated liquid oxygen, may then be explosively combined into carbon dioxide. The explosion of nitrated organic compounds such as TNT or nitrocellulose occurs due to the transformation of the original compound into several new ones. The more heat and gases an explosive produces per unit volume, the more powerful it is.

For general convenience, explosives have been divided into propellent and detonating groups, but the distinction is not sharp. Detonating explosives have been further classified as high explosives and initiating or primary explosives. Basically, primary explosives, upon ignition, explode almost instantly whereas high explosives may be burned under some conditions without exploding. Explosives are generally designed and compounded for specific use depending upon the ojectives desired. The high explosives are designed for military purposes and for

mining, excavation, construction, and even demolition in industry and commerce. The primaries are designed for detonation of the high explosives.

Dynamite has long been one of the more commonly used explosive compounds and, in plain language, embraces the cap sensitive materials containing nitroglycerin. Nitroglycerin is produced from glycerin, ethylene, glucol, nitric and sulphuric acid, and is generally considered as the most sensitive high explosive around today. It is often utilized by being absorbed in various compounds depending upon the need and explosive response. Some of these compounds are:

Ammonium nitrate
Apricot pits, finely or coarsely ground
Bagasse
Calcium carbonate
Charcoal
Chalk
Corn flour
Ground coal
Guncotton [nitrocellulose]
Paraffin
Potassium nitrate [saltpeter]
Lampblack
Oat hulls
Corn meal
Milo
Wood pulp [sawdust]
Wood flour
Sodium chloride
Sulphur
Zinc oxide.

An undesirable characteristic of most dynamites is their inability to resist water. This was overcome by adding nitrocellulose and other moisture resistant compounds. Certain dynamite has a tendency to deteriorate in storage, thereby becoming extremely unstable.

U.S. Military dynamite contains no nitroglycerin. Instead, it is a mixture of TNT RDX, engine oil, and cornstarch. It produces an explosive velocity of about 20,000 feet per second. Since it contains no nitroglycerin, it doesn't freeze and does not exude as does the conventional dynamite under adverse storage or aging conditions. It is nonhydroscopic, usually remaining effective under water up to about twenty hours.

BLASTING CAPS

Blasting caps are typically about ¼″ to 3″ long and made of bronze or aluminum. There are two types commonly in use: electric and nonelectric.

The electric caps traditionally have two wires ranging from four to twelve feet in length—these are the conductors. The nonelectric blasting caps traditionally have an open end for insertion of the safety fuse which will be described later and which communicates the flame through the fuse core and into the cup of the cap thereby activating the fuse.

In the electric cap, the introduced current is communicated to a bridge wire similar to the filament in a light bulb; this filament heats when the current hits it and thereby ignites the igniting charge in the cap. There are two basic types of electric caps:

1. The instant. In the instant, detonation is just that—instant.

2. The delay. In the delay, there is a powder charge which provides a delay that may be regulated for up to about fifteen seconds. Then the base charge is detonated.

Electric caps can and do malfunction and their residue may be found embedded in a soft surface at or near the scene of an explosion. Electric caps can also be accidentally fired by static electicity or accidental electronic transmission. Nonelectric blasting caps detonate when the "spit" or flame finishes its journey through the core of the cord and arrives in the safety fuse. This type of cap is not subject to accidental detonation from static electricity or electronic transmission as it is sensitive only to impact. This type of fuse may also be found in the debris of an explosion scene.

EXPLODING WIRE DETONATORS

Although not so commonly used, this type of detonator is generally available and occasionally used. The difference in this device is that the break wire explodes wherein the more common electric blasting cap bridge wire heats. The exploding wire detonator is used for less sensitive explosives such as PETN. The device is also considered safer since it is not prone to activation from static electricity.

SAFETY FUSE

This is a rope-like material used to transmit the flame to the detonator or nonelectric blasting cap. It is not unique as to color. A powder charge extends through the core. There are various types of fuses, both safety and waterproof. It is usually constructed much the same as detonating cord—wrapped with fabrics, plastics, and rubber, depending upon manufacture and intended use. It is identifiable from sec-

tions of the core filter material, according to mode of manufacture. Standard military burning time of an M700 time blasting fuse is approximately 40 seconds per foot. Average commercial burning time is 40 seconds per foot; 125 seconds per yard at 3,700 feet above sea level graduated down to 120 seconds per yard at sea level. Burning times deteriorate with age.

Blasting fuse residue may be recovered from explosion scenes. Where multiple charges may have been involved, there is always a chance that an unexpended fuse may be recovered and quickly identified.

IGNITER CORD & CONNECTIONS

These items are used to light safety fuses in blast situations involving multiple locations. The cord burns between one and eighteen seconds per foot, igniting the charged connector which in turn ignites the safety fuse. The connector looks like the blasting cap except where the end is slit for insertion of the igniter cord. The safety fuse is inserted, in turn, in the opposite end and then crimped into place. *Ignitacord* is available in black (rated at 4 seconds per foot), green (8 seconds per foot), and red (18 seconds per foot). It consists of thermite powder wrapped in textile and wire—about $1/16''$ in diameter.

DETONATING CORD

This is a cord or rope-like explosive wrapped in textiles, rubber, and synthetics. The inner core contains a high explosive: either PETN (Pentaerythrite) or RDX (Cyclotrimethyllenetrinitramine). The velocity is about 20,000 feet per second. Detonating cord has been in use for many years. Identification by color is unreliable and this cord can be confused with safety fuses by nonexperts—with sad results. More positive identification can be made by examination of the color of the central core filler material. The detonation cord core is either white (PETN) or pink (RDX) whereas the cord of the safety fuse is usually black or grey filler material (powder). Some inert training detonator cord is manufactured in blue, nonexplosive, jute core. RDX cord can stand about 325° F. for short periods. PETN is also more sensitive than TNT. Traces of bad sections may be found at suspected explosion scenes.

X CORD

This is an explosive in a metal-clad, linear container designed to provide time delays in microsecond range and to sever materials with explosive velocities extending upward from 20,000 feet per second depending on the core. The core is often contained in continuous metal sheath, lead, or other metals including aluminum, and is available in round, square, and rectangular configurations. It is commonly used in commercial blasting as well as aerospace, aircraft, and industrial operations.

ELECTRIC SQUIBS

Most squibs have the same basic appearance as blasting caps but utilize burning or deflagrating charges rather than detonating ones. Therefore, they are not practical in detonating charges; their use is basically for ignition or pressure development in closed chambers. Squibs can produce extremely hot flames, igniting powder, vapors, etc. They may be found in suspected explosive atmospheres where explosions have occurred. They may also be found where fires of criminal origin are suspected from electrical-mechanical delayed action means.

WATER GELS

Water gels or slurries are receiving increasing use. The terms are used interchangeably to describe mixers of oxidizers and compounds containing various percentages of water and are classified as blasting agents and explosives. Detonation may be by blasting cap or the compound itself may contain an explosive detonating ingredient; these combinations increase in use and variety.

The water gels have a base of ammonium nitrate with added thickeners to produce consistency and a sensitizer with aluminum possibly added. The compounds may also contain a gas forming, heat producing chemical. One major explosives producer estimates that water gels will virtually replace the traditional dynamite within the next five or six years because of its storage life, adaptability, and increased safety in handling.

BLASTING AGENTS

Blasting agents are defined as oxidizers intended for blasting but not otherwise classified as explosive. These have seen increased commercial use because of availability and relatively moderate cost; they are less sensitive than many other explosives and, according to some authorities, safer to handle. The most common formula is ammonium nitrate and fuel oil, usually about 94 percent ammonium nitrate and 6 percent fuel oil. Adding finely divided aluminum in-

creases the detonating velocity. Blasting agents usually require a booster in addition to the blasting cap. The size of the booster depends upon the particular make-up of the blasting agent.

TWO COMPONENT BINARY EXPLOSIVES

These are fairly new and contain two compounds which are mixed to make the explosive. One mixture includes a powder and liquid. The powder is white and the liquid yellow. The color may be altered somewhat. The mixture becomes explosive about five to ten minutes after the ingredients are introduced into the common environment. The powder form is a specially processed ammonium nitrate with combustion additives; the liquid is basically nitromethane. Detonation velocity is from 15,000 to 20,000 feet per second. Unlike dynamite, this compound has a good storage life if kept in tightly closed containers. It is easy to dispose of by dumping on the ground, in which case it will rapidly evaporate and is no longer sensitive. The mixed compound is also available in plastic sticks and flexible packaging for shaping to the need or configuration. The powder and liquid form is reported to be shock and friction resistant and is not sensitive to bullet impact. The compound reportedly has long storage life if maintained in sealed containers.

There are also liquid binaries on the market consisting of red and yellow colored mixers which become somewhat orange in color when merged and at which time they are subject to detonation.

BOOSTERS & PRIMERS

Boosters and primers have been developed to initiate the more recently developed, relatively insensitive blasting agents. It will be recalled that some of the newer blasting and explosive compounds are more insensitive to shock, friction, etc., than the older compounds; therefore, special primers and boosters have been innovated to insure the desired detonation. Some of these cast primers or boosters develop extremely high detonating velocity. Developments and usages are complicated, widely varied, and selected according to the particular assignment of the explosive. Casts and configuration vary depending upon the need.

MILITARY EXPLOSIVES

The investigator may encounter situations where so-called military explosives may have been used. The most common is TNT (trinitrotoluene). This is the least sensitive of the more common demolition block explosives. The rating is about 22,000 feet per second and it is not normally sensitive to bullet impact. It comes packaged in one-quarter, one-half and one-pound blocks and is yellow in color. The wrapping is usually labelled high explosive. Packaging may be round, square, or rectangular with the blasting cap well secured in the end.

Other military explosives include various size detonating blocks (tetrytol) which are yellow or buff in color and can be packaged for various transport capabilities including backpack/haversack or belt. It will detonate on bullet impact about 50 percent of the time and is being phased out of military use for this and other reasons. Explosive velocity is around 24,000 feet per second.

There are other compounds in highly portable configuration such as C-3 which is more powerful than TNT with an explosive velocity of about 25,000 feet per second; mixtures with RDX and plasticizers, usually yellow in color.

C-4, which is a steel cutting explosive, is light brown or buff in color; explosive velocity is about 26,000 feet per second. This has a putty-like consistency and becomes hard at low temperatures. Normally, it can be readily molded. It is not sensitive to bullet impact.

M 112 Demolition Charge is packaged C-4 and comes in 1″ × 2″ × 11″ packs, usually with 30 per packing carton. The unit pack is in a white plastic wrapper and may also be wrapped in olive colored nylar filon wrapper.

The M 118 Demolition block, Flex-X data sheet, or explosive is a two-pound block composed of four one-half pound sheets. Each sheet has a piece of pressure sensitive adhesive tape attached to one side. The sheets contain 63 percent PETN which is the same sensitive explosive used in detonating cord. The block is not bullet sensitive and is designed as a steel cutting charge.

M 186 Roll Demolition Charge is identical to M 118 except that the make-up is a 50-foot roll. The material is 3″ wide and ¼″ thick and can be quickly cut to any desired length. This versatile material is easily transported and capable of wide adaptation and precise use.

Cratering charges are in 40-pound water tight metal cans packed with 10 pounds of TNT and 30 pounds of ammonium nitrate. The TNT is the booster and is located in the middle. The explosive velocity is about 11,000 feet per second and the compound is used for building demolition, cratering,

and ditching. The container usually has a ring in the top for lowering the charge; there is usually a cleat on the side and a tunnel for the detonating cord.

The above are only the more common types of devices and charges; new developments are in progress. When in doubt as to the identity of an object or debris at a suspected explosion scene, clear the area and call in an explosives expert.

GUNPOWDER

Gunpowders are actually less explosive than flammable; however, when tightly confined in a container and ignited, they become explosive. Gunpowder consists mainly of saltpeter, sulphur, and charcoal. It ignites at about 480° F., generating a temperature of about 4,000° F. and a pressure of about 6,000 atmospheres.

The emphasis on gunpowder is its flammability. When the saltpeter in the powder is contaminated with chlorine, the autoexplosive compound nitrogen chloride is formed. If gunpowder is repeatedly heated and cooled, a chemical change may result in spontaneous explosion. The introduction of potassium perchlorate, even in fractional amounts, may produce spontaneous explosion. Gunpowder may be ignited by pressure, shock, friction, static electricity, spark, or flame.

It is well known by law enforcement authorities that gunpowder has been frequently used during recent years—and continues to be used—by individuals and groups generally classified as militants, dissidents, and protestors. Some of these groups improvise and utilize so-called bombs, including explosive and incendiary devices. Construction of the devices is only limited by the ingenuity of the individuals or groups using these devices. The more common improvisations are in the pipe bomb group. The pipe and powder are items easily obtained and difficult to trace. The pipe size depends upon the design and target. The ends are usually threaded and capped with detonation afforded by safety fuse or improvised cord.

Some of the more vicious individuals and groups occasionally load the pipe with glass or metal fragments designed to produce shrapnel effect. Improvisations vary with the plan and assignment. Property attacked includes law enforcement installations, public buildings and public utilities, such as power and transformer stations, and utility distribution stations. Some of the more easily detonated plastics that have been described earlier in this chapter are also used against these types of targets. For example, the improvised bomb or the more sophisticated plastics may be used in damaging transformers, opening selected fuel line locations where the release of gas or liquid may vaporize with the atmosphere and result in further explosions and fire.

Explosive type bombs are also utilized in conjunction with the incendiary device sometimes called a Molotov cocktail. Such incendiary devices were used against tanks in World War II, with considerable effect.

These devices, usually glass or plastic, are varied in size and design. The contents may be gasoline with a low flash point or a higher flash point fuel, depending upon the objectives required. For example, the gasoline or low flash fuel may be mixed with adhesive material which provides additional intriguing possibilities to the criminal using the device.

The incendiary bomb may be designed to shatter on impact or to leak upon penetration of a window, ultimately burn through, and then explode. It may be designed to burn slowly on the exterior of the container for a predetermined period until the jacket is penetrated whereupon the contents will spill with resulting explosive combustion. Again, these devices are as varied as the ingenuity of the criminal who uses them. The components and ingredients are available at any supermarket or shopping center.

The use of bomb-type explosive and incendiary devices is not limited to the so-called lunatic militant or dissident fringe. These devices are used by well organized intimidation groups, including labor dissidents as well as other criminals with specific design in mind. One example is the enterprising, hired torch or professional arsonist who is schooled in the methods of his trade and who is well aware that these incendiary and explosive devices are commonly used by militants and dissidents. What better diversionary tactic could he utilize to liquidate his client's property?

It is again emphasized that suspected explosives and explosive scenes should *always* be handled with extreme care. Again, when in doubt, clear the occupancy or area and call in qualified explosives experts.

Federal agencies, including the U.S. Treasury Department and the U.S. Army Explosive Ordnance Disposal Assistance (EOD), have special explosive units with equipment and expertise in the bomb and explosives field. An increasing number of State and local law enforcement agencies are training and staffing explosive and bomb details. Many public safety agencies now staff their own explosive and bomb units who work in harmony with Federal and State units.

Army regulations stipulate that the Army has the responsibility for disposal of all unneeded military explosive ordnances, regardless of type, age, or origin. Army regulations authorize the Army to assist civilian law enforcement whenever public safety is threatened by the presence of suspected or known homemade bombs or hazardous commercial explosives. The conditions under which Army assistance can be provided are generally: 1. The requesting agency has no EOD capability of its own, or that capability is already overburdened; 2. The requesting agency (Federal agencies excepted) executes a civil support Release and Reimbursement Agreement which is signed by the requesting agency and releases the government from liability as a result of EOD assistance provided by the Army. No charge is made for disposal of military ordnance or homemade bombs or arson devices or explosives which are abandoned.

An Explosive Ordnance Disposal detachment will not participate in searching for bombs or improvised explosive devices. When responding to a properly authorized request for assistance from civilian authorities, EOD personnel may function as technical advisers, initiate procedures to attempt to render a hazardous item safe, and dispose of or assist in disposal of the item or material. They will, within proper guidelines, assist local law enforcement agencies in developing their own capability in this field including training, safety, recognition, and reporting procedures pending arrival of EOD teams. EOD units are not located in every state and law enforcement officials who anticipate a need for this service should contact the nearest local Army base and initiate planning procedures which will provide the necessary assistance when required.

The same pre-planning procedures should be initiated with the U.S. Treasury Department and other Federal agencies within the scope of their authority to cooperate. Time is of the essence when bomb/explosion situations are involved. The arson investigator should establish a liaison with the agencies he expects to call on such occasions.

Over recent years, laboratory research has developed increasingly sophisticated equipment to locate and identify explosives and devices. Research continues. Some portable equipment is available for pre-detonation examination and scene search and also for post-explosion analysis. Most high explosives are organic residues and are often destroyed in the fire. Metals and fragments are important: detonators or parts thereof, parts of cords or fuses, container fragments, and squib or timer fragments may be found in the crater or surrounding environment. Occasionally these fragments can be put together, identified, and even traced. Dogs are becoming increasingly useful in identifying explosives.

Where it is apparent that a high velocity explosive device has been used, it should be beared in mind that the bomb or device may have been used to perform the same function as a firearm would in a homicide, or gasoline in an attack against persons or property in a fire where the device was intended as an instrument of arson. In the circumstance that a possible unexploded device remains, the procedures of the bomb disposal expert and the investigator may be quite different and should not be confused. Each must be utilized according to his particular area of knowledge and the considered objectives of his expertise.

It has been well stated that qualified bomb disposal personnel can be of great assistance at an explosion scene because they are familiar with the construction, components, and functions of most devices. They may recognize signs and fragments that would be missed by the average investigator regardless of how careful he may be.

Explosion scenes often attract large numbers of police, firemen, newspaper reporters, and all manners of bystanders. This not only presents a risk of additional injury but may also result in unwittingly destroying the integrity of the scene, losing key evidence, and hampering the assigned investigators in their search of the scene. In explosion scene examinations, suspected bombing or otherwise, much of the physical evidence which may be crucial to identification of the cause or specific device *and* to the suspect may be fragmented and scattered over a wide area.

Prompt isolation of the scene is extremely important. In earlier chapters, we have discussed the mechanics of fire scene examination in some detail. The procedures of isolation of the scene, preliminary survey and size-up of the examination problem, and how to go about it applies with even more emphasis and detail to explosion scene examination.

Additionally, the reality of the explosion may present the reasonable possibility of additional explosions, wilfully introduced to the scene, resulting from damaged or fractured gas or fuel lines, or from hazards created by structural conditions.

The officer in charge of the scene must be promptly designated. He, in turn, must determine what personnel and equipment resources will be required. He must decide what sectionalizing and diagramming of the scene is required. This will depend upon the size and complexity of the scene. He must assign selected personnel to examine the scene, in accordance with the size and complexity of that scene.

The officer in charge must further arrange for the logging, identification, and preservation of evidence collected, coordinating this activity with photography of key areas and evidence recovered. He must also assign the necessary personnel to interview witnesses and explore investigative leads as circumstances demand.

Explosion scenes, particularly major ones involving extensive fire loss, are subject to misinterpretation. This can grow out of initial confusion by the extent of the damage which is compounded by administrative "pulling and hauling," and the lack of qualified, assigned personnel at the scene. In such cases, explosions resulting from definite criminal acts can be classified as accidental! This leaves the criminal free to strike again on an occasion best suited to him. Conversely, accidental explosions can be labelled as "bomb caused explosions" and result in the expenditure of thousands of investigative man-hours that could have been more properly used in the investigation of a crime that actually occurred!

Recently, in a western city, a massive explosion and fire occurred in the early morning hours of a weekend. The building of origin was totally demolished in the explosion and fire with burning fragments blown over an area of several hundred feet around the perimeter and involved structures over a wide area around the perimeter.

Initially labelled as the work of a random bomber who was known to have been active in other parts of the city, the source and cause was later identified as a cargo of a highly unstable compound improperly cartoned and temporarily stored in the warehouse of origin under which conditions the explosion could only have been reasonably expected. At the other end of the spectrum, a theater fire occurred in the early morning hours in a suburban community; witnesses reported a low muffled explosion preceding the fire. Initial investigation by the Fire Department classified the cause as probable leaking gas explosion. Further investigation disclosed that the theater had been having serious problems growing out of the class of film being shown: there were financial problems. Residue recovered from the seat of the fire inside the theater disclosed that gasoline had been introduced into the ventilating system and ignited from a safe position outside the building. The cause of the fire was incendiary.

CHAPTER XIV

PHOTOGRAPHY IN ARSON INVESTIGATION

Photographs are silent witnesses that can be more convincing than the most eloquent witness. It is often difficult for even the most articulate investigator to accurately describe a fire scene, an object, its position, and when it was found, in a manner that will be understood (or fully accepted) by the judge or the jury. This is particularly true in some fire cases. Judges and juries are usually lay people with limited knowledge of fire. Occasionally, they entertain misconceptions concerning the behavior of a fire or explosion. Sometimes, they are misled or confused by previously introduced testimony or simply by what they have read in the newspaper about fires, firemen, or policemen and how they operate. A television, radio, or newspaper story of a fire may have termed it a holocaust. Later, a defendant is brought to trial charged with setting the fire. Expert witnesses testify to finding minute particles of glass from an incendiary bomb. The jurors, recalling the news coverage and holocaust description, cannot help but wonder about the credibility of the expert witnesses who now produce these small fragments of an incendiary device. They may even go so far as to disbelieve him! After all, they say to themselves, "How could this man recover those tiny fragments from the scene of a holocaust?"

There is much truth to the old adage, "What I can see I may believe." Jurors have often stated, when questioned by the trial attorneys, after the verdict is reached and accepted by the Court, "If those officers really found what they said they found, then why didn't they take pictures to show us so we could see it with our own eyes?" Judges, prosecuting attorneys and defense counsel often raise the same questions, and with probable cause.

It is often weeks, months, and sometimes years before fire cases come to trial. Usually the fire scene is no longer available. The jury cannot be taken to the scene because it has been materially changed.

In many cases, opportunity to photograph conditions and physical evidence depicting point of origin, pointers, and patterns of spread are irrevocably destroyed in overhaul of the fire scene or during demolition or repair which may be initiated within hours following control of the fire. The scene may be altered or its integrity discredited because of adjusters, repair people, and others trampling through critical portions of the area. Picking up and examining objects for good reason can alter the fire scene.

Photographic recording of how an important item of evidence was uncovered and how it looked at the time may be forever lost if the object and its immediate environment is prematurely moved. Its real credibility may be destroyed by neglect in recording the discovery and removal at the proper time. The proper time is at discovery. The scene may be inadvertently or deliberately altered minutes later.

Viewing an item of evidence in the courtroom may be completely out of context with its original appearance as found. The judge or jury (or both) may simply not understand how it could have been discovered and recovered in the condition it was reportedly found.

This is particularly true in cases of fragile items that might have been protected by falling ceiling tile, partitions, or drapes in the early stages of a flash fire or explosion. The collapsed materials may smother the items, thereby protecting them from further burning and preserving them for discovery by careful search procedures. As previously indicated, judges and juries do not always understand the behavior of fires and explosions and the sometimes curious phenomenon whereby fragile items can be preserved by the fire or even the explosion. Therefore, they are suspicious of testimony even produced by investigators and expert witnesses who attempt to explain without the support of step-by-step photographic verification. It might be fair to state that juries are not always impressed by theories and terminologies beyond their personal experience and perception. This is where good clear factual photographs may bridge that communications gap.

Photography of an object, as found, as removed, and from all sides, may spell the difference between the acceptance of the statements of the investigator or witness and disbelief of *what* he says he found, *how* he found it, and exactly *where* he found it. Factual supporting photography can spell the difference between conviction and acquittal.

Step-by-step photography, sometimes called progressive investigative photography, may be illustrated by the space-by-space and layer-by-layer examination of the fire scene which supports the testimony of the investigator that he carefully and systematically examined the entire fire scene; that he first conducted a perimeter examination noting the general characteristics, patterns, and initial areas of ventilation of the fire; that he next conducted a space-by-space examination; that he determined the general area of origin and through a more detailed examination he reached the specific point of origin; and that he next examined and identified certain described items of physical evidence from which he concluded the cause of the fire. A complete investigation will disclose that photography was utilized in recording the step-by-step process.

If the investigator has photographic documentation for his testimony, three important objectives will be achieved with the Court and the jury: 1. They will understand what the investigator is talking about because they can see it with their own eyes; 2. They will believe the investigator knows what he is doing and will be more inclined to accept his credibility; and 3. If they accept his credibility, they will be more likely to accept the integrity of the evidence as presented. This is particularly true where the fire or explosion has caused considerable damage and where detailed (delicate and possibly minute) items are allegedly recovered. It may be equally important in situations where damage has not been extensive but where physical evidence tells a particularly significant story, such as the existence of incendiary devices; plants; trails between spaces or buildings; incendiary arrangements in attics or ventilation and air-conditioning spaces; or the position of security switches, locks, or alarm systems.

A good photograph is worth a thousand words. If the scene is worthy of investigation, it is worthy of photographing without delay.

Progressive photography is often important in proving the *res gestae* (the full story) of the crime. Its importance in recording and illustrating the evidence of *corpus delicti* (body of the crime) cannot be overemphasized. Photographs are often very useful in illustrating the *modus operandi* (method of procedure) of the criminal. This is true in certain classes of fires set by so-called compulsive fire setters. (In one notorious series of incendiary fires of this type, the arsonist used greasy, oily journal box waste from railroad cars.) This is also true in certain classes of insurance fraud fires. (One example is the utilization of waste paper packed through attic spaces in order to provide the appearance of an electric cause in the attic.) It is also true in cases of certain classes of fires and bombings by revolutionary or civil disturbance types (i.e. explosive pipe bombs, certain specific types of Molotov cocktails).

Systematic early fire scene photography may become valuable at a later date when questions arise which may not have been foreseen at the time of the initial investigation. For example, the question may be, "Were the gas stove burners on or off?" In a recent gas explosion fire, the investigative picture changed from a possible suicide attempt to attempted murder. The Fire Department had responded to the explosion scene where the victim was rescued but badly burned. He was immediately transported to emergency hospital. There had been a flash explosion. The drapes, bedding, and the victim were burned; the utility company investigation determined that there were no faults or leaks on the service side and further eliminated line leaks inside. Several months later, questions were raised by police agencies concerning the matter. It was found, by inquiry with the Fire Department, that photographs had been taken of the kitchen range. They clearly showed that the burners were in full on position as was the oven burner control. There were no cooking utensils on the stove or in the oven.

Departmental and administrative objections are often made at the needless expense of fire scene photography. While such objections may be valid in some instances, the cost of a few packs or rolls of film and proofing is a very minor item when it is considered that even one or two out of the many may spell the difference between winning or losing a case, or when their availability, for reference, may answer questions unforeseen at the moment but are of major significance later. The availability of photographs for investigative reference has, time and again, saved countless man-hours of investigation. The comparison of the cost of even dozens of photographs is insignificant in comparison with the cost of investigative man-hours and probable continuing uncertainy as to what really happened because the evidence is no longer available to examine.

Where fatalities are involved in fires and explosions, the bodies may have been removed prior to arrival of the fire investigator. In such cases, the shadowed or protected areas, showing the original body position, will usually be apparent and should be photographed. In many cases involving fires and explosions, it is important to carefully scrutinize the areas adjacent to the shadowed or protected area of the body location for evidence as to cause of the incident. This applies to criminally caused incidents where the suspect may have been inadvertently trapped by premature ignition or detonation of the device he had installed. It is equally applicable to the accident scene because the victim may have been holding or using an instrument or item that will tell the story of what happened even though the victim is no longer able to relate what happened.

Very often, injured persons or bodies are removed in such a manner that what they were doing or what they were holding may forever be lost to the investigator. The importance of carefully photographing the shadow area and surrounding environment cannot be overemphasized. They are particularly important in showing the original location of objects during a fire, i.e., the location of a container used to spread accelerant. Photography of the item before and after it is moved shows the protected area of carpet or shadow. These protected areas are often apparent and show up well in careful photography. They confirm the presence of the incriminating item prior to and during the fire or explosion. Experience has shown that the defense occasionally raises the question as to "whether or not the incriminating item may just possibly have been planted there *after* the fire."

Reconstruction of items moved by firemen or through other means can be made by evaluation and photography of the shadowed or protected floor and wall areas in concert with physical reconstruction on the fire scene.

Photography of spectators at the fire scene is useful in cases involving series of incendiary fires or in fire and explosion incidents connected with dissidents or civil disorder. Arsonists and bombers often return to the scene after emergency crews arrive. Their planning of the incident may have been sophisticated. They may actually be extremely intelligent although their motives may appear unusual to the lay person. Generally, their curiosity concerning the response of the emergency and public safety crews and the reaction and investigative tactics of the police are usually intriguing to them, particularly the prima donnas of the fire setters and bomb tossers. Careful photographic recording and analysis of such scenes may produce reasonable human common denominators which can be definitely identified by further routine inquiry.

In this regard, where bystander photography may be relevant, it is good practice to contact trusted news and television sources who commonly appear at emergency scenes and can photograph spectators without rousing apprehension by the average suspect. Revolutionary types and dissidents are occasionally inclined to seek out news press photography even to the point of talking for the record. These comments and observations may later identify the person or group and connect them with the incident.

An example of photographic identification of a suspect at the scene was a case in which a large warehouse was destroyed by fire. The tenant/occupant claimed he was visiting in an eastern city, several hundred miles from the scene, at the time of the fire. He claimed that he did not return to the scene until the afternoon of the second day following the fire. He produced a witness to confirm his alibi. The investigators subsequently discovered the face of the tenant (and his "witness") in a photograph of bystanders taken while the fire was in progress. The alibi was blown and the tenant and his torch were connected to the scene.

Photography can be utilized to keep the record straight after a case goes to trial. For example, a major fire destroyed aircraft hangars, several aircraft, and other valuable contents. The origin centered around the malfunction of a gasoline pump. The cause focused on a manually disconnected vapor release line which permitted gasoline vapors and raw fuel to accumulate inside the pump casing and the pump area. A fire and explosion followed, although not necessarily in that order. A key witness interviewed at the scene, shortly following control of the fire, identified the disconnected vapor eliminator line. He indicated familiarity with the mechanical functions and purpose of the vapor eliminator line and the possible results of a disconnect of the line inside the pump cabinet. Photographs taken during interview of the witness showed him pointing and identifying the vapor eliminator line. A close-up was taken showing the hand of the witness, in detail, pointing to the disconnected section of the line.

Several months later, the same key witness took the witness stand and declared under oath that he never saw the disconnected vapor eliminator line and that he most certainly had not discussed it, on the scene, with the investigators. He denied he ever observed the uncoupled section of the line.

The color photographs were introduced into evidence showing the key witness pointing to the disconnected section of the vapor eliminator line; another photograph, interrelated by overlay with the above described photograph, showed the key witness talking to the investigator. The Court and the jury accepted the credibility of the photographs. The case was successfully concluded.

Factual photography can protect the innocent as well as identify the guilty. In a recent case, a fire caused extensive damage to a modern, well furnished dwelling in a suburban area. Responding firemen found that the premises were locked at the time of arrival of first witnesses and officers.

Neighbors advised that they observed the owner/occupant leave the house and drive away about a half hour prior to the discovery of the fire. An insurance company representative advised the fire authorities that the owner/occupant had materially increased his insurance coverage shortly before the fire and that the property was obviously overinsured. (What he neglected to tell the authorities was that the increase in the insurance had been upon the suggestion of the insurance agent, based upon recently inflated prices and alleged increased property values including replacement costs.)

Follow-up investigation by fire investigators resulted in a conclusion that the fire was of incendiary origin. This was based upon alleged multiple points of origin in the living room and hallway. The suspect was connected to the scene on the basis of alleged statements of witnesses that he had been observed leaving the premises shortly before the fire, that he had the only key, and that the premises were locked when the first witnesses arrived. He stated that he did not smoke. He admitted he had recently increased the insurance, thus establishing motive.

The owner/occupant was arrested and booked on a felony charge of arson.

A more detailed fire scene examination disclosed that the origin of the fire was in the wood paneled wall of the living room at an electrical duplex wall receptacle from which the fire extended up the wall, across the wood ceiling, and ignited drapes of the sliding glass patio doors and windows. The burning drapes ignited the shag carpet of the living room as they fell to the floor. This is what gave the firemen the impression of separate and multiple points of origin in the living room. The acceleration of the fire was aggravated by the heat displacement of the sliding glass doors and windows.

Qualified engineering and fire experts determined that the fire was caused by electrical malfunction resulting from incorrect and unlawfully joined aluminum and copper conductors and connections. This resulted in eventual loosening of the connections because of different heat coefficients of expansion between the two metals. This, in turn, resulted in arcing and heating which ignited combustibles of the insulation and the wall. The process can occur without activation or opening the circuit breakers.

The physical evidence was carefully photographed and preserved. This information was passed along to the District Attorney who thereupon dismissed the indictment.

Aerial photography may be valuable not only in the initial investigation of the fire but also in providing the Court and jury with a graphic picture of the scene and surrounding environment. This is particularly true of major fires such as shopping center, major multiple residential, and industrial conflagrations, as well as forest and wildland fires. During recent years, with the increased use of public safety helicopters, this type of photographic assistance has become more common. The service is also quickly available through the cooperation of the military and the news and television media.

In a recent major shopping center fire, which leveled a block of buildings during early morning darkness, aerial photos taken by helicopter patrol shortly after report disclosed the location of the fire to be in a single occupancy, with flames extending through a skylight. By the time ground emergency units arrived, the flames extended into adjacent occupancies and extended through a common attic. Early photographs by the press corroborated the space of origin. At the time of control, the entire center was leveled.

As is the case with many major fires, there were numerous conflicting statements (of witnesses) as to where the fire originated depending upon when they arrived, their point of observation, and many other human factors. There were natural conflicting statements of police and firemen for the same honest reasons. The demolition, following the fire, precluded exact analysis of the space of origin from the physical evidence alone. The aerial photographs were valuable in analysis of origin and probable cause of the fire.

A recent, major West Coast fire originated in a

brushy watershed area and rapidly spread into and through a modern residential area destroying a large number of homes. Aerial photography was valuable in showing the direction of the wind (through smoke direction), flame spread, and the rapidly succeeding ignition of wood shingle and shake roofs in the path of the fire. Photographs were valuable in explaining the apparent separate ignition in isolated areas which resulted from burning brands blown high and far in the cyclonic convection conditions created by the main fire.

Post-fire aerial photographs are useful in illustrating road and street systems where the movements or activities of the suspects may be relevant and in some instances are much more illustrative and impressive to a jury than the most carefully prepared maps and sketches. It should be emphasized that many jurors do not know how to interpret maps or sketches regardless of how much explanation and legendary data there may be.

Jurors are usually turned off by verbal or visual information which they do not understand. Most jurors do understand and appreciate photographs they can observe and evaluate, making up their own minds about questions placed before them. As a matter of fact, most jurors are very touchy about their prerogatives and that is probably as it should be.

Where distance or measurement is important, rather than merely illustrative, precise photography by skilled technicians, coordinated with altitude in flight and projection, may be necessary. This isn't usually the case, however, where fire position and behavior may be the more relevant factor. In some situations, geographic pre-fire photographs are available from Federal and other public agencies as well as construction agencies during the development of an area. These may be valuable in analysis of an entire area or project in relation to a fire, and equally valuable at the trial.

For many years, some officials have been prejudiced against color photography because of its possible inaccuracy. Some of the distrust remains. In recent years, color photography has been projected to a point of integrity and accepted by the most critical courts. Color helps because it shows colors as they are and tells it like it is.

One remaining criticism of color photography is that different people (juries, for example) interpret colors and photographs in different ways; the eyes of each individual act as a lens to transmit vision to the mind.

Color transparencies can be utilized to project life-size characteristics on a screen in a court room; this may be less costly than individual color prints as well as more illustrative, particularly when a good investigative witness can point out and identify important aspects of the projection to the Court and jury. Since the projections are on a large screen, they can see what the witness is pointing to and talking about. On the other hand, when the witness is handed a photograph, the Court and jury cannot always see and comprehend what he is pointing out while he is talking. Later, when they individually examine the exhibits, including that photograph, they may well have forgotten what the witness was talking about or missed its significance.

Good fire scene photography may be fairly compared with good autopsy photography. In autopsy photography, the full extent of the injury to the body surface is shown before and after the body is cleaned. After dissection, photos record the direction of the projectile, knife, or other implement of injury and the amount of damage done inside the body. They depict more vividly such details as trail marks in knife wounds and powder burns on gunshot wounds. So it is with step-by-step fire scene investigative photography: first, the overall or perimeter shots; second, the progress of the fire patterns, pointers, and ventilation; third, the general origin; fourth, the precise origin; and fifth, the cause. Perhaps this is an oversimplification but the procedures are comparable and equally important.

In recent years, cameras and film have been developed to the point where good photography is comparatively simple. Fire investigators have learned how to use their own photographic equipment with or without artificial light and under practically all ordinary field conditions. They have long since learned that knowledge of how to use this type of field equipment is often vital. It may be impossible to preserve a scene until a laboratory, special services, or professional photographer can get on the scene. Frequently, laboratory or special services photographers cannot remain on the scene during the often extended times necessary for step-by-step photography of a critical area as debris is removed. Department heads will not tolerate the photo lab being called back to a scene on a piecemeal basis. All too often, headquarters personnel is completely ignorant of this type of problem.

Again, it is the function of the photograph to show clearly, without distortion, the subject matter assigned to the photograph (what was found, where it was found, and in the precise condition it was found). It is not essential that the investigator be a professional photographer and it is not necessary that he be able to testify as to the light meter readings, shutter speeds, and manufacturing specifications of the film or of the processing or developing. This may have been true in the early years of investigative photography but it is no longer the case.

The Courts have repeatedly ruled, in plain English, that the test is whether or not the photograph fairly and truly reproduces the object or scene. The question is often asked of the investigator who took the photograph, "Does this photograph show the scene as you observed it?" Actually, the investigator need not have personally taken the photographs; they may have been taken under his direction or in his presence. The test then is, "Do the photos accurately represent the object or scene as he observed it?" The photos may not have been taken under the investigator's direction or in his presence; they may have been introduced into evidence earlier in the case. He may then be shown the photographs and, if they are relevant to the subject matter of his testimony, he may refer and comment in response to questions directed by counsel and according to the limitations of his expertise and understanding.

The Courts have repeatedly held that photographs need not be verified by the photographer so long as it is shown that they are not distorted and that they depict the conditions shown. The size of a camera is inconsequential. Generally, there are many excellent 35 mm cameras with automatic range finders and various light attachments that may be purchased for reasonable prices. The investigator should work out his own program of becoming acquainted with his camera and what he can expect in the wide variety of situations and environments he will encounter. The ingredients of success in investigative photography are modern reliable equipment, knowledge of the capabilities and limitations of that equipment, practice, common sense, ordinary prudence in taking the shots, patience, and, last but not least, good maintenance of the equipment.

The preparation and investigative cataloging of photographs should proceed in accordance with departmental instructions. No face markings should distort or prejudice the photo if it is expected to be introduced into evidence. Some circumstances require separate sets for use in interviewing witnesses, in which case the witness may be asked or may desire to make markings which would be desirable for statement and reference purposes. The photograph may carry a suitable date or classification or file reference number and may be further identified in reference to a map or sketch of the scene. Pre-control photographs often provide valuable information as to the origin of the fire, the identity of bystanders in situations where incendiary series type situations exist, and for the purpose of identifying suspects.

Finally, the quality and completeness of fire scene photography may spell the difference between success and failure of the investigation. If the Court and jury is presented accurate documentation of the investigation, they are more inclined to accept the objectivity and credibility of the investigation. Juries, like most other honest and reasonable people, accept and understand what they can see with their own eyes.

Figure A

The three fire incidents referred to in Figures A through O were of accidental origin. Investigation of these fires was conducted by Investigator Jim Upton of the Newport Beach Fire Department Fire Prevention Bureau under the direction of W.C. Noller, Fire Marshal.

The first incident (Figures A, B, and C and Drawings 1 and 2) occurred in the kitchen of a two story, single family residence at 2:30 in the afternoon. None of the occupants were in the house at the time the fire occurred.

Investigator Upton's examination of the scene determined that a portable broiler oven and a toaster (Fig. A) on the counter were both plugged into a wall receptacle (Fig. C arrow). The appliance cords appeared identical and were intertwined. The burn and char patterns indicated that these appliances were located in the area of origin. A close examination of the broiler oven determined that the appliance cord of this unit was plugged into the broiler circuit (Fig. B arrow). A separate connection was provided for the oven circuit.

The layout of the kitchen is shown in Drawing 1. Plastic storage drawers (see Drawing 2) had been mounted under the cabinets from one end to the other and were used for kitchen utensils, visible in Figs. A and C. The white "flow" pattern down the end of the broiler oven was from the melting and burning plastic drawers. The broiler oven control knob visible in Fig. B (arrow) was closely examined, but no on or off position could be determined.

The occupants were interviewed when they returned home in order to establish the sequence of events prior to the fire and determine who had been the last person in the house and, more importantly, in the kitchen. These interviews determined that all occupants had left the house by 10:00 a.m. that morning and had not returned all day with the exception of the owner's son, who had returned about noon for lunch. Only the mother and daughter were familiar with the use of the broiler oven and were the only persons to use it. They both informed Investigator Upton that the broiler oven had no on-off control, only a temperature control. Turning the unit on or off was accomplished by plugging and unplugging it.

The owner's son was again interviewed on a step-by-step basis. From this interview it was learned that he had come home and plugged in the toaster in order to toast bread for a sandwich. He had not used the broiler oven and was not familiar with its use. He remembered one appliance being plugged in at the time and plugged what he thought was the toaster into the open receptacle. He finished his lunch then left the house and did not return until later that evening after the fire.

Figure B

Figure C

The conclusion of the investigator in this case was that the toaster was already plugged in since the broiler oven would have been on if it had been plugged in, and since both appliance cords looked alike and were intertwined. Noting that one appliance was unplugged, the son confused the origin of the cord and inadvertently plugged in the broiler oven. The heat from the broiler later caused the plastic drawers, a few inches above it, to melt down on top of the appliance and then burn.

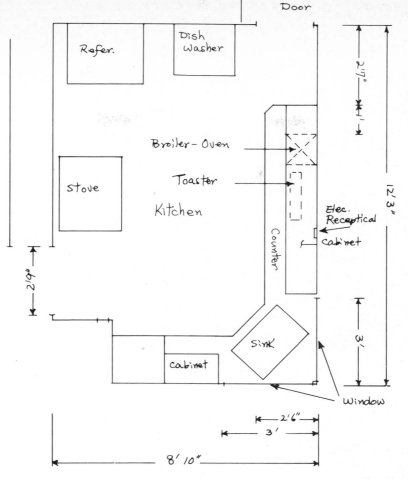

Drawing 1

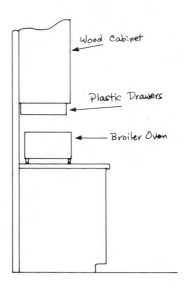

Drawing 2

It should be explained here that the mother and daughter always pulled out the cutting board, from under the cabinets, visible in Fig. A, and put the broiler oven on that when they used it.

It is of interest to note the importance the interviews played in this case as the evidence gained in that manner proved to be the key to solving the problem and provided an accurate cause determination as opposed to listing the cause merely as electrical or electrical appliance malfunction.

Figure D

The second incident (Figs. D through J and Drawing 3) will serve to illustrate the results that can be obtained if the investigator will take the time to make a careful, layer-by-layer, piece-by-piece examination of the fire scene.

This incident occurred in a single story, flat-roofed, commercial building having a number of separate occupants and was reported to the Fire Department about 4:30 a.m. The roof of the structure was burned along almost the entire length of the building. Heating and air-conditioning units were mounted on the roof above the areas they served.

A preliminary examination of the fire scene by Investigator Upton found that fire damage to all areas and rooms except one (Fig. D, Drawing 3) was at or near the ceiling and was obviously caused by a fire from above.

The heating and air-conditioning unit shown in Fig. E was found lying in the middle of the area shown in Fig. D and had been located on the roof where the rafters were burned away (Fig. F). This was the only unit to fall into the building. The investigator noted that the unit was on top of all of the debris and that all items beneath it appeared to be completely burned.

From interviews with the person discovering the fire and first arriving engine companies, the investigator was able to learn that, at the time of discovery, the fire was located in the area pictured in Fig. D; that the fire had penetrated the roof prior to discovery; and that at the time the first firemen made entry the heating and air-conditioning unit was still on the roof. Investigator Upton also noted that the drawer pulls on the steel file cabinets (Fig. G) had melted, even at floor level, and upon examination found all papers filed inside to be completely charred, including those in the bottom drawers. This condition would indicate intense heat at a low level for a long period of time and would be consistent with a long term fire originating inside the closed office space. A visual examination of the heating and air-conditioning unit indicated that it had been destroyed by a fire originating below it. However, to be certain no malfunction of the unit had occurred, an expert on that type of unit was consulted and his opinion, as was later learned, was in agreement with the investigator's.

Burn patterns, char depth, the collapse of the roof, and the observations of the firemen and witnesses indicated to the investigator an area of origin near the wall shown in Fig. D.

The investigator interviewed the occupant of the office for the location of all the items in the room (Drawing 3). He learned that a metal file cabinet and wooden credenza had been located against the wall

Figure E

Figure F

in the area of origin with a wooden desk and chair in front of it. An adding machine and calculator were on the credenza. Another calculator, a lamp, and a telephone were on the desk. A plastic waste basket was located on the floor at one end of the desk.

At this point a tail up-nose down, piece-by-piece examination of all debris began. This examination commenced outside the suspected area of origin and worked in toward it. From this examination and

Figure G

Figure H

over a period of approximately six hours, Investigator Upton was able to determine from the char and burn patterns on the remains of the credenza and the shelving within it that the fire had originated at or near floor level in that area. Further examination discovered a tangled mass of wires (Fig. H) that proved to be two extension cords plugged into a dual wall outlet (Fig. H arrow). One of the extension cords was a three-wire cord and the other was a two-wire cord. A notable difference was apparent between the two in

Figure I

Figure J

that the two-wire cord exhibited visible signs of beading and arcing along its length and the three-wire cord did not. The two-wire cord was carefully followed along the baseboard to a point near the corner of the room where the wires were found to have arced and separated (Fig. I). The baseboard at this point was burned in a "V" pattern. The tack strip was charred through to the concrete and the stud plate was charred through half its width (Fig. J). As the extension cord was lifted from this point one of the tacks

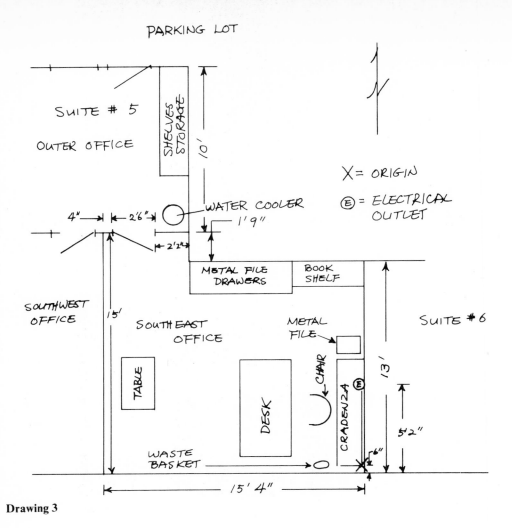

Drawing 3

from the tack strip came with it. The conditions found led the investigator to the conclusion that the extension cord had been forced down on the tack strip or had snagged on it, breaking the insulation. This resulted in a short that started the fire at this point. The other end of the wire led to the desk and provided current for the desk lamp and/or calculator. An accurate determination here was not possible because the heating and air-conditioning unit had fallen on top of this area and its removal disturbed the wires. When questioned, the occupant was not able to recall if one or both items received power from the cord.

The notable difference between the two extension cords indicates that current was available at the time the short occurred in the two-wire cord, but was not available at the time the insulation burned off the three-wire cord since the breaker had tripped prior to the fire's progress at that point. No other source of ignition was available at the point of origin.

Many workers in the area were interviewed by Investigator Upton. Among these he found one who had smelled smoke in the parking lot as early as midnight, but was unable to see smoke or locate its source. Other persons employed in the area who worked nights related that they had smelled smoke for two or three hours prior to discovery of the fire and had made a search of their respective buildings for its source. These interviews helped confirm the investigator's determination that the fire was of long duration and that it had originated from within the building rather than from a malfunction of the heating and air-conditioning unit on the roof as might have been suspected had the investigation been less complete.

The importance of a complete investigation cannot be overemphasized and no final conclusions should be drawn until all available facts can be properly evaluated. The investigator should never assume that an accurate determination is impossible simply because destruction appears to be complete at first glance. Time, patience, and attention to detail will very often provide accurate results.

Figure K

The third case, Figs. K through O and Drawing 4, occurred in a one- and two-story condominium separated by a common wall and was reported to the Fire Department at approximately 2:30 in the afternoon. This case will serve to illustrate to what extent the investigator may have to go to analyze his findings and arrive at a conclusion.

While fire fighting was still in progress, Investigator Upton began the investigation of this fire with an interview of the occupant of Unit #42. The occupant informed the investigator that while letting the cat out, she became aware of an unusual odor in her home at about 4:00 a.m. the night before. She searched the residence, but could find nothing unusual. Two hours later, she and her husband, still able to smell the odor now believed to be smoke, searched the house again, but were unable to find anything wrong.

Later that afternoon, while the occupant was sitting in the living room watching television, the gas-fed, decorative fireplace (Fig. K) self-ignited. This unit has an electric igniter and is controlled by a wall switch. She described the flame as having a green color. She went to the switch and attempted to turn it off, but the fire would not go out. She then noted that the painted wall above the fireplace was blistering and that it was very hot to the touch.

Investigator Upton questioned the occupant about the use of the fireplace and learned that it had been used for only short periods of time—one to two hours—on numerous occasions except at two previous times: once, for about four hours approximately twelve days before the fire and again for about seven hours the evening before the fire. She remembered when turning it off that it snapped and popped a lot. The occupant also informed the investigator that the house had been insulated for sound deadening purposes about six months prior to the incident.

Figure L

The investigator located the occupants of the adjoining unit, #44, and learned they too had become aware of an unusual odor, like rotten eggs or burned butter, about 4:00 a.m. that morning. Thinking it might be gas, they called the Gas Company and requested an inspection. The search of their residence gave no indication of the source of the odor.

An inspection was made by the Gas Company about 9:30 a.m. and no gas leaks were found. However, when interviewed by the investigator, the Gas Company employee indicated he too could smell the odor, but thought it outside the residence, as well as inside.*

The investigation of the fire scene began with a preliminary examination prior to overhaul. The investigator was able to determine from this that the fire had originated in the closet space in the bedroom of unit #44, or in the common wall between unit #44 and unit #42. It was evident that the gas fireplace was also built into this common wall and backed on the closet in unit #44. Overhaul in this area was limited to only what was necessary for extinguishment of the fire.

The investigator began with an examination of the debris in the closet and, finding no accidental source of ignition and the char and burn patterns indicating an origin at or in the common wall between the fireplace in unit 42 and the closet in unit 44, he proceeded to examine the debris located in the framed enclosure behind the fireplace.

The debris was skimmed off layer by layer (Figs. L, M, and N), and resulted in the determination that the space had been filled with an insulating material. This insulation covered the top of the metal fireplace box around the vent (Fig. M) and was installed to a depth of about 18 inches from the floor around the back of the unit (Fig. O). Carefully digging down into the insulation, the investigator observed alternate layers of charred and uncharred insulation (Fig. O) indicating that combustion had traveled horizontally through the material, as well as upward. This can be seen in Figs. M and O if studied carefully. The darker areas are the charred areas. The lowest point of this charring occurred in the area of the hole admitting the gas line through the back of the fireplace.

It might be pointed out here that the investigator has ruled out an incendiary cause in the closet and now has two and perhaps three possible causes for this fire: the possibility of a gas leak in the fireplace piping or gas valve; a possible accumulation of methane gas through a crack in the slab; or the possibility of heat trapped by the insulation initiating pyrolysis in the material itself.

*"Swamp gas" contains methane and hydrogen sulphide gas which is produced by the decay of organic substances and is often encountered at old dump sites and swampy areas. The condominiums were built over an old dump site. This gas is combustible and deadly.

Figure M

Investigator Upton then called in the Gas Company and had a pressure test put on the gas piping of unit #42 and found it to be tight. The fireplace unit was, in fact, still operable with only the electric control switch destroyed in the fire.

An engineering firm was brought in to test for the presence of methane gas. None could be detected and no cracks were evident in the slab.

The investigator contacted the insulating company and learned that the insulating material had a cellulose base with a borate additive for fire retardation and aluminum sulfate to kill bugs.

The investigator further learned from the occupant of unit #42 that part of the sales pitch by the insulating company was to apply a blow torch to the insulation to prove it would not burn.

Investigator Upton knew the material would support combustion since he had observed a small amount of the material still glowing red while digging down through it, even after observing firemen apply liberal quantities of water in that same area. What remained to be answered was why the borate additive did not retard ignition and how ignition had occurred.

The investigator then contacted the fireplace manufacturer and learned that an air space was required around the unit and its vent and that the temperature of its upper surfaces could be expected to be about 90° F. above the ambient room temperature. The manufacturer would make no guess as to what temperature might be reached if the air space was not provided.

Inspector Upton then researched the chemical possibilities of the cellulose, borate, and aluminum sulfate. He learned that when heated to a sufficient temperature, borate will burn with a greenish flame; that aluminum sulfate will hydrolize to produce sulfuric acid, which is an oxidizing agent that can cause combustion in the presence of a cellulose material. A sample of the insulating material was sent to two different laboratories and a third was taken to investigator Upton's own home for experimentation. The investigator found he could not ignite a sample of the material with a match, but after placing it in the oven (and smelling up the entire house) for one and one-half hours at 300° F., the material would ignite easily and glowing combustion would continue until almost all the material was consumed. He later learned from the laboratory that when subjected to heat, the fire retardant is baked off and decomposition of the insulating material results. This is accompanied by the production of water vapor and sulfuric acid, but in insufficient quantities to cause ignition.

The investigator then took some of the baked insulating material to a laboratory, placed a sample in a beaker, and allowed it to heat on a hot plate to approximately 300° F. The sample was observed to turn color from gray to brown and give off a visible vapor. A flame was passed over the beaker and through

Figure N

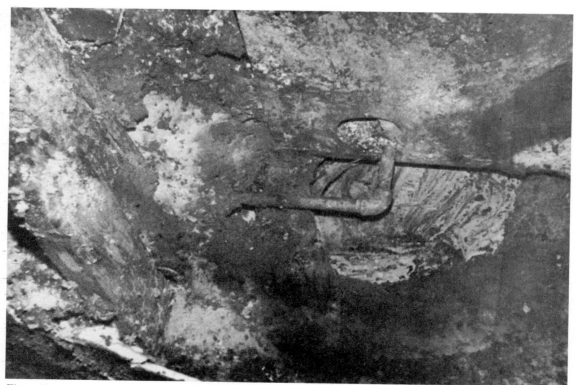

Figure O

this vapor. Ignition took place and continued on the surface of the material until it was entirely consumed.

Thus, from his own experiments and those of the outside laboratory, the investigator concluded that the fire had originated in the insulating material packed around the back of the fireplace and that the borate additive was baked off by the heat from the unit which no longer had the proper air space around

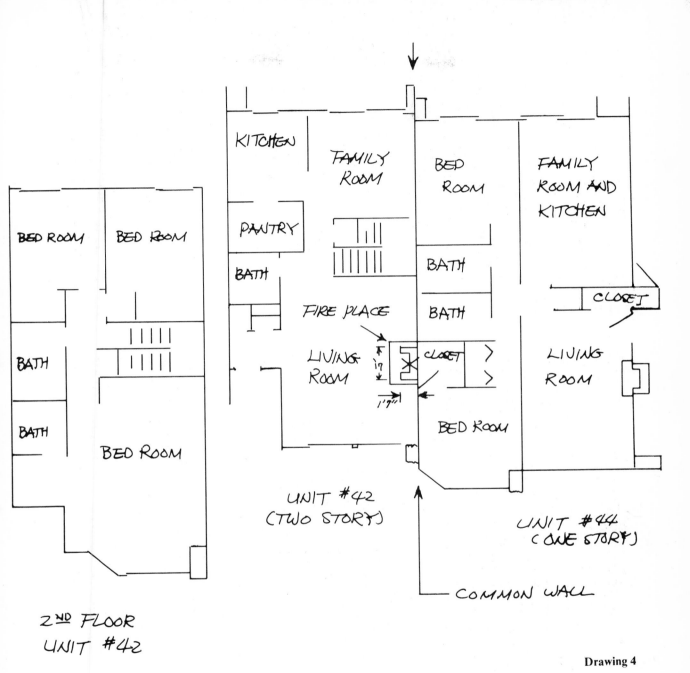

X = AREA OF ORIGIN

KITCHEN

FAMILY ROOM

BED ROOM

FAMILY ROOM AND KITCHEN

PANTRY

BED ROOM

BED ROOM

BATH

FIRE PLACE

BATH

CLOSET

LIVING ROOM

BATH

BATH

LIVING ROOM

BED ROOM

LIVING ROOM

CLOSET

1'7"

BED ROOM

UNIT #42
(TWO STORY)

UNIT #44
(ONE STORY)

COMMON WALL

2ND FLOOR
UNIT #42

Drawing 4

it. The heating of the insulating material also produced a flammable vapor, which was drawn by the flue action of the fireplace through the hole provided for the gas line (Fig. O). The vapor and the insulating material was then ignited over the open flame of the fire. Combustion continued in the insulation for several hours before visible burning in the fireplace and the wall above it was observed by the occupant of #42.

It should be noted here that although the investigator was reasonably sure that the fire had originated with the insulating material, it took several months to receive the laboratory results which led him to make his own test of the vapors given off by the heated material and to finally arrive at a conclusion that answered how the material had been initially ignited.

Figure 1

Figures 1 and 2.

Incendiary apartment fire. This was an attempt to disguise the origin as a wall furnace fire. Figure 1 shows the flash pattern extending from a wide base along the floor, actually extending diagonally away from the gas-fueled wall furnace. The fire was started by placing flammable liquids on the carpet extending from the wall at point X. The flammable liquid pattern extended across the living room as indicated in Figure 2. Approximately one quart of gasoline was applied across the carpet and was ignited from the apartment door.

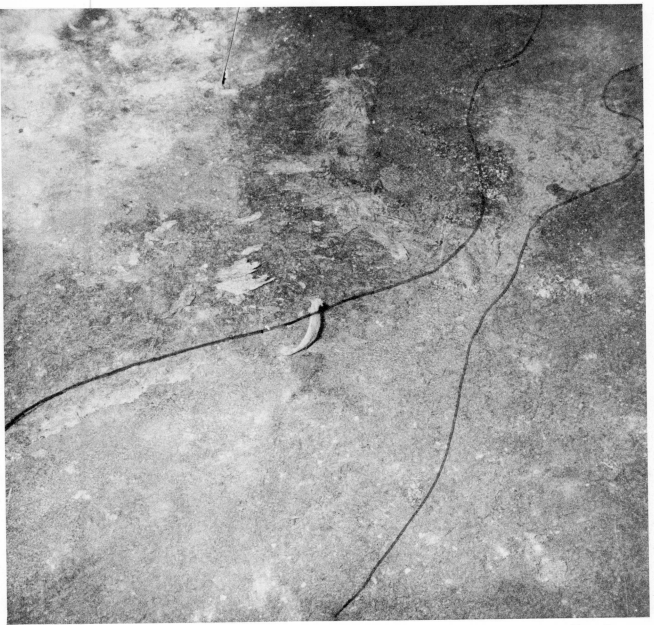

Figure 2

Household equipment and heat-producing appliances are commonly used by persons who set fires for financial reasons in order to mask the evidence of arson. Water heaters, kitchen ranges, gas furnaces, and electric irons are some of the more commonly used "dodges." The investigator should always remember that careful analysis of all physical evidence is required before a conclusion as to cause is reached.

Figure 3

Figures 3 and 4.

    Figures 3 and 4 show a fire pattern and alligatoring on a fir floor and the surface and underedge of a door. Fire investigators mistook the heavy char on the floor and beneath the door edge for a flammable liquid pattern, mainly because of the irregular flame pattern on the floor as well as the concentrated alligatoring along a wide base at floor level. Actually, this fire was a test fire set with wadded paper towels filling a standard office size waste basket and placed in a cardboard carton at the base of the door

Figure 4

shown in Figure 3. The cardboard carton and contents burned out in four minutes with the results indicated in Figure 3. The floor burn pattern is more clearly shown in Figure 4. This also shows the deeply charred and alligatored base of the door.

Char patterns can be deceiving. ALL factors must be considered and, where reasonable doubt exists, caution should be exercised in evaluation of a specific cause until laboratory facilities and expertise have been fully utilized.

Figure 5

Figures 5 and 6.

Figures 5 and 6 illustrate the fuel and ignition sources of an incendiary explosion and fire in a residential occupancy.

In Figure 5, arrows A and B point to what was originally a plier cut in the gas fuel connector. This connected the main gas fuel line to the forced air furnace indicated in the right portion of the photograph. The original cut or fracture in the connector widened during the progress of the fire as shown by the arrow in Figure 6.

The initial breach of the gas connector permitted gas to escape and gradually build in the space until it reached an ignition source in explosive (flammable) mixture. The ignition source was probably the

Figure 6

forced air furnace pilot or the gas burners when they activated. The furnace controls are shown at right center in Figure 5 and the burner manifold is shown immediately below it.

An insurance company investigator had attributed the cause of this fire as pyrolysis resulting from improper venting of the furnace. His "galloping analysis" of the origin and cause failed to take into consideration the very considerable and obvious interior wall lining and ceiling displacement.

Factual fire cause investigation cannot be done on a "hit and run" basis. ALL reliable evidence must be evaluated in an objective manner.

Figure 7

Figures 7, 8 and 9.

Figures 7, 8, and 9 are illustrative of fire damage caused by the careless use of heating torches by workmen during the process of sweating in plumbing joints. Good practice requires the cleaning of framing areas where sweating is to be accomplished. All sawdust, shavings, and other combustible waste must be cleared. Scorched framing areas must be wet down and work areas reinspected before leaving the construction site for the day. Practice and experience show that contractors and plumbers commonly hurry this process by cutting corners and failing to clean spaces where they use their torches. Fires commonly result—usually after the men leave the scene for the day. When fires do occur, they often appear as multiple origin fires. They are often classified as incendiary by reason of the apparent multiple origin hypothesis and also because of the intensity with which fires in buildings under construction commonly burn.

Figure 8

Figure 7 shows a completely demolished two-story dwelling which was under construction and adjoining dwellings under construction which were saved by the prompt and efficient action of the Fire Department. Plumbing sweating had been in process in the demolished house shortly before the workmen departed that evening. The fire was discovered shortly after they left. Figure 8 shows the scorching in the framing of the house. Figure 9 shows typical scorching of plywood at a plumbing joint that resulted from failing to clean combustible debris in the sweating area. Ignition can result in either smoldering or flaming combustion, depending upon ventilation and physical conditions at the specific location.

Figure 9

Figure 10

Figures 10, 11, 12, 13, and 14.

These figures show portions of a fatal fire scene. Figure 10 shows a duplex wall receptacle (A) and the base of the chair lamp (B), which had been plugged into the top connection in A. The worn appliance cord extended under the carpet across point X. The right rear leg of the chair shown in Figure 11 rested on the cord. The fire began at point X in Figure 10. It completely incinerated the rubber matting, baseboard, and carpet at that point, and proceeded up the back of the comfort chair. Note the pattern on the wall behind the chair in Figure 11 and along the base of the wall under the window. Also note localized heat damage which indicates a long-term, unventilated, smoldering fire. A close-up of the chair is indicated in Figure 12. The fire initially vented out the window to the right of the chair.

Figure 11

Figure 12

Figure 13 shows the time at which the electrical circuit servicing the lamp opened. The electric clock was on time as of noon the preceding day and was on the same circuit. The occupancy master circuit did not open.

Figure 14 shows the location in the kitchen where the asphyxiation victim was found. The victim was the sole occupant at the time of the fire. The condition of the victim's bed indicated that she had retired some time prior to the fire. Carbon deposits on the turned-back bed clothing indicated that she had left

Figure 13

Figure 14

her bed after considerable carbon (soot) had settled around the pillow. She had fallen at least once in attempting to escape through the kitchen door. Apparently only partially conscious, she fell in the kitchen before she could reach the door, her head striking at point 'A' on Figure 14 and her body extending across the floor over areas B and C. Items at D, E, and F are broken window glass blown into the kitchen by the Fire Department hose stream. Note that the glass is heavily carbonized, which indicates a long-term, smoldering fire.

Cause of fire was determined to be electrical. Cause of death was asphyxiation by carbon monoxide.

Figure 15

Figure 15.

This fire caused extensive damage to a split-level, modern dwelling and contents. The electrical circuits used romex and other nonmetallic conductors which were secured to the ceiling, wall framing, and joists by metal staples. The circled area is the point of origin of this fire. The arrow points to the metal staple which had been driven tightly into the insulation of the cable thereby destroying the integrity of conductor insulation. This resulted in electrical fault and ignition of the insulation with resulting ignition of the joist and ceiling space. The electrical conductors were welded at the staple location. The fire extended through the floor above and into the second level. It will be noticed that, following the fire, the area above the origin was boarded over for safety purposes. This fire was burning in the relatively unventilated ceiling space of the first level for a considerable period prior to the time it broke through the second-level floor.

Origin of this fire was initially classified by the Fire Department as suspicious because no one was at home on the evening of the fire. The true cause, as further confirmed by the power company and laboratory sources, was electrical—resulting from faulty installation of the NM cable.

Figure 16

Figure 17

Figures 16 and 17.

This apartment fire was caused by the ignition of wall framing by the BW wall furnace vent. The weather had been unusually cold and the occupants turned up the thermostat. Construction was recent and the furnace vent was insufficiently clear of combustible framing where it passed from first to second levels. Figure 16 is taken from the apartment of origin on the first level. Figure 17 shows where the fire entered the second-level bedroom of the adjacent apartment. Fortunately, there were no fatalities.

Fires can and do occur in wall and ceiling spaces because of inadequate or faulty heating appliance installation. These fires travel through walls and ceiling and attic spaces before detection and occasionally appear as multiple origin fires to inexperienced or impulsive fire investigators. Factual fire cause investigation is an exacting and often time-consuming process.

Figure 18

Figure 19

Figures 18, 19, 20, and 21.

Major shopping center fire. Fire originated in the mansard (Figure 18, arrow 1). Flames extended through the mansard towards the center background of Figure 18. Figure 19 shows the burned-out mansard and area of origin (circled). Figure 20 shows the area of origin in the unpartitioned area of the mansard. Figure 21 shows the burned-out ballast transformer taken from the area of origin. The transformer serviced advertising signs on the front of the mansard overhang.

The cause was classified as electrical fault. The origin was established by eye witnesses and physical evidence.

Figure 20

Figure 21

The entire center of the multioccupancy structure was a total loss. Investigators often become preoccupied with residual damage and destruction at the expense of factual determination of origin by analysis of pattern of spread and careful evaluation of the statements of witnesses. Contrary to the beliefs of some investigators, the area of greatest damage is not necessarily the area of the earliest fire. Neither is the lowest and deepest char necessarily indicative of the area of origin of this fire. Wind direction and methods and points of Fire Department attack and control are factors that must always be considered as well as fire load and structural design. Note the remaining mansard and framing in Figure 19 immediately to the right of the circled area of origin.

Figure 22

Figures 22, 23, 24, and 25.

These figures indicate the areas of origin of a major warehouse fire. Although building demolition and collapse was extensive, probable areas of origin were established by burn patterns on vertical support piling and by statements of eye witnesses who discovered this fire in its very early stages, identifying precise areas where flames were first observed inside the building. Fortunately, witnesses observed flames and smoke from three sides of the building enabling the investigators to formulate cross bearings on the position of initial flames.

Figure 22 shows residue of burned wood framing that had been piled for pallet construction. The arrows point to residue that appeared foreign to known materials in the area and later identified by laboratory analysis as residue of an incendiary device. The arrows in Figure 23 also show the white-colored residue settled into the remains of pallet material. Figure 25 shows an area of origin following detailed examination and removal of debris in the area. Figure 24 is a close-up of the area indicated in Figure 25.

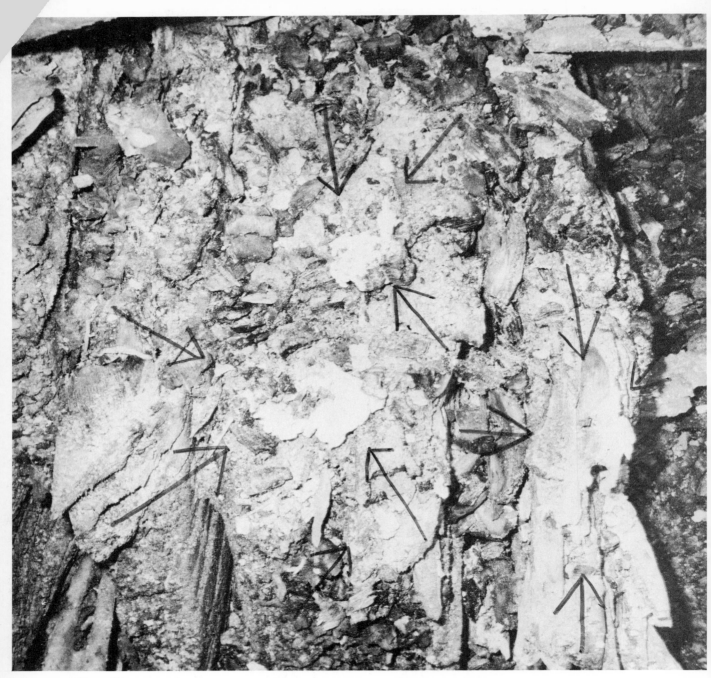

Figure 23

Fires causing extensive structural destruction and collapse often pose difficult, if not impossible, problems in determining area of origin and possible cause of the fire from physical evidence alone. The careful interview of all witnesses becomes extremely important in this type of situation. Location and interview of witnesses who passed the scene prior to discovery of the fire, as well as those who discovered the fire, often requires hundreds of man-hours of patient research and effort. Even then, careful interview by investigators familiar with the behavior of fire is often necessary for productive results. The origin and cause of the majority of our nation's major fire disasters is undetermined because of neglect of the fundamentals of sound investigative techniques: patient examination of the scene, location and interview of witnesses, and the use of competent laboratory expertise in evaluation of the physical evidence.

Figure 24

Figure 25

Figure 26

Figure 27

Figures 26, 27, 28, 29, 30, and 31.
   Scene of major industrial fire. This occurred shortly after one of the owners secured and departed late at night. Dull explosions were heard shortly thereafter. A police patrol unit observed flames extending from a window at the rear of the building (See arrow, rear center, Figure 26). The major building and contents were a total loss due to the rapid spread of the fire through the entire premises. Evaluation of a precise origin of this fire would have been virtually impossible from physical evidence alone. Again, many hours were expended in canvassing the neighborhood and questioning witnesses. The police officers who first observed the fire were questioned and provided information that was vital in establishing

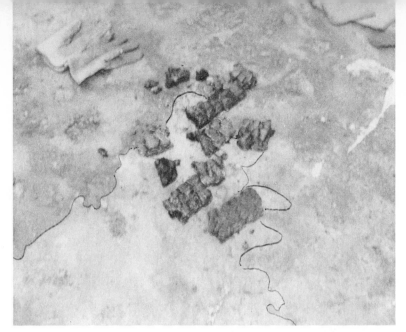

Figure 28

Figure 29

the origin of the fire. Figure 27 shows one point of origin. Residue of flammable liquids were recovered from debris in this area where piled merchandise had been located. Note intense fire pattern on wall and charring in a limited area at floor level (indicated by arrows).

Figure 28 shows another area of origin. The black outline shows the perimeter of flammable liquid pattern. Heavily charred crate bottoms are shown with their bottom sides exposed. Laboratory analysis produced evidence of residues of hydrocarbon compounds similar to gasoline. (No gasoline was stored on the premises or in the inventory.)

Figure 30

Figure 31

Figure 29 shows a container recovered from area. The lid had been inadvertently replaced by a fireman during overhaul. The fireman was located and interviewed. Laboratory analysis proved the residue in the container to be gasoline.

The cause of the fire was classified as incendiary.

Figure 30 shows the outside of forced open rear service doors. Figure 31 shows the inside of rear service door with the bolt in the condition it was found (circled).

Figure 32

Figure 33

Figures 32, 33, and 34.

These figures involved a retail mercantile operation. Merchandise was piled close to a gas-fueled hot water heater in a rear storeroom to simulate an accidental fire resulting from combustibles inadvertently placed too close to the water heater.

A trail of gasoline was extended through a ceiling mounted ventilator and across the roof to an alley where the trail was ignited. The flames followed the trail across the roof, down through the ventilator, and into the merchandise piled around the water heater. Initially classified as accidental, the final cause was incendiary.

Ventilator is shown in Figure 32. The faulted hot water heater is shown in Figures 33 and 34.

Figure 34

Figure 35

Figures 35, 36, 37, and 38.

    This fire caused extensive damage to a major apartment complex. Figure 35 shows a gas-fueled wall furnace. Arrow A depicts the origin of the fire in the furnace framing at the header plate. Figure 36, points B and C, show initial building frame char or pyrolysis at the header plate. Note, there is no insulation between the heater plate and combustible wood framing. Figure 37 shows the pattern of spread in the wood framing above the furnace. Note that, in this particular case, the BW Vent is insulated from the wood framing and, therefore, not faulted for this fire. The flame pattern followed the studs along each side of the wall furnace into the attic. The unpartitioned attic permitted the late night fire to spread

Figure 36

Figure 37

extensively through the attic involving several apartments before discovery. By this time, the Fire Department had a major fire on its hands. Fortunately, there were no fatalities.

Figure 38 shows an identical furnace in an adjoining apartment. Points A and A′ show the position of the top side or header plate in relation to the wood framing.

The reason the header plate in the area of origin became sufficiently heated to ignite the wood framing was that students residing in the apartment of origin had left a window open. The night was very cold. The apartment thermostat was located within six feet of the open window. Set at 72 degrees, the thermostat kept "telling" the furnace it was very cold. The furnace, at another interior location, continued to

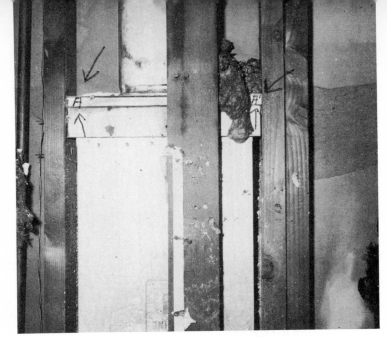

Figure 38

labor in a continuing burning cycle, attempting to raise the room temperature at the thermostat location. The continuing cycle of the furnace caused prohibitive temperatures at the header plate and resulting ignition of the wood framing.

Because the occupants were students, authorities initially suspected them of incendiarism. Not all fires are of incendiary origin. This one was clearly accidental.

Figure 39

Figures 39, 40 and 41.

An explosion and fire caused extensive damage in this two-level apartment building. The occupant of the apartment of origin was blown through the wall of the kitchen indicated by the arrow in Figure 39. The occupant expired in the emergency hospital. The investigation disclosed that the elderly occupant

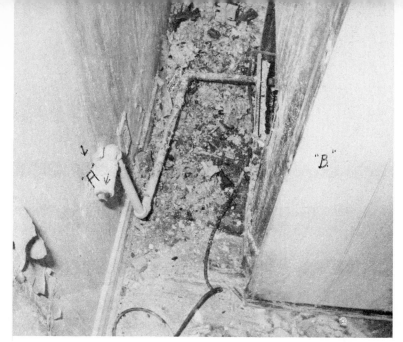

Figure 40

Figure 41

smelled gas late at night, got out of bed, walked to the kitchen, and turned on a light. The explosion followed. Occupant was found by firemen in the debris outside the building where she had been blown through the side of the kitchen. When the firemen arrived, the flames had extended through the common unpartitioned attic, thus involving several other spaces.

The original gas leak was traced to a faulty flex connector from the rigid gas line to the stove (Figure 40, points A and B). The stove burners were off. The controls and service lines were sound. The house service line was sound. The flame pattern indicated that the gas had leaked from the connector saturating the walls, ceiling, and attic area. The ignition source was the electric wall switch adjacent to the gas range in the kitchen (Figure 41). When the victim investigated the odor and turned on the light switch, ignition occurred.

Figure 42

Figure 43

Figures 42, 43, 44, and 45.

   This was an incendiary residential fire which had been originally classified as accidental. Allegedly, a faulty water heater flue had ignited combustible framing. More detailed investigation disclosed that the original flame pattern extended from a blind section behind the water heater, indicated by arrow C in Figure 43. (Figure 43 shows the hot water heater cabinet after the heater was removed.) Figure 42 shows the gas-fueled water heater in place. This was a butane- or LPG-fueled heater. The gas fuel is heavier than air.

Figure 44

Figure 45

Removal of ceiling and framing debris from around the base of the water heater disclosed that the water heater's main fuel line connector had been cut and deliberately fractured. (Figure 42, arrow B. The main gas line to heater control was on, arrow A.) The gas connector was attached to the house service line at arrow X in Figure 44. After the fuel line was cut, the heavier than air gas accumulated at lower levels and was ignited by the pilot light in the gas-fueled floor furnace indicated by arrow X in Figure 43 and arrow Y in Figure 44. The deliberately cut water heater fuel line connector is shown on a table in Figure 45.

The cause of this fire was clearly incendiary.

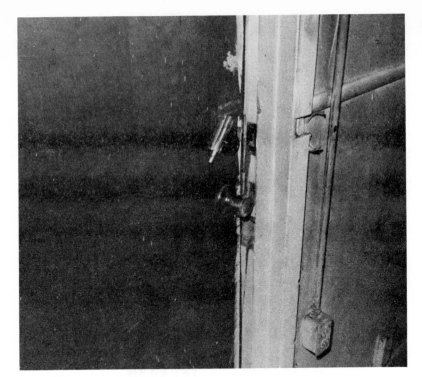

Figure 46

Figure 47

Figures 46, 47, 48, and 49.
   "Inside" burglary and arson. Figure 46 shows lock forced from the inside. Figure 47 indicates the position of the electrical equipment circuit utilized as an igniting source for flammables placed at various locations.

Figure 48

Figure 49

Figure 48 shows one area of origin. Note the arrow indicating the char pattern along the base of the shelf framing. Accelerant (kerosene) was poured on the floor and in shelving (2) and penetrated the floor beneath the shelving. Kerosene residue was recovered from area beneath floor.

Figure 49 shows the kerosene container which was recovered from a storage closet.

Figure 50

Figure 50.

This is an explosion and fire scene. The seat of explosion was a trailer truck loaded with unstable compounds and parked in a warehouse at arrow #1. Explosive force totally demolished the trailer and the shock wave displaced windows in the structure in the background and caused extensive fire and displacement damage around the perimeter. The warehouse where the trailer was parked was totally demolished as was one other building—the displacement damage extended several hundred feet from the explosion center. One of the explosions destroyed structures as indicated at the base of arrow #2.

Figure 51

Figure 51.
Trailer of origin was parked over the circled area. Explosive force from the interior of the trailer embedded trailer bed channeling in the pavement as indicated in the lateral lines at arrows. Note depressed and displaced paving and structural foundation in center foreground.

Figure 52

Figure 52.
    Displaced section of trailer near seat of explosion. Note direction of collapsed steel warehouse framing (arrow).

Figure 53

Figure 53.
Remains of part of trailer carriage and section that came to rest over 200 feet from the seat of the explosion. Note twisted heavy framing. Note missing tire from carriage assembly at the center of the photo.

Figure 54

Figure 54.
    Point of impact of one of the trailer tires approximately 200 feet from the scene. The tire was burning when it impacted (arrows).

Figure 55

Figures 55, 56, 57, 58, 59 and 60.

This incendiary fire caused extensive damage to a two-story dwelling and contents. Investigation by the Santa Ana Fire Department disclosed that the suspect had carefully planned the fire to avoid detection. In anticipation of the fire, the suspect removed pets from the scene, claiming that they needed the attention of a veterinarian. The absence of the pets, an open window (used by the suspect for egress after setting the fire), and a good investigator's curiosity and talent of observation were factors resulting in the solving of this case.

Figure 56

Figure 57

Figure 58

Patience and tact resulted in a confession by the suspect and subsequent prosecution and conviction of the crime of arson. Without these factors, the fire might reasonably have been written off as careless smoking or defective wiring. After all, it had occurred in the storage area of an old house. As it happened, however, the fire was set with gasoline, applied in liberal quantities.

Figure 55 shows the time electrical service was interrupted. Investigator McCalla reported that timing became progressively more important with the unfolding of the investigation. The suspect's confession was corroborated by the discovery of many physical factors, including the open window shown in the photograph. The carbon deposit in the framing indicated that the window had been open during the fire.

Figures 56 and 57 show the flooring of the bedroom and adjoining closet after the investigators had carefully removed debris and cleaned the floor. Note the burn pattern and deep char as well as the penetration.

Figure 59

Also note the low deep char on the baseboard and door framing. Investigator McCalla states he considered these factors, along with deep rolling alligatoring and smooth shiny blisters which suggested rapid temperature rise. These were inconsistent with a long, smoldering fire and consistent with the probability that an accelerant had been used. He further points to the burn configuration and floor penetration where the worn and very old flooring permitted penetration of accelerants. The suspect had applied accelerants in quantity to this area as well as to personal items in front of the chest of drawers in the closet. See the background of Figure 56 and Figure 58 which show the cabinet drawers. The patterns reflect rapid temperature rise as opposed to that which might have been expected from an accidental smoldering fire.

Figure 60

In Figure 59, Investigator McCalla holds a door which was adjacent to and above a point of origin in the bedroom. The lower hinge is intact. Note the contrast in char between the wood frame on the left side of the door and the left side of the door frame. Note the heavy char pattern on the door at floor level.

In Figure 60, Investigator McCalla holds the bottom edge of the door shown in Figure 59. Note that the char pattern only appears on part of the upper section. This was consistent with the burn pattern on the floor beneath the door where accelerants had penetrated floor through cracks and openings, prior to ignition.

Alligatoring and char patterns, interpreted by well-trained and experienced investigators, can provide clues and investigative leads that can reasonably result in factual conclusions. Such conditions must be evaluated with all other evidence before final conclusions are reached.

Figure 61

Figures 61, 62 and 63.

The fire indicated in these photographs was discovered, reported, and extinguished by neighbors. The Fire Department responded and completed overhaul. When investigators arrived, the scene appeared as shown in Figure 62. There were no apparent accidental ignition sources; the flame pattern, in itself, might have been regarded as suspicious. Note the limited vertical flame pattern and limited deep char in a localized area. A part of the deck against the wall was burned through there was deep char inside the shingle siding yet there was no heat source such as electrical wiring or an outlet.

Figure 63 shows the scene with two water-filled glass containers which were recovered and replaced by the investigators after they had interviewed witnesses and located the missing bottles. According to Investigator McCalla of the Santa Ana Fire Department, the investigation clearly revealed that the fire resulted from heat generated by the sun's rays through one or both bottles. Heat was concentrated on the shingle side of the exposure.

Burn patterns, relied upon without checking all the evidence, can be misleading.

Figure 62

Figure 63

Figure 64

Figure 64.

The Santa Ana, California Fire Department has a long-time reputation for thorough and successful arson investigation. They work closely with the police, cooperating agencies, and the District Attorney's office in this important phase of fire safety. Figure 64 tells an eloquent, if brief story, of productive investigative effort. Many otherwise careful arson investigators too often completely ignore the possibility of raising latent fingerprints from an object or objects at a fire scene. While the phenomenon of fire, with its byproducts, usually destroys or covers latent prints, this is not always the case. The illustrated incident was a comparatively small fire. It is the policy of the Santa Ana Fire Department to investigate all suspicious or incendiary fires. Their reasoning for this is sound. They say, "Little fires can become big ones."

In describing Figure 64, Captain Matt McCalla, an arson investigator for the Santa Ana Fire Department, stated that the "fire of incendiary origin involved a three-bedroom single-story residence. On arrival of the investigators, the fire had been contained by our suppression crews and largely confined to two bedrooms with residual damage throughout the premises. Disregarding the tired and often heard rhetoric that evidence is seldom available to prove the accused's participation, investigators lifted one good fingerprint from the protected underside of the can which had contained the flammable liquids used to set the fire. We were able to match the print with a suspect who did not live at the scene. He had a record. We connected him to the fire and the case was successfully concluded." The suspect was charged, arrested, and convicted of arson.

Fire Marshal Minchella and Captain McCalla, with the complete support of the Chief, hold frequent company training sessions emphasizing the importance of preservation of the fire scene during overhaul. This is essential to successful fire cause investigation. This particular case is an example of how it pays off.

Figure 65

Figures 65 through 78.

These photographs illustrate certain conditions found in a fire scene involving a single-story, three-bedroom modern dwelling in Orange County, California. Fortunately, the family was absent during the late night fire. Jealousy motivated this fire.

Orange County has long maintained an efficient arson investigation unit under the supervision of the California Department of Forestry and the Orange County Fire Department. Highly-trained investigative personnel work out of the department and in close cooperation with other fire authorities, law enforcement agencies, and the District Attorney's office.

According to Chief Wally Trotter, who supervises Fire Prevention and Fire Investigation, fire company personnel are trained to promptly summon investigative aid when undetermined, suspicious, or known incendiary circumstances appear. In this case, fire suppression units requested investigation immediately following control of the fire. Immediate investigation was initiated. This insures integrity of the fire scene and evidence recovered.

Fire scene examination disclosed four separate and distinct points of origin. The Orange County Sheriff's Office Crime Lab assisted at the scene. Investigation disclosed that low flash point, flammable accelerants were used at multiple locations inside the dwelling. The modus operandi indicated that the arsonist was familiar with the property. Interview of the victims, numerous witnesses, and the conduct and completion of investigative leads identified the suspect who, when confronted, denied his involvement.

Further investigation resulted in nailing down the time spectrum of the fire. Ignition was approximately fifteen minutes prior to discovery and thirty minutes prior to control. With this reliable time frame the investigators were able to disprove the suspect's alibi and, further, to place him at the scene of the crime at the time of the fire.

Figure 66

Figure 67

The District Attorney issued a felony complaint charging the defendant with two counts of arson of a dwelling. The case was tried and the defendant was convicted.

Figure 65 shows the living room. Note the limited heat and smoke damage evidenced by the curtains, windows, and furniture. Investigators' vehicles can be seen through the windows. The center window is in its original position. The conditions are consistent with a short-term fire considering damage and materials involved elsewhere in the dwelling.

Figure 66 shows the bedroom ceiling in the rear of the dwelling. Note the contrast between fire and heat damage in this space and in the living room. Note cracks in ceiling consistent with rapid temperature rise.

Figure 68

Figure 69

Figure 70

Figure 71

Figure 67 shows area of origin in bathroom doorway at floor level where accelerants were used.

Figure 68 shows the bathroom from the doorway in Figure 67 and again, pattern on the wall indicates rapid temperature rise from floor level.

Figure 69 shows origin in kitchen door area; again, at floor level. Note char pattern on doorway framing and condition of wall on both sides of doorway. Contrast this to the high flame damage in the center background of the kitchen.

Figure 72

Figure 73

Figure 70 shows an origin in a doorway area after a portion of the floor has been cleared of debris. Flammable liquid was poured in this area at the top center of the photo. Note that the asphalt tile is not spalled or deeply charred.

The arrow in Figure 71 shows a point of origin at the base of the kitchen cabinets.

Figure 72 shows the area where a limited quantity of accelerants was placed, but without much effect.

Figure 73 shows the same area as Figure 72 after the floor was cleared. The liquid pattern is evident. Note that the synthetic floor covering is not charred in depth.

Figure 74

Figure 75

Figure 74 shows the smoke pattern above where a limited quantity of accelerants was placed on the floor. This is before debris was examined and removed.

Figure 75 shows the liquid pattern on the synthetic floor after debris was removed.

Figure 76

Figure 77

Figure 76 shows a separate flammable liquid pattern on the floor after debris was removed. Again, note soot deposit but lack of floor char.

Figure 77 shows the floor-level origin at hall door. Note condition of carpet. Flammable liquids were used here.

Figure 78

Figure 78 shows top side of the door in Figure 77.

CHAPTER XV

THE WITNESS

This chapter is not intended as a legal discourse. Neither is it suggested to override department or jurisdictional procedures. The investigator should consult with his District Attorney or legal officer and with his department supervisor concerning applicable legal guidelines affecting the interviewing of all classes of witnesses and relevant policies.

The purpose of this section is to orient the investigator in the approach, interview, and evaluation of witnesses, and their importance to the success of the investigation of most fires. As in the vast majority of major crime, properly identified and intelligently interviewed witnesses spell the difference between the success and failure of investigative and prosecutive effort.

Many texts deal with the possibly too often repeated "tricks of the trade" in interviewing witnesses and interrogating suspects. This is done at the expense of practical common sense methods which have been proven over the years and accepted by successful, field-experienced investigators as well as by the legal profession and the Courts. It is unfortunate that the conduct of inexperienced and indifferent investigators has, during recent years, resulted in general suspicion of investigative procedures. The teaching of so-called psychological subtleties and unauthorized use of mechanical and electronic devices in a manner designed to persuade a witness to cooperate results in failure of the investigation and discredit to the officers involved.

There are numerous examples where resorting to questionable tactics results in complete alienation of the witness. Training texts are currently in use which advocate photography of the investigator and witness during the interview to show the friendly atmosphere: "See how the witness is smiling?"

The firm, official approach is stressed as such: "We have scheduled your interview at X o'clock at headquarters and I therefore assume you will be available." The instructor suggests that the prospective witness will usually succumb to this affirmative approach unless the investigator does something

further to intimidate or destroy the witness's confidence and loses control of the situation. While there is certainly nothing wrong with an honest affirmative approach in dealing with a witness, experience shows that the majority of American citizens do not respond favorably to an overly officious or pushy approach; neither do they respond affirmatively to gimmicks better left to television detective series and amateur sleuths.

DEFINITION OF A WITNESS

"A witness is an individual who has knowledge of facts or occurrence sufficient to testify in respect thereto." (Matter of Losee, 13, N.Y. Misc. Rep. 298, 299, 34 N.Y. Supp. 1120.) While this definition may be correct in the technical sense, "witness" means considerably more to an investigator who is looking for information he can rely upon and utilize in pursuit of his inquiry to the final solution. He may or may not expect the witness to take the witness stand, depending upon the circumstances and objectives of his inquiry. He may consider the witness who observed the subject in question as an informant whose information may guide him one step forward in his continuing investigation.

The witness spectrum is probably as broad as the human experience. Too often, perhaps, emphasis has been directed to the technical aspects of the interview at the expense of the human and psychological aspects of seeking out the witness, sizing him up, and establishing a rapport that will result in full disclosure of what he knows, in a manner that will insure his testifying fully and truthfully if circumstances require. This is really what it is all about.

How many times, in our individual experiences, have we observed a witness clam up? Perhaps he has drawn into his shell because he sensed that the investigator shined his badge in his eyes. Experienced and successful law enforcement officials have long since learned that over aggressiveness, such as unnecessary display of hardware and official insignia, rather than molding or humbling the average American citizen, simply raises his resentment rather than respect.

How many times does the "come on strong" approach close the door to further investigative leads? Certainly, there are situations where display of authority and the ability to back it up may be justified. There are, however, many more situations where the conservative approach accomplishes more reliable and productive results over the long haul.

WHO ARE WITNESSES?

Successful investigators recognize that witnesses do not conform to stereotyped patterns as suggested by some authorities, nor will they always conform to a pattern necessarily acceptable to the personal standards and expectations of the investigator. Witnesses are what they are and they range from young to old, poor to rich and come from all economic and educational levels. A witness may be a minister, banker, insurance executive, or adjuster. He may be a bartender, restaurant owner, hooker, bookie, or burglar. He may be, unknown to the investigator, the arsonist or, conversely, the investigator, after suspecting him as the arsonist, finds that he is actually a witness, perhaps even a *key* witness. Investigators all too often forget that the witness spectrum includes police officers, firemen, paramedics, utility employees, and even friends and neighbors. Witness information may be vital. Improperly handled, the witness and his information may be lost forever— by the turning of a careless word or the wrong approach.

One of the keys to the success of the investigator is understanding how to approach a prospective witness and learn what he knows. No textbook or set of rules will provide all the answers or procedures to cover all situations. Certain general rules may be applied to aid the investigator. These include training, working with experienced investigators who understand and succeed in witness interview and require basic human understanding, patience, and sense of balance. Every potential witness is a human being and the vast majority will react affirmatively under appropriate handling.

Much has been written concerning the environment of the interview, proper uniform or dress, and the affirmative approach which may not necessarily be true in proper perspective today. Whether we like it or not, customs, values, attitudes, and public reactions change, as do legal requirements and proce-

dures. While dress uniforms, shining brass, or gold braid may be desirable in some situations, they are resented in others. While a well groomed appearance, shiny shoes, and tasteful attire may be appreciated in department offices and other environmental situations, the same attire may be quietly resented by a witness down in the barrio. Insisting upon the interview of a witness downtown may result in his appearing (as directed) for the interview. The investigator, of course, will have touched base since he will have interviewed the witness "like it says in the book." Nothing, of course, will be said about how the witness closed the valve on the outflow of information he might well have provided had he been interviewed within the standards of reason and common sense.

This is why the more enlightened and successful law enforcement agencies have widened their perspectives in the crime investigation field including procedures permitting the investigator to meet the witness in his own environment under circumstances conducive to meaningful communication between the investigator and the witness. On the other hand, some department heads continue to insist that their investigators appear, at all times, in the uniform of the day even though it may be completely unsuited to the task and environment at hand.

Some witnesses, regardless of their environmental, educational, ethnic, or social positions or standards, are turned off by officiousness or display of authority. Whether justified or not, this is one of the realities an investigator must recognize if he is serious about obtaining facts from the witness which may be of importance in his inquiry. It is particularly important for department heads and supervisory personnel to recognize that they cannot control the personalities and instincts of witnesses and must permit their own egos and prejudices to bend in favor of allowing their investigators latitude, within reason, in accomplishing the investigative mission in a legal and ethical manner.

WITNESS INFORMATION IN GENERAL

For discussion purposes, perhaps we should classify witnesses in two general groups: 1. public service personnel; and 2. the general public. Investigators often overlook the special areas of assistance that public service employees may provide not only as lay witnesses but, in certain areas, as expert witnesses. Investigators often forget that public service personnel, like all other human beings, are subject to reactions in response to consideration and kindness. In fire cases, people in this category are often in possession of key information. Presumptuous treatment or short circuiting such witnesses with departmental policies and procedures may result in loss of meaningful cooperation.

Public service employees include fire, police, building and safety, utility, and public records personnel. Fire and police personnel, along with utility emergency personnel, are frequently the first witnesses in on the fire scene. They may be able to provide invaluable information as to location of the fire on arrival, progress of the fire, and any apparently unusual conditions; they may provide data on whether the premises were secured or which doors, windows, or hatches were open or vented. They may provide accurate information on progress of the fire *after* their arrival and identify or describe persons or vehicles on scene. Witnesses in this category may observe unusual items or conditions that may otherwise be irretrievably lost. The beat patrol officer may be one of the first on scene. He is all too often completely ignored by the investigators. Yet, he may be intimately acquainted with the neighborhood and what goes on there. He may even be familiar with the subject premises and its occupants. He may have his own informational grapevine that will provide the answers to what caused the fire. If he is not asked, the information he possesses may be lost forever.

The utility employee, dispatched to the scene to insure that gas or electricity is properly secured, may have observed conditions which may be misinterpreted or completely missed by the investigator. He may observe tampering that occurred prior to the fire or manipulation of circuit breakers or other safety devices.

In one important case, a garbage man, making his early morning rounds, was able to place the suspect at the scene shortly before the fire. Fire investigators had overlooked him. He made his observations known to his minister who called a city councilman. The Chief of Police was informed and assigned a detective. The detective conducted the interview and relayed the information to his Chief, who contacted the Chief of the Fire Department. The Fire Chief contacted his Fire Marshal who, in turn, passed the information to the fire investigator. It was then learned that the fire investigator had closed the case because he had been unable to place the suspect at the scene of the crime. Fortunately, the case was re-opened and the prosecution was successfully concluded.

It is always good practice to conduct a neighborhood inquiry for witnesses who might have been in the area at the time the fire occurred.

Fire investigators often neglect to question their own firemen. For example, a fire caused extensive damage to a suburban dwelling. Investigators arrested the occupant, charging him with arson. They were able to place him at the scene at the time of the fire. Disregarding his statement of trouble with a television set in his bedroom, they alleged there were at least two widely separated points of origin—one in the bedroom and the other at the opposite end of the house on the kitchen floor. Had the investigators taken the time and effort to interview firemen who originally forced open the kitchen door, they would have learned that there was *no* fire in the kitchen at that time. Shortly after entering the kitchen, the firemen were redirected to another area; during that period, the fire spread from the bedroom through the wood paneled halls and extended into the kitchen at high levels. There it ignited window curtains which, burning, fell to the floor, causing the suspicious floor patterns classified as arson by the investigators. Upon being advised of all the facts, the District Attorney very properly dismissed the complaint.

Basic information may be obtained from public service and public safety witnesses depending upon the circumstances of the particular scene. Perhaps all necessary information can be obtained on scene at the time. In such cases, it is good practice to suggest that the witness prepare a memorandum or report of his findings which may then be provided to the investigator through proper channels. There are, of course, situations where official confidentiality is required. In any circumstance, the witness' observations should be documented in a statement or report which may be utilized to refresh the witness' memory in the event that the case ultimately gets to court. This may be at a considerably later date.

A tape recording of the witness' observations should not be taken without his clear, recorded consent. Law and departmental policy varies somewhat in various jurisdictions. The use of monitoring and recording devices with witnesses and suspects must be in compliance with the law of the jurisdiction and departmental procedures. The investigator must know, *beforehand,* how far he may go. Departmental policy should be clearly enunciated in accordance with the current laws of the jurisdiction. It is well known that witnesses may become suspects and that persons who may have been originally viewed as suspect may turn out to be important key witnesses, rather than suspects.

Federal and State Law defines the conditions and circumstances under which conversations may be monitored and/or recorded. Not only are criminal penalties prescribed for violation of individual constitutional rights to privacy, but the courts have repeatedly excluded the use of information and evidence resulting from the use of prohibited procedures of investigative tactics.

Experience has shown that, after eliciting all possible factual information from a witness, it may then be appropriate to suggest that his statement be recorded with a copy provided to the witness if he so requests. The value of such recordings is to provide an accurate record of what has been said and which may be useful in assisting the witness to refresh his recollection at some future date.

More detailed information from public safety or service witnesses may be required than can be obtained at the fire scene and, under such circumstances, suitable arrangements should be made at an hour and place acceptable to the witness and his superiors. Observance of his department's procedures may prevent misunderstanding and further insure the utilization of the requested information in the form it can be used. Before the interview, the investigator should carefully list the information he requires and areas he wishes to cover during the contact or interview, particularly where the nature of the information required is technical or complicated. The contact may require only simple information such as, "When did you disconnect the power?" Or, it may involve checking of circuits, load capacity, and wiring plans.

The questions may embrace the on-scene observations of a police patrol officer and be as simple as: "Was the front door locked when you arrived?" or, "How do you know it was locked?" Or, the questions may be more complex. For example: "Do you know the proprietor?"; "Did you see him at the cafe earlier that evening?"; "What time did you see him?"; "Where was he standing?"; "If you know, who was he with?"; "Did you have a conversation with the proprietor shortly after the fire?"; "Who was present?"; "What did he say?"; "What did you say?"; "How was he dressed?"; and so on. Occasionally, patrol officers are inclined to write sketchy reports, often neglecting to include information which they feel is unimportant but may be vital to the investigator. Where the fire investigator reviews officers' reports, he should be cautious about accepting the officers' observations of the incident as all-embracing or conclusive. The officer should be contacted and interviewed, in detail and in depth as to his observations if he was or should have been in a position to make relevant or important observations.

When interviewing public service witnesses, it is often good practice to utilize sketches, building plans, layout sketches, and charts that are relevant to the subject matter of interview and permit the witness to mark the items of reference to illustrate his observations. This is particularly true in the case of firemen and police officers who are usually graphic in their recollections and observations if contacted without delay. Too frequently, delay will dim or confuse them because they have responded to numerous other incidents in the interim. The reference materials are particularly important if and when the case later comes to trial. It is not necessary that memoranda be fancy or precisely to scale so long as this is noted and taken into consideration as to accuracy and credibility.

Sketches and similar matter are particularly useful to building and safety and street department personnel who might be required to appear as witnesses. If they have something they understand and can refer to, their confidence as well as their recollection is enhanced. Building and safety officials are often of considerable assistance in producing and interpreting structural, mechanical, and electrical plans and diagrams vital in consideration of mechanical or electrical malfunctions or their elimination as a cause of the fire. They are also helpful in respect to evaluation of progress of the fire: through doors, hatches, or air-conditioning systems.

Perhaps, in light of what has been briefly covered, the reader may recognize the value of public safety and service personnel as witnesses or sources of information. Again, these informational resources are too often mishandled and occasionally completely ignored.

The second general category of witnesses, the general public, includes all types of people: the man on the street, the housewife, the business executive, and the student. In other words, anyone who may have knowledge, direct or indirect, that may be useful to the investigator in directing him to the objective of his inquiry. Inexperienced investigators too often overlook or dismiss a witness simply because he doesn't happen to have information which he feels might qualify him to testify in the first instance. Experienced investigators have long since learned that patience and analysis of what a witness may know can be important over the long haul although its initial relevancy may be obscure.

Experienced and successful investigators have learned to take their witnesses as they find them. He has learned that "this is how it is." His witness may not be clean and he may not be beautiful; his appearance may be less than credible. He may even be hostile. It has always been this way and it will probably continue to be this way as long as we have people and crime.

A witness may be identified to an investigator in a number of ways. For example, he may be "turned" through a routine fire or police report or a neighborhood check by the door rattling process and pounding the bricks. He may be identified directly at the fire scene by the investigator or by other officers or other witnesses. The means of turning up witnesses are as numerous as leaves on a tree. They are limited only by the ingenuity of the investigator and the time he is allowed to do his job.

Once the witness is identified, the investigator must plan his approach. The initial contact of the witness may spell the difference between obtaining valuable information and losing it. This planning of approach does not imply long term planning. With experience, planning may become nearly a reflex action.

An intelligent approach to a potential witness may well spell the difference between his relating what he actually knows and what he chooses to disclose. The intelligence of a witness often has less to do with his response to the investigator than his instincts and gut reactions. This is often the clutch. Here is the area where the difference between the men and the boys is often apparent in the investigative field. The average man on the street is fully aware that the overly aggressive approach by the officer or investigator is usually evidence of uncertainty or fear on the part of the officer. The witness' responses may be passive but not productive concerning the information needed.

Here is where the arson investigation (as in the case of most other major crime) may die a-borning. Here is one of the major reasons why only approximately one or two percent of the known arson cases are solved by arrest and conviction. Arson is a crime particularly dependent upon the use of circumstantial evidence and the utilization of reliable witnesses. The successful investigator must be well balanced and comfortable in his approach of the witness. If it is at the scene, circumstances may require obtaining

necessary basic information (including identification) and arranging for a subsequent interview when the investigator has more facts concerning the fire and when he can better evaluate what the witness may have to say. Whether we like it or not, the investigator must learn to play it by ear. No textbook or classroom instructor can provide hard and fast answers to all possible witness situations. These sources can only provide the investigator with technical guidelines and the basics to recognition of the more common pitfalls. Preferably, the inexperienced investigator may be assigned to work with a successful, experienced investigator. Hopefully, he will emerge with the knowledge and stability necessary to his survival in an exacting field and the ability to get the job done in an ethical, legal, and productive manner. In dealing with witnesses, this means the capability to make it easy for the witness to tell the investigator what he knows.

There are situations where the witness may seek to provide the information with the understanding that he will not be required to testify. The investigator should not make promises he cannot keep. Most prosecuting attorneys will agree that a witness who has been misled by investigators is of questionable reliability on the witness stand—at least until the atmosphere of deception has been corrected. In situations where the witness is uncertain or reluctant, "twisting him"—to use a questionably popular word in some circles—is dangerous and usually unproductive over the long haul. Legitimate arrangements may be made between the prosecuting attorney and a recalcitrant or reluctant witness but these should be avoided by the investigators except under legally monitored circumstances. "Deals" with witnesses and informants have a bad habit of boomeranging.

A witness may be able to provide factual information along with testifying; on the other hand, he may insist on remaining anonymous in which case the experienced investigator, reluctant to forever lose the information that may be vital to his case, elects to utilize him as a confidential informant. This practice has been widely and ethically utilized when witnesses have continued to supply valid information. Their identity is protected and, ultimately, sometimes with their consent, they appear and testify when the case goes to trial.

Informant witnesses have frequently become key witnesses after they have been convinced that they can trust the investigators and the prosecuting attorney.

Successful investigators make it a hard and fast

practice to double-check and analyze the accuracy of statements of all witnesses. This is particularly true in the circumstances of informant witnesses. The record is abundant with examples of honest mistakes of witnesses and with deliberately false statements. This is an investigative fact of life. It is the responsibility of the investigator to take the necessary and reasonable precautions to authenticate the credibility of the witness. One of the shortcomings of insurance-oriented and other classes of investigation, as well as in poorly trained or loosely supervised official investigations, is reliance upon unverified statements of witnesses; the condition has mainly resulted from outgrowth of case load, mass production techniques, and poorly trained and unqualified investigators.

Law enforcement and investigative agencies frequently rely on informant witnesses who may or may not appear on the witness stand. Such informants are commonly utilized in major crime cases including the activities of fraud/arson rings and organized crime. What has been said about checking credibility and reliability of information supplied is particularly relevant to this class of witness, whether he is called a witness or a confidential informant. It is difficult, if not occasionally impossible, to solve certain classes of well thought out crime without the use of an informant who may have access to conversations, meetings, activities, data, and plans of such conspiracies and groups. Such information, if accurate, is often indispensable in solving the case. The informant may be kept under tight security wraps for investigative reasons or for his own protection. His identity may remain unknown except to the investigator or the prosecuting attorney. In some circumstances, his position comes into the open when he appears as a witness. Circumstances alter procedures.

In a series of bombings and incendiary fires on the west coast involving laundry and dry cleaning establishments, it was learned that extortionists with long and interesting criminal records, including assault, bombings, and arson, were setting up for business in western cities. They were expanding their operations which had been successful in certain eastern and midwestern cities. It was mainly as a result of utilization of carefully selected confidential informants that the leaders were identified and exposed before a Federal grand jury. They quickly terminated their activities and moved out of the area.

PROCESS AND PHILOSOPHY OF INTERVIEWING WITNESSES

Much has been written about this subject by theorists as well as by field investigators. As earlier stated, there is a variance of opinion about techniques and procedures. Some theorists go so far as to delineate how the investigator should cut his hair and define his manner of dress. Others presumptuously define the positive approach as putting the witness on the defensive and placing him at a disadvantage to the point of destroying his ego, by which process he is more likely to tell what he knows. Still other pseudodetectives advocate the "knee to knee and eyeball to eyeball" doctrine, allegedly designed to place the witness in psychological retreat because of his personality uncertainties, causing him to reveal what he would otherwise conceal. Still others advocate the "kill with kindness" syndrome while at the same time utilizing the polygraph and other electronic and mechanical devices to convince the witness of the advances of science in the detection of deception.

Most experienced and successful investigators are aware that no single formula exists for all witness situations any more than would apply to all suspect situations or, for that matter, in dealing with human beings in any other spectrum of today's world. People are what they are. They usually react according to their background, environment, and current circumstantial surroundings; to the stress and climate of a given situation; and particularly, to the confrontation of the investigator who happens to be talking to them at the moment.

Quite naturally, the witness may react in accordance with the locus of the interview, the excitement, confusion, or stress of the fire scene, or the shock of emergency. On the other hand, his attitude (and reaction) may be entirely different once removed from the scene to the quiet of an office, schoolroom, or headquarters; or to his place of employment, his own office, or his home.

AT THE FIRE SCENE

The approach of the witness at the fire scene may be useful only to obtain preliminary data and identification. For example: Did you discover the fire?; Where was it burning when you first saw it?; How many other guys did you see?; Can you point them out for me?; What is your name and address? I would like to talk to you when we have more time and not when everyone is standing around. Is that O.K.?; and so on. In such circumstances, some very successful investigators seldom whip out a notebook (a la television) until they have established a conversational rap with the witness. It usually works; the witness all too often gets tongue-tied when the officer's badge is shined in his eyes or he whips out his scratch pad. Certainly, the average witness knows that he is required to identify himself; he also knows that if he talks too much he may be sitting around in court as a witness when he would rather be sipping a beer, watching the ball game, or fishing. Pushing him around isn't going to get the job done. By this route, the officer often misses the boat when it comes to picking up useful information.

Possibly illustrative of usually unproductive witness approach is the tactic commonly used by insurance adjusters and poorly trained investigators who are commonly observed at the fire scene with their electronic tape recorders cocked and primed as they approach a witness. Again, they may possibly elicit his name, but little else. A more conservative approach might have opened the door.

There are circumstances when it may be necessary for the witness to identify or point out items or conditions observed before he leaves the scene, while conditions observed are clear in his mind, and before the scene is changed. In such circumstances, tactful requests may be granted by the witness along with appropriate photographic recording of the witness pointing to the window, door, or other item he identifies.

In some cases, the witness will more readily cooperate if he is allowed to accompany the investigator to the scene after the emergency is ended and bystanders have departed. He should be permitted to do so whenever possible since he may feel at ease and become more cooperative. More reliable information may be obtained with the expenditure of a little extra time and his continued cooperation and appearance in court may be further assured.

INTERVIEWING THE WITNESS AWAY FROM THE FIRE SCENE

Most detailed investigative interviews take place at locations other than the fire scene. The fire scene may be visited to amplify or clarify points in question or otherwise covered in the basic interview. Circumstances alter specific procedures although general guidelines may apply. Again, it should always be beared in mind that the purpose of the interview is to obtain factual information in a form that will be useful to the investigator, including the appearance of the witness in court if circumstances require.

All too often, investigators consider contacting the witness as merely touching base. So long as he has touched base, nothing further is required. Either the witness says something or he doesn't. The officer all too often says, when questioned in this regard, "How the hell should I know what the guy knows? He doesn't tell me anything I can use so I go on to the next. I don't make a case, I close it. It's as simple as that." This is one of the principal reasons arson investigation is unsuccessful in many jurisdictions and it is probably one of the prime reasons why insurance companies are unsuccessful in bringing cases of fraud fire to a successful conclusion. Investigators or adjusters are seldom allotted adequate training for investigative interview and many are temperamentally unsuited to investigative interview. Even more are allocated insufficient time for witness contact and checking the credibility of information received.

Before arranging for situs of interview, the investigator should insure he has marshalled all facts relevant to the projected interview. He should have a clear picture of where he stands to date, what areas he wishes to discuss, and how he intends to conduct the interview. Perhaps, if the area he wishes to cover is detailed, he may set down his questions, in order, in his reference notes. By this process, he need not overlook vital points and he can proceed in a methodical manner. He can leave space for unforeseen information and unknown areas. Such a system is particularly helpful when the investigator sits down to dictate his report—perhaps many days later.

In working out a mutually agreeable place for the interview, the investigator should select a location which will insure privacy. For example, the headquarters office might be acceptable to the investigator, but not acceptable to the witness who may not wish to come downtown or may prefer, for the moment, to remain anonymous. He cannot be arrested since there is no probable cause; further, to pressure or lean on him might alienate him, in which case he would be useless.

Hitting him with a subpoena does not always produce constructive results unless the full context of what the witness knows has already been established. The old adage, "You can lead a horse to water but you can't make it drink," applies to witnesses, particularly where additional information and cooperation is required. Here is where many cases are lost: in the alienation of witnesses.

In the majority of cases, the average witness may be interviewed at a time and location of his own selection. While there are most certainly situations where hostile witnesses decline to cooperate, the majority of witnesses, if properly handled, are not hostile. Location and times selected at their convenience, rather than at the investigator's, usually produces the most constructive results. Places of employment during witness' work hours should usually be avoided. Under such circumstances, the witness can always terminate the interview if things get touchy, on the pretext that he must get back to work. He may also arrange for interruptions.

Generally, a witness may be interviewed at his home. He may or may not wish members of his family present; again, circumstances alter cases. Juveniles and female witnesses should always be handled with particular consideration and in accordance with departmental procedures. For example, juveniles may not be interviewed except with parental or school consent during school hours on the grounds; some jurisdictions require the presence of a parent or school official during such an interview.

Interview of females should be conducted in the presence of one other female regardless of the situs of interview, unless it is in the street or other public place with others present.

Various schools, colleges, and universities, both public and private, have special procedures for interview of students and school personnel; these procedures should be observed.

Witnesses should never be subjected to unreasonably long interviews. This is an elastic thing with factors such as the age of the witness, physical condition, situs of interview, weather, and time of day all being relevant. He should be afforded the opportunity to respond to his personal physical functions on request. So-called psychological pressures advocated by some theorists of investigative tactics, such as declining permission to smoke (if the witness smokes) or obtain a drink of water, or utilization of the straight-backed chair and strategic location of the interrogators, is inexcusable and usually unproductive.

INTERVIEWING WITNESSES IN THE ARMED FORCES

Interview of witnesses in the armed forces may be conducted off base in the same manner as the interview of any other witness. He may be subpoenaed for a criminal proceeding for a crime committed off a military reservation and he may be required to testify within the framework of the requirements of the laws applicable in the jurisdiction of the offense. Most law enforcement agencies have long followed established, uniform procedures in dealing with military personnel through policies of procedure established with military bases in the respective areas.

Interviewing military personnel on base must be conducted in accordance with the Uniform Code of Military Justice and in accordance with conditions prescribed by the military authorities on the particular base. Experience has shown that military authorities cooperate with local law enforcement agencies in permitting interview of personnel on base so long as legal, military, and ethical practices are observed.

UNIFORM CODE OF MILITARY JUSTICE

Article 31. Compulsory self-incrimination prohibited.

(A) No person subject to this code shall compel any person to incriminate himself or to answer any question the answer to which may tend to incriminate him.

(B) No person subject to this code shall interrogate or request any statement from, an accused, or a person suspected of an offense without first informing him of the nature of the accusation and advising him that he does not have to make any statement regarding the offense of which he is accused or suspected and that any statement made by him may be used as evidence against him in a trial by court-martial.

(C) No person subject to this code shall compel any person to make a statement or produce evidence before any military tribunal if the statement or evidence is not material to the issue and may tend to degrade him.

(D) No statement obtained from any person in violation of this article, or through the use of coercion, unlawful influence, or unlawful inducement shall be received in evidence against him in a trial by court-martial.

As a matter of procedure, military investigators are instructed to strictly observe the Uniform Code of Military Justice and to obtain a signed statement from an important witness that he has been fully advised of the provisions of Article 31 *before* he was interviewed and *before* the document or statement is signed.

When interviewing military personnel as possible witnesses to a fire that occurred in a civil jurisdiction, circumstances do not always permit prior contact of his military superiors. He should be afforded the full protection of the civil law in regard to subject matter and circumstances of interview; additionally, the Uniform Code of Military Justice, Article 31, should be observed as an additional precautionary procedure. Neglect and short circuiting of procedures has occasionally resulted in unfortunate misunderstandings, including lack of availability of key witnesses when their assistance is direly needed.

ITEMS TO CONSIDER IN THE INTERVIEW OF THE WITNESS

The success of the interview often depends upon the atmosphere created which, in turn, may be influenced by the attitude and ability of the investigator from the very outset. Much has been said and written about the necessity of wearing conventional clothing and projecting a stereotyped law enforcement appearance. Hopefully, we have learned much in the past decade. One of the things we have learned is that the investigator who has the ability to merge with his environment and surroundings creates a more favorable atmosphere aligned to obtaining information than the traditional type who may receive cooperation only in theory.

This applies to a one-on-one situation such as an interview. While an investigator interviewing an executive in an air-conditioned, carpeted suite might create hostility in the interviewee by appearing in faded blue jeans and sweater, such apparel might be entirely appropriate for interviewing a witness on a university campus or construction project. Appropriate demeanor and maintenance of equilibrium are not necessarily dependent upon attire alone. It is a fact of life today that, although most people respect authority and appropriate display of officialdom, they resent, actively or passively, the unnecessary display of bureaucracy, officialdom, and implied force. Tests have shown that the average citizen, square or otherwise, is not favorably impressed by plainclothes officers who make it a point to insure that his gun bulge is obvious. The average citizen (the witness) dislikes having the badge of authority shined in his eyes.

The investigator who is most successful refrains from the unnecessary display of authority, particularly in the environment of the interview. Certainly, it is necessary for identity to be established. If in uniform, this is accomplished, in part, by the officer's rank and position in the investigation, all of which may be explained to the witness. If the investigator is in attire other than uniform, his credentials should be displayed in a manner designed to inform the witness to his satisfaction, rather than to offend him or turn him off. Being overly pushy usually closes the door to a cooperative attitude on the part of the witness.

Suitable measures should be taken to minimize unnecessary interruptions or distractions during the interview. The location may have a bearing on this. If at an official location, it can usually be controlled by pre-arrangement by the investigator. If on the premises of the witness, his cooperation may be obtained in this regard. Investigators occasionally forget that a witness is a witness and his right to control his environment and conditions of interview can hardly be infringed upon. This is an area often misinterpreted or misunderstood by improperly trained investigators.

The interview should be conducted with an open mind and that stance should be continued throughout the session. Although the investigator may have a fair idea of what happened and how it happened, he should not reflect this to the witness. He should permit the witness to do the talking, interrupting as little as possible. If the investigator has done his homework, he should recognize cover-ups, honest mistakes, or ignorance of the witness well before the termination of the interview.

In some circumstances, it is good to permit a witness to completely relate his story without attempting to interrupt or correct him. Some witnesses do not have the faculty to narrate their observations and must be handled through a careful question and answer routine. In this regard, care must be exercised to refrain from suggesting answers or putting words in a witness' mouth. It is well known that some witnesses are susceptible to suggestion. These witnesses have a habit of coming unravelled when they get on the witness stand. Regardless of the procedure, the witness should be handled with understanding, patience, and tact.

Some of the more gung ho theorists have advocated control over the situation: If the witness decides to smoke, you assume control by instructing him there will be no smoking during the interview. Practical experience shows such tactics are usually unproductive, unwarranted, and unacceptable to intelligent investigators.

As a rule, the witness may be placed at ease by initial routine questions regarding his name, address, and occupation and friendly casual discussion of the inquiry in general. It is advisable to have a second investigator present and it is good to remember that anything said by any participants might be the subject of inquiry at some future time—including on the witness stand in Court. The investigator might be required to testify, under oath, as to what he and the witness said.

Any recording or monitoring of the interview must be in accordance with the penal laws of the jurisdiction and with departmental policy. The investigator should be fully cognizant of the law and departmental policy in such matters and must abide by them at all times. In some jurisdictions, today, it is unlawful to monitor or record conversations without the consent of a participant. In some jurisdictions, peace officers or law enforcement officers may monitor and record conversations of other parties without consent of any participant when investigating certain major crimes, by telephonic tap with court order previously received, and in some other circumstances.

An investigator, interviewing a witness in a non-official environment, should consider that his comments may be recorded or monitored; this also applies to telephone conversations. Investigators have been embarrassed by indiscreet or inappropriate comments during interviews and also where their telephone conversations have been recorded by prior participant consent.

A good practice during the early phases of the interview is to refrain from grabbing pen and notebook. This has a tendency to tighten the witness. A frequent practice by adjusters and private investigators is to charge into a situation with pen, lined notebook, tape recorder, or even a court reporter, showing a toothy smile and opening with: "Now let's have everything on the record so we can't misquote each other, shall we?" The witness usually responds with divulgence of no more information than is already known to the person who set up the interview. Certainly, there is a time and place for the notebook, the tape recorder, and even the stenographer. The successful investigator knows this time and place. He has gone over the ground carefully and is as sure as he can be that this is about all he is going to get from the witness and that it is factual in regard to the wit-

ness' knowledge of the events. Then is the time to suggest recording or a statement, with the explanation that a copy will be provided the witness. He can use the copy to refresh his memory if and when his testimony will be required sometime in the future; it will further prevent his being misquoted.

In either electronic or written record of the witness' statement, the time and date of the interview should be included along with the location and full names of persons present. In case of recording, the fact that the witness knows the interview is being recorded should be included along with the identification of the matter under inquiry. In the circumstance of interview and recording by statement, the witness' signature must be affixed at the end and his initials set down on each and every page.

Although some authorities categorize witnesses into friendly and hostile, this is somewhat of an amateurish approach. The fire investigator is supposed to interview all witnesses in an objective manner and it is up to him to maintain his cool and utilize his abilities and available facts to elicit the truth from friendly and hostile witnesses alike. Hostility doesn't necessarily prevent a witness from telling it like it is. Experience has shown that the sometimes friendly witness is the one who leads the investigator down the garden path to double cross and fabrication. The deceitful witness should be encouraged to talk and talk. The more he lies, the better the chance to point out his errors and finally obtain the truth. If he persists in deceit, he will probably be of little value to the prosecution unless he is subpoenaed by the opposition, in which case his repeated lies may be used to impeach his testimony. Then, he can be dealt with appropriately by the Court.

Interview of witnesses may be productively implemented by use of accurate reference photographs, plans, maps, and sketches of the scene as well as other relevant items. Such data are particularly useful when interviewing police, firemen, and expert witnesses.

Whether fire company personnel are interviewed individually or in a group depends upon the kind of information under inquiry. Often, when interviewed collectively, firemen indicate a more comprehensive response and are able to correlate the recollection of their movements, particularly when photographs or sketches are utilized. Upon these they may note and identify their observations which may be of value to the investigator as he continues his inquiry elsewhere. Extra prints and sketches may be utilized for this purpose since the marked documents may not be admissible into evidence. Such individual markings, however, may be useful in refreshing a particular witness' recollection since a considerable lapse of time between interview and trial is not uncommon.

A private witness may also appreciate the use of photographs and sketches, upon which he may wish to illustrate his observations. Extra photos or prints should also be used for this purpose. The markings should be the witness' own. Some investigators prefer the witness to initial and date the document of reference. Experience has shown that the average lay witness who is asked to examine photographs and sketches feels that obvious care has been taken in his interview, and that he is an important part of the investigation. As his interest is entertained, he becomes more cooperative.

IN SUMMARY

There is no panacea for interviewing witnesses and interviewing is not an exact science that will elicit precise answers for every situation or circumstance. General suggestions have been offered which, if used with fairness and common sense, should assist the investigator. Success in interviewing is an art requiring study, a proper temperament, and thorough knowledge and *observation* of legal and ethical procedures and practice. Its place in the law enforcement and investigative system cannot be overemphasized. The following reminders are set out:

1. Contact your prosecuting attorney or legal officer and familiarize yourself with the law and departmental procedures governing the interviewing of witnesses and suspects. (A witness may become a suspect or, a person originally regarded as a suspect may turn out to be a witness.)

2. Seek out an experienced and successful police or fire investigator and solicit his advice on the subject of witness interview.

3. During your initial experience as an investigator, seek assignment with an experienced and successful person in the field of interviewing. This need not necessarily be in the field of interview of fire witnesses; it has been said that, "the wider the experience, the better." This may be particularly significant when dealing with interview of witnesses and working with people.

4. Prepare your available facts *before* the interview.

5. Select the time and place best suited to getting the facts from your witness and try to achieve this location or an equally practical alternate without alienating your witness. It is sometimes necessary to bend a little rather than lose the opportunity of an interview.

6. Decide, *before* the interview, who is going to carry the ball during the session—you or your associate. Partners who are used to working together learn to do this naturally. In all other situations, if there are two or more associates, make the decision *before* the interview.

7. Make every reasonable effort to maintain order and privacy during the interview.

8. Remember, you are there to seek out information. Maintain control in a polite, friendly manner. Keep your cool and insist that your associates keep theirs. Let the witness do the talking even to the point, within reason, of permitting him to ramble. A good interviewer is able to steer a rambling witness or conversation back on the track without offense.

9. Keep your questions clear and as brief as possible. Take things step by step. Permit the witness to answer each question before proceeding to the next.

10. Avoid leading questions wherever possible, even though you feel you know what the answer should be. The witness is there to tell you what he knows.

11. Be thorough. Don't be satisfied with half an answer. Sometimes, it is good to leave the doubtful answer and move along. Later, come back to the half answer and the witness may fill it out. This is particularly true when it appears that the witness may be holding a few things back here and there. If you move into other areas, his mind will also move into those areas; returning to the partial or doubtful answer, he may supply the complete answer, uncertain of his earlier response.

12. Be patient and tactful. Avoid, wherever possible, antagonizing or embarrassing the witness.

13. Be politely discreet in what you relate to the witness and volunteer no more to him than he needs to know. Avoid providing him with the impression that you are guessing, bluffing, or that you do not know what you are talking about.

14. Be particularly careful when dealing with juveniles, handicapped, or elderly persons and unaccompanied witnesses of the opposite sex.

15. In all interviews, it is good to note the date, time, and place of the interview, the time the interview was terminated, and persons present. Although this information may be contained in recordings or statements, thorough investigators maintain a field diary which contains such information for his permanent future reference.

CHAPTER XVI

THE EXPERT WITNESS

It is well known that fires have a tendency to obliterate the evidence of origin and expertise is commonly required in evaluating and determining the point of origin and precise cause. Those who are experienced in the legal and practical aspects of arson investigation generally agree that, in the majority of criminal investigations and prosecutions involving fires, the turning point is proving the cause (establishing the *corpus delicti*).

In some cases, the proof of specific cause may be obvious. For example, a witness may have observed the suspect throw an incendiary device against the side of a building, observed the original ignition, and led the investigators to the remains of the device after control of the fire. This evidence, presented in court, may be acceptable and sufficient in showing that the fire resulted from a criminal agency without the testimony of an expert witness. On the other hand, perhaps there was no eye witness to the act, which is usually the case.

Let us suppose, for example, that investigators recovered the remains of an incendiary device such as a Molotov cocktail and residue from the point of impact, all of which was submitted to a crime laboratory. A properly qualified on scene investigator might later testify as to the identity of the item found and the odor of a petroleum substance similar to gasoline. He might further testify as to origin of the fire at point of impact, and that, in his opinion, the cause of the fire was other than accidental, i.e. set with human hands. Laboratory experts might further testify that debris and specimens recovered from the origin were submitted or described for laboratory processing and that analysis disclosed the residue to be gasoline. The tests might even further identify the gasoline and fire bomb fragments as being similar in chemical content and design to items and materials found in the defendant's possession.

The laboratory expert witnesses might not necessarily be fire experts. The fire experts, as a rule, are not laboratory experts. The testimony of each expert, in the above example, was utilized in establishing and corroborating the incendiary nature of the fire. The expert testimony of the laboratory specialists would have been further utilized to connect the defendant to the crime.

In the majority of arson prosecutions, the qualified fire expert is essential and it is upon his expertise, objectivity, and credibility that the Court and jury must rely in determining that important question: "Was the fire incendiary or could it reasonably have resulted from accidental means?"

Evidence placing the defendant at the scene prior to the fire is not generally considered to be part of the *corpus delicti;* neither is showing that the defendant had motive or opportunity to set the fire—or that he had been convicted of setting fires in the past. Any statements made, even a confession, may not be admitted until there is an independent showing, by separate reliable evidence, that the crime of arson was, in fact, committed.

Arson prosecutions are somewhat unique in that the expertise of a fire investigation specialist may have much weight in determining whether a crime was committed. It may rest upon his testimony alone whether a reasonable showing can be made of not only where the fire started but that it was caused by a criminal agency. The importance of this type of testimony becomes even more significant when it is considered that the testimony may rest upon observations and conclusions drawn from his examination of the fire scene. He may draw conclusions from evidence he has examined and from hypothetical questions put to him based upon evidence presented in court, even though he may never have visited the fire scene.

For example, the qualified expert witness may testify that he visited and examined the fire scene; that he found two separate and distinct points of origin; and that there was no connection between the two fires, one fire being in a storage room at the rear of the shop and the other in the office area at the front of the shop. On the other hand, the expert witness may never have visited the scene. He appears in court and is asked hypothetical questions by the prosecuting attorney based upon testimony of firemen who visited the scene and conducted investigations. Further, he is shown photographs of the scene that have been previously introduced into evidence. The qualified expert can formulate an opinion based upon previous testimony and upon his examination of the photographs, *if* he states that he feels he can form such an opinion. If his answer is affirmative, he may then state that opinion, which may be that the fire is of incendiary origin or that it is not. He may, of course, be cross-examined in depth concerning the reasons for his conclusions and opinions.

The importance and end effects of this type of expert testimony suggests sober reflection on the necessity of insuring that experts in this field receive the necessary authoritative training, supplemented by experience in the field. The necessity for complete integrity and objectivity of this class of expert witness should be obvious. This is undoubtedly why the Courts are cautious in the area of fire experts and why they usually permit wide latitude in cross-examination of expert witnesses, particularly in criminal fire cases. Under our justice system, this is as it should be. The suspect or defendant, regardless of his station in life or the size of the fire, is entitled to the benefit of reasonable doubt.

It is well established that reasonable doubt extends to the state's burden of proving that a crime, in fact, was committed. Experienced fire and law enforcement personnel recognize that arson is a heinous offense capable of destroying life and property and that it is occasionally difficult to investigate to a factual conclusion. They also recognize the need for maintaining investigative integrity within the guidelines of our justice system and without influence or pressure from possible interested parties.

QUALIFICATIONS OF AN EXPERT

The Courts have repeatedly held that the fire expert field requires special study, training, and experience and have rejected testimony in this area where examination has indicated a lack of such expertise. There is presently no widely accepted or uniform system of evaluation. In some areas, the testimony of firemen and fire chiefs has been rejected on matters of origin and cause; conversely, testimony of police and deputy sheriffs, as well as specialists in other fields, have been accepted.

Before an expert witness can be permitted to testify, his competency must be established by a preliminary examination. (Mathis v. State, 15 Ala. App. 245, 73. So. 122, Washington — Re: Gorkow, 20 Wash. 563, 56 P. 385; Pennsylvania Commonwealth v. Johnson, 265 Pa. 491, 109 A. 218; People v. Becker (1949) 94 CA 2d 434, 210 P 2d 871; and People v. Sunders, 13 Cal. App. 743 110 Pac. 824.) This does not necessarily mean that an experienced fireman or fire chief can testify as an expert on origin and cause unless it can be shown that he is especially qualified in those particular fields. (State v. Duelfas, 97 N.J. Law 43, 116 Atl. 865.)

The basic purpose of the expert witness is to provide the Court and jury with answers to relevant questions in technical areas concerning subject matter normally outside the generally accepted knowledge of the average person. For example, in cases involving the load-carrying capacity of electrical devices and conductors, an expert in the field of electricity might explain the voltage and amperage relationship in terms of use in watts, the hazards in terms of size of conductors and fuses, and the heat or arc potential from overload. As a technical expert, he might explain the fire-causing potential of electricity misuse in terms the jury would understand.

The behavior of explosive vapors, gases, or solids and their reactions to temperature and pressure is a subject not within the purview of common knowledge and the Court might permit a qualified expert to testify to explain the phenomenon and potentialities to the jury so long as his testimony remained within the confines of relevancy and materiality.

The Courts have generally considered that certain areas of the phenomena of fire and explosions are not within the spectrum of common knowledge and it is in these areas that the qualified fire expert may be permitted to testify. His opinions are frequently necessary in providing information that will assist the Court and jury in reaching decisions of fact such as where, when, and how the fire started.

Expert opinions are not admissible in areas where the jurors are qualified to draw their own conclusions from the evidence at hand. (Cochran v. State, 20 Ala. App. 109, 101 So. 73; People v. Beckman, 307 Ill. 492, 139 N.E. 91; State v. Rusher, 22 N.M. 275, 161 P. 337; and People v. Champion, 193 Cal. 441, 225 P. 278.)

However, before a witness may be permitted to testify as an expert, his competency must be established by appropriate examination by counsel and the Court, in its discretion (Mather v. State, 15 Ala. App. 245, 73 So. 122; Koons v. State, 36 Ohio,

195 Re—Gorkow, 20 Wash., 563, 56 P. 385). Other witnesses may be called to corroborate his competency (State v. Maynes, 61 Iowa 119, 15, N.W. 864; Copeland v. State, 27 Ala. App. 405, 173 So. 407; People v. Kimbrough, 193 Mich. 330, 159, N.W. 533).

Where the nature of the case involves scientific, mechanical, or other technical or specialized knowledge, the admission of expert opinion is considered proper (Nickolae v. U.S.C.C.A., 5th 48 F (2nd); People v. Lytle, 34 Cal. App. 360, 167 P. 552; People v. Freeman, 107 CA 2nd 44, 236 P. 2nd 396).

The Court may ask hypothetical questions of an expert witness to satisfy itself concerning the possibility of a fire occurring under certain prescribed conditions. (See People v. Freeman above.)

HYPOTHETICAL QUESTIONS

While the hypothesis contained in a question should have some evidence to sustain it, the question may be framed on any reasonable theory which can be deduced from the evidence. The statement may also assume any facts reasonably within the scope of the evidence upon which the expert's opinion is to be derived so long as the issues are material, relevant, and not unfair or misleading (People v. Becker, 94 CA 2d 434, 210 P 2d 871).

For example, in a prosecution for arson and burning insured property with intent to defraud the insurer, the evidence showed that the defendant's tightly closed residence burned after an explosion. A gas heater had an open valve and two flare pots, one uncapped, were in the adjacent debris. The facts warranted that an expert be questioned as to the elapsed time required to produce an explosive mixture of gas and air.

EXPERIMENTS BY EXPERT WITNESSES

In a prosecution for arson and burning insured property where the fire occurred in an unventilated room, there was no prejudicial error in permitting an expert witness to experiment for the purpose of showing the effect of insufficient oxygen in a closed space. Photographs were also admitted into evidence to show similar merchandise that had been burned under like circumstances. The experiment and photographs were offered and received not to prove the offense charged, but to illustrate the effect of insufficient oxygen in a closed room. The jury was admonished that the evidence was admitted for that limited purpose only. (People v. Mondshine, 132 CA 395, 22 P 2d 779).

EXPERIMENTS—MOTION PICTURES BY EXPERT WITNESSES

In a prosecution for willfully and maliciously setting a forest fire, it was not an error to admit the testimony of expert witnesses concerning a motion picture experiment near the scene of the subject fire. The film showed that, of a number of lighted matches thrown to the side of the road from a moving vehicle traveling at various speeds, only one of the matches did not remain lighted and start a fire. The pictures also showed the condition of the ground cover which was quite similar to that existing where the fires in question were started, although it was admitted that the wind and temperature conditions may not have been identical. (People v. Freeman, 107 CA 2d 44, 236 P. 2d 396.) In the same case, the appellate court held it was not an error to admit the testimony of the expert witnesses as to the cause of the fires because, even though the cause of some fires may be a matter within the realm of common knowledge, the situation involved considerations which called for the evidence of qualified experts. This included the charred remnants of ordinary kitchen matches which were found at the points where all the fires except one originated. There was ample evidence showing that these matches had not been placed after the fires started to burn and that none of the fires could have resulted from any of the others.

EVIDENCE—EXPERT OPINION (REVERSED)

Evidence showed that the defendant increased the fire insurance on his market shortly before a fire occurred there. The fire started near a light switch 15 minutes after the defendant and his employee turned off the lights, set the burglar alarms, and drove off toward the employee's home. An expert gave his opinion that the fire had been set although he conceded that it might have been caused by defective wiring. One burglar alarm switch was open and the defendant's statements concerning his income were inaccurate. Upon entering the building, the expert looked at the floor only to find that any evidence that there had been a fire had been removed. Held, insufficient evidence to warrant a conviction of arson and of burning to defraud insurer. (People v. Seltzer, 107 CA 2d 627, 237 P 2d 689).

DOCUMENTARY EVIDENCE—PHOTOGRAPHS

Photographs showing the bodies of persons inside the premises of a bar destroyed by a fire and the charred condition of the bar, used in connection with the testimony of a fireman who was called as an expert, were relevant in determining point of origin of the fire and were corroborative of the expert's testimony. (People v. Chavez, 50 CA 2d 778, 329 P 2d 907.)

CONCLUSIVE EVIDENCE IF KNOWLEDGE RESTS SOLELY WITH EXPERT WITNESS

It is only in cases where subject matter of the testimony is solely within the knowledge of the expert that uncontradicted testimony of the expert may become conclusive. (People v. Swain 200 CA 2d 344, 19 Cal. Rptr. 403.)

SUFFICIENCY OF CORPUS DELICTI FOR ADMITTING CONFESSION

In a prosecution for arson, there was sufficient evidence to establish the *corpus delicti* for the purpose of admitting the extrajudicial statements of the defendant. The testimony showed that one fire had started on the floor of the upholstery shop and another beneath the floor. Considerable cocoa fiber was on the floor and beneath the floor in the places at which the fires had been burning and some freshly burned matches were nearby on the floor. All doors were locked and no wires or devices of any kind which could have started the fire were nearby. The defendant was seen leaving his building early in the morning, about the time when the fire must have started. (People v. Sherman 97 CA 2d 245, 317 P 2d 715.)

The prevailing rule is that admission of expert testimony is not an invasion of the province of the jury even though it may involve the precise question upon which the jury is asked to pass. (Evans v. Comm., 230 Ky. 411, 19 SW (2d) 1091, 66 A.L.R. 360; People v. Baldwin, 36 Kan. 1, 12 P 318; and Williams v. State, 64 Md. 384, 7A 889.)

The general rule is that opinions of experts are not, as a matter of law, to be accepted by the jury in place of their own judgment. The expert testimony may be evaluated as to its credibility and appropriate weight, just the same as that of the credibility and weight of any other witness and also taking into consideration the apparent character, capacity, skill, opportunity for observation, state of mind, and con-

sistency of the expert witness as seen and heard by the jury and by the nature of the case and of its developed facts. (State v. Miller, 9 Houst (Del); and Comm. v. Moss, 6 Luz. Reg. Rep. Pa 31.) It should be noted that expert witnesses are human and subject to error and bias as are lay witnesses. Although expert witnesses are supposed to be objective in their analysis and opinions, it is well known that they may occasionally become overzealous which is always questionable in the spectrum of objectivity.

When the knowledge of the expert as to the particular fact in question is derived from his own personal observations, whether in or out of court, he may be asked his opinion directly on that fact. (Torshe v. State, Neb. 161, 242 N.W. 408; and People v. Young, 15 N.Y. 110, 45 N.E. 460.)

Where the opinion of the expert is based upon facts in the case which he has personally witnessed, he must first relate such facts to the jury before giving an opinion thereupon. (State v. Olson, 75 Utah 583, 287 P 181; and State v. Labbee 134 Mich. 55, 234 P 1049.)

An expert who has not made an examination of the scene may state an opinion on a hypothetical question which embraces facts entered in the evidence. (People v. Foley, 64 Mich. 149, 31 N.W. 94; and People v. Dunne, 80 Ca 34, 21 P 1130.)

The Courts are allowed considerable discretion in areas of expert testimony when admitting the testimony if the witness is qualified and then letting evaluation be made as to his weight and credibility. For example, it has been held that the flammability of certain substances, such as gasoline and petroleum products, is so well known that the Courts will take judicial notice thereof but the testimony of the expert may also be received. It is generally held that an expert may identify flammables by odor and color. (People v. Fitzgerald, 137 Cal. 546, 70 Pac. 554.)

Complete fire cause investigation may require expert assistance in many areas. The more common specialties may include the following:

Air Conditioning and Refrigeration Engineer
Construction Engineer
Consulting Engineer
Chemist
Electrical Engineer
Explosive Expert
Glass Expert
Laboratory Technician (physical evidence analysis)
Mechanical Engineer
Metallurgist

Pathologist
Petroleum Engineer

Public utilities, engineering, and service personnel are usually cooperative and reliable on services and testing equipment, including meters, service lines, conductors, and safety and overload factors. In industrial and commercial occupancies, as well as some institutional and habitational occupancies, experts on perimeter and interior intrusion and sensing systems may provide assistance in determining not only security of the premises at the time of the fire but other data possibly relevant to the origin of the fire that may be important to the investigation. This type of expertise may be unique to the particular security or alarm system in question.

When specialists are called upon for assistance, they must be provided with the information and physical evidence necessary to enable them to form factual conclusions. This may include examination of the scene, physical evidence removed from the scene, photographs, plans, specifications, and statements of witnesses. The expert may require additional information before he feels he can provide a definite opinion or conclusion that will withstand the scrutiny of skilled cross-examination. His request for such information should be complied with if reasonably possible. All of the above suggests the necessity of harmony and close cooperation between the general investigators and the specialist or expert.

There is a vast difference between investigative cooperation and collusion. Cooperation and understanding is essential in arriving at the truth in investigative matters. However, caution must be exercised, at all times, in order that investigative zeal does not result in a tilting of the investigative balance and a slanting of the facts to produce results that may not be consistent with the facts. History tells us that this has happened and will continue to happen; that investigators and expert witnesses, regardless of the best of original intentions, may be subject to the same temptations, pressures, and responses as anyone else. It is well known that specialists and experts appear in criminal and civil litigation, each with impressive credentials. Their testimonies can be poles apart, even when based upon the same background of investigative and evidenciary information. No doubt, most of the conflict of opinion may be attributed to honest difference of opinion. It is also reasonably possible that, in some cases, objectivity of investigative analysis and expertise may have been at least diminished in the maelstrom of financial interest or bias.

Some private authorities suggest that after the expert is retained, he should provide a rough draft of his report to the investigators for their review so that they may make suggested revisions before the final draft is completed and the finished report submitted. Although full and honest disclosure and discussion between investigators and experts is essential, the practice of supervision, review, and revision of the specialist's report by the investigators raises serious questions as to the independent integrity of the expert and his report, regardless of the good intentions of those who insist on such a practice.

The findings of the expert should be independent of the general investigators' report. Otherwise, the objectivity of his opinions and conclusions is diminished and the integrity of the entire investigative effort may be jeopardized.

CHAPTER XVII

THE WITNESS STAND

The importance of the witness was stressed in Chapter XV. It should be recalled that a witness is an individual who has knowledge of a fact or occurrence sufficient to testify; he or she may be the only means by which a particular fact in issue may be proven. The point may be discovery of the fire; it may be identification of the defendant who was observed running from the scene. The witness may be a fireman first on scene who will testify to the position of the fire or the position and condition of security doors or windows. He may be the only witness who can testify to accelerants vital to proving the *corpus delicti.* On the other hand, the witness may be the investigator who secured the scene, correlated the investigation and interviewed the witnesses.

The witness spectrum includes other private persons who may have knowledge that is material and relevant to the case, such as identity of occupant or suspect, his whereabouts at the time of the fire, motive, preparation, opportunity, and comments or declarations. The witness may be a laboratory specialist or an expert in some particular field such as electrical, explosives, heating and air conditioning, or specific origin and cause. In such cases, he is generally classified as an expert witness and his testimony might include areas of special knowledge and experience as distinguished from common knowledge. Such expertise might be of assistance to the Court and jury in arriving at a judgment of the issues alleged in the pleading. Details of definition and conduct of the expert witness will be dealt with later in this chapter. For the moment, our purpose is to discuss witnesses in general and their place in the picture as the case moves to trial.

Witnesses in general are the media whereby the evidence, be it visual, audio, or physical, is submitted to prove the matters at issue in a court of law. The witness spectrum and its use is as wide as the human experience. Here is the ultimate test of the arson investigation. The fire scene has been examined. The physical evidence has been identified and preserved. Witnesses have been carefully interviewed.

Investigative leads have been explored to factual conclusion. Reports have been submitted along with photographs and other relevant documentation. All of this investigation and preparation may appear to be a complete and carefully woven fabric authenticating the certainty of what happened, who was responsible, and why. Here, also, is the acid test of the alleged facts. Here is where witnesses must be placed on the witness stand, one by one, where each of them, under oath, must testify as to those facts within his or her knowledge concerning the case. The testimony may be simple or extremely complex; either way, the witness' testimony must not only be relevant and credible, it must withstand the scrutiny of searching cross-examination by the defense. Further, it must be admitted by the court and believed by the jury. Here is the place where the case will either proceed to a successful conclusion or fail, depending on whether the witnesses produced are accepted and believed. A witness' testimony may fail for any number of reasons including: 1. He may have been honestly mistaken and his story was not carefully checked out by the investigators; 2. His memory failed because of elapsed time; 3. Someone got to the witness; 4. Common fright of the witness on the witness stand; 5. Obvious bias or lack of credibility; and 6. Discredited (torpedoed) by defense attorney during cross-examination. There are also numerous other reasons a jury may not accept the statement of a witness.

Failure of a witness may be minimized by initial careful interview and checking his story, followed by an analytical re-interview of each witness shortly before he is placed on the witness stand. No witness should be called to testify without having first been carefully interviewed either by the attorney who expects to call him or the attorney's investigative assistant. Even though a statement was taken from the witness or his comments previously recorded, experience has shown, time and again, that things happen in the interim between investigative time and trial time that can materially alter the picture. The prosecuting attorney should be up to date on the witness before he calls him to the stand. With this pre-trial interview, the witness will usually be more comfortable when he takes the stand because he has at least met with the attorney and discussed the subject matter of his testimony, even though the discussion may be brief. Further, the witness will have refreshed his memory of the subject matter and will have a general idea of what it will be like and the ground that will be covered.

This applies to most lay witnesses as well as most firemen. Unlike most law enforcement and investigating officers, their experience on the witness stand is usually limited and often slanted by what they have seen on television and at the movies. It should be carefully explained to all witnesses that there is no stigma attached to discussing their testimony in detail either with the attorney who will call them or with the investigator assigned to assist. The witness should be clearly instructed, if he does not already know, that attorneys on both sides carefully interview their witnesses before the trial and instruct them concerning the areas they intend to cover and the conduct of the witness on the stand.

The witness should be informed that such procedures are perfectly proper so long as the witness answers all questions put to him fully and truthfully. The witness should be advised that he may be asked, by opposing counsel, if he has discussed his testimony with the prosecutor or his representatives before taking the witness stand.

WITNESSES IN GENERAL

In Chapter XV, we discussed the importance of establishing rapport and encouraging the confidence of witnesses in order to insure that they provide *all* information concerning the matter under inquiry and hopefully to insure that the witness would testify to those facts when the case proceeded to trial. The hard facts of life tell us that because a witness has provided useful information during an investigation, it does not necessarily follow that he will relate those facts once he assumes the witness stand.

The difficulties and inconveniences of appearing as a witness are not accepted lightly by the average person, regardless of the lectures he may receive concerning his duties as a private citizen. It is also a fact of life that, all too often, firemen and even policemen do not always step forward willingly when they must come downtown on their day off and climb onto the witness stand. This is particularly

true when the nature of testimony may be complex; it is also too often true when they have been treated in a cavalier fashion by the investigator and where they have been summoned out of a "clear sky" to stand around in crowded hallways waiting to be called. The problem becomes even more significant when the witness may be unfamiliar with courtroom procedures and apprehensive about what kind of treatment he or she will receive on the witness stand.

Perhaps the above briefly summarizes the reasons why *all* witnesses should be re-interviewed shortly before they are placed on the stand. In today's volume-oriented society, attorneys are so often overloaded with actual court time that they do not take the time for pre-trial interview. In far too many instances, they are forced, by circumstances, to rush to court and rely on outdated or incomplete witness summaries. The case is called, the jury is empaneled, and the trial begins. Witnesses are called. All too frequently, testimony falls far short of the expected mark even *before* cross-examination by some attorney who did his homework. Witness failure may be a key area in the linkage of the chain of evidence, broken beyond repair, the case injured beyond recovery. The post mortem explanation of the deputy D.A. to his boss and the investigator to his Chief will be, "Our witnesses came unglued."

Again, the importance of the witness cannot be overemphasized. Experienced and successful investigators and attorneys have long recognized the fact that, in court, the witness stand is where the issues are clinically and finally decided—the witness stand is the focal point. This is a fact too often completely misunderstood and even more often neglected by investigative theorists and case load statisticians with little or no actual investigative field experience or knowledge of trial practice and procedures.

Within reasonable proximity to the time of trial, the investigator should confer with the assigned prosecuting attorney and decide upon who will interview which witnesses *before* they are placed on the witness stand. At this time, the prosecutor should be familiar with the facts and with the order in which he expects to present his case including which witnesses he actually expects to call.

At this point, he and the investigator should decide which witnesses he should personally interview and which witnesses he may relegate to the investigator to re-interview. Many successful trial lawyers make it a practice to study a witness' statement for flaws. They expect the opposing lawyer, if he is on the ball, to do the same in considerable detail. They do not indulge in wishful thinking and should not accept the investigator's evaluation at face value that, "Hell, this witness is a tiger. Solid gold! He will knock them dead—a real eyeball witness." Too often, the tiger turns out to be toothless, blinded by the spotlight of cross-examination. The shining gold turns to brass.

Experienced lawyers make it a practice to personally study a potential key witness during a pre-trial interview. He needs to know what kind of an impression the key witness will make on the Court and the jury. Not only is he interested in how the witness looks in his office, but he is even more interested in how the witness will look and sound when he is sitting up there in the witness stand telling it to the jury. It is important to know, first of all, if he is credible and honestly willing to appear. His state of mind is important—is he reluctant? If so, is it because of ignorance, uncertainty, bias, hostility, or fear? Or a little bit of each? Although physical appearance and manner of dress are sometimes of some importance, the apparent appearance, often manifested in uncertainty or hostility, are even more important and are usually noted by the average jury.

Circumstances may alter the suggestions and instructions an attorney will give to a witness concerning his general appearance in dress and attitude. The suggestions may be made in a manner designed to help the witness rather than offend him. At the same time, the witness should not be required to appear as something he is not. Jurors are usually quick to sense anything phoney in the appearance of a witness.

For example, in a recent case involving a hotel fire, a key witness happened to be a well known "madam" in the community. A couple of local goons had attempted to burn her establishment. It was necessary to subpoena the lady as a witness for the prosecution and to testify as to prior threats and identity of the defendants.

After interviewing the distinguished madam in his office, the young deputy district attorney who tried to present the case for the State decided she would make a strong witness. After all, she hadn't taken kindly to an attempt to burn her out of business. He also believed that some of the jurors might be responsible members of the community, some of them ladies, and he was uncertain what kind of an impression the madam would make upon the jury since she was inclined to dress in a somewhat flamboyant manner. He therefore subtly suggested that she wear something slightly more conservative when she ap-

peared to testify.

When the time arrived for the witness' appearance in court, she appeared in somber black—no less. The effect was amplified by two of her "girls" who entered the courtroom with her and sat quietly in the rear while their mistress took the stand and testified. The jury's attention was mainly directed to the girls who appeared in the latest seductive street attire while the madam calmly put the finger on the two defendants sitting at counsel table. Most of the members of the jury readily accepted the witness for what she was and her testimony as truthful, which it was. They displayed the common sense and objectivity which has made our jury system the best in the world: they displayed the common sense to recognize that even madams can tell the truth.

The attorney may wish to go over the ground he intends to cover with a particular witness—permitting him to review photographs, sketches, and physical evidence he anticipates being used in the trial. If there are discrepancies between what the witness previously told the investigators and what he later states, *now* is the time to get the air cleared. If the witness has been interviewed by persons other than the investigating officers, it is important to find out what was said. Was the interview recorded? Was there a statement? Does the witness have a copy?

If the witness is a fireman, policeman, or other public employee, the attorney may wish to cover his knowledge of the scope of testimony including his duties, length of employment, special areas of experience, and the precise areas the testimony is expected to embrace. The investigative notes the officer has retained should be examined as well as any reports or other memoranda of reference utilized by the officer.

For example, in a recent case where two fires occurred in the same dwelling within a span of less than five hours, the Fire Department had investigated the first fire and classified it as caused by a defective fireplace. The origin and cause was so documented in the log and reported in routine reports. Investigation, following extinguishment of the second fire, which caused extensive destruction, reported the cause as rekindling.

A separate investigation, initiated about two weeks after the two fires, resulted in the investigative conclusion that the second fire resulted from incendiary means. In a trial of the issues, the original reports and documents were introduced to show that fire number one was reported as "faulty fireplace" and fire number two as "rekindling."

The above should emphasize the necessity of careful pre-trial examination of all reports and documentation that may affect the credibility of a witness.

The attorney may have a preference as to whether or not the officer or public employee appears in uniform. Some departments require officers to appear in full uniform unless otherwise instructed. Experienced attorneys often anticipate the climate of a particular case and make the determination on that basis.

Experienced and successful attorneys, during pre-trial interview of witnesses, instruct them to always listen carefully to each question—as it is asked—whether by the attorney on direct examination, opposing counsel, or by the Court. If the witness doesn't understand the question, he should respectfully say so. The question will then be read by the reporter or rephrased or asked again by the attorney who put the question. He will instruct the witness to wait until each question is completed before attempting to answer. This will provide his attorney with time to object to the question if it is improper. The witness will be instructed to refrain from volunteering information and to confine his answer to the question asked. The attorney should impress upon witnesses the necessity of remaining calm and objective and never engaging in argument or losing one's temper.

Attorneys often caution witnesses against falling into traps during cross-examination and to wait for the completion of the question. The attorney should be certain the question is understood and the witness should answer that question fully and truthfully.

EXCLUSION OF WITNESSES

Generally, courts have a procedure whereby witnesses to be called by either side may be excluded, on motion, from the courtroom during trial sessions. In such circumstances, witnesses must carefully abide by the instructions of the Court. These instructions usually require that witnesses remain outside the courtroom when it is in session, except when they are called in to testify. Witnesses are usually instructed to refrain from discussing their testimony with any other witness or person from that time on, except with their own attorney. (In the case of a State's witness, this would be the District Attorney or Prosecuting Attorney.) Any violation of the Court's specific instruction would be an act of contempt and punishable as such. The general objective

of such an instruction excluding witnesses is to insure independent and factual testimony of witnesses without the influence of what is said by others. The order is effective for the duration of the trial or until nullified by Court order.

THE GENERAL INFORMATION WITNESS ON THE STAND

The suggestions set out in this section may serve as a guide to the average fireman, police officer, or investigator. Suggestions for expert witnesses will be covered after this section.

We have discussed the importance of witnesses in proving or disproving questions of fact in our justice system. Our system is still the best in recorded history. It is important that each witness respect this system. It is even as important that *investigators* respect this system. The witness may or may not believe that his testimony in a particular matter is important. However, whether he is a lay person, fireman, police officer, or investigator, if he is subpoenaed as a witness, he must accept the full responsibility of appearing and telling the truth. Following are suggestions that may assist the witness in fulfilling his responsibility under the law as a witness:

1. The witness should review his notes and statements, if any, to refresh his memory before he appears in court. He may have been reasonably contacted and re-interviewed by the prosecuting attorney or his representative shortly prior to trial.

2. He should appear in court on time and be prepared to take the witness stand when called. His appearance should be neat and clean and as presentable as possible.

3. If the witness is required to sit in the courtroom and wait his turn to be called, he should refrain from jocular salutations with his associates during the session and avoid whispering, unless necessary. He should refrain from reading newspapers or magazines or engaging in other court distractions. Reviewing one's notes and reports while court is in session is considered bad form by some courts.

4. If witnesses are excluded, they should refrain from discussing their testimony with anyone except their respective attorneys. All other specific instructions by the Court must be carefully attended and strictly observed.

If waiting in the hall or elsewhere, the witness should be circumspect in his conduct, particularly during recess, when jurors may be where they can observe or hear what is said. Occasionally, witnesses and experienced investigating officers have inadvertently commented on the proceedings in the presence of jurors during recess. Innocent comments are occasionally misunderstood by jurors to the detriment of a case.

Casual answers to questions put by a juror, during recess, may be misunderstood by other jurors, by the defense, and by the Court. For example, in a recent case, a juror, after hearing a witness on the stand state he was from a certain state, approached him in the hall, commenting that he was from the same state and asked if things had changed much back there. The perfectly innocent question and response was misunderstood by the defense and the Court. Both the jury and witnesses were called in and admonished. It is best for witnesses to politely refrain from conversing with jurors.

5. Apparent carelessness or an indifferent manner in taking the oath manifests, in the opinion of some courts and jurors, an insensibility to the truth or a carelessness with the facts. Officers, and some experienced witnesses, occasionally succumb to the habit of taking the oath while still on the move toward the witness stand. This is not good practice. The witness should stand erect, listen respectfully to what is said by the court clerk, and then answer clearly. Only then should he proceed to the witness stand.

6. On taking the stand, the witness should maintain an attentive posture and attitude and refrain from slouching and resting on his elbows. He should listen carefully to questions and permit counsel to finish the question before answering. Officers are occasionally inclined to nod their heads in a manner suggesting that they know what question is being asked before it is completed. This makes a bad impression on the jury and may be embarrassing to the officer when he answers too quickly. Perhaps the question is not what he expected. A premature answer is a discourtesy to opposing counsel who may wish to interpose an objection before the answer is received.

7. The witness should speak clearly and direct his answer to counsel who asked the question unless counsel has asked the witness to explain something to the Court or the jury. For example, the witness may be asked: "Will you explain that to the jury, Mr. X?" Or: "Will you please step down and point out the window on the chart, Mr. X?"

It is recognized that there are various schools of thought concerning a witness directing his answers to all questions to the jury. Some respectable authorities suggest that witnesses who direct most or all answers to the jury sometimes create the impression that they are trying to ingratiate themselves or con the jury, whether the impression is intended or not. Further, this practice is sometimes considered a discourtesy to the attorney who happens to be asking the question.

8. The witness should answer all questions put to him fully and truthfully. His answer should be responsive only to the question. He should refrain from rambling and volunteering information and he should not attempt to explain his answer unless he is specifically instructed to do so.

9. Questions requiring yes or no answers should be answered "Yes, Sir" or "No, Sir." Some experienced witnesses fall into the bad habit of attempting to interject explanations to yes or no answers on the assumption that they should be allowed to explain. They should never attempt to do so unless asked or permitted to do so by the attorneys or by the Court. So-called experienced witnesses occasionally try to make their own rules in this regard. They usually wind up hurting their own testimony and the case. It is up to the Court and the attorney who called the witness to protect him in this regard.

10. The witness should avoid use of stilted or technical terms and phrases when plain language understood by the jurors would have been more informative and probably in better taste. Highly technical or bureaucratic terms are often misunderstood and, on occasion, resented by jurors.

For example, when the officer on the witness stand was asked the time he first observed the defendant, he replied, "I contacted the subject leaving his vehicle at exactly 1123 hours." While all this official jargon may be preferable in a report, it sounds too artificial on the witness stand. As the judge commented somewhat later, "Why do some of these official witnesses have to sound like a bugle on the witness stand? Why can't they come through like ordinary human beings, in language jurors understand?" Instead, the officer could have responded that he first contacted Mr. Smith (or the defendant) at 11:23 A.M. as he was getting out of his car (or automobile).

When an officer was asked where he first observed the defendant, he replied, "In the Greyhound depot. He was coming out of the head." The Court was forced to ask the witness, for the benefit of the ladies on the jury, and the gentlemen who have never been in the Navy, "What is a head?" The witness was then provided with the opportunity to elaborate on his expertise by defining what a head is. He stumbled from head, to latrine, to toilet. A long way around.

11. If the witness is requested to step down for the purpose of referring to a map or chart, he should make certain he understands the chart. If possible, he should refrain from standing with his back to the jury and from obstructing the view of the chart and reference points from the jury or the Court.

12. The witness should be equally courteous to opposing counsel, always maintaining composure and balance. Cross-examination is an essential part of our justice system in eliciting the truth. It should not be resented by the witness nor should it become a personal matter between counsel and the witness. The Courts are usually alert to the occasional hazards of cross-examination and usually maintain control. At the same time, they recognize the necessity of extensive cross-examination in exposing flaws and deceptions in testimony. Wide latitude is allowed, particularly where the witness may be very important or the significance of the evidence may be vital in the outcome of the case. The witness should never indulge in argument or a shouting match with counsel. In cross-examination, attorneys are quick to note low boiling points in a witness. Occasionally, they correctly diagnose these sensitive areas as uncertainty, passing over the area and then carefully returning, rather unexpectedly, to the area of uncertainty with a plan to upset the tempo of the witness in a manner he least expects. The trap is sprung. The witness, losing his temper or exploding with an answer he did not intend, is discredited in the eyes of the jury.

13. The witness should never attempt to guess or improvise an answer. He should never hesitate to say he doesn't know if, in fact, he does not know.

14. When the witness has completed his testimony, he will be so advised and the Court will authorize him to step down. He should respectfully ascertain if he is excused from further attendance before leaving the courtroom. If he is excused, he should leave. Remaining about the court or courtroom after one has been excused may be interpreted as bias or interest in the final outcome.

INVESTIGATOR ASSISTING COUNSEL

In most cases, counsel for the People and the Defense are authorized to retain an investigator or investigative assistant to sit with them at the counsel table, particularly where lengthy cases or technical matters may be involved. This includes cases where all other witnesses may be excluded. The Court's instructions to witnesses, where witnesses are excluded, applies to the investigator at the table if he is to be called as a witness. He must refrain from discussing testimony of witnesses with other witnesses and is bound in all other respects even though his presence at counsel's table is permitted.

Such assistants or witnesses perform various functions according to their ability and the need of their attorney. In arson cases, the assistant may be an investigator who correlated the investigation or he may be an expert on origin, cause, or any other relevant area of expertise concerning fire. Ultimately, he may be placed on the stand and, according to his competency, questioned as a general or expert witness.

In this category, the assistant who remains in court at all times must be extremely careful of his conduct. If other witnesses are exluded, he must avoid discussing courtroom testimony with his associates during recess. If witnesses are not excluded, he must be equally careful about comments to his associates concerning the credibility or characteristics of opposing witnesses, particularly within possible hearing distance of jurors. Assisting counsel usually includes listening carefully to the testimony of witnesses and keeping careful memoranda of critical or conflicting points which the assistant feels may be of interest to counsel. He should provide these notes to counsel as quietly as possible and refrain from whispering while a witness is testifying. Counsel usually likes to listen to what the witness is saying and needless interruptions may break his train of thought.

THE EXPERT WITNESS

"The nature of expert testimony is special knowledge of experience as distinguished from common and judicial knowledge and is in the nature of conclusions or judgments based on an assumed state of facts and rendered by any witness shown to be qualified beyond that of persons in general. Such testimony somewhat tends to invade the province of the jury, so as to supplant its work in proportion to the amount of reasoning in such testimony. In modern times, expert testimony has become a prominent factor both in civil and criminal trials. Our more specialized and complex civilization seems to afford an enlarged occasion for this class of testimony. This tendency to supplant the work of the jury by more general admission of opinions, inferences, and conclusions of the expert witness justly arouses the serious apprehension of students of trials by jury and also generally presents a question of interest". (Federal—Fry v. United States, 293 Fed. 1013, 34. A.L.R. 145; New Jersey—State v. Ehelers, 98 N.J.L. 236, 119, Atl. 15, 25 A.L. R999; Maine—121 Maine 128; Missouri—State v. Stapp, 246 Mo 338; and Utah—State v. Vance 38, Utah 110, Pac. 434.)

"The Court will go a long way to admit expert testimony on well recognized and generally accepted scientific principles." (Fed.—Frye v. United States, 293 Fed. 1013, ALD 145.)

"A proper foundation should be laid before opinion evidence is admitted." (California—People v. Stewart, 115 Cal. App. 681, 2 Pac. 2d 195; Michigan—Brown v. Detroit United R. Co., Mich. 520 185 N.W. 707.)

"The term 'expert witness' should not imply a willing witness to becloud or to thwart" (see C. E. McBride of the Ohio State Bar on the selection of expert witnesses in H. C. Underhill's *Criminal Evidence),* "and experts should not pass on the truth of the hypotheses on which their opinions rest unless it is within their own observations and experience." (Hammond v. State, 156 Ga. 880 120 S.E. 539.)

"Whether the facts assumed upon which the expert renders his opinion have been established is a question for the jury rather than for the expert." (Commonwealth v. Russ, 232 Mass. 58, 122 N.E. 176.)

"The judgment of the jury should not be surrendered to the opinion of experts." (United States v. Harriman, 4 Fed. Supp. 186; People v. Harvey, 286 Ill. 593, 122 N.E. 138; State v. Flory, 203 Iowa 918, 210 N.W. 961; Commonwealth v. Vallarelli, 273 Mass.; People v. Boggess, 194 Cal. 212, 228, Pac. 448; and Hodges v. State, 16 Okla. Cr. 183, 182 Pac.)

"The credibility of the expert witness and the weight of his testimony should be by the same rules used by the jury in determining the weight of other testimony." (People v. Lytle, 34 Cal. App. 360, 167 Pac. 552; People v. Singh, 136 Cal. App. 233, 28 Pac. (2d) 416; and People v. Farmer, 194 N.Y. 251, 87 N.E. 457.)

"Before experts testify, their knowledge and experience should ordinarily be inquired into so that the Court may determine their competency." (Federal—Samuels v. United States, 232 Fed. 536, Ann. Cas. 1917 A 711 Chemist; California—People v. Wilkins, 158 Cal. 530, 111 Pac. 612; also, California—People v. Hinkle.)

An expert witness may be required in various specialized fields in an arson prosecution. Most fre-

quently, perhaps, the expertise is in the area of origin and cause. This may entail a specialist with a background of training and experience in actual fire investigation. The fire expert may establish origin but further expertise may be required in eliminating electrical or mechanical cause, in which case the services of an electrical or mechanical engineer might be necessary. Where the use of accelerants or explosives may have been involved, the assistance of a laboratory expert, chemist, or physicist may be necessary. In reference to the security of the premises, the assistance of an expert on locks, alarm devices, or electronics may be required. Identification of latent fingerprints may require an identification specialist. In circumstances of fatalities, the expertise of a pathologist is necessary; for example, "Was the deceased alive at the time of the fire?"; "When did death occur?"; "What was the cause of death?"; or "What was the cause of the fire?"

It can, therefore, be conservatively assumed the investigation of arson occasionally requires the services of more than one qualified expert and certainly more than one area of expertise. If prosecution results, these experts must be called as *expert* witnesses. This is a fact frequently overlooked and often misunderstood by public authorities and by private industry. It is a fact of life frequently overlooked by the so-called expert who attempts to cover all technical bases when his competency may be limited to one area of expertise. Unfortunately, the incompetency of an expert is all too often not disclosed until he is on the witness stand and only then if opposing counsel has fully prepared for trial of the case, including evaluation of the competency of the expert witness.

Attorneys all too often assume that expert witnesses are expert witnesses without appropiate *voir dire* or cross-examination. The attorney either hasn't taken the time to research the subject or, by tradition, he is reluctant to question the expert in depth because of his impressive credentials. As he may have been told in law school, "Never question an expert unless you know what his answer will be and that the answer cannot hurt your case."

SUGGESTIONS FOR THE EXPERT WITNESS

Perhaps it goes without saying that an expert should fully expect that opposing counsel *will* come to court fully prepared to explore his credentials, his actual expertise, the accuracy of his inquiry of the facts, and his conclusions and opinions in respect to those facts in depth.

The expert witness should provide his counsel with a resume of his background, training, and qualifications. He should insure that counsel clearly understands the investigation he has conducted, the facts necessary to form his conclusions and opinions, and finally, those conclusions and opinions to which he feels he can testify. These areas must be thoroughly discussed and clearly understood between counsel and the expert *before* the expert is placed on the stand. Assuming facts not previously discussed is dangerous and can be disastrous to a case.

Most trial lawyers are fully qualified to decide what questions they will use and how to qualify an expert witness. It would be presumptuous for the expert to suggest to counsel what questions should be imposed other than to set out his qualifications, the areas of investigation he has covered, the conclusions and opinions he has reached, and the reasons for these conclusions and opinions.

Most expert witnesses are skilled in their field as well as experienced on the witness stand. However, like lay witnesses, they are human and therefore subject to reactions, pressures, and errors. Competent and experienced trial lawyers are usually well aware of this as they are aware of their own weaknesses and strengths.

It is assumed, of course, that the expert witness will observe the common rules of conduct expected of lay witnesses or general witnesses. These have been set out in some detail earlier in this chapter. The expert witness is expected to be fully cognizant of court procedure and his appearance on the witness stand is usually carefully scrutinized by the Court and the jury. He is always expected to be objective and completely factual.

In theory, he is not an 'advocate.' The adversary theory is a part of our system both in civil and criminal matters. Opposing counsel is an adversary under the system and usually appears as such. The expert witness is called to the stand—either by prosecution or defense—for one purpose: to provide a truthful, reasonable answer on a single or series of questions and to provide the triers of fact with the information necessary to permit them to come to their own conclusion of fact on the issues placed before them through the process of all the evidence. For example, the origin of the fire ("Where did it start?"), the cause of the fire ("How did it start?"), and the time of origin ("When did it start?") are all areas of expertise. It is not for the expert to offer an opinion or conclusion as to the involvement, guilt, or innocence of the accused.

It is obligatory for the expert witness to maintain his composure even under the stress of rigid and often deliberately castigating cross-examination. The expert should avoid using technical and stilted language where common language might be better understood. At the same time, he should avoid talking down to either the attorneys or the jury. Expert witnesses have a tendency to become excessively voluble. The expert witness should avoid volunteering information and should refrain from engaging in arguments with opposing counsel. Experienced attorneys are quick to size up an expert and if he is lured to the bait of argumentation or bias, he can be discredited with the jury. Many so-called experienced experts fall for this bait time and again; the word soon gets around and attorneys are able to shoot him down in flames.

In summary, it should be emphasized that the testimony of expert witnesses is especially significant in the prosecution of most arson cases. In the majority of cases, the *corpus delicti* must be established by opinion evidence. This opinion evidence may be determinative of whether a crime has been committed or not; it follows that it also is determinative of whether a defendant should have been charged or not. This is why the investigator and expert should be certain of all facts before moving forward and even more certain of all facts before testifying as to the precise cause. Unfortunately, there have been examples where experts have been drawn into the maelstrom of advocacy which more properly should have been left to the investigators assigned to that role.

CHAPTER XVIII

FIRE SCENE EXAMINATION AND THE FOURTH AMENDMENT

We have previously discussed fire scene evaluation in terms of recognition, evaluation, and preservation of evidence. Since the constitutional guarantees against unreasonable and unlawful searches and seizures apply to all persons and property in all jurisdictions, and since there continues to be some misunderstanding about how this applies to fire department and fire investigation personnel, perhaps it is appropiate to point out some of the general principles and guidelines in this field.

The fourth amendment of the Constitution of the United States of America specifies: "The people are entitled to be secure in their persons, houses, papers, and effects, against unreasonable searches and seizures," and "No warrants shall issue, but upon probable cause, supported by oath or affirmation, and particularly describing the place to be searched, and the persons or things to be seized." Similar provisions are found in the state Constitutions. The U.S. Supreme Court has held that the provisions of the United States Constitution in reference to self-incrimination and searches and seizures are binding in state and local jurisdictions. A "John Doe" warrant (not identifying the defendant or his property) has been held as violable of constitutional protection. It might be added that the Fourth and Fifth Amendments are intimately related, for unreasonable searches and seizures condemned by the fourth amendment frequently have the effect of compelling a man to give evidence against himself; for example, search and seizure (without consent or process) of private papers to be used against a party in a criminal proceeding is a violation of the fifth amendment of the United States Constitution. (Boyd v. United States, 116 U.S. 616, 6 S Ct. 524.) The protection against unreasonable searches and seizures extends to corporations. (Silverthonne Lumber Co. v. United States (1920), 251 U.S. 385, 40 S. Ct. 182; and 8 Cal. L. Rev. 347.) The fifth amendment of the Consitution of the United States of America speci-

fies that "No person can be compelled in any criminal case to be a witness against himself."

Fire Departments and all other related emergency units have been traditionally granted the right of entering private property (and all of their structures) including forced entry, if necessary, to extinguish fire. The courts have always held that this is in the public interest because of the hazards to life and property in the very nature of the phenomenon of fire. This emergency situation, excusing trespass, exists during the period of emergency which generally extends from the period of control of the fire through the necessary overhaul procedures whereby the emergency crews take what procedures are required to insure that the fire is out. The emergency situation may remain or continue through the reasonable precautions necessary to secure dangerous structural members such as roofs or walls that may fall at a later time or that may produce a hazard to persons. What is reasonable depends upon the circumstances of each case; the period may extend for a reasonable length of time to secure gas mains and electrical and industrial hazards. This is to protect the public from injury as a result of reasonably foreseen consequences.

During the above described period of emergency, it has been traditionally held that public investigative authorities may conduct investigation as to origin of the fire and as to the cause of the fire. In the course of this emergency presence on the property, they may examine such physical material as may be consistent with the emergency presence on the property and within their view. They may also photograph and remove physical evidence that points to the origin and cause.

Once the emergency is over and the Fire Department relinquishes the premises to the owner or such other person who may have the right of possession and control, the right to re-enter the property for purpose of continuing the investigation ceases unless such re-entry and continuing investigation is (1) With the clear and voluntary consent of the person with right to possession, or (2) With a search warrant issued by a magistrate who has competent jurisdiction, is based upon probable cause, and specifies the property to be searched and the items of inquiry. Any examination (search) of the premises outside the above described parameters has been held to be in violation of due process. In such a case the evidence observed or recovered must be excluded.

There are fine lines of distinction between lawful and unlawful recoveries of evidence and even the higher courts have occasionally puzzled over the distinctions. For example, does the presence of the Fire Department on the property for necessary overhaul of the fire give the right to the fire investigators to open office desk and file drawers on the pretext of overhaul when the desks and drawers were obviously not involved in the fire? Or, does the overhaul operation extend the right to either the fireman, fire investigator, or police officer to examine a residential garage area when the fire was confined to the house? The courts have said that the condition of reasonability must come into play. Suffice it to say that Fire Departments and investigative authorities should consult with their District Attorney or other competent legal authority when the question of unreasonable delay in retaining an investigative scene may be apparent. Most certainly, the investigators, fire or otherwise, should consult with the Prosecuting Attorney or other legal authority before re-entry of the scene unless the full cooperation of the party in lawful possession is absolutely certain and his voluntary consent has been obtained and can be verified by witnesses.

It has been stated in the law that the Constitution is blind to the differences between people. Its protection extends to all persons alike: to the young and the old, the poor and the rich, and the honest and the wicked. The Supreme Court has rightfully decreed that the rights of the most reprehensible criminal must be protected. While this is misunderstood in some areas, the Court's logic is far-reaching and sound. Information and evidence obtained in violation of a defendant's Fourth and Fifth Amendment rights are excluded under a procedure called the exclusionary rule.

The doctrine of the exclusionary rule was first promulgated in the Federal Courts and then expanded by the Supreme Court in 1961 to embrace every state and local criminal court in the nation. Prior to 1961, state and local law enforcement agencies, including fire departments, were not necessarily bound by the Federal rule. Even today, some Fire Departments and arson investigators misunderstand the application of the rule and the reasoning supporting it. Some investigators, aware of the general implications of the rule, attempt to alter its application to their particular convenience. For example, when the fire emergency procedures are clearly completed and no reasonable hazards remain, they remain in the "interest of safety" and continue to search the scene. In some circumstances, a fireman is left in charge on the pretext of emergency after the emergency condition has clearly ceased. The fireman or watchman remains to watch the property and protect it from trespassers. Again, in the absence of reasonable emergency, this is stretching the doctrine of reasonable search pretty thin.

Once the fire emergency is over and the Fire Department has turned over the scene, fire or law enforcement investigators should obtain a search warrant before re-entering the scene or have plenty of solid evidence that their re-entry and further examination of the premises was only after full consent was obtained from the person or persons in lawful possession of the premises.

In a recent case, the Fire Department responded to a fire that caused extensive damage to a dwelling. The Fire Marshal was summoned to conduct an investigation of origin and cause. Since it was late in the evening, the Fire Marshal conducted only a partial investigation during that visit. He departed with the fire companies when they turned the premises back to the owner/occupant. When the Fire Marshal departed, he advised the owner/occupant that he would be returning the following day to continue his investigation in better light. The owner/occupant said nothing.

On the following day, the Fire Marshal returned to the scene, accompanied by law enforcement investigators; a further investigation was conducted which caused them to believe that the fire was of criminal origin. Evidence was then removed for analysis and a criminal action was initiated resulting in the arrest of the owner/occupant.

The Court held that the return and search, the observations, and evidence seized at that time were unlawful. The case was dismissed.

In a similar action in another jurisdiction, the Court ascertained that the investigative reports disclosed the officers' suspicion that the fire was of incendiary origin when they departed from the scene after control and overhaul of the fire; that their return, the following day, and subsequent search and recovery of physical evidence were unlawful and in violation of due process. The Court further commented that, if the investigators suspected the fire was of incendiary origin when they departed the scene on the first day, they had ample opportunity to present their probable cause information to a proper magistrate and obtain a search warrant before returning to the scene. A return and search under subterfuge or pretext does not excuse the trespass. If, in the above instance, the investigators had consulted the District Attorney, they would have followed acceptable procedures and the critical error would have been prevented.

The arson investigator must be familiar with the rules of fire scene examination and searches and seizures in his jurisdiction at all times. If there is a question concerning a particular fire or search situation, he should contact appropriate legal counsel before proceeding.

Correct procedure is the difference between success and failure of many criminal actions including arson. Whether or not the investigator agrees with the law and the high court's decisions is really irrelevant. It is the officer's duty to obey the law in enforcing the law.

Generally, the courts acknowledge the legal presence of the authorities on the fire scene until the emergency ceases. This has generally been held to be a reasonable time for overhaul. Once that term or period expires, or the scene is released, further examination (search, if you will) must be in accordance with due process; that is, with consent or a warrant. Again, bear in mind that the search warrant may only be issued by a magistrate or court upon affirmation and probable cause. A search warrant is an order in writing, in the name of the commonwealth or jurisdiction, according to the local practice, which is signed by a magistrate, and directed to a peace officer. It commands him to search for personal property and bring it before the magistrate.

It has also been defined as an examination or inspection, by authority of law, of one's premises or person, with the discovery of contraband, stolen or illicit property, or some evidence of guilt to be used in the prosecution of a criminal action for some crime or offense with which a defendant may be charged (24 R.C.L. 701).* The courts have held that the warrant may only be issued upon probable cause

* R.C.L. refers to *Ruling Case Law* which is quoted in Ballentine, James, *Ballentine's Law Dictionary*, (Rochester, N.Y.: Lawyer's Publishing Co.), 1930.

and must reasonably specify the property to be searched and the items in question. Unless firemen or fire investigators in the particular jurisdiction are peace officers, the search warrant cannot be directed to them. Certain jurisdictions designate certain firemen and investigators as peace officers for the purpose of investigating the origin and cause of fires and enforcing the fire laws. The investigator should be thoroughly familiar with his particular authorization and designation before assuming an investigative assignment.

In reference to search and consent, judicial preference for search warrants has led the Supreme Court to observe that searches conducted without prior approval of a judge or magistrate are unreasonable under the Fourth Amendment (Coolidge v. New Hampshire, 403 U.S. 443, 454—1971; and Katz v. United States, 389 U.S. 347, 357—1967). However, while emphasis is on a preference for warrants, the Court has continued to recognize that a warrantless search, undertaken by law enforcement officers with the permission of a party empowered to consent, is lawful. This, of course, is the well recognized exception to the warrant requirement of the Fourth Amendment (Schneckloth v. Bustamonte, 412 U.S. 218 — 1973; and Davis v. United States, 328 U.S. 581 — 1946).

The case of Frazer v. Cupp (394 U.S. 731—1969) may be of interest concerning searches with consent. In that case, the defendant shared a room in his aunt's house along with his cousin Rawls. Frazier was arrested on a charge of murder. The place of arrest was at the aunt's home. Following the arrest and in the absence of Frazier, Rawls and the aunt consented to the search of Frazier's and Rawls' room. Rawls also consented to a search of the duffel bag they shared, which was divided into three sections containing his and Frazier's clothing. Garments of both were stained with what appeared to be blood. The clothing was seized and subsequently introduced against Frazier at his murder trial. Following affirmation of his conviction, Frazier appealed a Federal appellate decision, reversing the grant of *habeas corpus* relief by a lower court. Among other contentions, Frazier argued that his Fourth Amendment right against unreasonable search was violated when his clothing was seized following Rawls' consent; that Rawls had no authority to permit seizure of his clothing from the bag. The Court rejected his argument.

In United States v. Matlock (415 U.S. 164—1976) the defendant was arrested in the front yard of a home where he shared a room with a Mrs. Graff. At the time of arrest, the defendant was not asked by the officers if they could search his room; neither did they ask him which room he occupied. The officers went to the door of the house and were permitted entry by Mrs. Graff who was told they were looking for money and a gun from a bank robbery. She permitted them to search the bedroom she jointly occupied with Matlock. The room was searched and the money found in a diaper bag in the bedroom closet. On appeal by the government, one of the questions before the Court was whether Mrs. Graff was authorized to consent to the bedroom search. It was held that "when the prosecution seeks to justify a warrantless search by proof of voluntary consent, it is not limited to proof that consent was given by the defendant, but may show that permission to search was obtained from a third party who possessed common authority over, or other sufficient relationship to, the premises or effects sought to be inspected."

In his majority opinion, Justice White stated: "The authority which justifies the third party consent does not rest upon the law of property, with its attendant historical and legal refinements, but rests rather on mutual use of the property by persons generally having joint access or control for most purposes so that it is reasonable to recognize that any of the co-inhabitants has the right to permit the inspection in his own right and that the others have assumed the risk that one of their number might permit the common area to be searched." Other high court decisions seem to confirm the acceptability of search with consent but also indicate that questionable transactions will be scrutinized closely.

A consent to search should not be routinely substituted for a search warrant. Some recognized authorities suggest that where inadequate facts to justify the issuance of a search warrant are apparent, or where the exigencies of the situation make the warrant procedure impractical, a consent warrant may be in order. Under such circumstances, the officer must assure that he:

1. obtains the clear permission to search from a party in lawful possession;

2. that he avoids any action which would adversely affect the voluntary nature of the consent. The Supreme Court has rejected the argument that the state must prove a prior warning of Fourth Amendment rights in order to validate a search with consent. Nevertheless, a warning of the right to refuse consent is a factor to be weighed in determining its voluntariness and is considered sound police practice (DeVoyle v. State, 471 S.W. 2d 77, 80 Tex. Crim. App 1971);

3. carries out the search consistent with any limitations or restrictions imposed by the consenting party. Admissibility of evidence obtained under the above procedure may be expected. Again, the Supreme Court has upheld search with consent even when such consent has been given by third parties having the right of joint possession.

Questions have been raised concerning the propriety and legality of further re-entry and fire scene examination by officers after the premises have been released to the parties of possession (owners or tenants) and where a private or security guard has been posted either by the person in lawful possession or the insurance company. These situations pose fine points and, occasionally, such knotty questions as "What were the security guard's instructions and did he have express or implied authority from the owner or occupant to permit a continued search? Was his consent actually no consent at all?"

Again, the basic proposition of the law is that warrantless searches may be unreasonable in themselves, subject to certain well delineated exceptions. (Katz v. U.S., 389 U.S. 347, 357—1967; Vale v. Louisiana, 399 U.S. 30, 35—1970; and U.S. v. Goldenstein, 456, F. 2d 1006, 1009, 8th Cir.—1972.)

"Law Enforcement officers may enter private premises without either an arrest or search warrant to preserve life and property and render first aid and assistance, or conduct a general inquiry into an unsolved crime, provided they have reasonable grounds to believe there is an urgent need for such assistance and protective action, or to promptly launch a criminal investigation involving a substantial threat of imminent danger to life, health, or property, and provided that they do not enter with an accompanying intent to either arrest or search. If, while on the premises, they inadvertently discover incriminating evidence in plain view, or, as a result of some activity on their part that bears a material relevance to the initial purpose for their inquiry, they may lawfully seize it without warrant." (22 Buff. L. Rev. 419, 426, 427—1973.)

The utility of the exception to both the public and law enforcement is described in a frequently cited passage of a Circuit Court of Appeals opinion by Chief Justice Burger before his appointment to the Supreme Court:

"But a warrant is not required to break down a door to enter a burning home to rescue occupants or extinguish a fire, to prevent a shooting, or to bring emergency aid to an injured person. The need to protect or preserve life or avoid serious injury is justification for what otherwise would be illegal in absence of exigency or emergency. Fires or dead bodies are reported to police by cranks where no fires or bodies are to be found. Acting in response to reports of dead bodies, the police may find the bodies to be common drunks, diabetics in shock, or distressed cardiac patients. But the business of policemen and firemen is to act, not to speculate or meditate on whether the report is correct. People could well die in emergencies if police tried to act with the calm deliberation associated to the judicial process. Even the apparently dead often are saved by swift response.

"A myriad of circumstances could fall within the terms exigent circumstances: Smoke coming out of a window or under a door; the sound of gunfire in a house; threats from the inside to shoot through the door at the police; reasonable grounds to believe an injured or seriously ill person is being held within."

Again, even though the emergency doctrine justifies the initial warrantless entry, it may not sustain a subsequent search and seizure. For example, in the case of United States v. Goldenstein, 456 F. 2d, 1006, 1009, 8th Cir.—1972: "Where police officers were summoned to a hotel concerning a fight, a gunshot victim was found on the floor and the defendant, registered in the hotel, was last observed going up the stairs with a gun in his hand. The officer went to defendant's room and, on receiving no response to his knock, had the hotel clerk open the door. The room was searched but defendant was not present." The Court found the intrusion valid to this point for the purpose of rendering first aid and possible interrogation of the defendant concerning the fight. However, the subsequent warrantless search in which the incriminating evidence was found in a suitcase could not be supported under the doctrine since the reason for initial intrusion was to locate the defendant. Another limitation of the doctrine appears in cases where it cannot be shown that, at the time of entry, the police believed, or had reasonable cause to believe, an emergency existed. (Chimel v. Calif., 395 U.S. 752—1969.)

In summary, where investigating officers believe they have reason to conduct further examination of a fire scene after the normal emergency has ceased, they should consult with the District Attorney or other legal authority before returning to the scene. This precaution may spell the difference between a successful or unsuccessful conclusion of the case.

CHAPTER XIX

INTERROGATION

Interrogation is generally defined as a formal procedure of questioning or an examination. It has also been legally defined as seeking information with a positive factual purpose in mind or a meeting of persons face to face for a formal conference. Textbooks on investigation have occasionally attempted to distinguish interrogation from interview suggesting that interrogation means obtaining information in the form of confessions from suspects. Others suggest, quite literally, that interrogation is designed to force the truth from an adverse witness or suspect. One authority suggested that interrogation is an intensified questioning of a possible suspect.

Perhaps the difference in interpretation and understanding of the terms might be found in the so called means in which the process is used. The term interrogation is not offensive *per se*. It is the occasional use of the procedure that comes into focus or question and which has very properly resulted in judicial decisions defining rules of conduct for investigators and those representing our law enforcement and justice system in the investigative process. Whether or not the term interview is interchangeable with interrogation is really secondary to the actual conduct of the investigators.

The misuse of this information seeking process, whether it is called interview or interrogation, has caused the general public and the courts to be suspicious of any situation or environment associated with interrogation or any situation in which the term is used. In some areas, the term interrogation automatically carries the connotation of pressure or duress as to either witness or suspect. While this may not be true, the officer's comment, "We interrogated the suspect" is frequently misunderstood. Actually, the interrogation or interview may have been in an informal, low key, and friendly atmosphere. The officer, possibly appearing in court sometime later, calls the confrontation an interrogation and his demeanor on the witness stand may appear somewhat less than retiring. The Court and jury hears the word interrogation, and the die is cast.

Our courts have traditionally supported the necessity of investigative inquiry of witnesses and suspects within the bounds of constitutional limitations and ethical propriety. It is when we, as investigators, overstep or appear to overstep these bounds, either through ignorance or official zeal, that problems arise.

There is little practical difference between the process of interview and interrogation. The interview of a witness may be brief or considerably detailed. It may be in an informal or formal atmosphere. The situs may or may not have been carefully selected. The same may be said for interrogation.

Successful criminal investigators are aware that even the most casual witness may ultimately turn into the suspect. Conversely, and particularly in arson investigations which usually depend upon circumstantial evidence, the initial prime suspect may turn out to be completely innocent and his status may be factually changed, by the evidence, to that of key witness. As previously pointed out in the section covering the interviewing of witnesses, the approach to interview or interrogation may be the factor determining whether the true facts have been elicited from the witness or suspect. In the end, if he *is* the suspect, such information as he may provide can be used against him in a court of law, only if and when that confrontation was accomplished in a legal manner. *Further,* the conduct of the investigators may well determine whether any evidence or leads developed from the information provided by the suspect may be used in any further criminal proceeding.

Successful criminal investigators know that "investigative discretion is the better part of valor." The overly officious or come-on-strong approach is too often the indication of uncertainty and fear at the investigating end. This is nearly always recognized by experienced hoodlums and criminals who usually jump at the chance to exploit it into fatal investigative mistakes. Usually, the official weaknesses are also instinctively recognized by most other intelligent people.

On the other side of the coin, there are times when

the officer or investigator must move quickly and affirmatively in witness-suspect situations. However, in most arson investigations, these occasions are the exception rather than the rule. The more basic facts the investigator has at hand, the better he will be equipped to evaluate what information he receives from the witness or suspect.

Before launching into the procedures, it would be well to generally discuss the United States Supreme Court ruling in Miranda v. Arizona (June, 1966-July, 1967). This landmark case set down procedures covering interrogation by law enforcement authorities, or those acting for police officers under their instructions or at their suggestions. The Miranda Decision holds that "when a person is in police custody, or has been deprived of his freedom in any significant way, before he is interrogated, he must be given the following warnings:

1. He has the right to remain silent.
2. Anything he says may be used against him in a court of law.
3. He is entitled to an attorney.
4. He has the right to consult with a lawyer of his choosing and, if he cannot afford a lawyer, he will be provided one at the expense of the state.

The Supreme Court placed the emphasis upon the individual being in unfamiliar surroundings—out of touch with friends or relatives or others who could help him, and most certainly without a lawyer to advise him. The ruling applies to all Federal, State, and local jurisdictions and guarantees the rights specified.

To date, the courts have held that the warnings do not apply to situations where private investigators or private persons are interrogating suspects unless they are acting in concert or agency capacity for the police or law enforcement authorities. There are some rather fine distinctions that would be better left to attorneys and the courts. Situations where subterfuge between law enforcement officials and private persons or investigators is adopted to circumvent the intent of the ruling of course would invalidate any information received by the officers in the process. Further, private persons, including private investigators, may be held criminally and civilly responsible for violation of a person's civil rights in the process of interview or interrogation; for example, unlawful detention, threats, coercion, or trespass. Even though admissions or confessions obtained by private persons or private investigators may not be excluded under the Miranda Decision,

they may be excluded on evidence that they were not voluntary because of reasons such as even slight evidence of intimidation, real or implied show of authority, and other conduct which might have been construed in the vein of duress that negated the voluntary nature of the confession.

The same reasons may invalidate the confession made to law enforcement officers regardless of whether or not the Miranda Decision applies. The reasoning for exclusion of involuntary confessions is absolutely sound. For example, it may be the confession of an innocent person. Forms of pressure and duress can be very subtle, particularly where unsophisticated persons are concerned. The courts have always excluded all involuntary confessions on proper showing of cause, exclusive of any ruling imposed in the Miranda Decision.

The Miranda Decision applies to all officers acting in a law enforcement capacity and investigating criminal or suspected criminal acts in all Federal, State and local jurisdictions. Firemen designated as peace officers engaged in the investigation of criminal fires come under the rule, as do firemen who may be acting in a cooperating or agency capacity with the police who may be investigating the fire or with the District Attorney or other duly constituted law enforcement officials.

At the outset, if a person in custody is to be interrogated, he must be informed in clear and unequivocal language of his right to remain silent. For those unaware of the privilege, the warning is most certainly needed to make them aware of it. The warning is an absolute prerequisite in overcoming the inherent pressures of the interrogation atmosphere. Next, the warning of the right to remain silent must be accompanied by the explanation to the subject that anything he might say can and will be subject to use against him in court. Thus, the warning is needed in order to further provide the subject of the consequences if he does speak out. It is only through an awareness of these consequences that there can be a reasonable assurance of understanding and intelligently exercising the basic privilege. In advising the subject of his right to talk to a lawyer and have a lawyer advise him and be present during questioning, it has been held that an individual held for interrogation must be clearly informed that he has access to these rights. The right to this section of the warning is an absolute prerequisite to moving forward in the interrogation.

As previously indicated, the individual must also be clearly advised that he has the right to have a lawyer appointed, prior to questioning, at no cost or expense to himself. To fulfill this requirement, the individual must be clearly advised that if he has no money and no lawyer, one will be appointed before he is interrogated further. Without this additional warning, the admonition of right to counsel and the right to consult with him might reasonably be misunderstood. As a practical matter, it might also be a meaningless and hollow one.

The warning must be given in such a manner that the individual clearly understands what he is told, in language he clearly understands.

If the individual requests a lawyer, the interrogation must halt until he has the opportunity to talk to a lawyer; no further questions may be asked without the lawyer's permission or presence. If the individual requests a lawyer, but cannot obtain one, and the authorities do not provide one, the interrogation shall be terminated.

Many prosecuting offices and law enforcement agencies provide their investigators with Miranda Warning Cards which must be read, word for word, to subjects of interrogation and written releases to be signed by individuals who have waived their rights.

There has been much criticism of the Miranda Decision on the alleged grounds that it has handcuffed law enforcement in that it requires them to inform a person in a custodial or accusatory position of his rights in a manner he clearly understands before the interrogation can proceed; that this affords the hardened criminal a chance to catch his breath and collect his wits by which time he refuses to talk.

Experienced investigators who are used to doing their homework know that the objection is less than valid. Criminals, as a rule, already know their rights. Either way, the Miranda warning will mean little to them. Constitutional protection is afforded all persons: the young and the old, the unsophisticated and the educated, and those from all ethnic groups and levels of society. The intent of the protection provided by the Miranda Decision was to insure that no person is placed at an unlawful disadvantage by officers who, regardless of their good intentions, might be more sophisticated and knowledgeable than the subject of interrogation and certainly more adept at questioning than most laymen are at answering. The constitutional guarantees described in the Miranda Decision are the very basis of our democratic system and of what differentiates our justice system from that of the police state.

This does not imply that law enforcement officials

and the system aren't to be trusted. It simply means that individual freedoms and protection are the foundation of the guarantees set out in our Federal and state Constitutions; that these guarantees will not be circumvented in the interest of official convenience.

In further reference to the objection that the Miranda Decision handcuffed law enforcement, and increased crime, it should be emphasized that the same constitutional guarantees set down and imposed in the Miranda Decision have been observed long before that decision came down. For example, the Federal Bureau of Investigation, the Treasury Department, the Internal Revenue Service, and many other Federal law enforcement agencies have abided by the equivalent of the rule for more than fifty years—some of them much longer than that. Their excellent investigative and crime solution record, including murder, arson, bank robbery, counterfeiting, sabotage, and numerous other categories of major crime is a matter of record. They operated under Federal rules of procedure which, among other things, required warning individuals of their rights to remain silent and to the services of an attorney before interrogation.

So, let us not pay too much serious attention to the critics of the Miranda Decision. Interrogating suspects has not come to an end. The process does require knowledge and observance of those rules. In turn, this guarantees the credibility of the skilled and ethical investigating officer. True, it may help eliminate the lazy and unethical investigators but in the meanwhile, the professional will continue to do his job in a legal and ethical manner.

PURPOSE OF INTERROGATION

The basic reason for interrogation is to seek out information from the subject of the interview concerning his knowledge of the matter under inquiry. Again, this information may be to ascertain the subject's involvement, if any, or it may be for collateral information or for information pointing to investigative leads. Some authorities on the subject of arson investigation have written that the basis or basic purpose of an interrogation is to elicit a confession from the suspect. Such instructions are presumptive and often misleading, particularly to inexperienced investigators. Overly presumptive or aggressive attitudes often result in failure of the interrogation. The interrogation should not be conducted in a way to induce a confession. Interrogation is a valuable investigative tool, if legally and ethically used. If a person is innocent, the confrontation may provide him with the opportunity to produce or provide the necessary information to prove it. The first duty of the investigator is to provide the subject or suspect with the environment, atmosphere, and state of mind to furnish reliable information, whether it points to guilt or innocence.

As in many other types of investigations, physical evidence must be supported by the testimony of witnesses and, occasionally, suspects. It is essential for the investigator to develop this information, often through the process of interrogation, in order that it may later be utilized in the trial process in such a manner that the Court and jury will have it from witnesses or suspects rather than from the investigating officer or an expert witness. Juries are not always totally impressed by testimony of the investigating officer or the expert witness, either or both of whom are placed in the position of testifying to all things. Further, juries do not always clearly understand what an expert witness may be trying to say, regardless of his good intentions or the accuracy of his conclusions. They may not, therefore, be able to judge the facts fairly. By developing information from witnesses and suspects through the process of interrogation, and by later utilizing that evidence on the witness stand, the jury may then hear that testimony directly from the witness and in language they appreciate and understand.

The psychology of a jury is often uncommonly strange, particularly to investigators who may be abundantly familiar with all facets of a case and who do not understand when juries do not accept those facts or theories for granted. Regardless of the value of the physical evidence in a case or the apparent invincibility of the expert testimony, juries like to hear ordinary people like themselves testify. This may be because they are on more familiar ground, listening to what an ordinary witness has to say rather than the stilted terminology of many experts.

PREPARING FOR THE INTERROGATION

Circumstances do not always permit the time and environment that might be most favorable to this phase of the inquiry. Further, the investigator may have limited investigative facts at his disposal but believes he must move forward with the interrogation because he may not have a further opportunity. This happens. If, under such circumstances, his best judgment tells him this is the way to go, he must make the move. He must then play it by ear, feeling his way as he goes, so to speak—if the subject is willing to talk. Such off-the-cuff interrogations often pay dividends when handled tactfully and skillfully by experienced investigators. Even in this type of situation, experience and tact are the usual tests. Many major felony cases, including arson, have been solved through this procedure when they might not have been successfully concluded otherwise.

Conversely, unplanned, spur of the moment interrogations, with a "stranger" suspect and minimal basic information, is dangerous ground. The suspect may quickly learn how little the investigator knows; he may sense that the investigator is uncertain or bluffing. The investigator may well have burned his bridges behind him when there was no necessity for doing so. As a general rule, we, as the investigators, are the ones who have to "eat our mistakes." There is seldom a second go around. Therefore, the impromptu interrogation should be avoided if possible.

Arson investigation can usually be arranged so that key interviews and interrogations can follow a pre-arranged plan of gathering and evaluation of basic evidence. It is not good practice to engage in an interrogation with mind made up as to precisely what happened, how it happened, and by whom the act was committed unless it is clear, beyond any doubt. In preparing for an interrogation, the investigator should assemble and evaluate his information. This should include: interviews with firemen and other witnesses; information on origin and cause; information tending to connect the subject of interview to the scene; background information on the subject of interview, including his knowledge of and connection with the property involved in the fire and also including such information as may relate to motive; personality characteristics of the person to be interviewed, if known (i.e. how he may be expected to react and his possible credibility); and to formulate a list of key questions for which the correct answers are known to the investigator. These questions may be interjected at appropriate spaces during the interview and the answers received may be guides in evaluating the credibility of the subject of interview.

If more than one investigator is to participate in the interrogation, there should be a clear understanding of who will conduct the basic interview. General guidelines should be set down before the interrogation concerning what investigative information should or should not be divulged by those conducting the interrogation. Investigating teams who have experience in such matters usually function smoothly as a team, each knowing the *modus operandi* of the other. If such coordination is lacking, interruptions of one investigator can cause problems such as a break in the chain of thought of the other. Occasionally, this provides the subject or suspect with an opportunity to get his feet back on the ground. In the meanwhile, if he is reasonably intelligent, he will quickly conclude that the officers really don't know where they are going.

SELECTING THE PLACE FOR INTERROGATION

It is recognized that there are circumstances where the officers or investigators cannot always name the place or spot if cooperation and willingness to talk is to be reasonably expected on the part of the subject. Where the circumstance is custodial, the officers *do* have a choice.

If the circumstance is other than custodial, the location for interrogation should be other than at the subject's residence, place of business, or his other normal "diggings"; preferably, a neutral or official premises where the interrogation can proceed without unnecessary interruption either by associates, family of the subject, outsiders, or officers not actively participating in the interview.

While much has been written and said about the advantages of conducting interrogations in a plain room, experience has shown that the really important factor is quiet and privacy within the context of ethics and common sense. Some so-called experts have expounded on the investigative advantages of the pictureless, windowless room with three or four chairs as providing the most suitable environment for uneasiness of the subject. Experience has shown that the practice is impractical over the long haul and, further, that results are, more often than not, unproductive. The advocates of such practices are usually theoretical rather than practical investigators who must solve crime at street level. Environments that may be construed at some later time by defense counsel as "star chamber" atmospheres are self defeating right from the beginning.

The important factor in selecting a location for interrogation is quiet and privacy. The persons present should not exceed two officers, the subject of the interview, and a person designated by him if he so chooses, such as his attorney. The reporter or stenographer would be the additional person if the interview is recorded in this manner.

For example, if a female subject is involved, one of the interviewing officers should preferably be female, regardless of the current attitudes of equal rights and privileges. Defense attorneys are quick to note the odds in an interrogation situation where two burly officers have questioned one defenseless woman. If a juvenile is involved, consideration should be made as to whether a juvenile officer, teacher, or faculty member should be present. Again, circumstances alter options that may be exercised by the investigators in this regard. Remember, at a later test of the circumstances of interrogation, which may be on a motion in court, the fairness of the environment of the interview will be scrutinized.

Some official interrogation rooms are provided with the one-way glass. This has certain advantages. It has also been found that witnesses and suspects commonly recognize the mirror for exactly what it is—a glass through which he or she is being observed by others unknown to him or her. Most witnesses and suspects are really not stupid. They are usually sensitive. It has been found, as a practical matter, that the glass, in a supposedly private environment, really insults their intelligence and results in a general tightening of their attitude and in a lack of cooperation in terms of information provided.

Whether or not the interview is electronically monitored (recorded) depends upon the location of interview, the law in the jurisdiction involved, and department policy and regulation. It is generally accepted that the law in most jurisdictions permits electronic monitoring of conversations between officers and witnesses, and suspects and general third parties in the course of the investigation of crime.

This is subject to federal and state limitations on monitoring telephone conversations without the consent of one party or a court order.

In the subject situation, if the interrogation is to be electronically monitored or recorded, it should be accomplished only in accordance with federal and state law. Perhaps it should be emphasized that the right to electronically monitor conversations of witnesses and third parties without their knowledge and consent is strictly regulated in some jurisdictions and is prohibited to private persons (private investigators) by federal statutes under the omnibus crime bill. For example, private investigators, security personnel, and insurance representatives sometimes monitor and record conversations of third parties while interviewing employees, customers, and insureds. If the private investigator or representative is working for his employer or a company engaged in interstate commerce, the monitoring and recording may be in violation of the criminal statutes of the omnibus crime bill (federal statutes) by which the penalties for violation are severe. Before private investigators or private persons seek to monitor and/or record conversations or interviews, they should first seek guidance from a competent attorney, particularly if their client or company is engaged in interstate commerce.

THE INTERROGATION

Investigators assigned to conduct the interrogation should possess the ability to interpret reactions to questions. Regardless of the type of crime committed, the person being interrogated must always be handled in a civil manner. Whether the attitude of the investigator is friendly or not, he must attempt to keep the atmosphere impersonal and as quiet as possible. The use of profane language should be avoided. The unnecessary display of weapons and other hardware should be avoided.

Self control, under all circumstances, must be maintained regardless of possible provocation. The person in charge of the interrogation is responsible for adequate control of the situation at all times.

The following points are reminders for conducting a successful interrogation:

1. Be certain that the person, if he is in a suspect or custodial position, has been fully advised of his Miranda rights, that he fully understands them, and that he has otherwise made such written verification as required under jurisdictional or departmental procedure.

2. Be certain that the person being interrogated is reasonably comfortable and that he understands he may be permitted relief or comfort periods. At the same time, obtain his admission that he is not ill or otherwise incapacitated for the interrogation.

3. Try to create as pleasant and businesslike an atmosphere as possible under the circumstances.

4. As you proceed into the discussion, attempt to gradually gain the confidence of the subject; establish rapport. But make no promises you cannot keep.

5. Be polite but firm. It is seldom necessary to shine your badge in the eyes of the witness or suspect. He already knows who you are. Don't try to get familiar with him.

6. Don't exercise a superior moral attitude. The witness may react more positively to rationalization of what he knows or what he did by your appreciation that it is human to make mistakes. This may help him over a bad time in the experience and in the interview.

7. There are situations where a witness or suspect responds to an understanding of his ego and his feelings, and an understanding and appreciation of the reasons for what he may have done.

8. Let him tell his story in his own way. The important thing is that he is willing to talk and to tell you what he *says* he knows, in his own way. The good interrogator is a patient and sympathetic listener. There is always time to go back and identify inconsistencies or fill in the gaps.

9. Whatever questions are asked the subject, they should be phrased to elicit definite yes or no answers as far as possible. Be certain he understands the question. Then permit him to answer it without being interrupted with another question from another investigator. One question at a time.

10. Control the interrogation by directing it along the avenues you want to follow. At the same time, the investigator should keep an open mind and avoid controlling the interrogation to the point of keeping out information merely because it contradicts the theories of the moment.

11. Listen carefully to everything the subject has to say. Often impulsive and casual remarks may be revealing.

12. Pay attention to mistakes and contradictions.

13. Watch the subject and observe his physical reactions, which are occasionally more revealing than his verbal responses.

14. Do not appear overly officious, egotistical, or argumentative. There are occasions when disagreement with the witness or suspect is required. This can be accomplished without gum beating him or by divulging information he should not have in the impulse of the moment.

15. An uncooperative person may be persuaded to divulge what he knows only after the reason for his silence has been determined. Reminders of civic duty, social responsibility, or common decency are usually not too convincing, partiularly where there is a good chance the person is close to the suspect or that he may be personally involved. As a general rule, it is good practice to take the time to determine why the person chooses to remain silent—at least concerning the subject matter considered important. This usually requires patience, understanding, and diplomacy.

16. The interrogation should be terminated, if reasonably possible, in an atmosphere that will permit

further communicative contact with the subject. Leave the door open, so to speak.

In summary, the person interrogated should be favorably impressed by those who are asking the questions—by their conduct as well as by their words. Overaggressiveness or unnecessary officiousness should be avoided. Investigators and successful interrogators need not expect to be loved by those with whom they deal. However, they may be respected, even by the criminal. Time and experience have made this point repeatedly throughout the history of criminal investigation. If the person under interrogation distrusts or does not respect those who are questioning him, the odds that he will divulge what he knows are immeasurably reduced.

Experienced and successful members of the legal and law enforcement professions have long recognized the value of skilled interrogation. Attorneys carefully prepare for one form of interrogation in the trial process. It is called cross-examination. They also utilize it in the process of deposition when questioning opposing witnesses. Its skillful use usually means the difference between winning and losing their case. It has long been the valued tool of law enforcement in the fact-finding process, if properly used. Properly means legally, ethically, and by competent personnel.

It has long been known that successful interrogators have an underlying practical knowledge of human behavior. Study and experience have taught them that most human beings they will confront will react favorably to fairness, consideration, kindness, and reason. Usually, the reason must be bolstered with investigative knowledge of what happened and how. The use of these assets may well be the avenue to success in most investigative assignments and certainly to success in the professional career of the investigative officer.

CHAPTER XX

FIRES FOR PROFIT

While this text is oriented to the physical aspects of arson investigation, this chapter will be directed to one motivational class of incendiary fires that, during the past decade, has clearly created a great impact on society—the insurance fraud fire.

There are differences of opinion as to the extent of the economical impact from this class of fire. A recent survey by Aerospace Corporation, conducted for the National Institute for Law Enforcement and Criminal Justice, indicates insurance oriented arson accounts for approximately 17 percent of the nation's arson losses. The figure is probably conservative since the survey was conducted by science oriented personnel and based upon the most reliable information available. Other statistics suggest that the insurance fraud fire dollar loss may be at least 50 percent of the total national fire loss figure. In 1974, the U.S. Department of Commerce placed the direct fraud cost to insurers at approximately 1.5 billion dollars and it is still increasing. The gross economical loss has been estimated between the above figure and 4 billion dollars per annum. Again, all studies indicate that these fire are on the increase and the costs escalating. A recent report issued by the International Association of Chiefs of Police indicates that there is no uniformity in record keeping concerning arson fires (and, particularly, fraud arson fires) and no official uniformity in investigative procedures in dealing with analysis of cause of fires and reporting criminal fires in the National Criminal Index System. There is no present credible data on loss of life from arson or insurance or fraud motivated arson although presently available records disclose that approximately 12,000 persons died in fires (all classes) during 1976 and about 300,000 persons were seriously injured. Obviously, the gross figures do not take into account the lost work time and economical impact of those permanently liquidated or incapacitated.

The most experienced and best informed authorities agree on one point, however; that during the past decade, a significant impact has been made in most of our communities by arson for profit which is becoming an ever-increasing, lucrative field for the so-called white collar criminal and organized crime.

Generally, insurance fraud fires are carefully planned. This planning often includes a design to make the fire appear accidental, particularly where sophisticated criminals are involved. Major fraud projects are often expedited by skillful accountants and adjusters representing the insured's interests. This type of planning is frequently successful in executing the fraud fire and carrying it through to collection of the insurance, particularly where the authorities fail to diagnose the cause, and even more frequently, where there is no factual cooperation between the authorities and the insurance representatives.

Too often, this lack of cooperation grows out of a lack of knowledge of sound, practical, ethical, and legal investigative principles on both sides; each side sufficiently touches base to satisfy supervisory scrutiny. Soon, the officials move on to the next case after the dust settles and news interest dies. The adjusters settle the loss reporting "no evidence of arson" and "no evidence of fraud." In the meanwhile, the crooks are laughing all the way to the bank.

The weakest link in the investigative chain of the fraud fire spectrum is the lack of trained, competent investigative personnel at the official and industrial ends of the spectrum; the weakness may be further compounded by the very human and understandable frustrations growing out of unrealistic case loads. Communication and understanding between investigating officers and insurance representatives in a realistic pattern is necessary to the solution of this type of case.

Care should be exercised to maintain clear lines of ethical and legal responsibility between the investigating officers and the insurance representatives, including investigators retained by the insurance company. The insurance company has certain legal and ethical as well as contractual responsibilities to the insured. It may provide certain relevant information concerning a fire loss to the authorities within the framework of these responsibilities when the authorities have probable cause to conduct an investigation and make such inquiries. At the same time, the insurance company and its loss representatives must refrain from being drawn into an agency of the police relationship which may result in the loss of integrity of the investigative effort which, in turn, defeats the basic purpose of the investigation.

This type of investigative effort requires balance and propriety by the officials as well as the insurance representatives in disclosure of what the law and the courts have repeatedly held to be confidential official information and invasion of privacy through means other than the established methods of judicial process.

Practice and experience have shown, time and again, that arson-fraud cases have been properly and successfully investigated in the criminal and civil spectrums and through cooperation extended within the borders of established legal guidelines. The misunderstandings and exceptions occur as a result of ignorance, lack of appropriate training, indifference, and, occasionally, overzealousness.

The well planned arson-fraud fire may present problems with provable physical evidence which preclude satisfaction of the reasonable doubt requirements of a criminal proceeding.

At the same time, however, such evidence may satisfy the requirements necessary to prove fraud or justify recourse to the civil courts by injured parties. In this case, the results of official inquiry would be available through due process of the courts. This is not intended as a legal treatise but only to suggest to the arson investigator that there are procedures available under our system of criminal and civil jurisprudence providing alternate approaches in societies' remedies against those planning and committing violent crimes, such as arson, for profit.

Arson rings thrive in an environment that is indifferent to their presence; they thrive where dishonest and unscrupulous persons utilize fire as a vehicle to serve their requirements. Liquidation of distressed inventories is one of the more common and long-standing areas of activity; groups have recently been active in vacating distressed areas. Current investigations involve purchase of businesses by organized crime, under various fronts, followed by encumbering the assets through loans that are often based upon inflated values and inventories. Insurance coverage is usually obtained through cooperative or indifferent agents or brokers and, frequently, with in-

different fire insurance risk inspection. Often, there is simply no inspection. Occasionally, the inspection is farmed out to incompetent personnel who are paid on the basis of so many inspections per day—or else. Many of the inspectors would not recognize either a physical or moral hazard if it was staring them directly in the face.

The fire may be arranged by an approved torch who has the necessary expertise to pull the job in a manner ensuring that it will appear accidental. One of the more popular devices is to dress up the fire to make it appear to have been the act of vandals or burglars.

After setting the stage for the fire, the torch may make certain that evidence of forced entry is obvious even to the most casual observer. He may supplement this window dressing in the form of rifled files and cash boxes, missing typewriters, and other equipment usually removed by burglars.

During the 1970s, the increase in organized crime has been acknowledged across the nation by informed local, State, and Federal law enforcement authorities. A major segment of this type of crime is included in white collar crime, which often embraces arson and various forms of bankruptcy and insurance fraud. The impact of arson and fraud for profit has been felt in communities and cities across the nation where public safety and law enforcement authorities have combined their investigative personnel into task or strike forces working closely with State and Federal authorities in combatting the problem. The cooperation of the State and Federal authorities is vital because, in many instances, groups move on an interstate basis. They do not respect any particular jurisdiction. Areas where close cooperation between all agencies has shown constructive results include Los Angeles, Chicago, Milwaukee, Seattle, and other communities and jurisdictions where arson and arson for fraud is recognized for what it is—a serious criminal problem.

It has probably been correctly stated by experienced police investigators who have been where it is that, "Some guys go into crime because they are smart. The smart ones are usually the quiet ones who routinely and methodically go about their crime business. They avoid the headlines and newspaper and television coverage. After all, *they* are not running for re-election. They are out to make all the money they can, picking their spots and staying clear of the law except, perhaps, to purchase a connection here and there—again, one of the facts of life."

The sophisticated criminal, particularly the so-called white collar type, needs connections and he doesn't hesitate to pay what is necessary, whatever and wherever it may be, so long as he comes out ahead. In the fraud fire business, he may have to pay a public official, an adjuster, an insurance executive, a neighbor, or even a good witness.

Regardless of what some of our sociologists would like us to believe, our professional and white collar criminals do not always come from the ghettos and they are not necessarily the casualties of society.

As Harvard professor James O. Wilson, among many other experienced authorities, has said, there is no solid reason why crime must be diagnosed as the direct outgrowth of the ghetto or unemployment. This is particularly true when we deal with the professional criminal and organized crime which includes in its ranks the sophisticated and often the well educated; a wide spectrum of specialists exists in professions, including banking, insurance, contracting, real estate, management, labor relations, merchandising, and even, on occasion, the law.

Professional crime may be categorized as the planned illegal pursuit of money. The professional criminal goes where the "long green" is. He usually prefers the quiet road to the sure, untaxed buck, whether it is from hijacking, fencing, gambling, loan sharking, extortion, insurance or bankruptcy fraud, and, yes, even arson. Incidentally, arson is commonly used by the white collared hoods and organized crime elements in operations often overlooked or misunderstood by fire and law enforcement authorities. It is used in operations involving intimidation as well as property liquidation and fraud.

The professional criminal maintains his own "who's who" and is usually aware of the necessary mechanics and contacts essential to getting a particular task accomplished.

While it is undoubtedly true that much of the crime is disorganized, growing out of ignorance, poverty, frustration, and restlessness, among other reasons, the professional criminal proceeds with intelligent calculation and the assistance of other professionals in the underworld. When we have the meeting of the minds and concerted planning and execution of the crime for profit, with all of its ramifications, then we have what is generally known as organized crime. It doesn't necessarily originate or confine itself to any particular economical or ethnic group.

The professional criminal tradition in the United States may be reasonably traced back to the days of prohibition during which various groups acquired a fairly broad base of "know-how" in profit-making techniques via bootlegging and smuggling. They quickly expanded them into major crime enterprises within their various operating spheres. By the time of repeal of the eighteenth amendment (the prohibition act) in the early nineteen thirties, these various groups had expanded their control into activities such as loan sharking, gambling, vice, hot property, fencing, and real estate, among other things, including politics. They had refined their operations to the point where they could, if desired, control any criminal activity if they figured it would return a profit on their investment; again, usually tax free.

In 1975, it was officially reported that organized crime is presently a large and growing industry indeed; loan sharking, hijacking, organizing, and real estate gross over 100 billion dollars a year. Drug trafficking brings about 75 billion, illegal gambling about 25 billion. The above, of course, does not include the profits from bankruptcy fraud and insurance fraud via arson, auto theft, and garage accident repair rackets. These are in a class by themselves. These figures do not include personal property fraud scams through record manipulation and arson liquidation and assisted by the media of victimized insurance claims personnel and adjusters.

It is well recognized that the organized crime people are not necessarily the crude, rough and tumble, gun slinging hoods they were known as even a few years ago. Informed authorities recognize that they still utilize force when necessary but keep themselves well insulated by at least three levels from the direct action. They attempt to elevate their operations to an image status that is designed to encourage acceptance by society and nonobservance by law enforcement.

A spokesman for the United States Attorney General's office commented, in 1976, that the death of one Carlo Gambino, described as the most powerful Mafia Boss in the country, marks another turning point toward a native American brand of syndicated crime. The Attorney General's office further reported that the new generation of crime operators is now a younger group of people: many of them are born and educated here. An assistant Attorney General of the Criminal Division studying organized crime operations stated, "The influence of the so called Mafia, as it was once understood, is waning and younger men are taking their place."

The official continued, "The nation's crime syndicates are moving off the streets and into the corporate board rooms because they are finding business frauds are more rewarding than conventional racketeering. These people go where the money is. There is more money to be made quickly and with less risk in the so called 'paper crimes.' "

The Justice Department further reported in 1976 that "mobsters have infiltrated and taken over numerous businesses and have successfully infiltrated major labor unions." Examples were pointed out where businesses are selected whose assets are material but whose debts are heavy. This enables them to purchase the businesses for a nominal amount. They convert the assets to quick cash and escape via bankruptcy, the insurance fire, theft, fraud liquidation, or a combination of all.

Through these practices, plus the stock frauds and manipulation, the groups can "launder" vast sums of money already made in other rackets including gambling, narcotics, and vice. Although the offices may be pretentious and the personnel may be "smooth-smooth," and often accepted in the local service and country clubs, they still rely upon the old strong arm tactics including murder, arson, bombing, extortion, insurance manipulation, and fraud.

It is interesting to note that the Federal Government has recently recognized the seriousness of the growing problem. Former Attorney General Edward H. Levi recommended criminal strike forces on organized crime assigned to St. Louis, New Orleans, and some eastern communities in addition to assigning 14 strike forces along the east and west coasts.

The psychology of the top brass in organized crime is to trade upon and gain acceptance by modern society, concentrating upon those who evidence greed as a syndrome. They insulate themselves from street-level action and constantly improve their image. Until comparatively recent years, few law enforcement or investigative agencies have been trained or staffed to cope with the organized fraud fire operation which usually includes people who are sophisticated in fire cause, investigation, appraising, accountancy, salvage, and the underwriting and claims adjusting phases of the insurance operation.

CHAPTER XXI

SKETCHING FIRE SCENES

There are a number of sound reasons for investigative fire scene sketching regardless of the size or complexity of the fire. These sketches may be useful to the investigator who knows and cares what he is doing throughout the process of investigation and presentation of the facts to the prosecuting attorney for his prosecutive evaluation.

Sketches may be of the field note variety, set down progressively from the time the investigator arrives on the scene and continuing as the field inquiry unfolds. Such field note sketches should include dates and reference data relevant to the sketch and the stage of the investigation. This type of reference sketch, often recorded on a large size note pad (on gridded or quadrille paper), may also provide cross reference data concerning photographic position in relation to objects photographed; it may prove invaluable in refreshing an investigator's recollection, as to detail, during subsequent investigative conferences or possibly several months (or years) later at trial. For example, there are numerous examples on record where an arsonist has been apprehended in one jurisdiction and who admits to fires years or months before in other jurisdictions or is connected to such other fires by evidence developed in the current investigation. Unfortunately, prosecutive action on the earlier fires becomes impractical or even impossible because the investigators of the earlier fires simply failed to record the known facts and currently fail to recall sufficient detail concerning the fires for appropriate prosecutive action. All too often, in such cases, the prosecuting attorney is blamed by the investigators for refusing to prosecute when the fact of the matter is that the investigators have failed, from the outset, to properly document their findings.

Sketches are valuable as investigative aids during the interview of witnesses and suspects. Generally, care should be exercised as to the details of physical evidence in a particular sketch that might provide a witness or suspect with information that should have remained confidential at the moment, such as information as to means of entry, materials used to set the fire, location or origin, or other information concerning *modus operandi*. Usually, general outline or floor plan scene and area sketches should be used, allowing the person interviewed to supply any detail they can recall.

General sketches showing only outline or plan details can be reproduced by Xerox in any required quantity. A fresh copy should be utilized for each interview. Under such circumstances, the witness or suspect is provided with no suggestive information; he can do his own marking on the sketch, providing such detail as he recalls whereupon his sketch may become a part of the investigative file. In such case, he may be willing to initial the sketch or any markings he has made on the sketch.

Investigative sketches may be of the more sophisticated type wherein the layout of the scene is measured as well as all interior spaces, walls, bulkheads, doors, windows, and stairs. The sketch may be made on the scene, in which case at least two and preferably three persons are required. This may require time and care. In the more important investigations where physical detail is important, the sketch should be confined to basic structural, equipment, furniture, or stock data including streets, sidewalks, driveways, and fences.

This plan type sketch may be desirable in addition to the field note sketch. It will probably be finalized in sufficient scale for courtroom use and, therefore, should be in scale to the area and information it depicts. A copy of the basic floor plan may be utilized for filling in data on location of furnishings and equipment prior to the fire. Another copy may show the location of such furnishings or equipment after the fire. A third copy may set out detail as to electrical outlets, primary and secondary switch boxes and circuit breakers, stoves, furnaces, gas lines and valves, and other possible heat-producing sources. A fourth copy may be used to show the position and condition of doors and openings. A fifth copy may be used to show normal storage of flammables or combustible liquids. A sixth may be used to show the location of physical evidence, as found, with points of interest and reference identified by number or letter as coded in the legend of the sketch or chart.

For example, item A might appear on a chart. In the legend, it may be identified as a five gallon metal container with filler cap removed and containing residue producing the odor similar to that of gasoline. Item B might appear on the chart and be described in the legend as a screw-type metal filler cap. Item C might be described as a 14′ length of cotton clothesline producing the odor of kerosene.

Formal sketches prepared for court use should not be marked with such information as "arson fire," "incendiary area," or "location where fire was set." In brief, the sketch or chart should not contain the conclusions or presumptions that would provide the defense with grounds for moving for exclusion of the sketch because it assumes facts not in evidence or is prejudicial in its wording, composition, or form.

The formal sketch or chart to be used in court should contain basic information which is clearly not prejudicial to the rights of the defendant and which would not unfairly influence the jury. Each witness, as called, may then have the opportunity to refer to the sketch or chart, if he understands it, and point out and describe what he saw and what he found. The Court may then permit appropriate notations on the chart along with identification of the point or points with the particular witness.

Good sketches and charts are particularly important in complicated cases, involving numerous witnesses and items of physical evidence. Accurate sketches produced by the investigators are usually appreciated by the Court and the jury. Sloppy or obviously inaccurate sketches raise serious questions in the minds of the Court and the jury as to not only the investigative effort extended to get at the truth but to the basic competency of the investigators.

In most cases today, particularly in reference to fires involving industrial and commercial occupancies, governmental agencies have building, electrical, plumbing, and industrial plans on file. In the case of most dwelling and apartment construction during the past twenty years, building, general construction, and major repair plans are on file with the building and safety departments. Such plans are extremely valuable in double-checking electrical, mechanical, and other heat-producing or fire-causing equipment and in checking layout and measurement. The general layout plans can be utilized as a base for charts of floor plans produced in court.

Profile sketches and plans are occasionally useful where multilevel structural spaces are concerned; they may be utilized to depict or illustrate fire progress from the alleged seat of fire through the various spaces. The showing of the location of fire partitions and fire walls may be used to corroborate a position of multiple origin where suspected independent origins are found in opposing, separated spaces. Sketches can be used to insure that the Court and jury understand the arrangement of the premises and the evidence produced.

The investigator should be able to take the witness stand, perhaps several months after the fire, and, referring to his notes and field sketches, identify the areas he examined, pointing out exactly what he found and where he found it. For example, he may refer to the sketch and testify that, at point X, the executive office, he found the files opened and rifled; examining the carpet, he observed an irregular burn pattern; the area between the charred carpet and the carpet mat produced the strong odor of a flammable liquid similar to paint thinner; that he photographed the area, the files, and the carpet; that he removed the burned section of carpet after tagging it; and that he personally transported the section of carpet to the crime laboratory. All this should be recorded on his sketches, with time and date.

The investigator may then be shown the photograph of the section of carpet for identification for which he may relate to the sketch and his notes. He may, in turn, identify the section of carpet sample which may then be introduced into evidence along with the sketch.

Sketches do not take the place of photographs. Neither do photographs supplant sketches. Each has its place in the investigative picture. Neither should be discounted or neglected. Each medium supplements the other.

EQUIPMENT FOR SKETCHING

Sketching is basic to fire scene examination. Although it is too frequently avoided by investigators mainly because of its supposed complexity, it is actually well within the capability of even the novice investigator and should be practiced at every opportunity. With practice, the so-called mysteries will go away and the procedure will become routine. The necessary items can be carried in the briefcase and are as follows:

Pencils and pens—A small case of color ink crayons is very useful where the investigator may require a color code;

Legal or 8″ × 10″ note pad and clipboard;
Graph or quadrille paper;
A 1 ft. straight rule;
A 16 ft. tape measure;
A 50-100 ft. steel tape roll;
A magnetic compass; and
A small level.

Building and space measurements should be accurate, particularly in key areas and spaces involving origin, ignition sources, physical evidence relevant to the origin or cause of the fire, or those that may identify who is responsible for the fire. The scale may be set according to the extent of the scene and the detail required. For example, an 8″ × 10″ sheet may contain the entire scene or floor plan. A second sketch may demand more detail for smaller areas and the 8″ × 10″ sheet may cover only an 8″ × 8″ space to the scale of one inch to one foot. Again, a rough field sketch may be used for a more detailed and highly finished formal chart which can be produced with the use of conventional office drafting equipment.

Some departments use City and Council engineering staff members where more sophisticated charts are required such as for Board of Reviews and Court presentations. In such cases, however, care must be exercised that rough notes are properly interpreted and, again, that prejudicial information is not included that would render the chart objectionable in court. Prosecuting attorneys should be consulted as to what information should be set out. This consultation should not be postponed to the last minute before trial. The field investigator should maintain a close liaison with the engineering or drafting department if this system is utilized. For example, an elaborate chart was excluded because the engineers preparing it had labelled it "Arson scene—8006 South Crandall, _____, California." The Court sustained defense objection to the word "arson," which was also three times the size of the address lettering, on the grounds that there was no standing presumption the fire had been willfully and maliciously caused.

Another sketch was successfully objected to by defense on the ground it was distinctly labelled "Schultz's Fire."

A chart of a fire scene, carefully prepared as a Court exhibit, listed three points, #1, #2, and #3 as Set fire #1, Set fire #2, and Set fire #3. The chart was not admitted into evidence.

A sketch which showed a red, shaded area extending through several spaces in a warehouse was ruled improper because the legend on the chart labelled the shaded area as "gasoline saturated area." The Court ruled that this implied an unfair presumption that the fire was of incendiary origin before there had been any testimony to that effect.

A sketch outlining the location of the head, arms, body, and legs of a fire victim was permitted. A sketch with a point marked "matchbook" was admitted.

A sketch marked "Incendiary fire scene" was not admitted, again on the grounds that this posed an unfair presumption before the jury that the fire had been set. This was well before the prosecution had proved either the origin of the fire or the fact, if at all, that it had occurred by incendiary means.

Generally, a formal sketch or chart to be presented in court may be identified by the official case number, date of the fire, and address. It may also include such descriptive information as "Type V," "Group I or J," or other descriptive features.

In preparing a sketch, the investigator may find it convenient to use letters, such as A, B, C, etc., in designating walls, furniture, and fixed objects. If known, the spaces or rooms may be labelled with a descriptive word such as "Office," or "Kitchen." Items of evidence, such as incendiary devices, trailers, containers, gloves, equipment, can be identified with numerals such as Item 1, Item 2, etc. The system should be clearly identified with the field investigator keeping his personal identification notes on pages separate from the sketch: a case field notebook is good for this purpose. The sketch and field note identification of physical items must tally *exactly* with the evidence tags used in the procedure. This may prevent serious and embarrassing mistakes at the time of trial.

Further, the sketch and chart code system minimizes the chances of misunderstanding with witnesses during their interview and, later, when they take the witness stand. If the witness doesn't know the code the investigator is using, he will not know what the symbols mean unless the investigator wishes him to know.

The floor plan is the most commonly used type of investigative sketch. (See Figure 1.)

The exploded sketch includes the floor plan, as in Figure 1, and also the walls laid out flat with wall objects in their relative positions. This type of sketch is useful in providing illustrative background for the witness to use in explaining fire pattern or spread from the floor and up the walls—from the inverted fire cone or from a general area of origin. (See Figure 2.) In Figure 2, Area of origin #1 indicates the

File RW-2-97284
Bedroom-2nd level

Scale: 3/16" : 1'

Figure 1

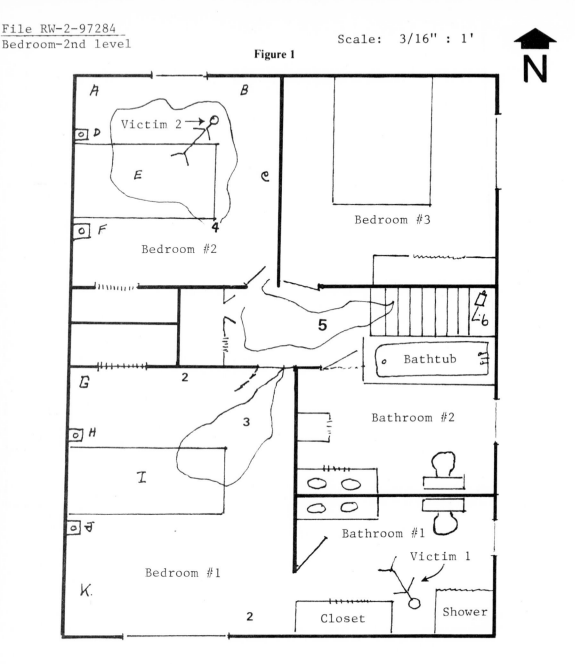

A – Chair.
B – Chair.
C – Television.
D & F – Nite stands.
E – Double bed.
G – 2--Chairs.
H & J – Nite stands.
I – Single bed.

1 – Victim. Male Caucasian.
    Face down.
2 – Victim. Female Caucasian.
    Face up.
3 – Point of origin.
4 – Point of origin.
5 – Point of origin.

6 – Two-gallon metal
    container of
    gasoline.

File RW-2-97066
Garage and Work Space

Scale: 5/16" : 1'

Figure 2

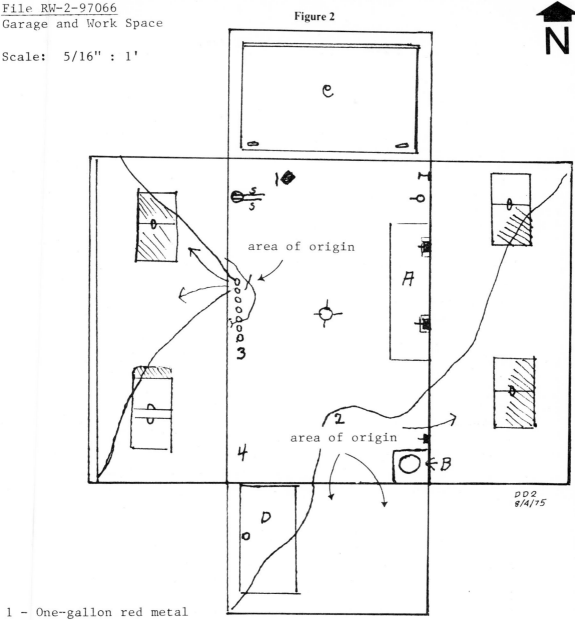

1 - One-gallon red metal
    container--empty with
    filler cap off.

2 - One-gallon metal screw
    filler cap.

3 - Sealed paint cans.

4 - Metal waste container
    with lid on--unburned
    contents.

A - Work bench.

B - Gas fueled water
    heater.

C - Tiltup garage door.

D - Pedestrian door.

/// - Broken, displaced
    window glass.

inverted fire cone pattern from the floor along the west wall. Area of origin #2 illustrates a more general pattern on the floor of the garage in the southeast corner surrounding the gas fueled water heater and with a more elaborate wide based spread along the south and east walls. Such a pattern might be expected where gasoline or any other low flash point fuel was spilled in quantity on the floor some distance out from the water heater. The fuel would vaporize and, when it reached the gas pilot light or the main burner of the water heater in explosive or flammable mixture, ignition would follow. The flash pattern would probably be general.

When measuring the inside of a room, measurements are taken from finished wall to finished wall. Inside trim and baseboards are disregarded. Windows, doors, and openings are measured along the wall in which they are located with windows and door trim also disregarded. Only openings are measured.

It is good practice for investigators to repeat or verify their measurement readings as they proceed. Measurements may become very important where critical areas or evidence positions are concerned. Fixed and reliable control points should be used.

There are certain accepted basic methods of spotting objects on a sketch. For example:

1. Triangulation.

In this system, a measurement may be made from two fixed objects along bearings to where the lines cross. The object to be spotted is at the intersection of the lines. The two points of reference and the object of interest would form the three points of a triangle.

2. Transecting baselines.

This system may be useful in sketching irregularly shaped outdoor areas where no natural baseline exists. In laying out a baseline, two stakes should be laid so that a line between them bisects the area to be sketched; next, locate the stakes by measuring in reference to fixed objects such as power poles and trees. Sketch a line between the two stakes. The objects within the area can then be spotted by measuring their distance at right angle from the previously designated baseline.

3. Rectangular coordinates.

This is a simple system by which a point is spotted by measuring at right angles from each of two walls in establishing an imaginary rectangle.

4. Straight line measurements.

The process of measurements taken from fixed points to either side of the object, such as items or objects on a wall.

Common scales convenient to field sketching are:
1″ equals 1′ for small rooms
¼″ equals 1′ for large rooms
⅛″ equals 1′ for very large rooms, small buildings, etc.
1″ equals 100′ for large buildings or outside areas.

The scale can be adjusted to the size of the sketch desired and the areas involved. For example, in industrial plant areas, where the number of fires may have occurred in several square block areas, smaller scale, such as 4″ to 300′ might be desirable. In fire cases involving forest and wildlands, a large scale sketch may embrace the area of origin in flat map layout. Additionally, a small scale or a series of graduated scale charts or sketches may be desired to illustrate the area of origin and its relative position in the general environment with reference to power lines, trails, truck trails, and road and highway systems.

There have been occasions, in major structural as well as forest and wildland conflagrations, when topographical and profile maps are desirable for illustrating: 1. Visibility and precise location of the fire when discovered; 2. Pattern of spread, considering topography, improvements, and accessibility; and 3. Probable access and movements of the person or persons responsible for the fire.

Careful sketching and mapping is often invaluable in studying the *modus operandi* and predicting the future operations of arsonists operating in forest and wildland areas. The procedure is all too often neglected by investigators who are inexperienced or indifferent to the problems of such fires and to their ultimate destructive capability. It is well known by dissidents that major forest fires and wildland fires tie up thousands of men each year and are extremely costly in their impact on the nation's resources.

The preparation of topographical and vertical profile maps requires a certain amount of expertise and patience in preparing in the interest of factual investigative integrity. (See Figure 3.)

Figure 3 sets out flat and topographical details of a major fire scene where several large warehouses and packing sheds were totally destroyed in an early morning fire. Initial limited fire fighting facilities, coupled with weather conditions and the very nature and character of the property involved, handicapped fire control methods. Ultimate property loss was considerable. Following control, several buildings were totally collapsed.

The extensive structural collapse handicapped the

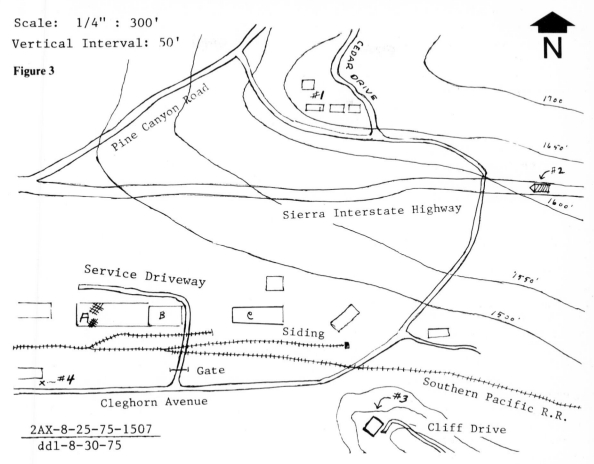

Scale: 1/4" : 300'

Vertical Interval: 50'

Figure 3

2AX-8-25-75-1507
dd1-8-30-75

investigators in evaluating origin of this fire from physical evidence or specific fire or burn patterns. Therefore, investigators literally interviewed scores of residents and occupants of the general area which included hills overlooking the involved area. A patient and time consuming canvass of the surrounding area produced certain key witnesses whose statements were carefully checked out and whose observations were utilized to triangulate the location where the first smoke and flame was observed at a time when the fire was probably very small.

Figure 3 shows the warehouse of origin and its location in the canyon bottom between the state highway and the railroad right of way. It shows the locations from which certain key witnesses observed the fire in its incipient stages. A, B, and C on the sketch are buildings ultimately destroyed in the flames. Witness #1 was standing on the high ridge north and east of the scene when she first observed the fire. It was located in the cross-hatched area on the north side of location A.

Witness #2 observed "a puff of smoke and flames come out of a ventilator on the top side of the warehouse at the west end of A." No other smoke or flame was visible. No persons were observed. It was broad daylight and witness #2 had direct and unimpeded visibility. Note contour lines indicating the vertical interval between valley floor and observation point. Witness #3 also looked directly down into the warehouse area. He resided about 150' vertically above the scene and at a lateral distance indicated by the scale. Witness #3 observed a small column of smoke and then flames burst from the cross-hatched area on the south side of the west end of building A. Witness #4 was standing level with the base of the warehouse, south of the west end, across the tracks, and observed heavy black smoke and flames emerge from the cross-hatched area of building A. He observed the flames spreading rapidly in an easterly direction.

The utilization of the cross bearings provided by the witnesses, from various vantage points around

Figure 4

HEATING

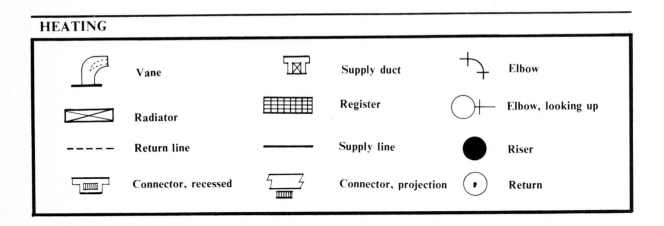

ELECTRIC

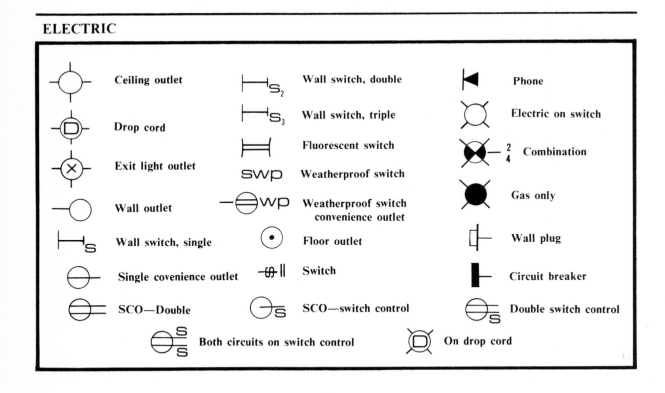

the scene, permitted a reasonably precise evaluation of the origin of this fire without the necessity of relying upon anyone's comments or stated observations. It should be noted that the witnesses were interviewed separately and without suggestive comments as to where the fire may have started and before the news media were aware of the existence of these witnesses. They had not discussed their observations with each other. Triangulation and cross bearings are of extreme importance where visibility is direct and where the physical evidence at the scene, in major conflagrations, cannot be relied upon in precise evaluation of origin. Triangulation is commonly utilized by forest fire lookouts in assessing origin of fires. The use of profile and topographical features is commonly utilized in illustrative sketches and charts of major conflagrations. Such charts are invaluable in showing a jury "what the witnesses are talking about."

Figure 4 sets out some of the more common heating and electrical symbols that may be useful to the fire investigator in preparation of fire scene sketches.

We have previously discussed the use of Xerox copies of "rough draft" fire scene sketches for investigative conference and review and for interview of witnesses and suspects. Separate copies should be marked by each witness or suspect. Such sketches can be supplemented, for investigative review and courtroom use by the master chart which, in turn, can be supplemented by transparent overlays with data or detail on the overlay as needed. By this process, if data set out on an overlay is objectionable to the court, only the overlay is lost for use in the presentation, not the base sketch or chart.

Although some investigators have recommended the use of "colors and dramatic identification to impress the jury," in the presentation of illustrative diagrams, experience has shown that such practices can boomerang in the form of court rejection of the entire display.

Conservatism and objectivity is the appropriate standard and the most professional in the long run.

CHAPTER XXII

THE INVESTIGATIVE REPORT

We must consider two classes of reports in this chapter: routine Fire Department reports and Investigative reports. Both classes must be considered in the investigative and prosecutive context. Fire Department authorities often mistakenly assume that since the fire department report is normally prepared only for statistical and administrative purposes, it has little or nothing to do with the criminal investigative report. This assumption is dangerous and has occasionally resulted in prosecutive failure because of the obvious contradiction between the information as to origin and cause in the two classes of reports.

At an early stage in any criminal prosecutive action, the defense has an absolute right, under the law, to be provided with any and all relevant official documentation and information that may be considered for use by the investigators and the prosecution. This includes all reports concerning the origin or cause of the fire, all investigative reports, and all other documentary data which is to be used or relied upon by the prosecution. This also includes the names, titles, and addresses of Fire Department personnel who had any part in examining the scene or compiling the routine fire department report, where the origin or cause or any other information relevant to the guilt or innocence of the accused may be at issue.

The regulation Fire Department statistical report, even though it may be merely a single page document, becomes a part of the investigative effort since it lists origin and cause and since it may become a part of the local, State, and Federal system. If this report has been carelessly or inaccurately prepared or if its identification, either as to origin or cause, conflicts with the investigative report, the error or conflict may be questioned in depth by the defense, if and when the case proceeds to trial.

Experience has shown that this conflict of information between the two reports has been embarrassing to the prosecuting authorities and has occasionally resulted in dismissal of the charges against the defendant on motion, appeal, and subsequent acquittal by juries on reasonable question of fact involving the specific cause of the fire.

Since the official Fire Department report must be generally considered as part of the investigative file, we will briefly deal with this class of report before moving on to the more detailed Investigative report.

Questions are frequently raised as to what information should be included in routine Fire Department reports. Obviously, it is not the prerogative or within the expertise of the criminal investigator or the prosecutor to make this determination other than to ask that such information be included, particularly in reference to matters and information pertaining to cause, and that they be as factual and accurate as reasonably possible and not relegated to untrained or irresponsible personnel.

Fire Department administrators usually prescribe what information shall be included in their departmental fire reports. Generally, this includes alarm date and time data; property identification and description; owner-occupant description; equipment, personnel, and aid response; insurance data and other loss information; injuries and fatalities, if any; and origin and cause. Information often varies, depending upon departments and jurisdiction. Responding officers' comments may be recorded or not depending upon department instructions or policy.

Origin and cause may be reported by one or more responding companies, again depending upon the instructions of the particular department. In the event of more than one company reporting cause, there may be obvious and apparent conflict in the findings and determination concerning cause. Conflicts of record to be faced by the prosecution may have to be explained in the event of a criminal prosecution. Too often, these conflicting reports return to haunt the probably more accurate investigative analysis and report of the investigators following their assignment to the case.

Routine Fire Department reports, as we have stated, are prepared basically for general administrative and statistical use. They are essential to overall administrative and public safety purposes. Some examples are equipment and manpower needs; occupancy conditions, code requirements, and violations; and human activities as related to fire causing activities. All of these are extremely important to fire control and efficient fire prevention. It is only natural, perhaps, that the average Fire Department administrative staff's preoccupation with the big picture sometimes causes them to overlook the urgency of maintaining precise report data in all reports dealing with a suspected criminal cause. This supervisory preoccupation often leads to or results in carelessness by the lower echelons in filling in the report column on origin and cause. There are numerous examples where it is common practice to fill in the cause column only as afterthought—several days after the fire.

Most Fire Departments maintain station and headquarters logs in which emergency and response entries are recorded separate from the company and Fire Department form reports. These log entries also note specifics or general comments concerning origin and cause of the fire. Such entries may be made by the company officer or other designated responding authority. Although Fire Departments have generally and traditionally considered such logs to be confidential official information, it is still a fact of life that such documents and included information are also a part of the official response and investigation picture and, therefore, subject to examination and question by a defendant if and when a case proceeds to trial. As in the case of the routine fire department report, log entries reasonably become a part of and relevant to criminal investigation reports and, by such reason, subject to scrutiny by the defense. It is therefore necessary for each Fire Department and investigator assigned to a case to insure that all such log entries are made by responsible officers familiar with the importance of accuracy rather than speculation. After companies return to the station, log entries are often made while memories are fresh. It should be impressed upon officers responsible for such logs that entries, if made, should be totally factual.

During the early 1970s, the acceleration of arson and incendiarism began to receive attention on a national scale, as earlier indicated in this text. The Nation's increase in incendiary fire losses has indicated the necessity of establishing a nationwide uniform fire reporting system covering the entire spectrum of fire causes—incendiary and accidental. The system is expected to include data on specific accidental causes as well as data for more detailed classification of incendiary and arson fires, including *modus operandi* and motive. The system is designed to evolve through the cooperation of each participating state.

Some states have already initiated a Uniform Fire Reporting System where *all* Fire Departments in the particular state are required, under the law, to submit uniform Fire Department reports to a state agency which, in turn, records this data for utilization on the state and in the local levels as well as projecting it into the National Reporting and Data System.

California initiated the California Fire Incidence Reporting System (CFIRS) in 1974. For example, the State was mandated by the Legislative Act, Section 13110.5, California Health and Safety Code, to collect all statistical information through the California State Fire Marshal's Office, beginning January 1, 1974. The law requires the Chief Fire Officer of each Fire Department of the state, including private entities providing fire protection, to furnish the State Fire Marshal certain data on each fire that occurs within his jurisdiction. The law authorized the State Fire Marshal to adopt regulations presenting the scope of information to be reported, the manner of reporting, the forms to be used, the time the information should be reported, and other requirements and regulations as he deems necessary.

The law further requires the State Fire Marshal to analyze the reported data, compile reports, and disseminate a copy of his report to each Chief Officer in the State. "The State Fire Marshal shall also furnish a copy of his report and analysis to any other person interested upon request" *(State Health and Safety Code, Sect. 13110.5, Jan. 1, 1974).*

The State Fire Marshal prepared a coded uniform report implemented by a code book based, in part, on the National Fire Protection Association Coding System (NFPA 901, 1973 Edition) of the Uniform Fire Incident Reporting System, limited to California's needs and conforming to California statutes.

Generally, this report includes the specific departmental and jurisdictional identification, incident number, alarm data, address, and ownership and occupancy data. Coded information includes property classification, type, damage, location, and cause. Coded information also includes area, materials involved, smoke spread data, protection facilities, and miscellaneous information including injuries and deaths. The use of the reverse side of the one sheet form is for optional general fire department information in uncoded form.

For use of this type of form in any central file and data system, it is important that complete factual input is carefully entered on the form and properly identified as to the code. As State Fire Marshal Albert E. Hole very properly stated in his comments to all participants in the California Reporting System, "Undoubtedly, data obtained from these reports will ultimately reflect in the technologies of Fire Prevention, Protection, and Suppression. To this end, I urge each user to exert the effort necessary to make this a successful program." Chief Hole's comments and plea for accuracy are particularly relevant to the coding sections referring to origin and cause in reference to incendiary and arson fires. Miscoding or conflict on a single report may become relevant in a prosecutive criminal action since, as previously indicated, the original fire report may reasonably become a part of the entire investigative report and prosecutive file.

While it may well be true that Fire Department officers or the investigators may explain an open contradiction between the Fire Department report and investigative reports as to origin and cause, it remains for the Court and jury to accept or reject their explanation.

Even in the sophisticated Uniform Reporting System, errors can occur. An expert and objective analytical investigation was recently conducted of one of the systems currently in use. The investigation studied the accuracy of input into the data and computer system as well as the accuracy of what the system might produce on demand. The report reflected, in part, that "This information is critically important for establishing fire patterns, so that effective programs may be implemented where they are most needed." It could be reasonably stated that this specific need and programmed response could be applied practically to acts of incendiarism or arson, where particular *modus operandi* or patterns might be reflected in the data system.

The critical examination of the computer system and a very objective report reflected that information carelessly recorded on the reports, mistakes by reporting Fire Department officers in code designations, and erasures or other human indifference or error at the field level resulted in inaccurate answers from the computer. The scanner reports what it sees. The analysis noted: "Some fires reported could not have occurred under the circumstances reflected in the reports. Discrepancies were discovered between the source of heat, form of heat, type of material, and form of material reported.

"This suggests failure by personnel filling out the forms and the possible lack of understanding various categories established in the Fire Incidence Reporting System Manual."

Thus, the errors were assigned to lack of understanding of codes in the manual, overabundance of paperwork, and possible general apathy. Again, these routine fire reports may reasonably become a part of the investigative file and subject to scrutiny by the defense. It is therefore necessary, where incendiary fires are suspected, that qualified supervision of the preparation of this category of report must be something more than casual.

THE FORMAL ARSON INVESTIGATION REPORT

There is continuing controversy concerning what information should be included in an arson investigation report. One of the long-standing dilemmas facing arson investigators is the occasional variance between what his department superiors require and what the District Attorney or prosecuting attorney expect.

Traditionally, Fire Department administrators and supervisory personnel have been oriented to fire control and personnel management procedures rather than the techniques of criminal investigation and preparing investigative reports that will be acceptable in the criminal justice system. This has long been conspicuously evident in the lack of emphasis on criminal fire cause investigation (and the priorities attached therewith) in the majority of Fire Departments throughout the nation. It is not the intent or the place of this text to comment upon where emphasis should be placed. It is, however, the purpose to call attention to the need for more realistic handling of the preparation of routine and investigative reports where incendiary fires may be involved.

It is necessary that prosecuting attorneys insist upon complete accuracy in information submitted to them. It has frequently been their experience, in arson reports submitted for prosecution, that such reports are based upon speculation and information growing out of hearsay. Conclusions are too often based upon conflicting or incomplete information or investigation by improperly trained or unqualified personnel. Investigative leads are not fully explored.

One highly respected authority on criminal prosecution, including the prosecution of arson cases, stated that "unfactual and incomplete information, including that which was supplied by insurance claims people, when subjected to the scrutiny of cross-examination, was often lacking in objectivity and factual integrity."

Several prosecutors, each with experience in prosecuting arson cases, seem to agree that whatever the motive for a particular incendiary fire may be, what the prosecutor must really know, when he is receiving an investigative report is, "Can we prove this fire was set with human hands? That it was of criminal origin in the eyes of the law and in a manner the Court will accept our proof? Can we identify the person or persons responsible for the act? Can we place him or them at the scene of the crime WHEN it was committed?" One experienced prosecutor added, "Although we don't have to prove a motive under the law, it's pretty handy to know why a guy did what he did, particularly if his hands have been clean, by the record, in the past. Juries are just like you and me—they aren't going to buy a serious felony package on a guy unless they can be shown a reason which makes common sense to them why he did it. It's as simple as that."

As an afterthought, he added, "That's the way I'd want it if I was in the defendant's shoes. I always try to remember that."

One prosecutor commented, "Quite naturally, we would expect our investigators to have been completely objective in their findings and I would expect that they had conducted their own investigation and I would want that reflected in the report. We recognize that, in most white collar types of crime, including insurance fires and insurance fraud, we must have the cooperation of certain institutions and the insurance people but I would expect that all information submitted by them be double-checked by the arson or fraud investigators from the public agencies before the report assumes its accuracy and before I proceed to a prosecutive stance. We have learned this from the hard road of experience."

The responsibility of the prosecuting attorney is a very serious one and not always clearly understood by the average citizen. It is occasionally misunderstood by investigators in the police and fire service. It is the responsibility of the District Attorney or prosecuting attorney, when a case is presented to him as a suspected arson case, to protect the innocent as well as prosecute the person or persons suspected where there is reliable and probable cause to believe the crime was, in fact, committed and that the suspect or suspects committed the crime. Suspicion is usually not enough.

The District Attorney is interested in all the facts in order that he may properly weigh those facts and, possibly, check them out before he takes the case to a preliminary hearing or before the Grand Jury. The record shows that the majority of the Fire Department reports, including those covering major fires, evidence a preoccupation with response and control tactics; involved and exposure property damage; insurance data and insurance loss; structural and electrical/mechanical code violations; and possible occupancy hazards discovered during post fire overhaul. Certainly, the above factors are very properly necessary in the interest of appropriate fire prevention, safety, and response capabilities and vital to fire and administrative personnel. However, if the fire is of suspected criminal origin, the District Attorney or prosecuting attorney may or may not be interested in such information but he will require considerably more, in completely factual and verified form with which he, as a prosecutor, is familiar and which, when reviewed, must also ultimately be provided to the defense attorney at a certain stage in the prosecutive procedure. This is a fact of life not generally understood by most fire officials.

Differences of opinion as to origin and cause, submitted in separate fire response and investigation reports from different responding fire companies, have often been utilized to discredit evidence of cause during a prosecutive action.

Supervisory notations and remarks superimposed on Fire Department reports have often been utilized to discredit evidence of cause in a subsequent prosecutive action.

It is with the arson investigator's report, prepared for the prosecuting attorney, that we will attempt to deal at the moment. The routine Fire Department investigative report may be used as a basis if it is found to be factual. Such a report must be accurate and as complete as the particular circumstances permit. If hearsay is included, the hearsay character of the information should be so identified and the investigative leads should be identified whereby the related information may be authenticated. If the quality or integrity of certain physical evidence is questionable, the report should so indicate. If the credibility of a witness is subject to question, this should be pointed out in the report.

THE REPORT SHOULD BE OBJECTIVE

The prosecuting attorney is entitled to all the facts before he should be expected to make a decision on prosecutive action. Again, it is his duty to protect the innocent as well as prosecute the guilty. He has a right and duty to question each and every item of fact before he makes his decision.

One of the more common comments of experienced prosecutors concerns lack of full disclosure of investigative information in submitted reports. The criticism is more at the quality of the contents rather than the form.

Detail and content of investigative reports may, as a practical matter, depend upon the policy of the particular prosecuting office and, in some circumstances, upon the ramifications of a particular case. Successful arson investigators make it a practice to get acquainted with the prosecuting attorney, or someone designated by him in his office, before it becomes necessary to seek a complaint or specific prosecutive advice. In this manner, the department, through its investigative staff, may determine what the particular office expects in the way of investigative information, and in what form. Some prosecutors' offices assign a special deputy to advise the investigators from the outset concerning who takes the case from its inception, right on through the trial of the case in the Superior or District Court. Many of the larger offices assign one prosecutor to supervise in the earlier stages including the preliminary hearing. If the defendant is held to answer, another senior deputy prepares the information and follows the case through trial in the Superior or District Court. In at least one major jurisdiction, which is one of the largest metropolitan areas of the United States and where arson investigation and prosecution has been successful for years, the Fire Authorities have built up liaisons to the level where the District Attorney's Office will supply an experienced prosecutor at the very outset, at the request of the Fire Authorities, who will supervise and follow the case through preliminary trial or grand jury, and through trial in the Superior Court. This is a highly successful procedure since the Prosecutor is intimate with investigative details from the outset. In all the above circumstances, the record indicates that the prosecutors insist on an investigative report before final determination is made concerning prosecutive action.

FORM OF THE INVESTIGATIVE REPORT

Most modern fire and law enforcement agencies require standard forms with designated space provided for selected material. These spaces set out case designation; location; date of incident; time of report; statistical data and information including owner, occupant, and reporting person; and other preliminary data. The reports usually include preliminary data on suspect or arrest information.

Identified spaces are provided for the narrative report of investigating and arresting officers. The Department form and procedural reports include fire scene examination and investigative conclusions as to origin and cause, naming the evidence and/or expert witnesses who will testify to origin and cause. Such information usually includes time of origin of the fire which is an important factor in placing the suspect on scene at the time of origin of the fire or at the time the crime is alleged to have been committed. Standard form and format reporting is useful to supervisory investigators in analysis of what has been accomplished in an investigation as well as identifying investigative gaps and setting out necessary or desirable investigative leads. A standard and required format is important and valuable in that it provides uniformity if other investigators are assigned to the case. It is further useful to the prosecutive staff who become familiar with standard form reporting and know where to look for information expeditiously.

In the event that there is no standard departmental format for the investigative report, the following suggestions may be helpful:

REPORT OF FIRE INVESTIGATION
File Number
Case Designation

Date of incident _____ Day _____
Time of Alarm _____
F. D. Incident number _____
Address _____
Owner of Property _____
Address _____ Telephone _____
Occupant* _____
Address _____ Telephone _____

*Usually with reference to occupancy or space of origin.

DESCRIPTION OF INVOLVED PROPERTY

This description usually includes at least the involved structure and the occupancy or space of origin. It may include other occupancies or spaces as circumstances require. This description should be as brief as possible without overusing technical terms or structural or occupancy classifications. The Prosecuting Attorney wants to know, in plain language, what is involved and, hopefully, without having to refer to a building code or other technical data, learn what the investigator is talking about. For example, some departments insist that department reports describe buildings and occupancies in terms of types and groups. A report might describe a property as a "Type V, Group H" when all the prosecuting attorney wants to know is, "Is it a dwelling, an apartment house, or what? Is it a concrete building or is it a frame-stucco?" An investigative report described the involved property in one instance as a "single story Type I, Group E." The report should have informed the busy D.A. that "the involved was a steel truss, masonry and concrete, commercial structure with the space of origin consisting of a dry cleaning plant using flammable materials." If the division, type, or group of the structure or space becomes relevant, that technicality may be used at a later time. Again, in the description of the premises, make it plain and make it brief.

In the descriptive narrative, the investigator may wish to make appropriate cross reference to photographs. For example, "The plant fronted on South Broadway. (See Figure 1.) Main power panels were in the southeast corner. (See Figure 2.) Service entrance was in the south end at center. (See Figure 19)."

The investigator may refer to charts and sketches in his descriptive data. For example, "The involved property is a two story frame-stucco, commercial, multiple occupancy structure with frame and shake roof (See Figure A: 1st level floor plan and Figure B: 2nd level floor plan)."

NARRATIVE STATEMENTS OF WITNESSES WHO DISCOVERED AND REPORTED THE FIRE

This section should contain brief statements of early witnesses, in the investigator's narrative form, for the purpose of further acquainting the reader with the story of the fire as it unfolds. For example, "This fire was discovered by Mr. A, further identified in the investigative index, who states that he was waiting for a bus directly across the street from the involved premises. He had been waiting for the bus about ten minutes and had direct visibility of the front door of the cocktail lounge on the opposite side of the street. While he was waiting, the premises were dark. Mr. A states that he observed two men emerge from the front door, close it, walk rapidly east along the opposite side of the street, turn the corner, and disappear. At this time, he heard a muffled explosion and the front windows of the cocktail lounge were blown onto the sidewalk; immediately thereafter, he observed the interior of the cocktail lounge in flames. Mr. A states that he pulled the fire alarm box which is located on the same corner as the bus stop. At this time, flames were emerging from the front and side windows of the cocktail lounge and he could hear other explosions inside the premises. Mr. A states he looked at his watch and it was 3:55 a.m.

Mr. A states he can identify one of the two men he observed emerge from the cocktail lounge immediately prior to the explosion and fire.

Mr. B is a cab driver for the Triple A Cab Company. He is identified in the witness index. He states he was sitting in his cab in a parking lot at the rear of the cocktail lounge. He had been sitting there about five minutes. He states the rear of the cocktail lounge was dark except for the glow of an interior night light. He heard an explosion from the direction of the cocktail lounge. Immediately thereafter, he observed flames inside the lounge through the back door which had blown open. He radioed the report of the fire to the dispatcher. Immediately thereafter, he observed two men run from the side street into the alley at the rear of the cocktail lounge. He observed them get into a pickup truck and drive away; he cannot identify the truck except to make out that it was black in color, and about a 3/4-ton pickup truck. He states that he did not recognize either of the men."

NARRATIVE STATEMENT OF FIRST OFFICERS ON SCENE

Traffic Sgt. D. Gilhooley, Badge 999, received dispatch at 0357 hours and arrived on scene at 0359 hours. He states that the interior of the Cactus Club was totally involved in flames upon his arrival. He parked his patrol unit in the parking area at the rear and as he approached the premises, he heard two explosions from the interior of the Cactus Club. The rear doors were open, with flames pouring out. He ran around to the front and observed that the sidewalk along the front was covered with glass. He observed that the front door to the cocktail lounge was blown open. The door frame was off the hinges. He heard the fire equipment approaching and proceeded to clear the intersection of traffic.

Chief Matheney, Battalion 66, was the first fire officer on the scene. He observed that the interior of the Cactus Club was heavily involved. Front and rear doors were blown off the hinges. Flames were also extending from side windows of the cocktail lounge and out of the top side ventilators. He called for a second alarm and assigned responding units as they arrived on the scene. The fire was controlled at 0431 hours.

At 0438 hours, Captain Breeze, during the course of overhaul behind the bar, observed 2 one-gallon containers which produced the strong odor of gasoline. At about the same time, Captain Mills called his attention to two more plastic containers on the floor of the office; also, one in the front hall and one in the rear hall. He immediately called for the assignment of an arson unit and requested a Police Guard on the premises.

Captain Breeze and Captain Mills can confirm the findings as above related. See their detailed statements in the index file.

NARRATIVE OF FIRE SCENE EXAMINATION BY INVESTIGATING OFFICERS

This section of the report should contain a factual summary of the investigating officer's examination and include when he arrived on the scene. It should include security measures taken from the time of control of the fire scene, until his arrival and until release of the scene. It should contain his observations concerning the entire premises including reasonably possible accidental fire causing sources in the area of origin. He should identify such possible sources on sketches and photographs which will be illustrative of conditions found.

The area and point of origin should be described with reference to illustrative sketches and photographs. Physical evidence of cause should be identified by reference to the sketches and photographs. For example, "A one gallon plastic container rests on its side in front of the office file cabinet (See Figure A in first floor sketch and Figure 9 in the photo file). A small quantity of liquid remains in the container. A sample of this liquid produces an odor similar to gasoline. A sample, placed in a saucer, burns when a match flame is applied. The vapors continue to flash when a match flame is applied above the saucer. The plastic container is sealed and

evidence tagged and transported by undersigned to Fire Department evidence locker."

This section should include narrative description of the pattern of spread and progress of the fire from the point of origin. For example: "The flame damage in all spaces except the office is residual. The lowest fire is at the base of an inverted char cone pattern extending vertically up the wood panel wall to the ceiling—from the office carpet between the file cabinet and the desk. The pattern of spread extended into the open files and also vertically to the ceiling with flame pattern extending into the reception office area and thence, at high levels, into the hall. There is residual heat and smoke damage throughout the other four office spaces."

The report should set out conditions of doors and windows including, if possible, means of entry and egress of the arsonist. For example: "The rear office entrance was barred on the inside. The slide and dead bolts were engaged securing the door from the inside until it was forced open by the Fire Department (See Officer Gold's statement). The front entrance door is secured by a mortice lock which was in a closed and locked position until the Fire Department arrived (See Captain Cruz's statement). The executive suite office door (area of origin, see Plan A) was in an unlocked and open position during the fire. The locking mechanism is undamaged (See sketch B, Figures 11 and 16). All windows were closed. Window frames are steel barred. The bars are intact (See Figures 21-23)."

The investigative narrative should cover physical evidence which identifies or 'connects' the arsonist to the scene. For example: "One government issue flashlight, 3 cell, Ser. #NAS 9-658 864, is recovered from the inside of the master electrical panel closet. It is tagged and turned over to crime lab for examination for latent fingerprints and for further identification (Figure 34)."

The narrative should include evidence indicative of time of origin of the fire. For example: "The executive office electric clock, circuit #4 on the secondary panels, is mounted on the wall directly above the point of origin. The hands of the clock are heat warped against the face at the position 4:59 (See Figure 44). The company time clock hands are frozen against the clock face at the position 5:03, circuit #7 on the secondary panels (Figure 45). These above designated clocks are set and synchronized to Western Union time by the office superintendent each morning (See Mr. R. Block's statement in index of witness statements). Each clock is evidence tagged and transported to F.D. evidence locker. The master financial file cabinet lock is not forced. The lock is in an unlocked position and the drawer was open during the course of fire (Figure 48)."

This section should indicate if laboratory or other expert assistance is brought in and, if so, what physical evidence is removed by them, with appropriate cross reference made to each item by the special file numbers.

The section should report conditions found which suggest either *modus operandi* or motive. For example, preparation or evidence that the fire was anticipated may appear in the form of moved or missing property. As a further example of *modus operandi* or common pattern, one burglar who made it a practice to cover his tracks with arson always carried a one-quart, metal container of charcoal lighter fluid. After saturating certain furnishings, he would ignite the combustibles and always leave the empty container near the point of origin.

Automobile pyros often utilize the gasoline siphoned from the victimized vehicle to set fire to the car and leave the gasoline filler cap adjacent to the origin. Professional arsonists occasionally fall victim to habit and leave telltale signs of their *modus operandi*. Therefore, the investigator should be careful to note and report unique conditions that are found.

INVESTIGATIVE CONCLUSIONS AND OPINION AS TO ORIGIN AND CAUSE

This space should briefly and concisely include the conclusions and opinion of the investigator concerning where the fire started, how the fire started, and, if reasonably possible, when ignition occurred. For example: "It is the undersigned's conclusion that the origin of this fire was in the executive office space (See Floor plan A; Figures 40-44). The cause of this fire is incendiary. This fire was willfully set with human hands by means of placing gasoline on the carpet of the office and pouring it into the master files. Paper matchbook was used to ignite the gasoline (See figures 46-50). The physical evidence is consistent with ignition between 4:45 and 4:59 a.m., July 4, 1977. Undersigned has qualified as an expert witness on origin and cause of fires in the Superior Courts of this State. In further support of cause, as above indicated, see Crime Lab report #_____ which is cross referenced to this report as to Gas Chromatograph and laboratory readings and findings identifying the suspect accelerant at the scene as gasoline."

NARRATIVE OF WITNESSES INTERVIEWED

This section of the report should include an index reference to the complete statement of witnesses and an investigative statement describing the interview of witnesses. This section of the report is to provide the supervising officer and the prosecutor with ready reference as to the crux of a witness' testimony. For example: "Miss Mary J is the executive secretary of Mr. X. She states that Mr. X had been drinking heavily in his office during the afternoon preceding the fire. He called for the internal audit reports at about 3:30 p.m. She obtained them from the master file cabinets in his office and relocked the file. Mr. X has the only other key. She observed Mr. X place the audit reports in his briefcase and depart at 3:40 p.m. Miss J states she locked the executive offices at 4:30 p.m. She was at her home with her husband, Davey J, all evening on the night of the fire. She first learned of the fire when she showed up for work at 8:55 a.m. and found the police waiting at the door.

"Mr. Zack Z, office superintendent, states that he locked the suite at 5:15 p.m. the evening preceding the fire. He checked all spaces. Everyone was out. The janitor has keys to all offices except the executive office. No one has keys to that office except Mr. X and Miss J.

"Stanley B states that he is the janitor. He has keys to all doors except the executive office. He cleaned the offices and dumped the waste on the evening prior to the fire. He does not smoke. He secured the offices at 12:30 a.m. The executive office door was closed and locked. There was no light on in the office. There was nothing unusual at the time he secured. He double-checked the hall door when he locked up. He left a night light on in the reception office."

Investigator's note—See witness index for detailed statements of witnesses.

NARRATIVE OF INTERVIEW OF SUSPECT

This is one of the key sections of the arson investigation report and, under certain circumstances, it may be one of the most sensitive from a legal perspective. This depends upon when suspicion focused on the suspect, the custodial circumstances of his interview, other factors relevant to whether or not his statements or remarks were free and voluntary, and whether or not he should have been fully advised as to his constitutional rights against self-incrimination and rights to counsel before answering any further questions or making further statements. However, it is the purpose of this section to deal with report writing and the Investigative Report and to set down all information in written form. It is for the prosecuting official to determine what portions of that report may be used.

One of the basic investigative failures is inaccurate investigative reporting of the statements and comments of witnesses and suspects. All too often, investigators avoid putting the information into report form until it is too late for reliable, accurate recollection. Too many investigators overlook the pratical fact that such information, when accurately recorded, may prevent distortion of the facts by the suspect or by others.

In the majority of arson investigations, it is seldom that the precise identity of the suspect immediately comes into focus. He may be regarded as a victim or as a routine witness during the early stages of the inquiry. This is true in the case of pathological fire setters; it may also be true in the case of insurance and financial fires and in fires occurring because of social unrest or domestic difficulty. There are numerous other hypothetical circumstances where late focus on suspicion may occur. In such circumstances, the witness may have talked to the investigators or other persons on numerous occasions concerning the fire. For example, he may have discovered or reported the fire, or he may have been the last known person in or at the premises prior to discovery of the fire. The statements or comments of this witness may seem overly routine or even boring to the inexperienced or careless investigator who usually fails to record them. Shortly, they are forever forgotten. Suddenly, such statements from this type of witness may come into focus; they may develop a significance that may become a key to the solution of the case, including identity of the suspect. Again, if the information was not included in the report, it becomes subject to question. Accuracy as to what was said and when, may have been lost forever. As every competent prosecuting attorney knows, there are legal as well as practical reasons for reducing investigative information to writing.

In a not unusual case, for example, the authorities were plagued with a series of costly incendiary fires, all occurring in the dead of night and many involving dwellings where people were sleeping. Many of these fires were discovered or reported by an alert security patrolman. In some cases, the investigators were careful and set down their comments and statements in their reports. Ultimately, when suspicion finally focused on the security patrolman, he was advised of his constitutional privileges against self-incrimination and his right to an attorney and he quickly elected to remain silent from that point on. However, his earlier statements and comments that had been carefully set down in writing were admitted and were the key to the successful conclusion of the case. The arsonist was convicted and the fires ceased.

Statements of possible suspects should be carefully reduced to writing—even in report form. It is for the prosecuting attorney to evaluate their usefulness if the case proceeds to trial. Overlooked, they are useless. The time, location, and circumstances of interview and persons present should be set down in the report.

A routine conversation between a possible suspect and the investigating officers might occur as follows:

"Undersigned arrived at the fire scene at 0815 hours and initiated fire scene examination. Sgt. Cagle, who had been in charge of the fire scene since the Fire Department released the scene, was relieved by undersigned. Sgt. Cagle left the fire scene at 0820. Undersigned is assisted by Officer Meyers.

At 0915, Dr. C arrived and identified himself as the proprietor and occupant of the involved medical offices. His identification is verified through his medical identification and confirmation with Mr. M, the building superintendent. Dr. C states that he wishes to enter his offices to check the fire damage and examine his medical cabinets. Officer Meyers and the undersigned accompanied Dr. C on a tour through his offices. As we arrived in his private office, Dr. C stated, "So this is where it started, huh?" We did not comment either on the origin of the fire or the cause. Dr. C stated, "I see my narcotics locker is unlocked. That's funny—I have the only key and I locked it before I left on the weekend." Dr. C volunteered that he had left the city on last Friday evening, July 1, for a fishing trip down on the Keys. He stated he had only flown into Miami Beach this morning at 6:30 a.m. He lives alone in an apartment at 2266 Sealane Drive and found, under his door, a note on white note paper, written in long hand and in ink, stating: "We burned your pad." He stated that this was his first knowledge of the fire. He stated that he called his attorney who advised him that his office had been burned out. He stated, "I gave the note to my attorney."

Dr. C further stated that he had been forced to

discharge his secretary the day before he departed on his fishing trip. He stated that he suspected her of hitting his narcotics cabinet. He stated that she had been in his employ for two years and that "She has a key to my office and didn't turn in, but I don't know how she opened the cabinet." He states that he will inventory the cabinet and provide us with a report of missing narcotics.

Dr. C departed from the premises at 9:53 a.m. We continued our fire scene examination.

Another example of interview of a witness and possible suspect is as follows:

Investigator A and the undersigned arrived at subject fire scene at 5:23 a.m. The alarm time was 0357 hours and Chief K is completing overhaul. The involved space is a beauty salon. Chief K introduces the undersigned to one Charles Martin X who states that he is the proprietor of the involved salon. He states that he was notified of the fire by the building janitor, William J., who called him at his apartment and said, "You'd better get down here, your joint is burning." Mr. X states that he lives in an apartment at 2466½ Broadway and that this address is two blocks from the scene. He had dressed and walked to the fire. "It was all burned out when I got there." Mr. X states that he locked the salon at 9:30 p.m. the previous evening and walked to his apartment. He states that he resides with Joseph Glenn L who is vacationing in San Francisco at this time. He states that the janitor and himself have the only keys to the place. He states that he smokes and added, "I might have left a cigarette in the waste basket or something. I am very nervous lately." Sitting in the undersigned's vehicle, with the dash and dome lights on, it is noted that Mr. X's hands appear to be slightly scorched. The hair on the back of his hands is singed; the eyebrows appear scorched, and his face is very red as if sunburned. He is extremely nervous.

Mr. X states he would prefer not to continue the conversation at this time, that he is very upset about the fire, that his health is bad, and he must get some rest. The interview is terminated at 5:29 a.m. Mr. X is observed walking from the scene in the general direction of his apartment.

The undersigned interviews the janitor, Mr. J, who states that he observed Mr. X run from the side door of the beauty salon as flames broke out the rear windows into the alley. Mr. J states that he knows Mr. X very well by sight and that he got a good look at him under the street light as he passed the corner. He is positive that it was Mr. X. Mr. J states that he had janitored the salon earlier in the evening; he has a girl friend, Julie M, who lives across the alley and had been visiting with her. Just as he was leaving, via the alley, he heard a "sort of" muffled explosion. He saw X run out of the salon, the flames bursting out the back windows. J states, "I stayed out of sight so he wouldn't see me." J further states that he called the Fire Department, using Julie's phone. He then called X's apartment. No answer. He called a second time, right after the Fire Department arrived on the scene. No answer. He called about fifteen minutes later. X answered. "He claimed he'd been sound asleep. I told him he'd better get down to his joint— it's burning. He never said nothing—just hung up."

The above exemplary narrative report of the statements of a proprietor and a witness are taken from an actual case. The investigators, at the time of the interviews, had no evidence as to the specific cause of the fire. They had only arrived on the scene at the time of the above interviews. Subsequent fire scene examination disclosed that the fire originated in the beauty salon and that alcohol had been used, in quantity, in the rear of the salon and in a rear storeroom. The proprietor had been scorched at the time he ignited the flammables. The statements of the janitor were accurate. The proprietor subsequently denied any conversations with the investigators wherein he had, at any time, described his movements on the evening of the fire. The denial was not believed by the Court or jury.

NARRATIVE INFORMATION REFLECTING MOTIVE

This section should contain information and cross reference to evidence concerning motive. As a practical matter, it is usually necessary to make a reasonable showing of motive, either by direct or indirect evidence. In some cases, usually the simpler ones, it is manifested by the act. In others, it is somewhat more subtle. The prosecuting attorney should have this information provided in the report submitted to him.

For example, in insurance fraud fires, the investigator may wish to indicate the following:

1. Name of the Insurance Carrier—building and contents or business interruption.
2. Amount of Insurance—including dates of policies, increases, loss payables or mortgage clauses, etc.
3. Name and address of agent or broker.

4. Name and address of Insurance Adjusters—including public adjusters.
5. Names and addresses of Insurance Investigators with specific identification of who they represent.
6. If available, previous fire and insurance loss history of the subject of inquiry. This should be personally checked out by the investigating officials before relying on it in presentation at trial or in official report.

In fires motivated by other than insurance or white collar fraud, supporting information might be in the form of:
1. Prior acts.
2. Statements of witnesses concerning threats of violence or admissions concerning previous fires.
3. Supporting physical and documentary evidence such as a previous record of setting fires to cover burglary and/or other crimes.
4. Information connecting the suspect with individuals or groups known to set fires for reasons of civil or social unrest.
5. Reliable information that may be used to show, directly or indirectly, the state of mind and motivation of the suspect at the time he committed the act—establishing the reason why.

INDEX TO PHYSICAL EVIDENCE

This section lists physical items removed from the scene and provides cross index to photographs, sketches, and evidence tags. For example:
1. Two gallon atlas metal container (Evidence Item 1-22-c).
2. 8″ × 10″ section shag carpet from area A (Evidence Item 1-23-c). This sample placed in sealed clean glass container and transported by EDC to crime lab. 7-4-77, 3:00 p.m.

INDEX TO SKETCHES

This section provides a catalogue and a guide to sketches and charts to be utilized with the report. For example:
1. Master floor plan, 1st floor.
2. Master floor plan, 2nd floor.
3. Living room floor plan (area of origin).
4. Master bedroom floor plan (area of origin).
5. Field chart of involved property and surrounding environs.

INDEX OF PHOTOGRAPHS

This section provides a catalogue and a guide to all photographs utilized in the investigation which are cross referenced to reports and sketches. For example:
1. Figures 1 – 6:   Perimeter of exterior of involved premises.
2. Figures 7–12:   Electrical and gas service entrances, panels, and equipment.
3. Figures 13–36:   General photographs showing interior spaces.
4. Figures 37–48:   Area and points of origin.
5. Figures 49–62:   Detail of physical evidence.

INDEX OF WITNESSES

This section should list witnesses by full name, address, occupation, and telephone number.

EXPERT WITNESSES AND OFFICIAL WITNESSES

This section should list official and laboratory witnesses by department and telephone number; witnesses, such as from utility services, fire experts, and private laboratories, should be listed by their office and telephone numbers and by areas of expertise in this particular case.

Investigative reports should be signed by the officer conducting the investigation and by his supervising officer with the date noted for signing and approval.

THE INVESTIGATIVE SUMMARY

Some arson investigations involve considerable investigation and detail reporting. This may result in what may appear overly voluminous material. Frequently, this is neither understood nor appreciated by administrators with limited or no investigative experience. Such detail may be unneeded until the case goes to trial. When, as the saying goes, the chips are down, if the factual detail is not available, the prosecution will probably fail. The investigative effort will have been basically wasted. On the other hand, already overburdened prosecutors frequently do not have the time to review a complete detailed report before prosecutive action is initiated. What they want to know at the time is "Has the crime been committed?"; "Is there reliable evidence to show that the crime was committed?"; "Is there reliable evidence to show that a certain identified person committed the crime?"; and "Is there reliable evidence to connect that person to the crime?" Hopefully, a motive for the act can be shown. From a practical point of view, most prosecuting attorneys would like to know whether or not they have a reasonable chance of obtaining a conviction on the basis of evidence reportedly available. Is it the kind of a case that the Court and a jury would believe? As one experienced prosecutor put it, "We must present our case mainly through the testimony of witnesses. Witnesses are people. People, whether they are firemen, policemen, experts or whatever, are subject to honest mistakes, error, and even prejudice; judges and most juries understand that. Under our system, the suspect is also entitled to a fair shake. So, we like to know the facts, the good and bad, before we take a case to preliminary or to the grand jury."

A summary of witnesses, an outline of their testimony, and listing those witnesses in the projected order they may be called is occasionally helpful to the prosecutor in proving the necessary elements of the case. The prosecutor, after reviewing the summary, may point out flaws in the case or the testimony or apparent investigative gaps that are not covered in the brief or, upon reference, in the investigative report.

Perhaps an actual case should be cited for illustrative purposes. This was a fire which caused extensive damage to a resort property and resulted in the loss of one life. Mr. A owned a valuable vacation and recreational facility. He leased some of the spaces for certain so-called therapy purposes to a businessman from the east whom we will identify as Mr. B. After a few months, it was indicated that the therapeutic venture was unsound, whereupon Mr. B applied to Mr. A for a cancellation of the lease. Mr. A declined, leaving Mr. B stuck with a very expensive, long-term lease. Mr. B had also gone to considerable expense in furnishing and equipping his facilities. He was heavily indebted to some of his associates in the east on very short-term, high interest loans. When he defaulted, they began to "turn on the heat." Mr. B discussed his options with some of his associates on the project and decided that the best one was to terminate the lease and liquidate his investment to the insurance companies by the process of fire. Through one of his associates, he increased the insurance on his furniture and equipment and obtained a very sound policy on business interruption insurance. He named the eastern loan sharks on the loss payables. Following a conference with his east-

ern financial backers, he was advised that a Mr. T would be visiting him shortly.

Mr. T appeared in due course and, following a conference with Mr. B and two of his associates, C and D, a date was set for the projected fire. Before the target date, much of the valuable equipment was moved, piece by piece, to a safe warehouse late at night. On the projected date, at the end of the tourist season, Mr. T moved to complete the job. During the late hours of the night, he spread quantities of gasoline through the targeted spaces. Although he was an experienced hand, he neglected to turn off one automatic furnace pilot light. As he was spreading the gasoline through an adjoining space, the heavier than air vapors reached the pilot light and the explosion and fire occurred.

Although severely burned, Mr. T was able to maintain his cool sufficiently to escape from the space and run down a driveway. As he ran, he threw the five-gallon gasoline container into some bushes behind a garage. He was barely able to make it to D's apartment which was in another building on the grounds. (B and C had decided to be out of town on the evening of the fire.) In the meanwhile, neighbors had heard the explosion, noted the flames and called the Fire Department. Mr. D, noting Mr. T's burned condition, immediately placed him in a bathtub of cold water as a first aid measure and provided medication to quiet him until he could somehow get him off the property without being observed.

In the interval, fire and police authorities arrived at the scene and the fire was controlled after extensive damage to the building and remaining contents. Following control, an officer was left to maintain security until an investigation could be initiated the following morning.

After the emergency apparatus and most of the police units departed, Mr. D wrapped Mr. T in a blanket and was able to leave the premises with him unobserved. He drove Mr. T to a hospital about one hundred miles from the scene, thus avoiding the local hospitals. The hospital accepted Mr. T who was in very critical condition. Mr. D advised the hospital authorities Mr. T had been injured in a vehicle accident on a country road. The hospital accepted the reason for Mr. T's injuries without further question.

In the meantime, fire and police authorities, working in cooperation, determined that the fire was of definite incendiary origin. They recovered gasoline residue from the carpeting in one of the offices and found the five-gallon container behind a garage some distance from the scene. The container evidenced flash fire damage and laboratory examination disclosed that it contained a residue of gasoline. The filler cap was missing as was the spout cap. Laboratory examination further disclosed residue of flesh on the handle of the container which was later identified as human skin. Other investigators recovered the filler cap and spout cap from inside the space of origin.

A survey of local area hospitals for unaccounted burn victims, within the time spectrum category of this incident, was negative.

At this point, the local authorities called upon the District Attorney's office investigative staff for guidance and cooperation in further investigation. There was reason to believe that they had a homicide on their hands. The District Attorney's office provided two additional experienced investigators.

Through information obtained by the police, suspicion was directed to B who was placed under surveillance which led to the location of Mr. T in an intensive care burn ward of a northern hospital. Physicians advised the authorities that they did not expect Mr. T to survive the injuries received in the fire.

A representative of the District Attorney's office and an investigative associate were permitted to visit Mr. T who stated that he had been medically advised that he was going to die and that he wished to make a statement to the investigators concerning the injuries he had received in the fire. He thereupon described the manner in which he had been approached by Mr. B and others to set the fire. He described meeting with B, C, and D and inspecting the property to be burned at which time a date and time was set and he was provided with a key by D. He detailed how he had set the fire and how, when things went wrong, he was concealed by D and then transported to the northern hospital. He described the payments he had received from B and C. (The visits by B and C, under assumed or fictitious names, were confirmed by the hospital authorities who later identified them.)

Mr. T's deathbed statement was recorded by a court reporter. He expired two days later.

When interviewed by investigators, B and C refused to discuss the matter and referred the officers to their counsel. D, after considering the matter, decided to tell the investigators the entire story as he knew it. B, C, and D were indicted on the charges of conspiracy to commit arson, arson, feloniously burning personal property to defraud an insurance

company, and murder. All three defendants were subsequently convicted of counts one, two, and three but the murder charge was thrown out on appeal to a technicality since the deceased was considered one of the co-conspirators.

Here was an example of a major investigation which required considerable detail in the basic report. In this case, an investigative summary of the report was prepared for the convenience and quick reference of the District Attorney. The summary was, in substance and form, as follows:

District Attorney's Case File #_____

Re: In the case of the People of the State of _____
    v. A, B, C, and D.
    Sections _____, _____, _____,
    and _____ CPC
    Conspiracy to commit arson, arson, burning personal property to defraud an insurer, murder.

Witnesses

TO PROVE THE FIRE

Fire Chief _____

1. As to date and time of response.
2. As to property involved.
3. As to physical burning of real and personal property and as to property involved.
4. As to his request for police and Fire Marshal's investigation.
5. As to securing the premises pending investigation.

TO PROVE CORPUS DELICTI

Fire Marshal _____

1. Basics as to his duties and experience in investigating fires.
   Qualify as expert witness.
2. As to time he initiated the fire scene investigation at subject address.
3. As to general and specific observations of physical evidence.
4. Opinion as to area of origin.
5. Opinion as to point of origin.
6. Opinion as to cause.

Witness: _____
Laboratory Expert

1. Duties and qualifications.
2. Date and time he examined the scene.
3. Location and identification of 5-gal. can.

4. Location and identification of can cap.
5. Location and identification of can spout.
6. Examination of can and report on contents and identification of flesh/skin on can handle.
7. Location and removal of carpet samples.
8. Tests conducted on carpet samples.
9. Identification of gasoline.
10. Flammability and explosive characteristics of gasoline (Describe flash point, explosive range, ignition, and burning temperatures).

TO CONNECT DEFENDANTS B, C, AND D

Investigator M_____
1. Will testify to death bed statement of Mr. T.

Court reporter Ms._____
1. If necessary, introduce transcript of statement of T's dying declaration.

Witness: Mr. A
1. Describe real property he owns (Involved premises).
2. Introduce copy of lease to B.
3. Financial difficulties related by B, C, and D.
4. B and C's conversations concerning voiding the lease.
5. Moving equipment out of spaces, late at night, shortly before the fire.
6. Conversations with B and C, shortly before the fire and threats by B telling him to keep his mouth shut if he wanted to survive.

Witness: _____
1. Observations of B and C moving property in rented moving van from involved spaces to warehouse (Five trips all late at nite; Observations at the time he followed the van).
2. Observed B purchase 2 five-gallon cans of gasoline, place them in van, and return them to his garage two nights before fire.

Witness: _____
Service Station Proprietor
1. Identifies B.
2. Testifies to sale of gasoline, in 2 five-gallon cans, to B. Identifies date by sales slip.
3. Identifies van.
4. Identifies C who was riding in the van. (C got out of van and got change for the coke machine. Also identifies C by scar on nose.)

Witness: _____
Insurance Agent
1. As to conversations with B and C regarding insurance policies at the time coverage was written — six months prior to date of fire.
2. As to conversations with B ten days before fire regarding increase in insurance on furniture and equipment and business interruption insurance. As to putting the increase in effect at that time.
3. As to the check that bounced and as to his conversations with C concerning the check.
4. As to B calling him on the morning following the fire. Conversation concerning possible cause and assigning a 'reasonable' adjuster who could be 'handled.'

Witness: _____
Claims Adjuster
1. As to his assignment on this case.
2. Policy information, coverage, and detail.
3. Describe duties as adjuster.
4. Describe and relate conversations with B and C.
5. Describe conversations with D.
6. Introduce physical inventory he took of equipment in spaces.
7. Introduce inventory presented him by B and C.
8. Explanation of difference between inventory B and C presented and his personal inventory.
9. Conversation with B concerning inventory discrepancy.
10. Offer of reward by B if he would cooperate.

Witness: Mr. D (also defendant).
1. Describe experience and occupation. (Expert in insurance matters)
2. Background and acquaintance with B and C.
3. Nature of their joint operation.
4. Financial contributions of each partner— B, C, and D.
5. Arrangements with the landlord—Mr. A.
6. Financial situation of the business two weeks before fire (including tax problems).
7. Delinquent loans — describe conversations with B's eastern associates.
8. Conversations with B and C concerning raising the insurance.
9. Conversations with B and C regarding moving out the valuable equipment prior to the fire.

10. Leasing the warehouse space for the equipment.
11. Conversations with B, C, and T shortly before the fire.
12. Providing T with key to spaces that were to be burned.
13. Description of events immediately following the fire. T's injuries, his treatment of T, and hauling T to northern hospital after authorities departed.
14. Conversations with B, C, and the insurance adjuster after the fire.
15. Conversations with B and T at the northern hospital shortly before T died.
16. Identification of inventory of loss prepared by B and C.
17. Identification of long distance telephone call data concerning a call he made to B immediately following the fire.

AS TO CAUSE OF DEATH OF T

Dr. _____
1. As to his observations and treatment of Mr. T following his admission to the hospital.

2. Identification of the body following death.
3. Observations and conclusions at autopsy.

Mr. _____
1. Identification of deceased as Mr. T.

Coroner _____
1. As to conclusions and opinion concerning cause of death of the deceased.

Serious and productive arson investigation requires understanding of the basic problems, expertise in techniques, dedication, and attention to detail. As I have said before in this text, the criminal justice system sets procedural and legal standards which cannot be short-circuited, even by the exponents of mass production and convenience.

Appreciation and support of the standards of our justice system is the measure of the difference between the men and the boys. Perhaps, the ultimate answer is quality rather than quantity.

APPENDIX

CLASSIFICATION OF FLAMMABLE AND COMBUSTIBLE LIQUIDS

Most jurisdictions classify combustible and flammable liquids in accordance with standards established by the National Fire Protection Association for fire safety and protection purposes and as set out in NFPA Pamphlet #30, *Flammable Liquids Code.*

Liquids are those fluids having a vapor pressure not exceeding 40 psi absolute at 100° F.

The code defines flammable liquids as those having a closed-cup flash point below 200° F. and are subdivided into the following described classes:

Class I—Those having flash points at or below 20° F.

Class II—Those having flash points above 20° F. but at or below 70° F.

Class III—Those having flash points above 70° F. but below 200° F.

According to Section 6, NFPA Fire Protection Handbook, the volatility of a flammable liquid is increased when heated to a temperature equal to or higher than its flashpoint. When heated, a flammable liquid which might otherwise be a Class II or Class III liquid may become subject to the applicable handling and storage recommendations for Class I or II liquids.

According to Title 16, Code of Federal Regulations, Revised 1976, flammable liquids are included in a further classification within the regulation of the Consumer Products Safety Commission which, in Section 1500.3 states:

"Extremely flammable means any substance that has a flash point at or below 20° F. as determined by the method described in Section 1500.43.

"Flammable means any substance that has a flash point of above 20° F. up to and including 80° F. as determined by the method described in Section 1500.43."

The section goes on to describe flammable solids and setting out packaging, transportation, and labelling of flammable and extremely flammable liquids and solids.

EXAMPLES OF FLAME TEMPERATURE

Large illuminating flames, when burning free, are less hot than small, intense, and sometimes less visible ones. The flame temperature of the latter most approximately denotes the temperature of combustion of the substance though never actually reaching it. The reason for this is that flame temperature is always lower than the temperature of combustion because of certain chemical processes. Auto consumption goes on within the atmosphere of the flame and exhibits considerable variations of temperature according to the different parts of the flame. The following may serve as examples of flame temperatures but which may fluctuate according to apex, base, or flanks of the flame.

	TEMPERATURE IN DEGREES FAHRENHEIT
Alcohol	2150
Carbon disulfide	3290
Coal gas	1700 to 2600
Fire damp or pit gas	5500
Petroleum lamps	1436 to 1900
Stearin candles	1184 to 1700
Sulphur	3200

AVERAGE SURFACE TEMPERATURES OF STANDARD LIGHT BULBS IN OPEN SOCKETS

WATTS	VOLTS	TEMPERATURE IN DEGREES FAHRENHEIT
40	120	260
60	120	252
75	120	272
100	120	261
100	230	285
150	120	278
200	120	297
200	120	389
500	120	374
300	120	389
1,000	120	480

251

Temperatures vary at various locations on the bulb, the hottest area generally being the top surface at the opposite end from the socket base.

HEAT-PRODUCING CAPABILITIES OF VARIOUS MATERIALS

A British Thermal Unit (BTU) is the amount of heat required to raise the temperature of one pound of water one degree Fahrenheit (measured at 60° F.).

A calorie is the amount of heat required to raise the temperature of one gram of water one degree Centigrade (measured at 15° C.). One BTU equals 252 calories.

In terms of energy, as heat can be used to do work, it is occasionally convenient to convert BTU's to joules. One BTU equals 1,055 joules or 0.0236 horsepower.

MATERIAL	EXPRESSED IN BRITISH THERMAL UNITS PER POUND (BTU).
Petroleum products	18,000 to 20,000
Coal, bituminous and anthracite	10,000 to 14,000
Coke	12,500
Peat	10,000
Timber	8,000
Asphalt	17,000
Bitumen and pitch	15,000
Coal tar	18,000
Straw	6,000
Wool	9,800
Cotton	7,200
Flax	6,500
Hydrogen	61,000
Ethyl ether	22,000
Napthalene	17,300
Ethyl alcohol	13,000
Glycerin	7,000
Sulphur	4,000
Rubber — hard sulphur	14,900
Rubber — soft low sulphur	18,700
Edible grains	6,000
Bread	4,500
Butter and margarine	13,500
Bacon	11,300
Nuts	10,000 to 13,000
Vegetable and animal oils, fats and waxes	17,000
Sugar	7,000
Cellulose	7,500
Paper	7,000
Starch	7,500
Guncotton	1,900
Dynamite	2,300
Magnesium	10,900

The above figures are general averages and may vary between specimens.

SPONTANEOUS IGNITION TEMPERATURES OF THE MORE COMMON FUEL COMPOUNDS

MATERIAL	TEMPERATURE IN DEGREES FAHRENHEIT
Acetone	1000
Acetylene	635
Ammonia (anhydrous)	1204
Amyl acetate-n	714
Amyl alcohol	621
Aniline	1418
Benzene	1076
Benzine - petroleum ether	475
Butane-n	806
Butane-iso	1010
Butyl alcohol-n	693
Butyl cellosolve	472
Camphor	871
Carbon disulfide	1204
Castor oil	840
Denatured alcohol	750
Dichlorethylene	856
Diethylcellosolve	406
Diethyl ether	366
Ethane	950
Ethyl acetate	907
Ethyl alcohol	799
Ethylene	1009
Ethylene glycol	775
Fuel oil #1 thru #4	490 to 505
Fuel oil #6	765
Gas, coal	1200
Gas, natural (methane)	999
Gas, oil	637
Gasoline	495
Hexane-n	477
Hydrogen	1076
Hydrogen sulfide	500
Kerosene (same as fuel oil #1)	490
Linseed oil	820
Lubricating oil	500 to 660
Methane (natural gas)	999
Methyl alcohol	878
Mineral spirits	475
Methyl cellosolve	551
Methyl ethyl ketone	960
Naptha (coal tar)	900 to 960
Naptha (stoddard solvent)	450 to 500
Naptha (V.M. & P.)	450 to 500
Octane-n	450
Petroleum ether	475
Phosphorus (red)	500
Phosphorus (yellow)	86
Pine tar	671
Propane	864
Propyl alcohol-iso	852
Resin oil	648
Soya bean oil	833
Sulfur	450
Tun oil	855
Turpentine	488

AUTO-IGNITION OF BLASTING COMPOUNDS

The temperatures at which blasting compounds will detonate differ considerably but, in general, these temperatures are lower than those for explosive gases and may vary with condition of the compound and rate of ambient temperature rise.

BLASTING MATERIAL	AUTO-EXPLOSIVE TEMPERATURE IN DEGREES FAHRENHEIT
Blasting gelatine	396
Cellulose dynamite	330
Celluloid	380
Collodion wool, air dry	332
Dynamite, with 50% nitro	380
Guncotton, compressed	334
Guncotton, air dry	360
Gunpowder	518
Kieselguhr, with 50% nitroglycerin	336
Nitroglycerin	494
Mercury fulminite	347
Picric acid	572
*Blasting gelatine, with camphor	310

* For flash point, flammable limits, vapor density, etc., see Hazardous Chemicals Data, *NFPA Handbook on Fire Protection,* Table 6-126; Flash Point Index of Trade Name Liquids, Pamphlet 325 A (1972) City of Los Angeles Dangerous Chemicals Code, 1951 Edition; or Factory Mutual Engineering Loss Prevention Bulletin #36.10.

IGNITION TEMPERATURE OF MISCELLANEOUS MATERIALS

MATERIAL	IGNITION TEMPERATURE IN DEGREES FAHRENHEIT
Cotton, absorbent	446
Cotton, batting	511
Cotton, sheeting	464
Cane fiberboard	440
Filler paper	450
Newsprint paper	448
Viscose rayon	546
Wood fiberboard	424 to 444
Aluminum paint flakes	949
Magnesium, fine powder	883
Magnesium, coarse powder	950
Magnesium, ribbon	1004
Magnesium, cast	1144
Tin, powder	842
Tin, coarse powder	1094
Zinc powder	1202
Nitrocellulose film	279
Matches, common (heads)	325
Carbon soot	366
Crude Pine gum powder	581
Shellac, scale	810
Paint film—oxidized linseed oil, varnish	864

VARIOUS WOODS	IGNITION TEMPERATURE IN DEGREES FAHRENHEIT
Basswood	482
Birch	399
Douglas fir	500
Long leaf pine	442
Oak, tanbark	448
Ponderosa pine	446
Sitka spruce	446
Redwood	572
Spruce	500
Tamarack	510
White Oak	410
White Pine	446
Western Larch	460
Western red cedar	378

Reliable tests indicate that treatment with certain chemical fire retardants (fireproofing) raises the ignition temperatures to as much as 1,000 degrees in wood products and with the lasting qualities varying with materials used, application, and the particular environment such as temperature changes and weathering.

Ignition temperatures in wood vary depending upon milling, age, and weathering. Wood pyrolysis may occur during periods of extended heating when loss of hygroscopic water may be expected up to approximately 212° F. At about 400° F., decomposition causes the wood to darken in color with loss of strength although the internal structure may be retained; at approximately 932° F., carbonization occurs and additional volatile spirits are lost. The reaction in absence of air becomes exothermic at about 530° to 570° F. and with pyrolysis completed at about 932° F. although the residue of wood charcoal remains. The remaining charcoal will continue to produce gases on further heating up to approximately 1500° F.

Tests have shown that the ignition temperature of wood decreases with extended exposure time. For example, when Long Leaf Pine is exposed for six minutes, it will ignite at 442° F. It will ignite at 315° F. when exposed for forty minutes. The ignition temperature may be further reduced by exposure for longer periods as the pyrolytic action progresses. Wood framing in brick walls exposed to conducted, long-term heating from steam pipes have been known to completely pyrolize over a period of years—sealed inside the walls but in proximity to the heat-producing pipes.

The National Bureau of Standards' method of establishing ignition temperatures of solids includes heating the specimen to the lowest temperature from which exothermic reaction of oxidation can self-accelerate to ignition which is defined or apparent by the glow or flame of the subject material; the specimen is in the air at constant, self-ignition temperature, flowing at the optimum velocity. Air flow is varied with the type of material and the intensity of oxidation is so that the air passing around or through the specimen will be sufficient for normal oxidation without excessive cooling of the reacting masses. The optimum velocity is usually experimentally determined for each material as indicated by the self-heating that results.

METAL COLOR AS INDICATOR OF TEMPERATURE

COLOR	TEMPERATURE IN DEGREES FAHRENHEIT
Incipient red heat	970
Dark red heat	1252
Cherry red heat	1462
Pale red heat	1742
Yellow heat	2012
Incipient white heat	2372
Full white heat	2732

MELTING TEMPERATURES OF CERTAIN BUILDING MATERIALS AND METALS

MATERIAL	TEMPERATURE IN DEGREES FAHRENHEIT
Wrought iron	2732
(Note this is the 'white heat' indicated in the above table)	
Mild steel	2462
(Structure failure at 842)	
Cast iron	2500
Brickwork	2600 to 3000
Brass	1714
Glass	1400 to 1600
Aluminum	1200
(Structure failure at 437)	
Zinc	762
Lead	617

CALCULATIONS IN FIRE LOADING FOR THE MORE COMMON OCCUPANCIES

OCCUPANCY	*BRITISH THERMAL UNITS PER SQUARE FOOT
Hospital ward occupancy	8,000 or less
Residential occupancy	27,200
Residential timber floor	20,800 68,400
Residential wood trim	20,400

OCCUPANCY	*BRITISH THERMAL UNITS PER SQUARE FOOT
School classrooms	29,600
Office occupancy with light files	58,400
Library	200,800
Heavy file store	332,000
Textile factory	200,000
Textile warehouse	500,000
Bookstore, filled	2,000,000
Rubber warehouse	2,000,000 and up

*A British Thermal Unit, BTU, is the amount of heat necessary to raise the temperature of one pound of water 1° Fahrenheit on the temperature scale. For example, the heat output of wood products is gauged at approximately 7,500 BTU's per lb. The heat output of coal is gauged between 11,000 and 14,000 BTU's per pound. The fire loading of an occupancy or space is gauged on the total pounds in relation to the space—in the terms of the total heat output of the fuel (such as furnishings or stored items) in the space. The seriousness of the fire in a given space may be estimated to a reasonable degree upon contents, construction, and ventilation.

The above are time-temperature curves, as reported by the NFPA, and compared with the standard time-temperature curve indicating the relative severity of fire growth and temperature rise depending upon different fire loadings as indicated above.

The standard time-temperature curve generally represents a condition of high fire severity encountered in stages of actual fires when combustibles are such as to favor rapid temperature rise. The curves may only be considered as a general guide because of variance in ventilation and structural characteristics.

COMBUSTIBLE CONTENT	HEAT POTENTIAL	EQUIVALENT FIRE SEVERITY
Total, including finish floor and trim Lbs per sq ft	Assumed Btu per sq ft	Approximately equivalent to that of test under standard curve for the following periods:
5	40,000	30 min
10	80,000	1 hr
15	120,000	1½ hrs
20	160,000	2 hrs
30	240,000	3 hrs
40	320,000	4½ hrs
50	380,000	7 hrs
60	432,000	8 hrs
70	500,000	9 hrs

GLOSSARY OF TERMS
AND DEFINITIONS

Accelerant   In chemistry, a catalyst (a compound that may speed up a chemical process). In fire investigation, the term is used to describe liquids and compounds utilized by arsonists in the setting of fires, such as alcohol, gasoline, kerosene, charcoal lighter fluid, and paint thinner.

Acetylene   A colorless hydrocarbon gas, C-2 and H-2, that is produced by the action of water upon certain carbon compounds and used principally in welding and cutting operations.

Alligatoring   A term used by fire investigators in the discussion of fire spread patterns and fire point indicators. The general usage is to describe visual indications of the degree of the carbonizing process of wood when exposed to flame or sufficient heat. This results in structural deterioration of the wood. Usually, the remaining surface appearance is characterized by cracks and ridges. The term is used by some experts in conjunction with their consideration of depth of char and also in conjunction with their analysis of the speed of the fire, whether or not accelerants were present. There is presently no scientific support for the reliability of estimates on this basis.

Amperage   The strength of a current measured in amps.

Ampere (Amp)   A unit of rate of flow of electricity. Flow of electricity depends upon the pressure in volts and the resistance, identified as impedance, in alternating current circuits. Electrical current is generally classified into two types—direct (DC) and alternating (AC). Direct current provides continuous flow in the same direction while alternating current reverses flow with frequency and is measured in cycles per second.

Arc   When an electric current is interrupted, either intentionally (by a switch), or accidentally (because of a loosened terminal), heating that results from high resistance or arcing may occur. Either condition may cause ignition of insulation or adjacent combustible materials. The degree of heat or intensity of the arc depends upon the amount of current in the circuit. Electric arcs can ignite combustibles because of sparks being thrown in the general vicinity of the fault, whereas fault type heating alone, in an overloaded conductor, may result in the ignition of insulation and of combustibles in the immediate proximity of the conductor. Either of the above conditions can result without opening the circuit breaker or other circuit safety device.

Area of Origin   The term used by fire investigators to describe the general area where a fire may have started. It is not limited to the specific point of origin: the term is elastic and may describe an entire building in a multibuilding fire; a room where the fire is limited to one structure; or, in a forest fire, an entire canyon or front in a major conflagration.

Arson   The common law felony of maliciously and voluntarily burning the house of another or sometimes, the willful and malicious burning of the dwelling house of another. Under common law, it was an offense against the security of a habitation and referred to possessions rather than to property. Hence, it was considered an aggravated felony, and of greater enormity than any other unlawful burning because it manifested a greater recklessness and contempt of human life than the burning of any other building in which no human being was presumed to be. The crime is now statutory in most jurisdictions, but many of the statutes define the crime substantially as it was in common law. There are statutes, however, which apply the crime to all sorts of property. (*See* 2 R.C.L.496 and Ballentine on the Law of Arson, 107.)

Atom   Atoms are generally defined as the extremely minute particles of which all matter is composed. Each element consists of one or more identical atoms; the properties of elements are determined by their individual structure of atoms. Gold, for example, is an element, as are Aluminum, Antimony, Iodine, Helium, Sodium, Silver, Uranium, Tungsten, and Zinc. The chemical formula shows the number of atoms of the various elements in the molecule and can be identified by breakdown and arrangement. The atomic weight of an element indicates the weight of its atom as compared with the weight of an atom of oxygen. The molecular weight of a compound is the sum of the weights of all atoms in one molecule.

Auto-Ignition Temperature   This is generally used in discussing ignition temperatures of liquid, solid, or gaseous compounds or substances. It is rated at the minimum temperature to which the material must be heated to initiate or create self-sustained combustion, independent of any outside heat source. The term is also used in the discussion of spontaneous heating resulting from physical, chemical, and biological reactions.

Avogadro's Law   Generally, this law states that, under constant temperature and pressure, equal volumes of all gases contain the same number of molecules and that the densities of various gases may be computed from their molecular weights.

Bimetal Control   A common method of applying the principal of differential expansion is to weld or braze together two thin layers or strips of metal having widely different coefficients of thermal expansion. This procedure forms an element called a bimetal which, when heated, bends toward the metal having the lower expansion of the two metals combined. The change in length of either strip composing the bimetal, for a given chance of temperature, is always proportional to the original length of the strip although the ratio may vary for different metals. The elements are arranged in various shapes for various purposes, including activation of heat and temperature controls.

Boyle's Law   The behavior of gases is based on certain gas laws which are sufficiently reliable to predict this behavior under the more commonly encountered conditions and environments. Boyle's law states that the volume occupied by a given mass varies inversely with the absolute pressure if temperature is not allowed to change or where PV is constant. The relation between temperature, pressure, and volume for most gases may be determined by accepted formulas. These formulas are set out in publications of the American Gas Association and by the National Fire Protection Association.

British Thermal Unit (BTU)   The amount of heat necessary to raise the temperature of one pound of water one degree Fahrenheit, measured at 60° F. One BTU equals 252 calories. It is important to recognize the difference between heat and temperature. Heat is the quantity of measurement whereas temperature is the measure of intensity. Specific heat or thermal capacity of a substance is the number of BTU's required to raise the temperature of one pound of the substance one degree Fahrenheit or the number of calories to raise one gram of the substance through one degree Centigrade.

Burning Point   The temperature which a substance must attain before it will ignite on the application of an ignition source or a flame. The burning point is usually higher than the flash point although the levels may coincide such as in ether, carbon disulfide, petroleum ether, benzol, and certain other compounds.

Burn Pattern   The term used by some fire investigators in defining and illustrating the progress of a fire by means of visible charring, decomposition, and displacement. It may be used to define carbonization from luminous and nonluminous combustion, spontaneous ignition process, and pyrolysis. It may be used in describing major fire progress or limited progress inside walls or isolated areas and spaces. When used by experts, they should be required to define the concept behind its use.

Calorie   The amount of heat required to raise the temperature of one gram of water one degree Centigrade, measured at 15° C. One BTU equals 252 calories. As heat can be converted to energy, it may be said that one BTU equals 1,055 joules; one BTU per minute equals 0.0236 horse power.

Carbon   A nonmetallic chemical element found in many inorganic and all organic compounds. Diamonds and graphite, of course, are pure carbon. Carbon is also present in substances such as coal, coke, charcoal, soot, and smoke. Wood and some fabrics commonly deteriorate to carbon and charcoal in the process of decomposition. Coal and charcoal are subject to spontaneous heating in piles and further deterioration in the carbon process.

Carbon Black   This may be formed by the incomplete combustion of natural gas and a liquid hydrocarbon or by a liquid hydrocarbon alone. It occludes oxygen and slow smoldering combustion may easily result if stored without proper cooling and ventilation. After thorough cooling and airing, carbon black will not heat spontaneously although heating may result from mixture with oxidizable oils. Dust explosion hazards may exist where carbon black is processed or stored.

Carbon Dioxide   A gas which may be a product of combustion.

Carbon Monoxide   A gas which may be a product of combustion. Its ignition temperature is 1128° F.; flammable limits vary from 12.5 to 74 (percent by volume); vapor density is 1.0; and it is water soluble.

Cause   As used in fire investigation, identifying and describing the igniting agent or heat source of a particular fire. For example, some causes could be: "match ignited and thrown into combustibles," "friction from electric motor belt from thrown bearings," and "incendiary origin—Molotov cocktail ignited and thrown into window of dwelling which then ignited draperies and carpet."

Centigrade   One Centigrade degree is 1/100 the difference between the temperature of the freezing and boiling points of water at one atmosphere of pressure. 0° is the freezing point and 100° is the boiling point of water.

Charcoal   A black form of carbon produced by partially burning or oxidizing wood or other organic matter and compounds. Under certain conditions, charcoal reacts with air to heat spontaneously and ignites into self-sustained flaming combustion. The more finely the charcoal is divided, the greater the hazard of combustion. Spontaneous heating may result from lack of sufficient cooling; lack of ventilation; becoming wet, then drying without ventilation; friction; being finely divided without ventilation; or leaving the residue in a chemically unstable condition.

Charles' Law   This states that the volume of a given mass of gas is directly proportionate to the absolute temperature if the pressure is kept constant. V/T (the ratio of volume to temperature), is constant.

Circuit Breaker   A type of electrical overcurrent device. There are circuit breakers and oil circuit breakers; adjustable and nonadjustable; and instantaneous and delay, with thermal tripping mechanisms. (*See* the National Electrical Code.)

Overcurrent protection devices include thermal cut-outs which are not intended to open short circuits or grounds but may be used to protect motors and heavy branch circuits from overload, and plug fuses which are produced in several types including the one-time and the time delay (Type S), which is designed to discourage tampering or bridging. Overcurrent devices also include thermal cutouts which are not intended to open short circuits but may be utilized to protect motors and motor branch circuits from overload. Others include various types and classes of cartridge fuses which may be equipped with drop out links, one-time fuses, super-lag renewable, as well as dual element fuses of the blade and ferrule type. (*See* National Electrical Code.)

Circumstantial Evidence   Proof of circumstances surrounding the transaction; proof of certain facts and circumstances in a given case from which a jury may infer other connected facts which usually and reasonably follow according to the common experience of mankind (8 R.C.L. 180.)

City Gas   This gas may be natural, manufactured, or liquified petroleum gas, or mixtures of any of these. Natural gas seems to be in most common use today and consists mainly of methane, a small amount of ethane, possibly some propane, butane, small amounts of carbon dioxide, and varying amounts of nitrogen. In compound, the result is a lighter than air mixture at the meter. Service main pressures may be from 5 psi to 10 psi or higher; it is usually a 3½- to 8-inch water column on domestic consumer premises.

Combustible Liquids   Liquids with a flash point at or above 200° F. are sometimes referred to as combustible liquids. When a combustible liquid is heated to or above its flash point, it may have some of the hazards of a flammable liquid. (*See* **Flammable Liquids.**)

Combustible Solids   Those solids found in greatest abundance in properties which constitute the greatest bulk of property destroyed by fire. These include all materials which will ignite and burn or undergo substantial chemical change when subjected to heat or flame. The chemical make-up of most ordinary combustible solids is carbon, hydrogen, and oxygen with lesser percentages of nitrogen and other elements. Cellulose is the main component of wood by weight; paper is almost pure cellulose. Cotton consists of 90 percent cellulose. Animal fibers consist of protein molecules containing high percentages of nitrogen as well as carbon, hydrogen, and oxygen.

Competency of a Witness   A person is competent to testify if he has sufficient understanding to receive, remember, and narrate impressions, and is sensible to and understands the obligation of an oath (28 R.C.L. 447). Competency also entails an adequate ability to observe, mental capacity, and other relevant factors (*See* Blythe v. Ayres, 96 Cal. 532, 586, 19 L.R.A. 40, 50, 31 Pac. Rep. 915).

Conduction   The process by which heat is communicated from one body to another by direct contact or through an intervening solid-, liquid-, or heat-conducting medium. Some examples are: a steam pipe in contact with wood; a chimney flue in contact with attic or ceiling framing; and a pair of pliers in contact with electrical conductors that are grounded through an electrode. The amount of heat transferred depends upon the heat conductivity of the materials and the area of thickness of the conducting mass. The rate of transfer is in direct proportion to the temperature differential between the points of entrance and departure.

Contract   An agreement by which a person undertakes to do or not to do a particular thing. Within the meaning of the federal contract clause of the Federal Constitution, the term includes not only contracts as the word is ordinarily understood, but all instruments, ordinances, and measures which embody the inherent qualities or purposes of contracts and carry reciprocal obligations of good faith. (*See* Ballentine's definition of contracts.)

Contract Mala in Se   This term includes all contracts of an immoral nature, iniquitous in themselves, and those opposed to sound public policy. Where both parties are *in pari delicto* (in equal fault), neither, as a general rule, will be accorded relief in a court of law (Holland v. Sheehan, 108 Minn. 362, 23 L.R.A. (N.S.) 510, 511, 122 N.W. Rep. 1).

Contract of Insurance   An agreement by which one party in a consideration promises to pay money or its equivalent, or do some act of value to the assured, upon the destruction or injury of something in which the other party has an interest. (*See* Cooley's briefs on the Law of Insurance, Vol. 1, p. 5.)

Convection   The process by which heat is moved by air differences, usually in a rising or circular pattern. For example, in the case of air circulation in a room, heat from a stove will move laterally if there is an obstruction to vertical movement such as a ceiling, and vertically if there is an obstruction to horizontal movement such as a wall.

Conversion of Centigrade to Fahrenheit   The formula for converting Centigrade to Fahrenheit is: $F = \frac{9}{5} C + 32$. To convert 10° C. to Farenheit:

$$F = \frac{9}{5} C + 32$$
$$F = \frac{9}{5} (10) + 32$$
$$F = 18 + 32 = 50° \text{ F.}$$

The equation for converting Fahrenheit to Centigrade is: $C = \frac{5}{9} F - 32$.

Corpus Delicti   The body of the crime, assuming that the specific crime charged has actually been committed by someone. The *corpus delicti* is made up of two elements; first, that a certain result has been produced (i.e. a man has died or a building has been burned); and second, that someone is criminally responsible for the result. (*See* Ballentine on *corpus delicti* and 7 R.C.L. 774.) The *corpus delicti* specifically implies the body of the offense, or the substance of the crime.

In homicide cases, it has at least two elements; first, the fact of death; and second, that the criminal agency of another person was the cause thereof. (*See* Ballentine on *corpus delicti* and 13 R.C.L. 736.) In larceny, the *corpus delicti* is composed of two elements; first, that the property was removed from the possession of the owner; and second, that it was taken without the consent of the owner by another person or persons with willful design.

In an arson case, the *corpus delicti* consists of two elements; first, that the fire occurred (the burning or fire must at least extend to a charring of the wood or fabric to satisfy the legal requirements of burning); and second, that a fire resulted from the willful and intentional ignition by a criminal agency. The first must be shown by affirmative evidence. The second may be shown by direct or circumstantial evidence. For example, if flammable liquids were present in the library of a dwelling and ignited by a trailer extending from the front door, the *corpus delicti* may be established by proving the occurrence of the fire and, second, eliminating all reasonable, accidental sources of ignition such as electrical, mechanical, smoking, lightning, etc.

Crime   Under interpretations in our system, crime is a wrong of public character because it possesses elements of evil which effect the public as a whole and not merely the person whose rights of person or property have been invaded. The term includes felonies and misdemeanors (Morrison v. Texas, 6 A.L.R. 1644). Crime is also defined as an act committed or omitted in violation of a public law either forbidding or commanding it (4 Blackstone's Commentaries, 5; and 29 A.L.R. 413).

Criminal Charge   A charge which, strictly speaking, exists only when a formal written complaint has been made and a prosecution initiated against the accused. In the eye of the law, a person is charged with crime only when he is called upon in a legal proceeding to answer to such a charge (United States v. Patterson, 150 U.S. 65, 68, 37 L. ed. (U.S.) 999, 1000, 14, Sup. Ct. 20).

Criminal Conspiracy   A combination of two or more persons attempting to accomplish, by some concerted action, some criminal or unlawful purpose, or to accomplish some purpose not in itself criminal, by criminal or unlawful means. (*See* Harris v. Commonwealth, 113 Va 746, 38 L.R.A. (N.S.) 458, 460, 73, S.E. Rep. 561.)

Criminal Information   A formal declaration of the charge or offense against a person, made by the prosecuting or district attorney, and filed in the court in which the person is to be tried.

Criminal Intent   That evil state of a person's mind, accompanying an unlawful act, in the absence of which no crime is committed. In some crimes, the law requires specific intent such as in some statutes making it a felony to file a proof of loss with the intent to defraud an insurance company. In other crimes, the intent may be general as long as the act is willful and intentional, such as the willful and malicious act of setting fire to a railroad bridge. In certain crimes, the intent may be implied from the obvious willfulness of the act in which case malice may be inferred. It is important for the investigator to distinguish clearly between intent and motive. Motive is the reason, real or fancied, that a person has for committing an act. Intent, express or implied, is required under the law. Proof of motive is not a requirement under the law.

Criminal Offense   As used in statutes permitting the introduction of evidence of commission of a criminal offense to affect the credibility of a witness, the term is generally held to include both felonies and misdemeanors, but not to include violation of a municipal ordinance.

Under constitutional provisions for prosecution of all criminal offenses by presentment or indictment of a grand jury, acts of a militia man which merely constituted a violation of the military code do not amount to a criminal offense (State, ex. rel. Madigan v. Wagener, 74 Minn. 518, 42 L.R.A. 749, 752, 77 N.W. Rep. 424).

Criminal Proceeding   The prosecution of a person charged with a criminal offense, the subsequent contemplation of the conviction, and the punishment for the offense of the person so prosecuted. A proceeding against a juvenile offender is generally not a criminal proceeding since such proceedings do not generally contemplate punishment for the offense but prevention of deterring minors from becoming criminals (State v. Freeman, Mont. 262, Pac. Rep. 168, 171).

Criminal Prosecution   A prosecution in a court of justice, in the name of the sovereignty of the jurisdiction involved, against one or more individuals accused of a crime. Although instituted by an individual, a criminal prosecution is not in any sense an action between the person instituting it and the prisoner. (*See* Concordia Fire Ins. Co. v. Wise, 46 A.L.R. 463.)

Criminal Statute   A statute which describes an act or the omission of an act as a criminal offense. A statute authorizing punishment for contempt is a criminal statute (Langenberg v. Decker, 131 Ind. 471, 16, A.L.R. 108, 113, 31 N.E. Rep. 190). Statutes in this category may be either felonies or misdemeanors.

Criminal Syndicalism   A California statute defines the term to be any doctrine or precept advocating teaching, aiding, or abetting the commission of crime, sabotage (defined as meaning willful and malicious physical damage or injury to physical property), or unlawful acts of force, violence, or methods of terrorism, as by means of accomplishing a change in industrial ownership or control, or effecting any political change (20 A.L.R. 1544; *See* State v. Diamond, 20 A.L.R. 1544 and *Ballentine's Legal Definitions*).

Current, Electric   Electrical current is of two kinds: direct (DC), and alternating (AC). Direct current is a continuous flow in the same direction, as in batteries; alternating current, now widely used, creates a flow which is periodically reversed and creates a system of waves. The number of cycles is the number of waves per second. As a rule, alternating current circuits are in single- or three-phase. Single-phase is carried by a two-wire circuit although a third or neutral wire is often used which does not alter the principle. In a three-phase, three-wire, balanced (delta) circuit, the current flow in each conductor leads or lags the current in the other two conductors and the algebraic sum of the three is zero. Any of the two wires of a three-phase circuit may be used to supply a single-phase circuit and balance may be obtained when three two-wire circuits are connected so that they are equivalent to one three-wire, three-phase circuit. The common voltages are 120/208 and 277/480. (*See* National Electrical Codes.) The flow of electric current creates magnetic force and a change in magnetic field surrounding a system of wires. This produces an electric voltage which, in turn, creates current flow. These facts are the basis of the generator and the electric motor. Voltage is produced in the windings of motors and generators. In a motor, voltage created by the rotor is known as back electromotive force; to some extent, this restricts the flow of current through the motor. The current required to start a motor is much greater than that required to operate it once it is in motion or at normal speed.

Curtain Boards   An incombustible barrier suspended to bank heat along a ceiling in order to enhance the effectiveness of a sprinkler or extinguishing system.

Cryogenics   This is the science of dealing with the behavior of materials at temperatures close to absolute zero. It is utilized in the handling of gases such as argon, oxygen, hydrogen, and nitrogen, for purposes of liquification, transport, and storage. *(See* NFPA 6-31: Cryogenic Properties of Gases.)

Decomposition Explosions   Certain compounds are capable of decomposing almost instantaneously. Examples are commercial explosives, ammonium nitrate, and carbon disulfide. In addition, certain other endothermic compounds are subject to explosion under certain conditions. Explosive decomposition is usually accompanied by the release of large quantities of hot gases and, in general, it is correct to say that the speed of release of the gases is proportionate to the violence of the explosion. Explosions and detonations may result in the formation of pressures attaining several hundred pounds per square inch. A pressure wave may spread in all directions at velocities from a few thousand to more than twenty-five thousand feet per second and which, in turn, can cause damage to buildings and fixed objects. Some authorities classify explosions as low order (explosions of gunpowder and similar explosives) and high order (in groups of dynamite, nitro compounds, etc.).

Decomposition, Heat of   Heat of decomposition is the heat released by the decomposition of endothermic compounds, i.e., those requiring the addition of heat for their formation.

Detonators   The term commonly used to describe the device employed in initiating the decomposition of explosive compounds such as dynamite and blasting gelatine. Detonators generally require two types of explosives; one being sensitive to heat or fire, such as the safety fuse, which will explode a second more powerful charge that detonates or boosts to the principal explosive. Lead azide is commonly used as the first detonator because of its high sensitivity. The detonators are usually designed to attach to the safety fuse or another remote triggering device and are contained inside a tubular copper or aluminum case, with an attachment suitable for crimping. Detonators are commonly designed for electrical activation.

Diffuse Explosion   The instant decomposition of combustible gases in appropriate mixture with air. In a limited space, this phenomenon may displace walls, bulkheads, and fixed objects. The combustion produces a great amount of sudden heat with expansion dependent upon volume. This is not a high velocity type explosion but is heat-producing and capable of displacement damage as well as continuing fire.

Direct Evidence   Evidence given by witnesses who testify directly concerning their own knowledge of the main facts to be proven. Eye witnesses are a good example: A takes the witness stand and testifies that he saw B toss a burning object through the window of the dwelling and that, immediately thereafter, flames burst from the window and B ran from the scene.

Distillation   As used in fire investigation, a laboratory process utilized in the recovery and analysis of accelerants. In simple distillation, the evidence specimen is heated to vaporize the residue and the vapors are condensed to reform as a liquid. In the process of steam distillation, the residue recovered from the scene is flooded with water and heated to the boiling point. Steam and vapors are introduced into the process and the condensed results are then separated. The accelerant, if any, is then identified. Vacuum distillation is a process in which any accelerant present in the suspected specimen is removed by simultaneous application of suction and heat.

Dust Explosions   The rapid order combustion of finely divided particles of combustible solids in an atmospheric oxygen environment when an igniting source is present. The fine particles or dust may be from coal, plastics, grain, explosive powders, wood, cotton, industrial waste, or light metal. The phenomenon may be accompanied by considerable heat but is not considered in the high explosive order although low order explosive damage and displacement may result.

Dynamite   A high explosive, principally consisting of nitroglycerin absorbed in inert solid materials to reduce sensitivity to shock. Absorbents include a type of infusorial earth, wood compounds, etc. At present, dynamite is probably the most commonly available high explosive. Its purchase and use is regulated in most jurisdictions; however, it is commonly used in criminal activities. Straight dynamite is essentially nitroglycerin absorbed in a combustible absorbent such as wood pulp and extra oxidizing materials such as sodium nitrate with a small amount of calcium carbonate or zinc oxide. Ammonia dynamite consists of ammonium nitrate with nitroglycerin in smaller percentage and may also include sulfur and cereal products along with a neutralizing zinc oxide. Gelatine dynamite broadly covers a variety of compounds with the common factor consisting of the substitution of smokeless nitrocellulose powder for relatively inactive wood pulp. The compounds are gelatinous and plastic in mass and are sometimes called blasting gelatine. It is generally considered more potent than ordinary dynamite.

Dynamite is produced in a low freezing formula by introduction of a number of compounds which are explosive and may be substituted for varying portions of the nitroglycerin which has a tendency to freeze and become very unstable. The introduction of other mixtures reduces the freezing point of the nitroglycerin; some of these compounds include nitrosugar, nitropolyglycerine, nitrotoluenes, and nitroydrins.

Dynamites are considered far more stable to shock than nitroglycerin although the dynamite compounds will explode on overheating and exposure to heavy shock, such as impact by a bullet. The dynamites become unstable in conditions of improper storage, aging, and crystallization. Disposal should be restricted to explosives experts.

Electricity   In the context of flowing through conductors, electricity is composed of identical particles called electrons that are much lighter than atoms. Electrons weigh only 1/1837th as much as an atom of the lightest chemical element, hydrogen. (In this context, electricity may be described as "an electric current; a stream of moving electrons, setting up a magnetic field of force through which it produces kinetic energy"—*Webster's New World Dictionary.*)

Electricity is also a form of energy which may be generated by friction, induction, or chemical change and has magnetic, chemical, and radiant effects; it is a property of the basic particles of all matter consisting of protons (positive charge) and electrons (negative charge) which attract each other. *(Webster's New World Dictionary.)*

Electricity carries the potential danger of causing fire due to improper utilization, fault, improper grounding, arcing, short circuiting, overcurrent, etc.

Evidence   That which makes clear or ascertains the truth of the very fact or point in issue, whether from the defense or the prosecution. Those rules of law whereby we determine what testimony is to be admitted, what is rejected in each case, and what weight is to be given to the testimony so admitted. (*See* Ballentine on Evidence & 10 R.C.L. 859.)

Experimental Evidence   This is proof of a fact or theory in the form of an experiment made during the course of the trial of an action, in the presence of the jury, and usually in the courtroom. The admission of such evidence is entirely within the discretion of the court and neither party can demand it as a matter of right. (People v. Levine, 85 Cal. 39, 22 Pac. Rep. 969, 24 Pac. Rep. 631.)

Expert Opinion Evidence   The testimony of an expert in which he is permitted to state his opinion on a question of science, skill, or trade. Thus, the opinions of medical men are regularly admitted as to the cause of disease, death, consequences of wounds, sanity, and state of mind. Numerous other professionals' testimony is similarly considered. (*See* Estate of Toomes, 54 Cal. 509.) In many Federal and State jurisdictions, witnesses who qualify to the satisfaction of the Court that they are especially skilled in the chemistry and behavior of fire are permitted to form and express opinions to the jury as to origin and cause of the fire. They are never permitted to testify as to who set the fire; that is the exclusive province of the jury.

The jury may believe or disregard the opinions and conclusions of an expert witness or weigh his credibility in the same manner they can weigh the testimony of any other witness.

In some jurisdictions, courts only allow an expert fire witness to testify as to his findings; for example, that he found evidence of a bomb, accelerant, or separate and distinct points of origin. Courts in those jurisdictions that are more conservative about the admission of expert testimony will not permit the expert to state his conclusion or opinion as to cause. They hold that this area is the exclusive province of the jury or the triers of fact.

Expert Witness   An expert witness is one who has acquired such special knowledge of the subject matter about which he is to testify, either by study with recognized authorities on the subject or by practical experience, so that he can give the jury assistance and guidance in solving a problem of which their good judgment and average knowledge is inadequate. (11 R.C.L. 574. *Also see* Ballentine's Legal Definitions.)

Explosion   An explosion is an instantaneous decomposition of a solid or liquid substance, extending throughout the entire mass, and accompanied by considerable disengagement of heat. The substance is partly or wholly converted into gaseous decomposition products.

Explosive Limits (Flammable Limits)   In the context of gases and vapors which form flammable mixtures with atmospheric oxygen (oxygen and nitrogen) and pure oxygen, there is a minimum concentration of vapor in air or oxygen below which flame propagation does not occur on contact with an ignition source. There is also a maximum proportion of vapor or gas in air above which flame or explosion will not occur. These boundary line mixtures of vapor or gas with air are known as the lower and upper flammable or explosive limits and are usually expressed in terms of percentage by volume.

Generally, it may be said that if a mixture is below the lower flammable or explosive limit, it leans toward exploding or burning; above the upper flammable or explosive limit, the mixture is too rich to burn or explode. (For example, in pumping liquids such as hydrocarbon fuels from storage tanks, it is a common safety practice to replace the volume with inert gases, thereby eliminating the possibility of the introduction of an explosive mixture in the oxygen-gas vapor spectrum. An inert gas will neither flame nor explode.)

EXAMPLE OF EXPLOSIVE LIMITS
PERCENT BY VOLUME OF VAPOR-AIR MIXTURES

SUBSTANCE	LOWER LIMIT	UPPER LIMIT
Acetone	2.15	13.0
Allyl Chloride	3.11	11.1
Butyl Alcohol	2.4	8.0
Gasoline	1.4	7.6
Hydrogen	4.0	75.0

Explosives   Solid or liquid explosives represent gases or vapors condensed into the smallest possible compass. The substances used in the blasting or explosive arts are generally termed explosives or blasting materials.

Their detonation results in a sudden and enormous expansion of gases and vapors which are liberated from the previous condition of chemical combination.

In addition to the commonly known and special industrial explosives, certain fertilizers and chemical-industrial compounds are unstable and require special handling in packaging, transportation, and storage and will explode violently under conditions of mishandling or misuse. These compounds are described in various industrial and public safety manuals. Some of the more common blasting explosives are ammonite, blasting powder, chlorate powder, carbonite, explosive gelatine, guhur dynamite, gelatine dynamite, wetterdynamite, nitroglycerin, and nitrocellulose.

Fahrenheit Temperature   A temperature scale which sets the boiling point of water at 212 degrees and the freezing point at 32 degrees above the zero point on the scale.

Felony   In common law, a felony was any crime which, like treason, worked a forfeiture of the offender's lands or goods. This definition is obsolete, and currently whether a criminal act is a felony or misdemeanor is usually distinguished by the character of the punishment provided in the statute. As a general rule, all crimes punishable by death or imprisonment in the state prison are felonies; all others are misdemeanors.

Fire (Combustion)   As used in the discussion of combustion, fire is the process whereby substances, or individual constituents of the same, combine with oxygen accompanied by the liberation of heat. Three factors are necessary to the process in the general sense: the body or supporting factor (oxygen); the substance to be consumed (such as wood, coal, etc.); and the disseminating factor (heat).

Fire Gases   Fire gases generally refer to the gaseous products of combustion. Most combustibles contain carbon which, when burned, form carbon dioxide when the oxygen supply is good and carbon monoxide when the air supply is poor. Other gaseous products of combustion may include hydrogen sulfide, ammonia, sulfur dioxide, hydrogen cyanide, nitric oxide, phosgene, and hydrogen chloride. The products of gases depend mainly upon the chemical composition of the fuel as well as ventilation and combustion temperatures during the process.

Fire Load   The fire load of a space or occupancy is the expected amount of combustible materials in the area or space under consideration. It can generally be expressed in the terms of the weight of the total combustibles per square foot of the occupancy in relation to their heat-producing capability in calories or BTU's. Most fuels, such as wood, fibers, petroleum products, books, papers, and furniture may be rated in BTU's per pound and the fire load thereby generally computed. However, construction in or ventilation of the space may produce substantial variables. Predictions can only be general. American and British laboratories have produced standard time-temperature curves for various classes of occupancies based upon calculated fire loads which may be utilized for references. (*See* NFPA Standard Time-Temperature Curve, #251.)

Fire Partition   A partition serving to restrict spread of fire but not rated as a fire wall. (*See* **Fire Wall.**)

Fire Point   The lowest point in temperature at which a flammable liquid in an open container will produce vapors in continuing combustion. The fire point is usually a few degrees above the flash point except in certain unstable compounds.

Fire Resistance   Uniform building codes define fire resistance as a relative term used with a numerical rating or modifying adjective to indicate the extent to which building materials, structures, or other materials resist the effect of fire; for example, resistance of two hours as measured on the standard time-temperature curve.

Fire Triangle   A term used in some fire training courses to illustrate the need for the three factors essential for fire: fuel, heat, and oxygen. (*See* **Combustion.**) Basically, combustion depends upon the substance to be consumed, oxygen (the supporter of combustion), and the disseminating factor which is heat. The disseminating factor may result from physical, chemical, or biological reactions.

Fire Wall   Broadly defined as a wall erected to prevent the spread of fire. Effective, approved walls must have sufficient fire resistance to withstand the effects of the most severe fire that can be expected in the building and must provide a complete barrier, along with any openings suitably protected. (*See* NFPA Fire Protection Handbook and Uniform Building Code for specifications and standards.)

Flame   It is generally conceded that burning materials, when supported by sufficient oxygen, produce luminosity called flame. It is generally accepted that flame is a distinct product of combustion. The sufficiency of the flame and its extension depends upon the fuel, availability of oxygen, and quality of fuel or fuel load. The color of the flame may vary with the type of fuel and also with conditions of draft; it may also vary with degree of temperature. For example, a natural gas flame, under poor conditions of draft and ventilation, may appear lazy and yellow or orange; under appropriate and well adjusted ventilation effects, it may appear blue.

Flamespread   Once ignition occurs, the propagation or movement of flame from layer to layer and/or across surface exposures without regard to the source. There are a number of accepted methods of testing materials and surfaces for flamespread and scaling possible rate of spread under fire conditions. These include the tunnel test, room burn-out tests, as well as full scale building fire tests conducted in Great Britain. Forest Products Laboratory, Madison, Wisconsin, conducts flamespread and rate of spread tests under actual conditions. Some tests are done in simulated occupancies to scale with various fire loads and to determine flash-over at certain temperatures reached under actual fire conditions.

Flammable   Generally used in fire investigation and code standards to describe combustible material that ignites readily and burns intensely with rapid flamespread. The term is used in a general sense without a clear definition of ignition temperature, surface burning rate, or other defined guidelines. The term is preferred to inflammable in order to avoid possible confusion due to the prefix "in" which suggests the negative, such as in the term incombustible. (Incombustible has the same meaning as noncombustible.)

Flammable Liquids   Fire protection authorities, including the National Fire Protection Association, have established an arbitrary division between liquids and gases which is defined in NFPA #30 of the Flammable Liquids Code. Liquids are those having a vapor pressure not exceeding 40 psi absolute at 100° F.—approximately 25 psi gauge pressure.

Flammable liquids are those having closed cup flash point below 200° F. and are divided into three classes in the Flammable Liquids Code as follows:

Class I—includes those having flash points at or below 20° F.

Class II—includes those having flash points above 20° F. but at or below 70° F.

Class III—includes those having flash points above 70° F. but below 200° F.

(Combustible liquids are those with a flash point at or above 200° F. When a combustible liquid is heated to or above its flash point, it may have some of the hazards produced by flammable liquids.)

The volatility of a flammable liquid is increased when it is heated to a temperature higher than its flash point. For example, if a flammable liquid in the Class III range becomes heated, it may produce the characteristics of a Class II liquid.*

Title 49—Transportation—U.S. Code, defines flammable liquids and extremely flammable liquids. Extremely flammable liquids are those with a flash point below 20° F. This code regulates packaging and shipment in interstate commerce and other areas wherein the Federal Government has jurisdiction.

Flammable (Explosive) Range   This is the range of combustible vapor or so-called gas-air mixture between the lower and upper limits commonly described as the flammable or explosive range. For example, gasoline (115-145 Aviation Grade) has a flash point of –50° F. Its rated ignition temperature is 880° F. Its flammable limits (explosive range) is approximately 1.4 at bottom and 7.6 at the high end of the spectrum. For example, the lower limit of the flammability of gasoline of this order at ordinary ambient temperatures is approximately 1.4 percent vapor in air by volume while the upper limit is about 7.6 percent. All concentrations by volume of gasoline vapor in air falling between 1.4 percent and 7.6 percent are in the flammable-explosive range. Flammable or explosive ranges of vapors and gases vary widely. For example, the explosive range of Hydrogen gas is 4.0 at the lower and 75 at the upper limit. Ethyl Alcohol—lower, 4.3 and upper, 19. Butyl alcohol—lower, 1.7 and upper, 9.8. Carbon monoxide—lower, 12.5 and upper, 74.

Flashover Point   Initial progress of a fire may be slow or fast depending upon the characteristics of initial ignition and basic fuel. Important factors are the nature of the fuel or fabric, its surface, finish, environment, and available oxygen. If the fire continues, it may eventually reach a stage where all exposed combustible surfaces simultaneously burst into flame. This is what is generally known as flashover or flashover point and is significant in the communication of fire from space to space, even in supposedly separated areas. Flashover is a common phenomenon—a product of fuel load, combustible surfaces, temperature, and available oxygen. The results of flashover may be mistaken by inexperienced or indifferent fire investigators as separate and distinct areas of origin; this sometimes creates the mistaken illusion that a fire was incendiary when, in fact, it was not. Flashover must also be considered in forest and wildland fires under certain conditions of weather and terrain.

Flash Point   The flash point is the lowest temperature at which a substance gives off vapor sufficient to form an ignitible mixture with the air near the surface of the substance. In respect to its use in the terms of vapors and flammable liquids, the term ignitible mixture is used in the context of flammable range. When ignited between the upper and lower limits, it is capable of flame propagation away from the source of ignition. Combustion may not be continuous at the flash point, depending upon fuel, extent, and environment. As indicated above, the term flash point most commonly applies to flammable liquids although there are many solids that may slowly deteriorate, sublime, or become chemically active at normal ambient temperatures. Many others will react in slightly higher temperatures or when exposed to direct rays of the sun, producing vapors which will flash while the substance retains its basically solid state.

Fraud   Conduct which operates prejudicially on the rights of others and is so intended; a deception

---

*Specially refined petroleum products, initially developed as Stoddard Solvent, but currently merchandised under various trade names by different companies, have solvent properties approximating those of gasoline but also have fire hazard properties similar to kerosene. According to reliable authorities on flammable liquids and gases, a danger in their use lies in the practice of persons using the solvents believing they are using a safe solvent without fire hazard. They may neglect ordinary precautions which would be observed with a liquid such as kerosene. When heated above their flash point (about 100° F.), these solvents produce vapors as flammable as those of gasoline at its flash point temperature, which is approximately –45° F.

practiced to induce another to part with something of value, or surrender some legal right and which accomplishes a desired end. As commonly used, the word implies deceit, deception, artifice, and trickery. (United States v. Summers, (D.C.W.D. Va) 10 Fed. Rep. (2d) 627.)

Fraud In Law   To constitute fraud in law, a representation must be an affirmation of a fact, and not a mere promise or matter of intention. A statement of a matter in the future, if affirmed as a fact, may amount to a fraudulent misrepresentation, but it must amount to an assertion of fact and not an agreement to do something in the future. If a promise is made to do something in the future, and at the time it is not intended to perform the promise, that fact does not constitute a fraud in the law. (Miller v. Sutliff, 241 Ill. 521, 24 L.R.A. (N.S.) 735, 738, 89 N.E. Rep. 651.)

Fuel Break   An artificially created or natural separation between buildings and improvements and forest or flammable vegetation, or through wildlands to enable fire crews to combat and control advancing fire. The construction, permitted cover, and widths depend upon code and official discretion in relation to the risks involved, terrain, and adjacent natural vegetation.

Fusible Link   Metal parts designed to separate at desired temperatures to release or otherwise activate self-closing fire doors or openings. Fire doors, for example, may be made self-closing by a system of weights suspended by wires, or pulleys restrained by a fusible link or other fixed temperature release or heat responsive device. Other heat responsive devices are used, such as thermostatic releases, where the spread of fire might be so rapid as to pass through a fusible link, restrained door opening before the fusible link could operate.

Galvanism   Electric current in energy resulting from a chemical reaction.

Gas   Gas is an aeriform fluid of matter lacking independent shape or volume, which tends to expand indefinitely. It has been authoritatively declared that matter or material existing in the gaseous state is difficult to describe because it has no apparent size or shape that is identifiable with liquids and solids. The properties of gases, and their behavior, can only be explained by assuming that they are composed of extremely minute particles in constant motion—the higher the temperature, the more violent the motion. This may be illustrated in vapors subjected to extreme temperatures and during the introduction of flame. For fire protection purposes, gases are generally divided into two broad categories: flammable and nonflammable. (*See* **Flammable and Combustible Liquids** and Flammable Gases, 6-27 NFPA Vol. 12.)

The hazards of flammable gases are generally similar to flammable liquids and there is really no sharp line of demarcation between gases and the gases of liquids in respect to fire hazard; further, any actual gas, at a sufficiently low temperature and high pressure, becomes a liquid and any flammable liquid at a sufficiently elevated temperature becomes a gas.

Gasometer   An instrument designed to measure gas, such as an explosion meter.

Globule   A small particle of matter, usually fluid or liquid in form, and of special pattern.

Gram (g)   The basic unit of mass in the metric system.

Gravity (g)   In physics, gravity is used in terms of weight in resistance to terrestrial gravitation. The rate of acceleration of gravity is approximately 32 feet per second. It is also used in terms of the weight of liquids and oils.

Halogens   The members of this group are chemically active and have similar chemical compositions. Some halogens include bromine, chlorine, fluorine, and iodine. They differ from each other only in the degree of activity. They are noncombustible but will support combustion of certain compounds. Turpentine, phosphorus, and some finely divided metals will ignite spontaneously in the presence of halogens. Halogen fumes are poisonous, corrosive, and extremely irritating to eyes and throat.

Hardwood   Hardwoods such as oak, ash, mahogany, and gum are commonly used in finishing and veneers, and also in certain key construction members. Coniferous woods such as pine, cypress, and some of the cedars are softwoods used in framing. There is very little difference between hard and soft woods in reaction to fire except in some redwoods.

Heat   As related to combustion, heat may be manifested in the form of rapid oxidation, with the evolution, under certain circumstances, of flame, smoke, and light. A knowledge of the conditions that determine whether rapid oxidation of a substance with evolution of light will occur is essential to the principles of fire control and investigation.

All substances are made up of atoms or groups of atoms (molecules). Each atom consists of units of energy in the form of electrons, protons, and neutrons in continuous motion—ultimately expressing individual composition in the form of energy. Energy can be expressed in the form of heat.

Chemical reactions are endothermic or exothermic. Exothermic reactions are those which produce products with less total energy than the reacting substance whereupon the energy has been *released* in the form of heat. Endothermic reactions produce products with more total energy than the reacting substances whereupon energy in the form of heat has been *absorbed*.

Oxidation reactions involved in fires are exothermic in the sense that one of the products of the reaction is heat. While, by far, the most common oxidizing material is the oxygen of the atmosphere (one-fifth oxygen and four-fifths nitrogen), certain chemicals, such as sodium nitrate and potassium chlorate, can also readily release oxygen under favorable conditions thereby supplying the flame environment or even creating an explosive environment. Certain pyroxylin plastics contain sufficient oxygen combined in their molecules to produce combustion without an outside source; zirconium dust may be ignited with carbon dioxide. Other explosive and industrial compounds, as earlier stated, will produce oxidizing conditions sufficient for graduated or instantaneous decomposition accompanied by the disengagement of heat.

Heat Explosion   A term used by some firemen and investigators which they interpret synonymously with flashover or flash fire. There is considerable doubt about the accurate usage of such a term since it has been utilized to categorize widely different situations of fire behavior under the same classification.

Heat of Combustion   The amount of heat released during the process of complete oxidation, generally referred to as calorific value. Heat of combustion depends upon the arrangement and numbers of atoms in molecules. Calorific values are commonly expressed in BTU's per pound or in 1-gram calories per gram. (Sawdust produces approximately 8,490 BTU's per lb.; cotton about 7,000 BTU's per lb.; while cottonseed oil produces approximately 17,200 BTU's per lb.; and crude oil approximately 18,000 BTU's per lb.)

Humidity   The amount or degree of moisture in the air. Relative humidity is the amount of moisture in the air as compared to the amount that the air could contain at the same temperature. It is expressed as a percentage. For example, a relative humidity of 25 percent means that the air contains one quarter of the saturation value at that temperature. If the temperature is raised without a change in moisture content, the relative humidity would drop to a lower percentage on the spectrum. While relative humidity has only a moderate effect on structure fire once ignition occurs, it is a factor in the moisture content of wood and vegetable materials as well as fabrics. Relative humidity is a definite factor where forest and wildland fires are concerned and it is an important factor in terms of fire growth in that class of fires, along with temperatures, wind, and slope conditions.

Hydrocarbon   Any compound containing only hydrogen and carbon. Benzene and methane are examples of hydrocarbons.

Ignition   The heating of a compound or substance to the point of continuing combustion or chemical change.

Ignition, spontaneous   In general terms, this is the process wherein substances or compounds ignite as a result of an increase in temperature of the substance or compound without an independent outside ignition source and without drawing heat from its surroundings. It is sometimes called spontaneous combustion by laymen although it may occur over a long-term period such as in unventilated, piled, green hay or other vegetable products; coal dust; charcoal; and oil paint rags. The rate of heat generation, air supply, and insulation properties of the suspect fuel and surrounding environment have definite relevance to whether or not spontaneous heating will occur in the first instance and also as to the rate of heat generation before flaming combustion may occur. In most vegetable compounds, the process may be slow; on the other hand, with unstable or rapidly oxidizing compounds, heat generation may be rapid and even explosive. The process may be luminous or nonluminous. It may occur with or without smoke.

Ignition Temperature   Ignition temperature is generally defined as that point of minimum temperature to which a solid, liquid, or gaseous substance must be heated to initiate or cause self-continuing combustion, independent of the heating or igniting source. Experience and tests have shown that ignition temperatures may vary with change in conditions and environment and listed ignition temperatures should be considered as only approximations. For example, ignition temperatures of flammable liquids and vapors may vary depending upon vapor or air-gas mixture, size and shape of the contained environment, and other chemical and physical factors. This is why there is some variance in reported ignition temperatures by different laboratories. The ignition temperature of combustible solids may be reasonably influenced by the rate of airflow, rate of heating, surface conditions, and size of the particular solid.

Impedance   In reference to alternating electric current, the apparent resistance corresponding to the true resistance in direct current; a combination of inductive reactance and resistance is referred to as impedance. The symbol is Z and the quantity is measured in ohms. There are two methods of determining the impedance of a circuit that is made of both inductive reactance and resistance. These are the vector or impedance triangle method and the computation method. (Load and resistance have relevancy to fire cause.)

Inert   The term indicates a physically neutral or inactive substance. Used in connection with gases, it describes gases such as nitrogen, helium, and other gases which present no fire hazard and can be utilized by various methods to neutralize atmospheres which would otherwise be explosive. For example, inerting sytems are used to pump inert gases into contained explosive atmospheres as when oil tanks are pumped out during discharge of tanker cargoes. Inerting systems may also be utilized to extinguish fires.

Insurance   A contract whereby one undertakes to indemnify another against loss, damage, or liability arising from an unknown or contingent event.

Insurance Adjuster   An agent of an insurance company whose general duty it is to adjust and report losses to the principal officers of the insurance company. Under relatively recent usage, adjusters may be direct employees of the insurance carrier or agents by retainer or special assignment. Insurance adjusters may also be retained directly by the insured to represent the interest of the insured in his negotiation with the insurance carrier.

Insurance Agent   One who negotiates policies of insurance for a commission paid to him by the insurance company.

Insurance Broker   One who acts as a middleman between the insured and the insurer and who solicits insurance from the public under no employment from any special company, but, having secured an order, places the insurance with a company selected by him. A broker is the agent for the insured, though at the same time, for some purposes, he may be the agent for the insurance carrier. Any acts and representations within the scope of his authority as such agent are binding on the insured.

Insurance Carrier (Insurance Company)   Within the general context, a company engaged in the business of making contracts by which it agrees to indemnify the other parties (the insured or designated) from a loss or damage which they may suffer from a specified peril.

Insurance Contract   A contract whereby one person undertakes to indemnify another against loss, damage, or liability arising from an unknown or contingent event.

Insurance Money   Money recoverable on a policy of insurance by the insured against the insurance company which issued the policy. (*See* Stacey v. Fidelity & Casualty Co., 21 Ohio App. 70, 73, 152 N.E. Rep. 794, 795.)

Insurance Policy   An agreement by which one person for a consideration promises to pay money, an equivalent, or do some act of value to another, upon the destruction or injury of something by specified peril.

Insure   To contract to indemnify a person against loss from stated perils; to enter into a contract of insurance as insurer.

Insured   When used as a noun in fire policies, it is the person whose property and legal representatives is insured, but it should not be extended to include any other persons, such as the mortgagee of the property.

Insurer   A person who, by contract of insurance, agrees to indemnify another person, called the insured, against loss from certain specified perils.

Intent   In the legal sense, intent is distinct from motive and may be defined as the purpose of using a particular means to effect a certain result. On the other hand, motive is the reason which leads the mind to desire that result. *(Ballentine's Law Dictionary*—Baker v. State, 120 Wis. 135, 97 N.W. Rep. 566.) Intent is ordinarily an inference of law from which acts are proved. (State v. LaPage, 57 N.H. 245, 24 Am. Rep. 69.)

   In a trial for arson, the prosecution must show that the act of setting the fire was intentional as opposed to accidental.

Investigative Lead   The continuing inquiry resulting from basic information. For example, A interviews witness B who states that he observed C leaving the scene of the crime. The investigative lead requires interview of C who states he was not at the scene but was with D in a distant city at the time alleged by B. The investigative lead extends to D to determine the accuracy of the statement of C or B. Investigative leads are indispensable in factual investigation. The pursuit of investigative leads is all too often neglected.

Kindling   Some fire authorities classify the ordinary fire fuels into three categories: tinder, kindling, and bulk fuel. In British fire studies, for example, combustible material defined tinder as material ignitable by a common domestic match and which will thereafter continue to burn of its own accord. Common examples of tinder are textiles, cardboard, paper, and celluloid. Kindling is defined as material that will ignite and burn if associated with sufficient tinder but in which a match will not produce a continuing fire; a typical example might be thin match boarding or plywood. Bulk fuel includes the heavier constructional timbers such as joists, floorboards, and rafters, baled or compressed combustible materials, and items such as books.

Kindling Temperature   *See* **Ignition Temperature.**

Kinetic   Movement resulting from motion.

Kinetics   The science that deals with the motion of masses in relation to the forces acting on them (as in explosions).

Kinetic Theory   The theory that the minute particles of all matter are in constant motion and that the temperature of a substance is dependent upon the velocity of this motion. Increased motion is accompanied by increased temperature. According to the kinetic theory of gases, elasticity, diffusion, pressure, and other physical properties of gases are due to the rapid motion (in straight lines) of the molecules; to their impact against each other and the walls of the container; to weak cohesive forces between the molecules, etc.

Latent Heat   In general, the additional heat required to change the state of a solid to liquid at its melting point or from liquid to gas at its boiling point after the temperature of the substance has reached either of these points.

Latent Heat of Vaporization   Latent heat of vaporization is the heat which is absorbed when one gram of liquid is transformed into vapor at the boiling point under one atmosphere of pressure. It is expressed in calories per gram or BTU's per pound. (*See* **Calorie, British Thermal Unit,** and **Latent Heat.**)

Malice   In the legal sense, a condition of the mind which shows a heart devoid of social duty and fatally bent on mischief, the existence of which is inferred from the acts committed or words spoken. Malice means an intentionally wrongful act without just cause or excuse, or as the result of ill will; it does not necessarily signify ill will toward a particular individual. Hence, the law implies malice where one deliberately injures another in an unlawful manner (*Ballentine's Law Dictionary* and 18 R.C.L. 2).

In arson prosecutions, proof of malice is necessary. As indicated above, malice may be implied from the nature and circumstances surrounding the act.

Misdemeanor   Any crime which is neither punishable by death nor by imprisonment in a state prison. The Courts have generally held that where a crime may be punished as a misdemeanor or as a felony, it will be considered a misdemeanor only (*Ballentine's Law Dictionary,* R.C.L. 55).

Motive   In criminal law, motive is that which leads or tempts the mind to indulge in a criminal act. It is an inferential fact and may be inferred not merely from the attendant circumstances, but, in conjunction with these, from all previous occurrences having reference to and connection with the commission of the offense.

It is never necessary to establish motive for a conviction, though it is often useful to lend color to and explain the actions of the parties, and even connect the defendant with the offense charged (*Ballentine's Law Dictionary;* also see 13 R.C.L. 747, 761).

Although it is not legally necessary to prove motive to sustain a conviction, most district attorneys or prosecuting attorneys will very practically decline prosecution on an arson case particularly where there are no eye witnesses to the setting of the fire by the defendant, no confession, or no clearly connecting admissions by the defendant. The principal reason for the practicality of proving motive is that courts and juries are reluctant to make a finding against a defendant in a serious charge of arson unless there is a showing as to why the defendant would have committed the act.

Nuclear Explosion   The release of energy produced by nuclear fission and the chain reaction process accompanied by release of heat energy, explosive force, and dispersion of radioactive substance. The environment exposed may be unusable for long periods of time as a result of radioactive contamination, the extent of which depends upon the extent of the reaction and environment exposed; contamination may be in the form of dust, vapor, and other direct and indirect residue of the phenomenon.

Ohm, Ohm's Law   An ohm is the unit of electric resistance. The relationship between volts, amps, and ohms is expressed in Ohm's Law which is stated as follows:

I equals current in amps.
E equals electromotive force in volts.
R equals resistance in ohms.

$I = \dfrac{E}{R}$, $R = \dfrac{E}{I}$, and $E = IR$

Ondometer   An instrument for measurement of radio or electronic wavelength.

Oxidation   Generally, the union of a substance with oxygen; the process of increasing the positive valence or decreasing the negative valence of an element or ion; the process by which electrons are removed from atoms or ions.

Oxide   A binary compound of oxygen and some other element.

Oxides   Oxides of metals and nonmetals react with water to form alkalines and acids respectively; this reaction may occur violently with sodium oxide. Calcium oxide, more commonly identified as quicklime, also reacts with water accompanied by the evolution of sufficient heat to ignite combustible materials such as cloth, paper, and wood.

Oxygen   A colorless, odorless, tasteless, gaseous chemical element that is the most abundant of all elements. It occurs free in our atmosphere of which it forms one-fifth, in volume, along with nitrogen. Oxygen is very active and is able to combine with most other elements. It is essential to the life and growth processes, as well as to combustion.

In an atmosphere of pure oxygen, combustion is more intense than in an environment of atmospheric oxygen which is approximately only one-fifth pure oxygen and four-fifths nitrogen. Oxygen may be manufactured by liquifying air and separating the oxygen from the nitrogen by a process based on their differences in boiling points called fractionating; oxygen may also be produced by the electrolytic decomposition of water—separating it into its constituents: hydrogen and oxygen. Hydrogen gas is lighter than air, extremely explosive, and with a fairly wide explosive range.

Liquid oxygen is used widely in industry. Liquid oxygen, reduced to the liquid state under extremely low temperatures and container stored, weighs about 71 lbs. per square foot and, at atmospheric pressure, its temperature is $-297°$ F.

Carbonaceous material, mixed with liquid oxygen, is used as an explosive.

Ozone   An allotropic form of oxygen usually resulting from or formed by electrical discharge in the air; also used as an oxidizing, bleaching, or deodorizing agent in the purification of water.

Ozonic Ether   A solution of ethylic ether, hydrogen peroxide, and alcohol.

Ozonides   Series of compounds of ozone.

Pattern of Spread   The term used by fire investigators to describe the remaining physical evidence of the progress of the fire from origin to control.

A great deal of fire terminology is utilized by investigators such as fire pointers, depth of char, char pattern, alligator pattern, heat pattern, and structural collapse. There is no presently known scientific authentication and no evidence that any one combination of the terms or methods is precise in any given fire. It is generally agreed among authorities that utilization of the terms must be predicated on actual field experience. The pattern of spread of some fires may be clear cut or well pronounced in some cases. In others, including major structural and forest and wildland conflagrations where buildings collapse, topography, terrain, or varying weather conditions were a factor. Physical factors of pattern or spread may be altered beyond reasonable or precise interpretation regardless of presently available, reliable methods of inquiry.

Pilot Light   In general, a gas fueled burner, utilized to rekindle a principal burner (main burner) and commonly used in domestic and industrial gas fueled appliances. The more modern devices are utilized and regulated with automatic safety controls.

Plastics   Plastics may be generally described as compounds consisting of small molecules known as monomers that are linked together into long chains to form polymers and copolymers. In respect to their reaction to fire, plastics may generally be classified as either thermoplastic or thermosetting depending upon their behavior when heated. Thermoplastic compounds soften when heated; thermosetting plastics, once set, cannot be resoftened. Modern chemical-industrial development has produced plastics from a wide range of basic materials; the finished products are more widely used in clothing, structural, industrial, and transportation activities as time progresses. Much is yet to be learned about the reaction of various plastics to heat and fire as well as toxicity of their combustion products. Laboratory and field tests of certain commonly used plastics have suggested considerable variation in the reactions from limited tests and major conflagrations.

Plug Fuses   Devices used for overcurrent protection. These are of several types including the ordinary one-time type, the time delay type and the S type which does not have to be time delay. The S type may be designed so that the 16- to 30-amp classification cannot be used in fuseholders of the two initially described. Plug fuses are sometimes called buss fuses. (*See* National Electrical Code for specifications on all types of fuses including plug fuses, thermal cutouts, circuit breakers, cartridge fuses, etc.)

Point of Origin   In the context of fire investigation, point of origin means the precise location of initial ignition of the substance involved; usually, the location of the heat source is indicated: match, arc, spark, or other ignition source. Point of origin is more specific than area of origin.

Pressure, explosive   Explosions may be characterized by energy release apparent in effect but not cause. Depending upon their causes, explosions are of four principal kinds: energy release generated by rapid oxidation of gasoline vapor; release of energy generated by rapid decomposition such as in a dynamite explosion; release of energy caused by excessive pressure such as in a boiler explosion; and energy release created by nuclear fission or fusion, such as a hydrogen bomb explosion.

A practical method of differentiating between fire and explosion is that an explosion develops forces which may cause violent displacement of structures or other objects, and indicates the presence of pressures developed by the explosion of vapors and other materials. Explosive pressure tables have been worked out on the more common explosive compounds and gases.

Products of Combustion   The term is usually used in the context of physical and visible results of a fire in the form of combustion gases, flame, and smoke.

Most combustible materials contain carbon, which burns to form carbon dioxide when the air supply is ample. When the air supply is limited, carbon monoxide may be apparent. Some of the other gases may be formed when the materials burn and these may include ammonia, hydrogen cyanide, hydrogen chloride, nitric acid, phosgene, hydrogen sulphide, sulfur dioxide, and other gases, depending upon the subject of combustion and temperature rise in the combustibles.

Pyrolysis   Generally defined, pyrolysis is physical and chemical decomposition by heat. The phenomenon has been known for a long time; however, with the exception of its process in certain compounds, there is much to be learned. Since the organic nature and structure of commonly combustible fuels vary, the process varies. When heated, organic compounds, such as wood, are subject to complex deterioration to simpler compounds which progressively may become more volatile and therefore more flammable than the previous structure. The heating need not occur in the form of apparent flaming combustion; it may be accomplished by exposure to steam pipes, electrical heat producing sources, or inert gases. Pyrolysis has occurred in wood framing in sealed walls where adjacent heat producing steam pipes have gradually carbonized (pyrolyzed) the wood framing over the years. The process will ultimately produce flaming combustion. At the other end of the time spectrum, the phenomenon may occur in a relatively short period of time.

Pyrophoric Materials   These are compounds that may ignite spontaneously. They may be called pyrophor and include materials such as titanium; hafnium; uranium; and thorium as well as phosphuretted hydrogen; ethyl, methyl, and propyl compounds; and potassium sulfide.

Radiation   As used in fire investigation, radiation is one of the three methods or media by which heat is transferred; the three methods being conduction, convection, and radiation. Radiation is the heat transfer, from one body to another, by heat rays, through intervening space, in much the same manner as light is transferred by light rays. Two examples are heat from the sun and heat from an electric heater adjacent to a wall. Radiated heat passes freely through a vacuum and through gases. Like light, heat is reflected from glass or another bright surface. Heat radiation is largely in the red and infrared light range and is similar to sunlight but differs somewhat in absorption and refraction properties because it has a longer wavelength.

Sabotage   The malicious damage or injury to the property of an employer by an employee. (*See* State v. Moilen, 140 Minn. 112, 1 A.L.R. 331, 332 167 N.W. Rep. 345. *See also* **Criminal Syndicalism**.)

Self-Incrimination   The giving of testimony as a witness against one's will. The United States Constitution provides in the Fifth Amendment that no one shall be compelled to testify against himself in the Federal courts and nearly every state has embodied the same provisions in their respective constitutions. The guarantee extends to self-incrimination situations during interviews by peace officers and certain governmental representatives.

Smoke   The vaporous matter resulting from some forms of combustion and made visible by minute particles of carbon suspended in the vapor. In chemistry, suspension of solid particles in gas. Under the usual conditions of insufficient oxygen for complete combustion, there may also be present methane, methanol, formaldehyde, and formic and acetic acids. The combination of the combustible, rate of heating, oxygen concentration at or near the combustible surface, along with temperatures, usually determines the composition of fire gases and the resulting smoke, if any. The apparent color of the smoke may vary with the composition of the combustibles and can also be influenced by ventilation and application of water or other extinguishing agent.

Smoke particles may cool to the extent where water vapor, acids, and residues of the combustibles involved may be identified if recovered from areas such as windows or other surfaces. It is, of course, well established that moisture-laden particles, if inhaled, may carry highly poisonous or irritating compounds into the respiratory tract and eyes. If allowed to accumulate in a building, hot unburned products of combustion will ignite explosively when a supply of oxygen is suddenly made available. (*See* **Flashover.**) Some firemen and investigators call this phenomenon a smoke explosion. This is one of the prime reasons why firemen vent fires, usually by opening windows, doors, or by cutting holes in the roof.

Specific Gravity (sp.gr., s.g., or G)   The ratio of the weight or mass of the given volume of a substance to that of an equal volume of another substance used as a standard. (Water for liquids and solids, air or hydrogen for gases.) The specific gravity of gasoline and other petroleum products, for example, is commonly measured in Degrees API (American Petroleum Institute).

Specific Heat (sp.ht.)   The ratio of the amount of heat required to raise the temperature of a unit mass of a subsance one degree to the amount of heat required to raise the temperature of the same mass of water one degree; the number of calories required to raise the temperature of one gram of a given substance one degree Centigrade.

Oxidation reactions always produce heat and are not always clearly understood even by firemen and fire investigators. Reactions, including flamespread, fire pattern, and possible explosion reactions are greatly influenced by fireload in the area of origin, combustibles involved, and initial availability of oxygen. (*See* **British Thermal Units, Calorie**).

Spontaneous Heating   *See* **Ignition, spontaneous.**

Static Electricity   Designated as stationary electrical charges or discharges in the atmosphere; frictional electricity such as produced in movement of bodies or fabrics on surfaces. It is relevant to fire investigation in that electrical charges, without proper bonding or grounding, may introduce a spark or arc into an explosive or combustible environment. Some examples are improperly bonded or grounded fuel lines, tanks, and pumping facilities. (*See* National Electrical Code.)

Subrogation   As used in civil actions, the substitution of one for another so that the new party succeeds to the former's rights or legal claims. It is frequently referred to as the doctrine of substitution. It is a device commonly used in insurance litigation, adopted or invented by equity to compel the ultimate discharge of a debt or obligation. It is the mechanism by which the equity of one man (or party) is worked through the rights of another. The right of an insurer on payment of a loss to be subrogated *pro tanto* to any right of action which the insured may have had against any third person whose wrongful act or neglect caused the loss insured against by the insurer is one example. (14 R.C.L. 1404.)

Temperature   The degree of hotness or coldness of any substance or body, usually measured in terms of a Kelvin or a Rankine temperature scale. (*See* **Centigrade, Fahrenheit.**)

Thermostat   Thermostats are widely used, fixed temperature heat detectors used in signaling systems. Probably the most common type is the bimetallic type which utilizes two metals with different expansion coefficients resulting in movement of the strip and closing or opening of the contacts regulated to the temperature function. There are also thermostatic cables, snap action disc thermostats, and other heat reaction devices.

Tort   An injury or wrong committed either with or without force, to a person or a person's property. Such injury may arise out of nonfeasance, malfeasance, or misfeasance.

Trailer   A term used to describe the means utilized to extend an ignition point from a location outside an occupancy into the space where the plant or booster may be located. Trailers often connect various plants or sets inside a space to insure complete involvement within a short period of time. Flammable liquids such as kerosene and charcoal lighter fluid have been frequently used. Gasoline is seldom used as a trailer because of the rapid evaporation characteristics that makes its use unpredictable. Various types of window cord, rope, and wrapping cord have been commonly used, saturated in kerosene or other medium flashpoint fuels. Blasting cord has been used, particularly where explosions are desired. Arsonists occasionally improvise using oil-saturated, twisted newspaper trailers or any other tinder type fuel that insures communication through the target premises.

Transformer   Generally, an apparatus or device for transforming or converting the voltage of an electric current. There are two types: a step-down transformer which changes high voltage to lower voltage; and a step-up transformer which changes lower voltage to higher voltage. Transformers vary in size and capacity over a wide range, constructed or designed for specific functions, from the liquid and mechanically cooled types found in substations and primary facilities right on down to the smaller units in primary service entrances and secondary areas.

Vapor Density   Vapor density is the relative density of a gas or vapor (minus air) as compared to air. A figure of less than 1 indicates that a vapor is lighter than air; a figure greater than 1 indicates that the vapor is heavier than air. The vapor density of a compound equals the molecular weight of the compound divided by 29. In the formula, 29 is the composite of the molecular weight of air.

Vapor Pressure   The pressure of a confined vapor that has accumulated above its liquid. It is determined by the nature of the liquid and the temperature. Vapor pressure figures for many substances may be found in chemical handbooks; vapor pressures of petroleum products are usually determined by the Reid method as recommended by the American Society for Testing Materials, ASTM Standard D-323.

Voir Dire   To speak the truth. An oath is so called when it is administered to a prospective juryman or a witness as a preliminary step to examining his qualifications as a juror or witness.

Volatile Liquids   Those that may be readily vaporized. The hazards depend upon their flash point and explosive range. Examples of volatile liquids are acetone, allyl alcohol, ethyl alcohol, gasoline, and kerosene. (*See* Table 6-156, NFPA Fire Protection Handbook, for table on hazardous chemicals and liquids.)

Volt (v)   Volt is a unit of electrical pressure, the force which causes electricity to flow through a conductor. Voltage is not necessarily a measure of fire hazard; for example, 1.5 volts through a very fine wire can cause that wire to become red hot. The heat of the wire, if in contact with combustibles, will result in fire. Certain size conductors may have high voltages and low carrying capacity. (*See* **Ampere** and its relevance to voltage and current flow.)

Watt   The watt is a unit of power. A current of one ampere flowing under pressure of one volt equals one watt. For example, a 100-watt light bulb rated at 110v takes a current of 0.9 amp and has a resistance of 120 ohms. It is the demand for power when using items such as light bulbs, heaters, stoves, and motors that places the load on the conductors. If the demand is more than the size or capacity of the conductors can carry (are rated for), heating of the conductors will follow. A fire may follow the heating or arcing growing out of the overload since circuit safety devices, such as fuses or circuit breakers, may not open the circuit before ignition of combustibles occurs.

BIBLIOGRAPHY

Aerospace Corporation Law Enforcement Development Group, *Survey and Assessment of Arson and Arson Investigation.* Aerospace Report ATR 76 (7918-05-2), 1976.

American Bar Association, *Criminal Investigation Standards,* 1973.

Asch, Sidney H., *Criminal Investigation Rights of the Individual.* New York, Arco Publishing Co., Inc., 1967.

Ballentine, James A., *Ballentine's Law Dictionary.* Rochester, N.Y., Lawyer's Publishing Co., 1930.

Barnes, Harry Elmer, and Teeters, Negley K., *New Horizons in Criminology.* Englewood Cliffs, N.J., Prentice-Hall, Inc., 1943.

Barr, Martin, M.D., *Mental Defectives.* Philadelphia, Blackerson's & Sons, Inc., 1904.

Battle, Brendan P., and Weston, Paul, *Arson: Detection and Investigation.* New York, Arco Publishing Co., Inc., 1978.

Bird, Eric, and Docking, Stanley, *Fire In Buildings.* London, Adam & Charles Black, 1949.

British Home Office, Research Analysis Section, *Fire Protection/Air Raid Precautions Review,* 1940.

Browning, B.L., *Chemistry of Wood.* Interscience Publications. New York, John Wiley & Sons, Inc., 1963.

Brunswig, Dr. H., Montroe, Charles, E., and Kibler, Alton L., *Explosives.* New York, John Wiley & Sons, Inc., 1922.

Caldwell, Robert G., *Criminology, 2nd ed.* New York, Ronald Press Co., 1965.

Conant, Ralph Wendell, *Problems in Research: Community Violence.* Washington, D.C., Institute on Mental Health, Research Branch, 1969.

Cressey, Donald R., *Criminal Psychology.* Philadelphia, J.B. Lippincott Company, 1974.

Curtiss, Arthur F., *The Law of Arson.* Buffalo, N.Y., Dennis & Company, 1936.

Ebaugh, Franklin A.B., M.D., *Clinical Psychiatry, 4th ed.* Philadelphia, P. Blackeston's & Sons.

Eichner. H.W., *Basic Research on Pyrolysis and Combustion of Wood.* Madison, Wisconsin, U.S. Forest Products Laboratory, 1962.

Federal Bureau of Investigation, *Handbook of Forensic Science.* Washington, D.C., Government Printing Office, Publication #027-001-00014-9.

Freimuth, H.C., and Gettler, A.O., "Carbon Monoxide and the Blood." *American Clinical Pathology,* 1943.

Haines, John E., *Automatic Controls: Heating and Air Conditioning.* New York, McGraw-Hill Book Company, 1961.

Hawk, P.B., Oser, B.L., and Summerson, W.H., *Practical Physiological Chemistry.* Blakiston's Sons, 1947.

Herman, Stephen L., *Bomb Scene Investigation.* Stephen L. Herman, 1977.

Inbau, Fred Edward, *Criminal Investigation and Criminal Law.* Radnor, Pennsylvania, Chilton Book Company, 1972.

Inbau, Fred Edward, and Reed, John, *Criminal Interrogation and Confessions.* Baltimore, Williams-Wilkins Company, 1967.

Inbau, Fred Edward, Moenssens, Andre A., and Vitulio, Louis R., *Police Scientific Investigation.* Radnor, Pennsylvania, Chilton Book Company, 1972.

International Association of Arson Investigators, Stuerwald, John, Ed., *Selected Articles on Arson Investigation.* Marlboro, Massachusetts, International Association of Arson Investigators, 1975.

International Conference of Building Officials, *Uniform Building Code.* L.C. #29247, 1973.

International Conference of Building Officials and the Western Fire Chiefs Association, *Uniform Fire Code.* L.C. #73-77250, 1973.

International Association of Mechanical Officials, *Uniform Mechanical Code.* L.C. #73-77246, 1973.

International Association of Plumbing and Mechanical Officials, *Uniform Plumbing Code.* L.C. #52-18889, 1973.

Inciardi, Fred, "The Adult Fire Setter: A Typology." *Criminology.* Volume 8, 1970.

Kennedy, John, *Fire Investigation.* Chicago, Investigations Institute, 1977.

Kind, Stewart, *Science Against Crime.* New York, Doubleday & Co. Inc., 1972.

Kirk, Paul L., *Fire Investigation.* New York, John Wiley & Sons, Inc., 1969.

Kirk, Paul L., with Bradford, L.W., *The Crime Laboratory.* Springfield, C.C. Thomas, 1965.

Lenz, Robert, *Explosives and Bomb Disposal Guide.* Springfield, C.C. Thomas, 1976.

Los Angeles, City of, *Dangerous Chemicals Code.* Los Angeles, Los Angeles Fire Department, 1951.

Mach, Martin H., *"Gas Chromatograph, Mass Spectometry."* Aerospace Corporation Report ATR 76 (9472-2), 1976.

National Fire Protection Association, *Arson: Some Problems and Solutions.* Boston, NFPA Publication SPP-38, L.C. #76-7887, 1976.

National Fire Protection Association, *National Fire Codes, Volumes 1-12.* Boston, National Fire Protection Association, 1977.

Olsen, Alten L., and Green, John W., *Laboratory Manual of Explosive Chemistry.* London, John Wiley & Sons, 1943.

Robinson, Clark S., *Explosives: Their Anatomy and Destructiveness.* New York, McGraw-Hill Book Company, n.d.

Sadler, William S., M.D., *Theory and Practice of Psychiatry,* St. Louis, C.V. Mosby Company, 1936.

Schafer, Robert S., *Introduction to Criminology.* Englewood Cliffs, N.J., Prentice-Hall, Inc., 1926.

Sisco, Donald, *The Militant's Formulary, Volume 1.* An underground publication, date and publisher unknown.

Snyder, LeMoyne, *Homicide Investigation: Practical Information for Coroners, Police Officers, and Other Investigators.* Springfield, C.C. Thomas, 1973.

Soderman, Harry, *Modern Criminal Investigation.* New York, Funk & Wagnall's, 1963.

Stevens, Richard E., *National Fire Code, Volume 3*. Boston, National Fire Protection Association, L.C. #38-27236, 1973.

Stewart, C.P., and Stolman, A., Eds., *Toxicology: Mechanisms and Analytical Methods, 2 vols.* New York, Academic Press, 1960-61.

Stolman, E.S., and Khauslovich, G.P., *Mechanations and Methods.* New York, Academic Press, 1960.

Strecker, A.M., *Clinical Psychiatry.* Philadelphia, P. Blackeston Sons., n.d.

Stuerwald, John E., *Fire and Arson Investigator.* International Association of Arson Investigators, Vol. 27, #3, January 1977.

Suchey, John T., and Tipton, Howard O., *Arson: America's Malignant Crime.* Columbus, Ohio, Battelle Columbus Laboratories, 1976.

Thompson, Norman, *Fire Behavior and Sprinklers.* Boston, National Fire Protection Association, 1964.

Tyron, George, *Fire Protection Handbook, 12th ed.* Boston, National Fire Protection Association, 1962.

Underhill, H.C., *Criminal Evidence.* New York, The Bobbs-Merrill Co., Inc., 1973.

United States Government, *Combatting Crime in the United States.* Washington, D.C., U.S. Government Printing Office, 1967.

United States Government Commission on Violence, *Causes and Prevention of Violence.* Washington, D.C., U.S. Government Printing Office, L.C. #76-604085.

United States Government General Services Administration, *Transportation and Storage of Explosive Compounds, title 49.* General Services Administration Archives, CFR 170.1.

Von Schwartz, Dr. Karl, *Fire and Explosion Risks,* trans. by Charles T.C. Salter. London, Charles Griffin & Co., 1926.

Watt, John H., *National Fire Protection Association Handbook of the National Electrical Code.* Boston, National Fire Protection Association.

Weingart, George W., *Pyrotechnics, 2nd ed.* New York, Chemical Publishing Company, 1947.

Wellman, William R., *Elementary Electricity.* New York, Van Nostrand Reinhold Co., 1947.

Wilson, James Q., *Thinking About Crime.* New York, Basic Books, 1975.

Zemansky, Mark W., and Sears, Francis Weldon, *College Physics.* Reading, Pennsylvania, Addison-Wesley Publishing Co., 1957.

INDEX